BARRON'S

AP*

UNITED STATES GOVERNMENT & POLITICS

9TH EDITION

Curt Lader, M.Ed.
Former AP U.S. Government and Politics Teacher
Northport High School
Northport, New York

BARRON'S

*AP and Advanced Placement Program are registered trademarks of the College Board, which was not involved in the production of, and does not endorse, this product.

About the Author

Curt Lader taught Social Studies for 36 years and AP U.S. Government and Politics for 13 of those years at Northport High School on Long Island before retiring. He holds a Master's degree in Education from Queens College and Professional Diploma in Educational Administration from St. John's University. Lader is currently teaching "Inside Politics Today" at the C.W. Post campus of Long Island University.

All inquiries should be addressed to:
Barron's Educational Series, Inc.
250 Wireless Boulevard
Hauppauge, New York 11788
www.barronseduc.com

ISBN: 978-1-4380-0744-1 (Book)
ISBN: 978-1-4380-7606-5 (Book/CD Package)
ISSN: 2150-6329

PRINTED IN THE UNITED STATES OF AMERICA

9 8 7 6 5 4

CONTENTS

PART TWO: CIVIL RIGHTS AND CIVIL LIBERTIES

PART THREE: THE INSTITUTIONS OF GOVERNMENT

PART FOUR: POLITICAL PARTIES, ELECTIONS, POLITICAL BELIEFS, THE MEDIA, AND SPECIAL INTEREST GROUPS

PART FIVE: PUBLIC POLICY ISSUES

PART SIX: MODEL EXAMS

As you review the content in this book and work toward earning that **"5"** on your AP U.S. Government and Politics Exam, here are five essentials that you **MUST** know above everything else:

Barron's Essential

1 **Know the principles of the United States Constitution.** You will find multiple-choice questions relating to the elitist and pluralist theories of government, and free-response questions about separation of powers, checks and balances, and federalism. Make sure you understand the relationship between the federal and state governments as well as the interrelationship among the three branches of government.

2 **Apply the principles of the U.S. Constitution to the formal institutions of government.** This is the biggest part of both the multiple-choice and free-response questions. You should understand that the phrase "formal institutions of government" refer to the three branches of government and the federal bureaucracy. Discuss with your classmates which branch of government has the most power and look at the size and scope of the federal bureaucracy. Understand the "iron triangle" concept.

3 **Understand how civil liberties and civil rights have played an important role.** Know the difference between civil rights and civil liberties. There are key Supreme Court cases that apply to these topics and there have been multiple-choice and free-response questions. Explore the concept of "selective incorporation" of the Fourteenth Amendment to the United States Constitution, another topic that has repeatedly appeared on the exam.

4 **Explore the importance of "linkage institutions."** Linkage institutions are political parties, elections, special interest groups and the mass media. You should be able to understand the purpose, goals, development, organization, and the philosophies of political parties and how they conduct elections. The exam has stressed the changing nature of elections and the significant role the media plays.

5 **Develop confidence and you will get that "5."** After reviewing the material in the book, taking the practice multiple-choice and free-response questions at the end of each chapter, and taking the practice exams, you will be ready for the exam!

Preface

The Advanced Placement U.S. Government and Politics course and test, unlike the other Social Studies AP courses and tests, is contemporary in nature. Students taking the course and the test are among the best and brightest and most politically aware.

Updating this book reflects a 17-year cycle of test changes that were first incorporated when the first edition of the Barron's *AP United States Government and Politics* was published. The 9th edition includes significant political events that have taken place between 2013 and 2015, including the second term events of the Obama administration, the battle between the Republicans and the President over domestic and foreign policy issues, the 2012 mid-term elections, and other key political events that help explain the material that make up the Advanced Placement U.S. Government and Politics course and exam. Sample multiple-choice and free-response questions follow each chapter, with answer explanations for all multiple-choice questions and rubrics for the free-response questions.

In preparing the revisions for this edition, I included the events that contributed to the foundation of the course curriculum, and changed the model exams to reflect this. Material was obtained from many sources and includes updates to statistics, charts, and graphs. Particularly helpful were the many government websites. Another resource that complements this book is *Barron's AP U.S. Government and Politics Flash Cards.*

If you purchased this book with the optional CD-ROM, you will have access to two electronic sample exams. These exams have been updated to reflect the latest examples of multiple-choice and free-response questions. The automatic scoring on the CD-ROM has also been updated. Points will not be deducted for incorrect answers. Therefore, you are encouraged to answer all questions in order to give you an accurate simulation of the exam.

Lastly, I particularly want to recognize a few individuals. Thanks to my colleagues at Northport High School. I would also like to recognize my editor, Kristen Girardi, who provided guidance and support, especially during the update of this book. Finally, I thank my wife, Phyllis, who without a doubt is the best editor I have ever known; my children, Craig and Glenn, who throughout the process kept reminding me to "get a life" when it came to getting political information for this project; and my parents, who have always encouraged me. I could not have completed this book without their support.

Curt Lader

June 2015

Introduction

USING THE BOOK

The Advanced Placement U.S. Government and Politics Examination is offered once a year, in May. More than 280,000 students nationwide took the test in May 2015. This book offers a comprehensive review of the key concepts taught in the AP U.S. Government and Politics course, with many historical examples cited for illustration. In addition, each chapter contains:

- an overview of the topic
- key terms
- both historical and contemporary examples
- multiple-choice questions and answers
- free-response or data-based questions
- rubrics following each free-response question or data-based question

The last section of the book offers students the opportunity to take two model exams, including free-response and data-based questions with suggested answers. A complete glossary of terms and an index related to government and politics follows the model exams.

Suggested Uses

- If you are taking the course for a full year, read each chapter as you complete the same unit of work in your class. Answer the multiple-choice questions and the free-response question at the end of each chapter. Highlight significant areas such as key terms and create index cards for each unit. Because you are taking AP U.S. Government and Politics over the course of an entire year, you have the advantage of using this book as a supplement to your text. When you start reviewing for the test in the spring, go over the key terms and index cards that you made and take the model exams as part of your review.
- If you are taking the course in the fall, begin using this book in the spring semester. Starting in January, review a chapter a week. Answer the multiple-choice questions and the free-response question at the end of each chapter. Highlight significant areas such as key terms and create index cards for each unit. In late April, take the model exams and after scoring the exams, review the material that you had difficulty with. If you are taking the course in the fall, you must establish a timeline for a review of the material that was learned months before the actual exam.
- If you are taking the course in the spring, you should follow the timeline for each unit that is set by your teacher and use the book as a supplement to your class instruction. Answer the multiple-choice questions and the free-response question at the end of each chapter. Highlight significant areas such as key terms and create index cards for each unit. When you start reviewing for the test, go over the key terms and index cards that you made and take the model exams as part of your review.

- Answer the questions following each chapter. Keep track of the types of questions you answer incorrectly so that you can analyze why you got them wrong.
- Take the model exams under test conditions.

A Note to Students

Because of the manner in which each chapter is organized, you have the opportunity to pretest your skills in each area related to U.S. government and politics. You can also apply the chapter overview, key terms and contemporary connections to current issues, and use the glossary as you study current events in government and politics.

How you use this book depends to a certain extent on how your school offers the course. Nevertheless, by answering the sample questions at the end of each chapter and by taking the model examinations, you will have an indication of how well you will do on the actual exam.

If you organize your time and systematically review the material in the book, and then intensify your studies in March and April, you will have an excellent foundation for the test in May.

A Note to Teachers

Suggest to your students that they use this book along with their text. They can use the overview section of each chapter in conjunction with class assignments, evaluating current trends in each area. They can also use the key terms to develop additional free-response and data-based questions. The sample multiple-choice questions can be used to develop test-taking skills. Particular emphasis is given to the types of questions posed so that students can better understand the nature of what is being asked.

The book offers you the opportunity to use the material for review. Those of you who are teaching a semester course can appreciate the value of having review material available for study at a more leisurely pace than what sometimes takes place in a semester class. For those of you who are teaching a full-year course, the book and test material can motivate your students to improve their understanding of the material as well as their ability to take the test.

A Guide to the Exam

One of the keys to doing well on the AP U.S. Government and Politics Examination is to have an understanding of the structure of the test as it relates to the course itself. The next section explains how the test is organized and developed. Percentage ranges are given for the multiple-choice section, and a thematic topic breakdown is given for the free-response questions. In addition, an analysis of the manner in which the exam is graded will help you create test strategies for success.

STRUCTURE OF THE TEST

The Advanced Placement U.S. Government and Politics Examination is 2 hours and 25 minutes and consists of

The multiple-choice section takes 45 minutes. Students should try to answer every question because there is NO penalty for guessing.

- Section 1—60 multiple-choice questions (45 minutes)
- Section 2—Free-response questions (100 minutes)
  Four mandatory free-response questions (25 minutes each)

The free-response section takes 100 minutes. Students are given four mandatory questions. One or more of the free-response questions may be data based (consisting of graphs, charts, cartoons, excerpts of documents, etc.). These questions require that the student specifically respond to the data-based material.

The multiple-choice section of the test is worth 50 percent of the total grade. The free-response section is also worth 50 percent of the grade.

SKILLS NEEDED TO SUCCEED

Students taking the AP U.S. Government and Politics Exam should be able to demonstrate proficiency and competency in the following areas:

- Political theory, political beliefs, and the political process
- Linkage groups, including special interest groups, the media, political parties, and elections
- The Constitution
- Formal institutions of government (Congress, Executive, Judiciary, the bureaucracy)
- Civil Rights and Civil Liberties
- Public Policy

Furthermore, they should be able to:

- analyze, interpret, understand, and respond to stimulus-based data including charts, graphs, cartoons, and quotes
- interpret data and support it in free-response questions

HOW THE TEST IS SCORED

The Educational Testing Service sends scores in July. Depending upon the student's choice, the scores are also sent to colleges and universities. The scores are reported on the following scale:

Score	Average College Grade
5—Extremely well qualified	A
4—Well qualified	B
3—Qualified	C
2—Possibly qualified	D
1—No recommendation	F

TEST OUTLINE FOR MULTIPLE-CHOICE SECTION

A. The Constitutional Foundations of the United States—5 to 15 percent
  - Historical development and adoption of the Constitution
  - Separation of powers
  - Checks and balances
  - Federalism
  - Theories of modern government

B. Political Theory and Beliefs and Their Influence on Individuals—10 to 20 percent
  - The theories of modern government including elitist, pluralist, and hyper-pluralist
  - Views that people have about government and their elected officials
  - Characteristics and impact of public opinion
  - Voting patterns of citizens
  - Characteristics of political beliefs and the differences between liberals and conservatives

C. The Development and Philosophies of Political Parties, Elections, Interest Groups, and Mass Media—10 to 20 percent
  - Characteristics, organization, and history of political parties
  - Nominations, campaigns, and elections
  - Voting patterns and the effect on the political process
  - Laws that affect elections
  - Interest groups and political action committees
  - Legislation affecting the political process
  - The mass media and its effect on politics

D. The Formal Institutions of Government, the Bureaucracy, and the Development of Public Policy—35 to 45 percent
  - Characteristics and power of each institution
  - Relationships among each institution
  - Linkage between these institutions and the political process, political parties, interest groups, the media, and public opinion
  - How public policy is formulated and implemented
  - The impact of the three branches of government on public policy
  - The impact of the bureaucracy on public policy

E. Public Policy—5 to 15 percent
  - The nature of public policy
  - The creation of public policy
  - The relationship between public policy and linkage institutions

F. Civil Liberties and Civil Rights—5 to 15 percent
  - The Bill of Rights and how it evolved
  - The incorporation of the Fourteenth Amendment
  - Judicial review and key Supreme Court cases
  - The fight for minority rights

Most colleges and universities accept a score of 4 or 5 for credit and placement. Many colleges and universities may accept a score of 3 for credit and/or placement. Scores of 1 or 2 are not accepted by colleges and universities for either credit or placement.

The rule of thumb in determining how well you will probably do on the exam is to look at the number of multiple-choice questions you answer correctly. If you consistently get between 50 and 60 percent correct, you should be able to score a minimum of a 3. If you score consistently between 66 and 75 percent of the multiple-choice questions correctly, you should be able to achieve a 4, and if you score 80 to 100 percent correctly you can get a 5. (This assumes, of course, that you adequately answer the questions in the free-response section.)

In a statistical breakdown of a recent test, approximately 50 percent of the students taking the test achieved a 1 or 2, 26 percent achieved a 3, 13 percent achieved a 4, and 12 percent of the students received a 5.

STUDY STRATEGIES

Unlike courses in American history or European history, U.S. government and politics has a more contemporary approach. Even though you must understand the historical perspective of each topic in the review chapters, more often than not examples are drawn from 1960 to the present.

In a U.S. government and politics course, the structure and goals of government are explained in much greater detail than in the typical civics course. There is an in-depth approach to the organizational components of the institutions of government as well as the application of how government works in relation to achieving public policy goals. Because many students have an inherent bias when it comes to politics, you must be careful to separate your opinions from the study of politics. Even though most students use one major textbook for a U.S. government and politics course, you should be able to see clearly the manner in which the author(s) analyze the subject matter. If you use supplementary books, you should look for any biases and understand that it is important to evaluate different points of view.

Using the Internet, reading a daily newspaper (including columns and editorials) and a weekly news magazine, and watching the Sunday morning political discussion television programs are as important as any text or supplementary reading on U.S. government and politics. Through those media you will develop a complete understanding of the nature and function of government and politics in America. Additionally, you can also get involved in the political process by volunteering to work in a local campaign.

Tips for Getting the Most out of This Book

- **Read the preliminary paragraph.** Each chapter begins with a "Contemporary Connection" and an overview of the topic, which establishes a perspective and outlines each area.
- **Study the key terms.** Since generalizations are such an integral part of any understanding of government and politics, you should be able to give examples to support the thesis statements found in each chapter.
- **Connect the key terms to specific test questions.** Most test questions incorporate the key terms.
- **Develop a working vocabulary.** So much of the content related to U.S. government and politics is vocabulary and concepts. Study the list of key terms in each chapter and check their definitions in the glossary. These words appear in many of the multiple-choice questions and answer choices.
- **Look at the model answers and rubrics that follow free-response questions.** They will guide you on how best to answer the question.

Getting the Entire Picture

In studying U.S. government and politics, you should understand the details related to each governmental institution as well as the impact of politics on the success or failure of government. In doing so, you must be familiar with the cast of characters, vocabulary, historical context, and bias of the author. One important way a student of government can master this material is by prereading. Anytime you are unfamiliar with any subject matter, this method will be helpful.

PREREADING THE MATERIAL

Before reading any specific text, supplementary book, document, or article, look at the material as if you were surveying a landscape. In this survey you should:

1. look at the table of contents
2. determine the flow of chapters or specific readings
3. read the overview
4. study the key terms
5. underline the cast of characters and key terms
6. read the author's conclusions
7. look over any review material at the end of each chapter, and
8. read the info tabs in each chapter

Through this process, you will be able to cull sufficient material prior to any in-depth reading and note taking.

MINING THE MATERIAL

After you preread any material, you should do what any good surveyor does—mine the material. Through a detailed excavation you should use a series of focus statements to direct your attention to the specifics of the material presented.

- What general principles of government and politics are presented?
- What historical examples are given to illustrate these principles?
- Who are the main personalities related to these principles and historical examples?
- Why are these principles, examples, and personalities significant?

As any good prospector, you are looking for the gold ore rather than fool's gold!

READING THE TEXT

After you have finished prereading and have mined the material, you should be ready to go through the text slowly and systematically. It is highly recommended that you highlight the material if you own the book. If you don't own it, you will have to develop a system of note taking.

TIP
Use a highlighter sparingly. Mark only key points.

If you highlight the material, be careful not to *over* highlight. There is nothing to gain by highlighting paragraph after paragraph of material. In fact, you have more to lose—your valuable review time. Highlight key phrases, key people, key terms, and key statements. Even if you own the text, you may want to go one step further and transfer the highlighted material as notes on index cards.

If you use index cards for your notes, you will be forced to conserve space. You can also use the cards as flash cards. For example, one side of the card can have the topic, and the other side of the card can have specific examples from the text. You can create separate cards for vocabulary terms, key court cases, presidential decisions, legislative acts, bureaucratic agencies, and the list goes on.

As an alternative to highlighting and taking notes, some students prefer to outline the material. If you use this technique, you should purchase a notebook and in an organized and consistent manner create an outline going from general topics to specific examples. The advantage of outlining over highlighting is that you get a much more complete picture of the chapter. The drawback is that it is much more difficult to study an outline than individual note cards or highlighted material. The best way to summarize the material is really up to each student.

SAMPLE READING WITH UNDERLINING, NOTES, AND AN OUTLINE

<u>Interest groups</u> and their relatives, <u>political action committees</u>, or <u>PACs</u>, were formed to influence the political and legislative agenda. Utilizing <u>lobbying techniques</u>, individuals representing <u>special interests</u> attempt to gain the favor of elected officials. Some examples of interest groups are the <u>National Rifle Association (NRA)</u>, the <u>National Education Association (NEA)</u>, <u>Pro-Choice</u>, and <u>Pro-Life</u> organizations. Many of these groups also make contributions to the coffers of specific politicians or political parties. Attempts to reform the amount of money PACs can give resulted in the passage of the <u>Federal Election Commission</u>. There are many supporters of interest groups who claim that because of the knowledge of these organizations, legislators acquire a great deal of valuable information regarding proposals.

Underlined Example

Interest Groups
   AKA political action committees using lobbying techniques.
   Special interest groups such as NRA, NEA, Pro-Choice, Pro-Life try to influence legislation.
   Reform—Federal Election Commission.

Notes

Interest Groups

   I. Nature of Interest Groups
      A. Political Action Committees
      B. Lobbyists
  II. Examples of Interest Groups
      A. National Rifle Association (NRA)
      B. National Education Association (NEA)
      C. Pro-Choice Organizations
      D. Pro-Life Organizations
 III. Impact of Interest Groups
      A. On politicians
      B. On legislation

Outline

SUMMARY OF READING TECHNIQUES

1. Get the entire picture—look at the overview, key terms, vocabulary, and test questions.
2. Preread the material—determine the flow of chapters, underline the cast of characters, and look for conclusions.
3. Mine the material—look for principles of government and politics, historical examples, main personalities, and principles.
4. Read the text—highlight, underline, or take notes.

Building Your Government and Politics Vocabulary

Just as you have become familiar with those key words that reappear in a historical context, you will also see a repetition of terms, phrases, and concepts related to U.S. government and politics. The more you use them, the faster you will internalize them. Become familiar with the terminology through readings, your own writing, debating topics with your classmates, and answering test-related questions. When you watch the news, listen for the lingo. You will be surprised at how fast you start using the same language as politicians and elected officials. Be sure to review the extensive glossary at the end of the book.

EXAMPLE: A newspaper article talks about the prospects of a presidential veto of a rider to the Defense Department appropriations bill.

TRANSLATION: The president may not sign a piece of legislation because an amendment he did not agree to was included as part of a revenue bill for the Defense Department.

MULTIPLE-CHOICE QUESTIONS

TIP

As a general rule, you must answer 50 percent of the multiple-choice questions correctly and get an acceptable score on the free-response sections in order to receive a score of 3 (qualified).

There are 60 questions and each question has five answer choices. You have 45 minutes to complete this section, which accounts for 50 percent of the grade. This section covers the following topics:

- 5 to 15 percent: Constitutional Foundations of Democracy
- 10 to 20 percent: Political Theory and Beliefs and Their Influence on Individuals
- 10 to 20 percent: The Development and Philosophies of Political Parties, Interest Groups, and Mass Media
- 35 to 45 percent: The Branches of Government, the Bureaucracy, and the Development of Policy
- 5 to 15 percent: Civil Liberties and Civil Rights
- 5 to 15 percent: Public Policy

Strategies for Answering Multiple-Choice Questions

- Read the entire question. Underline key words in the question such as: all of the following EXCEPT, which of the following, increases, decreases, are commonly used, is responsible, principles, most accurately compares, is recognized as, best describes, is correct, results, reflects, is most likely, is true, all the following are true, least likely, and which best DEFINES.
- Look for and underline key vocabulary words in the questions and answer choices.
- Read all answer choices. Using the process of elimination can usually increase your ability to find the correct answer. In questions where there is an "All of the above" or more than one correct choice, make sure that you look for multiple answers.
- Be aware of "negative" questions such as "All of the following EXCEPT."
- Answer all of the questions. Since there is no penalty for wrong answers, try to eliminate any obvious incorrect choices, and then guess. If you guess correctly, you will increase your score! An incorrect guess will not affect your score. You should be able to answer at least 50 of the 60 questions.
- Go with your first instinct. Usually, your first response is the correct one. Only change answers if you are absolutely certain.

- Be aware of the time limitation. Unlike other AP history tests, you have only 45 minutes, rather than 60 minutes, to answer all the questions. Try to give yourself a breather between the time you complete the section and that last check to determine if you want to answer any of the circled questions.

Types of Multiple-Choice Questions

The AP U.S. Government and Politics Examination relies on a variety of multiple-choice questions, including identification and analysis. Those kinds of questions can be further identified as generalizations, comparing and contrasting concepts and events, cause-and-effect relationships, definitional, solution to a problem, and chronological.

In addition to identification and analysis questions, there are stimulus-based questions that rely on your interpretation and understanding of graphs, charts and tables, political cartoons, short narrative passages, surveys and poll data, quotations that come from primary source documents, and Supreme Court decisions.

In this exam the trend is to increase the number of these stimulus-based questions in the multiple-choice section of the test.

IDENTIFICATION AND ANALYSIS QUESTIONS

1. Which best reflects the principle of separation of powers in the U.S. system of government? | **Definitional**

    (A) Political linkage institutions
    (B) The division of power between the federal government and state governments
    (C) Qualifications for U.S. senator
    (D) Congress having the ability to make laws that are necessary and proper
    (E) Federal regulatory agencies

2. Incumbents would most likely be successful in their reelection campaigns because of which of the following factors? | **Cause-and-Effect Relationships**

    (A) Voter identification
    (B) Rejection of PAC money
    (C) Limited services to their constituents
    (D) An aggressive campaign by a young opponent
    (E) A third-party candidate entering the race

3. In *Miranda v Arizona*, the Supreme Court based its decision on which constitutional principle? | **Generalization**

    (A) Convicted felons cannot be tried for the same crime twice.
    (B) Citizens can exercise free speech except when there is a proven clear and present danger.
    (C) People have the right to exercise their religion freely except when that religion is supported by public funds.
    (D) The rights of the accused are protected by the due process right of a lawyer being present at the time of interrogation.
    (E) A person's house cannot be searched without a warrant.

4. Which of the following individuals would be most likely to register to vote?

(A) A person with a college education

(B) Somebody who moves from job to job

(C) A senior citizen living in a nursing home

(D) An unemployed person on welfare

(E) A felon who is pardoned and is eligible to vote

5. Which election is an example of a shift of party realignment?

(A) The election of 1932 and a shift of business executives to Roosevelt

(B) The election of 1960 and a shift of Catholic voters to Kennedy

(C) The election of 1976 and a shift of religious conservatives to Carter

(D) The election of 1980 and a shift of blue-collar Democrats to Reagan

(E) The election of 2000 and a shift of African-Americans to George W. Bush

6. Which of the following statements most accurately compares the political, social, and economic philosophy of the participants at the Constitutional Convention regarding the debate over the inclusion of the Bill of Rights into the document?

(A) Federalists favored the inclusion of a bill of rights.

(B) Anti-Federalists favored a bill of rights as part of a constitution.

(C) Wealthy property owners favored the inclusion of a bill of rights.

(D) Farmers were against the inclusion of a bill of rights.

(E) Slave owners favored the inclusion of a bill of rights.

7. All of the following are powers of the Supreme Court EXCEPT

(A) judicial review

(B) preside over impeachment trials of the president

(C) hear cases on appeal from state courts

(D) decide cases deriving from original jurisdiction

(E) rewrite congressional legislation that the Court declares unconstitutional

Answer Explanations

Once you identify the specific kind of identification and analysis question, you must then proceed to answer it by process of elimination or through specific knowledge of the concept or information. Unlike stimulus-response questions, where the answer can be found in the data, identification and analysis questions are factually based.

1. **(D)** Question 1 requires an understanding of the definition of separation of powers as well as definitions of political linkage institutions (choice A) and division of power (choice B). You also must have factual knowledge regarding the role of federal regulatory agencies (choice E) to understand that qualifications for office do not represent a power of a branch of government (choice C). Choice D is correct because the only stated power is the elastic clause giving Congress the power to make laws necessary and proper.

2. **(A)** Question 2 asks what factor (the cause) would result (the effect) in the reelection of incumbents. Choices B and C are completely wrong and can be eliminated right away. Choices D and E are not directly related to the cause and effect nature of the question. Choice A is correct because the only factor that has a direct impact on the success of the incumbent is voter identification.

3. **(D)** Question 3 gives you a specific event and asks you through analysis to identify the general principle that came about as a result of the event. In order to answer it, you must know what the event is all about. In this case you must know something about the *Miranda* decision. You may be able to eliminate two of the choices (B and C) if you know that the decision had to do with a criminal. But, to answer the question, you really had to know that Miranda did not have a lawyer present when he was interrogated (choice D).

4. **(A)** Question 4 presents a problem. Which type of individual would most likely register to vote? You probably could eliminate three choices (B, C, and E) because logically people in these groups would not have an incentive or desire to vote. That leaves you with two choices related to socioeconomic status. Even though it would be to the advantage of an unemployed person on welfare (choice D) to register, it is highly unlikely that a person on welfare would do so, thus you would have to eliminate that choice as well. This leaves choice A as the correct answer.

5. **(D)** Question 5 really combines two forms of identification and analysis questions—the definitional and chronological. You must know the definition of *party realignment* and something about the history of presidential elections. The only election in the choices given that resulted in a dramatic party shift was choice D, the Reagan election of 1980 where many traditional blue-collar Democrats voted Republican. They became known as Reagan Democrats.

6. **(B)** Question 6 compares and contrasts the differences between the participants at the Constitutional Convention in relation to their attitude toward inclusion of the bill of rights. This is an extremely difficult question because you must have factual knowledge about the issues. You must know that in fact certain groups and individuals did not want a bill of rights as part of the original Constitution; you must know the characteristics and names of the groups represented at the convention, and you must know something about the socioeconomic status characteristics of those groups. If you knew the differences between the Federalists and Anti-Federalists, then the question is much easier to answer because choice B gives a straightforward factual response.

7. **(E)** Question 7 presents the problem of determining which of the listed choices are legitimate powers of the Supreme Court. The strategy for answering this question is to look for the factually correct statements. By doing so, you will end up with the one incorrect or negative answer, which is the correct choice. In Question 7, the powers of the Supreme Court are outlined in the Constitution and have developed as a result of judicial practice. Choice A is factually correct because of the decision reached in *Marbury v Madison*. Choices B, C, and D are all listed powers found in Article III of the Constitution. Choice E, the correct choice, is factually incorrect because though the Court can declare congressional legislation unconstitutional, only the Congress can rewrite the law.

STIMULUS-BASED MULTIPLE-CHOICE QUESTIONS

Here are a few examples of the more common type of stimulus-based questions found in the multiple-choice section of the test.

Short Narrative Passage | Many critics of presidential poll taking point to the manner in which polls are taken and the number of polls released prior to election day. We have Democratic-sponsored polls, Republican-sponsored polls, daily tracking polls, polls that ask registered voters who they are voting for, and polls that ask likely voters who they are voting for.

1. What is the primary impact of a poll driven election?

   (A) It determines the outcome of the election.
   (B) It usually favors the incumbent.
   (C) It helps the candidate understand the state of the horse race.
   (D) It enhances the policy issues of a campaign.
   (E) It motivates undecided voters.

Short Quotation | 2. Former presidential candidate John McCain said, "They said money is free speech. Since when is money free speech?" Which of the following would agree with this statement?

   (A) advocates of political campaign finance reform
   (B) The Supreme Court
   (C) Political Action Committees
   (D) Independent Expenditure Committees
   (E) proponents of the First Amendment

Supreme Court Decision | 3. "If there is a bedrock principle underlying the First Amendment, it is that the Government may not prohibit the expression of an idea simply because society finds the idea itself offensive or disagreeable. . . . We have not recognized an exception to this principle even where our flag has been involved."

The *Texas v Johnson* Supreme Court decision quoted above did which of the following?

   (A) made flag desecration legal for nonpolitical reasons
   (B) upheld the Texas statute, which resulted in Johnson's arrest for burning the flag
   (C) made Congress pass a constitutional amendment prohibiting flag burning
   (D) recognized that burning a flag for political reasons is a form of symbolic speech protected by the First Amendment
   (E) expanded the ways government can prohibit freedom of speech because of offensive actions

Grill our experts with your food safety questions. Call the USDA Hotline.

4. The subject of the cartoon presents what point of view?

(A) It is the responsibility of the consumer to be aware of potential food hazards.
(B) The U.S. Department of Agriculture fought for the passage of the Meat Inspection Act.
(C) Congress should conduct oversight hearings regarding food safety.
(D) A major task of the Department of Agriculture is to provide public information related to regulations.
(E) The president supports the Department of Agriculture's efforts in establishing regulatory reform.

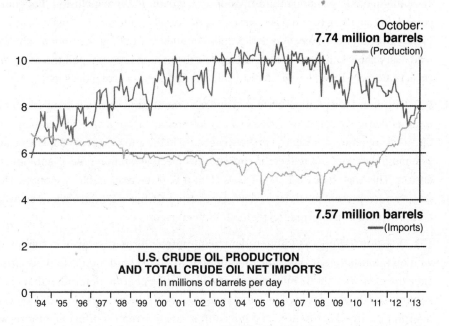

5. According to the information in this chart, which of the following statements is true?

(A) The amount of domestic crude oil production has increased from 1994 to 2008.
(B) Overall imports of crude oil have remained constant from 1980 to 2010.
(C) The amount of crude oil produced was equal to the amount of oil imported from 1980 to 1990.
(D) A trade surplus resulted from the overall production of domestic crude oil.
(E) The increase of domestic oil production has led to a decline in gas prices.

Answer Explanations

1. **(C)** The passage makes the point that there are many different polls that are utilized during a campaign. The question asks you to explain the consequence of these polls on the election. Choice C is the correct answer because the impact of these polls on a race is to increase what is called the horse race component—who is ahead at any given time. Choice A is incorrect because polls change, and the voters determine the outcome. Choice B is incorrect because a poll can favor the challenger as much as the incumbent. Choice D is incorrect because polls tend to distract from the policy debate. Choice E is incorrect because studies have found that the proliferation of polls turns off undecided voters.

2. **(A)** Question 2 requires you to apply the context of McCain's quote to a group that would disagree with it. The quote refers to the Citizen's United Supreme Court decision in which they equated political donations as a form of free speech. As a result, there was a tremendous increase in the amount of allowable political donations by independent groups. Choice A is correct because advocates of political campaign finance reform would agree with the idea that money should not be equated with free speech. Choices B, C, and D are incorrect because these groups favor the increase in campaign contributions. Choice E is incorrect because not every proponent of the First Amendment equates money with free speech.

3. **(D)** Question 3 incorporates an excerpt from a Supreme Court decision, *Texas v Johnson*, which received a great deal of notoriety. Even if you didn't know the background of the case, the quote gives enough information to lead you to the conclusion that choice D is correct, because flag burning is a symbolic political act protected by the First Amendment to the Constitution. Choice A is a trick answer aimed at catching the student who does not read every choice. In fact the decision made a distinction between political and nonpolitical acts. Choices B and E refer to results that contradict the actual decision.

4. **(D)** Question 4 is a political cartoon that deals with the theme of a federal cabinet providing a service to the consumer. It asks you to determine the *point of view* of the cartoon. This direction sometimes presents a problem because in the choices there could be an accurate statement that does not reflect the cartoon's perspective but that reflects another accurate answer. This was the case in choices A, C, and E, three reasonable responses. However, they do not represent the point of view of the cartoon. Choice D is an obvious answer based on the caption and information pictured in the cartoon.

5. **(E)** Question 5 simply asks the student to interpret information given in a graph dealing with oil imports versus domestic oil production. All the student has to do is cross reference the choices with the information provided in the chart to determine that choice E is correct. The only knowledge required to answer this question is the ability to accurately interpret the trends presented and not confuse the line representing oil imports with the line representing domestic oil production. The pitfall in this kind of question is when the student superficially looks at the information. In that case, some students would pick choice A as the answer because oil imports have risen consistently over the period.

A Final Word About the Multiple-Choice Section

Throughout the course of study, your instructor should be giving you a variety of sample multiple-choice questions with five possible answers. These questions can come from this review book, other books that have test banks, self-generated tests, or sample questions available from the Educational Testing Service. You should become sensitive to the kinds of questions you score well on as well as those questions that give you trouble. Keep an ongoing list of vocabulary concepts you are not familiar with.

Also be aware that, statistically, the multiple-choice questions when scored provide for a wide range of students correctly answering any given question. The percentage of students answering questions correctly on a sample test ranged from a high of 94 percent to a low of 14 percent depending upon the difficulty of the particular question. Taking the average of the percent correct of all 60 questions on a sample exam, for the students attempting to answer the questions, the percent correct was 65 percent. This does not correlate to the final score of the exam but provides an insight into the range of difficulty of the questions.

As far as the actual scores are concerned, of those students with multiple-choice scores of 51 or higher, most earned scores of 4 or 5. Of those with multiple-choice scores of 41–50, the majority received a score of 4, whereas most others earned scores of 2 or 3. Of those earning 31–40, the majority got a score of 3, whereas most others earned a score of 1 or 2. Students scoring between 11–20 usually earned a score of 1. And of the test takers with scores of 16 or less, the majority got a score of 1.

FREE-RESPONSE QUESTIONS

You must answer four mandatory questions in 100 minutes (25 minutes per answer). This section is worth 50 percent of your grade.

As a general rule, if a student scores above 50 percent on the multiple-choice section and scores in the middle to upper range of the free-response questions, that student probably will receive an overall score of 3.

There are different approaches that the student can take in answering the four required free-response questions. Depending on the specifics of the question you may have to write an answer that is based on:

- an introductory statement that lists the tasks you are going to answer (i.e., give examples that illustrate, discuss the nature of . . .)
- data (graphs, charts, quotes)

The following text provides the general criteria for scoring the free-response section:

Each of the four free-response questions is worth 12.5 percent and, together, the answers total 50 percent of the exam's overall score. In scoring the answers, raters are given a rubric (general scoring criteria) that ranges from 3 to 9 points. These totals are then converted into an overall score for the free-response section.

Depending on the criteria established for a question, students receive 1 point for each task successfully completed. Full credit is obtained for each part of the answer when, for example, students identify the correct answer and then explain it through the use of examples. Students can also receive partial credit if they fail to answer a question completely.

It is important to remember that when answering a free-response question the goal is to fully address the listed tasks. You must then give specific examples to support your answer. Students

TIP

Without a doubt, the best way to improve your multiple-choice test-taking ability is through practice and repetition.

TIP

Learn to recognize the major components of a free-response answer. They are relatively easy to pick out. Key words include:

1. list
2. identify
3. describe
4. explain
5. evaluate

who answer the questions completely and correctly and provide adequate examples will receive full credit.

The four questions are worth 50 percent of the examination. Each answer is weighted equally.

Notice how the key phrases are very similar and call for the completion of a task. Additional sample and practice free-response questions appear in the review chapters and in the model tests.

Free-Response Question Topics

Here are some topics that have appeared in recent years as free-response question prompts. They illustrate the nature of the question and in no way are meant to reflect the exact language.

- the extension of the Bill of Rights to the states through Supreme Court cases such as *Gitlow v New York* (1925), *Wolf v Colorado* (1949), and *Gideon v Wainwright* (1963)
- the balance of power between the executive and legislative branches as exemplified by the War Powers Act and the Budget and Impoundment Control Act
- the contrast between the candidate-oriented and issue-oriented presidential campaigns of the 1990s and how the media and the candidates have contributed to these types of campaigns
- how special interest groups target the federal government and how these groups use specific tactics and resources to achieve their goals
- the weaknesses of the Articles of Confederation and how they were remedied by the adoption of the Constitution
- how the appointment process of Supreme Court justices has become politicized by looking at the characteristics of nominees and showing how interest groups affect the process
- why it has been so difficult to pass campaign finance legislation by looking at the Supreme Court decision in *Buckley v Valeo* (1976), soft money, and the issue of congressional incumbency
- why the Fourteenth Amendment to the Constitution is so important by examining two specific provisions and applying the first to a landmark case such as *Brown v Board of Education* (1954), *Baker v Carr* (1962), or *Regents of the University of California v Bakke* (1978) and applying the second provision to another landmark case such as *Mapp v Ohio* (1961), *Gideon v Wainwright* (1963), or *Miranda v Arizona* (1966)
- why it is difficult to create effective public policy as a result of divided government, weak party discipline, and the increase in the number of special interest groups and political action committees (PACs)
- why voter turnout has declined in federal elections and why voter turnout is greater in presidential elections versus midterm elections
- factors that increase or decrease presidential approval ratings
- the identification of formal constitutional powers of the president and Congress in making foreign policy, informal constitutional powers used by the president in making foreign policy, and how those powers give him an advantage over Congress
- the definition of divided government and how it has contributed to a decline in the trust of government: how the increased cost of elections has contributed to the decline in trust of government and how the decline in trust in government has impacted individual political behavior
- how the judicial branch is both immune from and responds to public opinion
- how the federal government has increased its power over the states through the budget process, the elastic clause, and the interstate commerce clause. How specific legislation

such as the Americans with Disabilities Act, Civil Rights Act of 1964, and Clean Air Act illustrate how the federal government's power has increased

- how the Supreme Court has used incorporation to apply the Bill of Rights to the states in such areas as Fourth Amendment privacy rights and search and seizure, First Amendment and Fifth Amendment issues, and Sixth Amendment rights of the accused
- how campaign finance proposals such as eliminating soft money, limiting special interest group independent expenditures, and raising hard money limits have been debated over the past 10 years
- how specific bureaucratic agencies make policy and how Congress uses oversight over these agencies
- the characteristics of a bicameral legislature and the different powers held by the House and Senate
- the nature of the electoral college winner-take-all system, how it hurts third party candidates, and why the electoral college has not been abolished
- the components of the First Amendment religion clause as they relate to *Engel v Vitale* (school prayer), *Lemon v Kurtzman* (state financing of religious schools), *Reynolds v United States* (polygamy) and *Oregon v Smith* (drug use by Native Americans as part of their tribal rites)
- the constitutional dispute between the executive and legislative branches over the War Powers Act: how provisions of the War Powers Act limit the war-making power of the president. What other powers Congress has in its ability to deal with wars
- what congressional reapportionment means and its relationship to the states. What congressional redistricting means. The results of gerrymandering, and when it is used to redistrict. How Supreme Court decisions related to congressional redistricting have placed restrictions on redistricting
- the balance between presidential influence over Congress versus how a president is limited in exerting influence over Congress in the area of public policy as exemplified by the enumerated powers of the president that help him influence public policy. How mandatory spending, party polarization, and the lame-duck period limit a president in influencing Congress in the area of public policy
- the relationship between fiscal policy and monetary policy, and their impact on the economy of the United States. Why the Federal Reserve Board has independence in influencing monetary policy, and how the president and Congress influence fiscal policy
- the impact that the Fifteenth Amendment to the United States Constitution had on voting rights, and how civil rights laws have changed African-American voter turnout. What states did prior to the 1960s that had an impact on African-Americans. Examples of unconventional political participation that African-Americans used to bring about changes in civil rights laws
- the connection that Federalist No. 10 had to majority and minority factions regarding the power they could have in government. How the United States Constitution not only created a democracy but also established rights for the minority against majority rule. Which part of the government represented the people and how the Constitution protected minority rights. How primaries, the direct election of senators, and the expansion of voting helped create a more representative government
- the concept of linkage institutions and how elections (as one example of a linkage institution) connect people to elected officials. While low voter turnout can negatively weaken this link, what other examples of linkage institutions positively help connect people to their

governments. How the factors of age and education impact voting. One factor that hurts voter turnout. An example of another linkage institution that increases the connection of people to their elected representatives

- the consequences of majority party rule in Congress in relation to the lawmaking process. How majority rule does not necessarily mean that a law will be passed by Congress, because the rules of each House can influence whether a law is passed. In the legislative process in the House of Representatives, what types of things the majority party can do to pass a law. Examples of different rules that the House and Senate have that help each chamber pass legislation but sometimes result in the same legislation not being passed in both houses

- interest groups are formed with the purpose of favoring their positions. The Constitution also has different parts that protect individual rights and their interests. Explain how the Bill of Rights protects the rights of individuals and their right to promote political positions. Explain how grassroots mobilization, lobbying, and litigation are used by interest groups to promote public policy. Describe how the federal government regulates special interest groups.

- the federal bureaucracy has many roles in the executive branch carrying out its policies and programs and exerts independence in carrying out this function. Many employees in the federal government are civil service workers hired under the merit system. Describe what is meant by the merit system. Describe how the independence of the federal bureaucracy is impacted by its structure and the complexity of public policy positions. Explain by using examples from the Constitution how the Congress, the judiciary, and special interest groups check the federal bureaucracy.

- one characteristic the framers of the Constitution developed is the concept of a limited government. One of the goals that the Founding Fathers had in drafting the Constitution and Bill of Rights was to restrict the power of the federal government. The powers of state governments were also limited by future constitutional developments. Explain how federalism and checks and balances limit the powers of the president. Explain how the Establishment Clause and the right to a public trial limit the power of the national government. Explain how the citizenship section of the Fourteenth Amendment and selective incorporation limit the powers of state governments.

- the U.S. Supreme Court handles many different types of appeals. On average the court hears around seventy-five cases a year that are taken up as a result of different factors that also influences the decision the courts make. What is a judicial review? What impact does a judicial review have on the power of the Supreme Court as it relates to checks and balances? Explain how the Supreme Court grants a writ of certiorari. What impact does stare decisis and judicial activism have on the Court's decision-making process?

- public opinion polls are an example of linkage with congressmen and women and other elected officeholders. They use the results of polls in different ways, such as what their constituents favor and the political impact of what the results reflect. What are the characteristics of a scientifically accurate poll? How does public opinion influence how a member of congress votes? How does public opinion impact close reelections of representatives? How do the voting records of representatives and party leadership reduce the importance of public opinion?

- every 4 years each party has a national nominating convention at which time the delegates choose a presidential and vice-presidential candidate. The delegates are selected in different ways by states and the parties. What is an open primary? What is a caucus? What is the impact of a winner-take-all primary that is used by the Republican Party? What is the impact of the Democratic Party having superdelegates and show how they increase the power of party leaders during the nominating process. Why does a candidate have a different approach to the primaries than the general election?

- one of the characteristics of the U.S. Constitution is separation of powers among the three branches of government rather than power being concentrated to a single branch. This often results in conflicts between the executive and legislative branches. How is Congress impacted by the president's veto power, the president's power to issue executive orders, and the president's power as commander in chief? How is the president impacted by Congress's power of legislative oversight, the Senate's power of advice and consent, and Congress's budgetary power?

- Congressmen have many responsibilities including writing legislation, oversight, and constituent service. Describe how the Senate filibuster, House Rules Committee, and the Conference Committee impacts lawmaking. Describe how Congress uses oversight of the federal bureaucracy. Explain the role of casework and how it impacts legislation.

- The judiciary is considered not to be influenced by politics. But in reality, politics does impact the courts. Describe two political features that impact the confirmation process and explain how these features make it more difficult for a nominee to get confirmed. Explain one power of the president that is a check on the decisions of the court.

- One of the goals of special interest groups is to influence the political process in a way that has positive results for their members. Describe two methods used by special interest groups to influence elections. Explain how special interest groups use issue networks (iron triangles) and amicus curiae briefs to influence governmental policies. Explain how the media and pluralism limit the influence of special interest groups.

- Our democracy has differing theories of representation. Define direct democracy. What is a republican form of government? Give one reason why a republican form of government was selected by the framers of the Constitution. Describe the trustee model and delegate model of congressional representation and explain why a congressman would choose the trustee model over the delegate model.

- There are many different roles that political parties play in elections and the institutions of government. Describe two activities that political parties perform in elections. Describe one significant job that a political party plays in Congress to advance the party's agenda. Explain how direct primaries and candidate-centered campaigns have lessened the role of political parties in the political process. Explain how the polarization of political parties has increased a party's influence in Congress.

- Creating public policy is a complicated process. How policies are formed, enacted, and implemented involve different institutions of government. Explain how the media and elections impact the creation of public policy. Describe how congressional committees and executive orders help enact public policy. Explain how bureaucracies and iron triangles help implement public policy.

- Federalists and Anti-Federalists battled over the ratification of the U.S. Constitution. Ultimately, political compromises were made before the ratification was approved. Modern day political debates also reflect the political differences of each group. Compare what the Federalists and Anti-Federalists believed regarding the power of the central government. Explain how the First and Tenth Amendments reflected the Anti-Federalist positions. Explain how either the due process or equal protection clause of the Fourteenth Amendment changed the relationship between state and national governments.

- Amendments to the U.S. Constitution, voting laws, and changes in demographics have impacted voter turnout. Identify how the Fifteenth, Nineteenth, and Twenty-sixth Amendments have impacted voters. Explain how the motor voter law and voter photo identification impact voter turnout. Describe how either education or age determines whether a person will vote. Explain why presidential elections and midterm elections have different voter turnout rates. Explain why primary and general elections have different voter turnout rates.

■ Foreign policy is determined by both the president and congress. Even though the power of the president has increased, the president still is prevented from making all foreign policy decisions. Describe how foreign policy is made by choosing two congressional enumerated powers. Describe how foreign policy is made by choosing two presidential expressed powers. Explain the importance of the use of the president's executive agreement power in carrying out foreign policy. Explain how either elections or the president's job approval ratings can reduce how the president can carry out foreign policy.

■ Even though the president seems to have the upper hand in making policy, there are still limits to presidential power. Describe how the president's role as Chief legislator, chief bureaucrat, or chief administrator has resulted in presidential power. Explain how civil service employees and the Supreme Court limit the president's ability to make power. Describe how divided government impacts policy making.

■ One of the consequences of the creation of the Constitution by the Founding Fathers was a federal system of government that resulted and impacted the relationship of state and national governments. Compare how state sovereignty and national sovereignty differed under the Articles of Confederation and the Constitution. Explain how the commerce clause and mandates increased the power of the national government over the states. Explain how block grants and Supreme Court decisions have impacted the devolution of power from the national government to the states.

■ Civil rights and civil liberties have been protected by the Fourteenth Amendment to the Constitution. Describe how civil rights and civil liberties differ from each other. Identify what is the primary clause of the Fourteenth Amendment that furthers civil rights. Describe a piece of legislation that resulted in increased civil rights to women and persons with disabilities. Identify what is the primary clause that furthers civil liberties. Explain how two of the following Supreme Court cases incorporated civil liberties—*Gideon v Wainwright*, *Mapp v Ohio*, and *Miranda v Arizona*.

KEY TERMS USED IN FREE-RESPONSE QUESTIONS

Explain

Explain how incorporation of the Bill of Rights has had an impact on the states.

Identify and Explain

Discuss how demographics influence voter turnout.

Define

Define incorporation and explain its effect on the states.

Compare

Compare the differences between an open and closed primary.

Identify and describe

Identify and describe the role that special interest groups play in policymaking.

Using the information from the chart

Using the information from the chart, identify and explain how the creation of the budget impacts public policy.

List and identify a solution

List problems associated with the Articles of Confederation and *identify* how the Constitution helped to solve those problems.

Using the map

Using the map, identify those sections of the country that voted Democratic and those sections that voted Republican.

Perform the following tasks by defining, describing, or identifying or explaining

Perform the following tasks in identifying the advantages and disadvantages of congressional incumbency by: defining the franking privilege, discussing the impact of a political party's endorsement, and explaining the role of mid-term elections on a challenger's chances for success.

Strategies for Answering the Free-Response Questions

- Read all of the questions, looking for tasks.
- Read the entire question. Underline key words (listed in a previous section) that will help you understand what the question is looking for.
- On the exam, jot down references to data and specific examples that relate to the question.
- Outline your argument with references to data; make sure you provide a specific example for every statement made.
- Use factual data, both historical and current, to support your answer. If you are not sure of a specific name, date, or term, don't use it. However, if you can describe an example, filling in most of the details, do so.
- Make sure that your supporting evidence and data support what the task(s) ask(s).
- Start writing your answer following the format of the question: answer task (a) first, then task (b), etc.
- Using your outline, use the specific factual data and examples. Make sure that your answer refers to the tasks mentioned in the question.
- If the question gives you specific data areas to comment on, be sure your examples and answer refer to those areas in the question.
- Reread! Revise. Be aware of the 25-minute time guide.

How to Write a Free-Response Answer

Once you follow the strategy advice, actually writing the free-response answer is an easy task. For some inexplicable reason, students have a phobia about writing. Try to approach this task as if you were creating a multilevel building using building blocks.

The foundation would represent the premise of the question. The first floor represents the first task, usually asking you to identify an issue, statement, policy, or the like. The second floor explains what you have identified. The third floor represents the second task, and the next floor describes or explains what you have previously identified as part of the second task. Most answers can have two or more tasks. Other answers are based on an illustration, and will be covered later in this chapter.

BUILDING BLOCKS OF A TYPICAL FREE-RESPONSE ANSWER

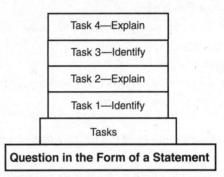

The most important start to your answer is to understand what the question is all about. Typically, the answer will start with a statement related to a topic. Then the question will ask you to complete a series of tasks. Then proceed to follow the "building block" model discussed earlier and complete each task. These building blocks of information will help demonstrate your knowledge of the subject matter that you have decided to write about. There is no need to include a formal conclusion.

Let the reader know what you are doing every step of the way, and make sure you identify each task by writing the number and letter of the task (e.g., 1a).

Things to Avoid in Answering the Free-Response Question

- statements that are implausible, can't be proven, or don't relate to the question
- unsubstantiated generalizations in your answer
- imposing your own opinion—your own thoughts and feelings are not evidence
- incorrect data or irrelevant information
- avoid lengthening your answer with excessive wordiness to make it appear as though you are saying more than you are—you are not fooling anyone. If you use what may be called building slippage (BS), your building blocks will begin to tumble under their own weight.

Sample Free-Response Question

For illustrative purposes, some model free-response answers in this book may include more material than the question requires. For example, the question may say to choose two out of three topics, but the model answer will address all three topics to give readers the most thorough information. Students should practice writing their answers to the free-response questions that address all the parts of the question and complete the answer within the 25-minute time limit.

Directions: You have 25 minutes to answer the following question. This question is based on your knowledge of U.S. government and politics and it may contain materials from charts, graphs, and tables that you will have to analyze and draw conclusions from. Make sure you provide sufficient information and examples in your answer.

Some people have made the claim that the Supreme Court's decision to hear controversial cases has the potential of altering public policy (4 pts.):

Using the Defense of Marriage Act (DOMA) and *United States v Windsor*

(a) Identify and explain the provisions of the Defense of Marriage Act.

(b) Explain two ways how *United States v Windsor* altered public policy.

Following this answer you will find a scoring rubric that describes the number of points that is allocated for this question and a brief explanation of some of the possible answers to the question.

SAMPLE RESPONSE

(a)   In 1996, Congress passed the Defense of Marriage Act, aka DOMA, and President Clinton signed it into law. The law was passed in response to the potential of Hawaii making gay marriage legal in that state. The act allowed states not to recognize gay marriage laws passed in another state. This kind of law was unique since the Constitution's full faith and credit clause lets states recognize the laws of other states including marriage. But, since the law defined marriage as only the union between one man and one woman, and that means a person of the opposite sex, it would exclude any recognition of gay marriage. States would have the option of recognizing the legality of gay marriages in their own states, but any gay couple who married would be denied over 1,000 federal benefits including Social Security and welfare programs.

(b)   In 2013, the Supreme Court ruled in a case called *United States v Windsor* that the Defense of Marriage Act violated the Fifth Amendment's liberty clause, and ruled that the law was unconstitutional. The impact of the law was significant and far reaching. As a result of the decision, gay couples who were married in states that recognized gay marriage or performed gay marriages were able to get all the federal benefits that were previously denied to them by the law. In addition, those gay couples who were legally married in a state that recognized gay marriage and moved to a state that banned gay marriage would still be able to receive federal benefits. In 2015, the Supreme Court legalized gay marriage throughout the United States.

TIP

1. Read all the questions.
2. Look for key terms and any specific information contained in the questions.
3. Outline your argument using building blocks as a way of organizing your information.

SCORING GUIDELINES FOR SAMPLE FREE-RESPONSE QUESTION

Part (a) 2 Points

One point is earned for identifying what the Defense of Marriage is, and one point is earned for explaining the major provisions of the law.

Answers may include, but are not limited to, the identification and explanation of the following:

- The Defense of Marriage Act was a law passed that allowed states not to recognize gays who were legally married in other states.
- The Defense of Marriage Act defined marriage as the union of one man and one woman.
- The Defense of Marriage Act permitted gay marriage in states where they were performed.
- The Defense of Marriage Act prevented legally married gay couples from receiving federal benefits.

Part (b) 1 Point

Two points are earned for citing two ways the court's opinion had an impact on public policy.

Answers may include, but are not limited to, the following:

- The Supreme Court in ruling the Defense of Marriage Act unconstitutional sanctioned the legality of gay marriages in those states that permitted them.
- The overturning of the Defense of Marriage Act meant that legally married gay couples would receive federal benefits.
- Legally married gay couples would also receive federal benefits even if they moved into a state that banned gay marriage.

DATA-BASED QUESTIONS

Questions that are based specifically on data such as charts and graphs may be historical or contemporary in nature. Students are expected to analyze, evaluate, and interpret material from a variety of sources. AP readers will look for evidence that the student understands the data, explains the data in relation to the question, and gives specific examples to answer the question as it relates to the data. Examples of data material include, but are not limited to:

- charts
- graphs
- tables
- political cartoons
- survey or poll results

Key Terms Used in Data-Based Free-Response Questions

The directions are very clear that the student must analyze and integrate an analysis with a general understanding of U.S. government and politics. Be especially aware of the following phrases:

- using data, identify
- explain
- using data, describe
- using quotation, identify and explain
- identify trends

Just as in the multiple-choice section, you should underline the key terms used in the question. You should also highlight significant points within the data itself. For example, underline the title of a graph and the graph's statistical parameters.

Topics in Data-Based Free-Response Questions

The following topics represent ones that have appeared on the test in recent years. In no way are they meant to reflect the exact language of the questions.

- Analyze the nature of discretionary and mandatory spending through pie charts and how they create barriers that impact lawmaking.
- Describe voting patterns in presidential elections using a map and identify geographic regions that voted strongly Democrat and strongly Republican.
- Explain how congressional reelection patterns have created an advantage for incumbents using a pie chart and describe the impact that incumbency has on the political process.
- Describe, identify, and explain a chart regarding the distribution of government benefits for children and the elderly from 1965 through 1986.
- Identify trends in a graph comparing the number of federal and state employees and how block grants and federal mandates impacted these trends.
- Identify the point of view of a political cartoon dealing with Ralph Nader's candidacy in the 2000 presidential election. Explain how the electoral system hurts a third party's chances in winning elections and describe how third parties make a contribution to the political system.
- Define what an entitlement program is and explain "where the money comes from to pay for Social Security." Identify the problems Social Security faces in the future.
- Define what is meant by policy agenda and how the media uses it to impact the political agenda. Why is the president better able to use the media than Congress? Interpret a table that deals with how often viewers in different age groups watched the evening news, and explain how the pattern changed. As a result of this change, what would be the consequences for the president in relation to how he uses the media to accomplish his policies?
- Identify a trend in a graph that shows how shifts in Democratic and Republican party identification have impacted presidential and congressional elections in the South. Explain how the advantage of incumbency, gerrymandering, and differences between state and national parties resulted in more Democratic candidates being elected to the House of Representatives than the presidency. Explain how Catholics, labor union members, women, and social conservatives have changed the party identification of the Democrats and Republicans over the past number of decades.
- Using a graph of minority representation in Congress, compare the differences of minority representation in Congress between 1960 and 2000. Explain how the Voting Rights Act of 1965 and the Twenty-fourth Amendment to the U.S. Constitution helped remove minority voting barriers. Identify one thing that prevents minority representation in Congress. Explain *why* this feature you identified prevents minority representation.
- There are many different considerations that presidents use when appointing people to the federal courts and the confirmation process may be very hard. Using the chart of Presidential Appointments to the Federal Judiciary by Selected Demographic Characteristics Between 2000 and 2011 describe one way President Obama's appointments and President George W. Bush's appointments to the federal judiciary were the same. Using the chart describe two ways President Obama's appointees were different from President George W. Bush's appointees. Explain why what party the president comes from creates differences in

presidential appointments to the federal courts. Describe one way a president can positively influence the success of his appointments being confirmed to the federal court.

- Based on a chart that illustrates the extent of party polarization in the House and Senate from 1879–2007, give a definition of party polarization, identify one ideological difference between the parties, describe two reasons why there is party polarization in Congress, and describe the impact of party polarization on the ability of Congress to make policy.
- Based on a map that shows five swing states that influences the campaign strategies of presidential candidates in the general election; describe one reason why the Electoral College was chosen to elect the president; describe the meaning of the cartoon; explain why states such as California, Texas, and New York are not highlighted in the cartoon; and describe two campaign strategies used by candidates running for president highlighted in the cartoon.

How to Write the Data-Based Free-Response Answer

The data-based questions require you to interpret, analyze, and evaluate a base of information and then to make conclusions related to specific questions. In looking for the question you want to respond to, keep in mind that much of the data provided can be used as part of your answer.

After you have completed reading the data-based question(s), you should methodically follow a series of steps:

1. Highlight or underline the key terms in the question.
2. Provide specific examples that illustrate your understanding of the data.

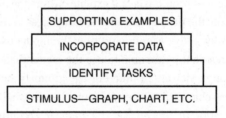

3. As you can see, just like the non-data-based free-response answer, you should identify the tasks and give supporting examples.

SAMPLE STIMULUS-BASED FREE-RESPONSE QUESTION

Use the following chart and your knowledge of U.S. politics to complete the tasks below:

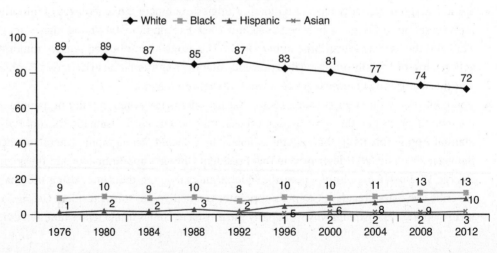

(a) Using the chart above, compare the trend of the share of the white vote to the Hispanic vote from 1976 to 2012 and explain why this trend was an important factor in determining the winner of the 2012 presidential campaign.

(b) Explain how each of the following contributed to the trend in (a)

- The 2010 Census
- The Get-Out-the-Vote operation

(c) Identify one law proposed by some states that could have decreased minority turnout in 2012. Explain how the law you identified reduces minority turnout.

SAMPLE RESPONSE

(a) Based on the information in the chart, the white voter turnout has decreased from 89 percent in 1976 to 72 percent in 2012, while the Hispanic voter turnout increased from less than 1 percent in 1976 to 13 percent in 2012. This trend was one of the key factors that contributed to the reelection of President Barack Obama over Governor Mitt Romney. Because the white vote dropped by 17 points and the Hispanic vote increased by almost 13 percent, Barack Obama was able to overcome the deficit in the overall percentage of voters who voted for him.

(b) The 2010 Census results were a key in understanding why the Hispanic vote increased so much from 1976 to 2012. The Hispanic population was the fastest-growing minority group according to the 2010 Census and that growth took place in many of the key battleground states that Obama ultimately won contributing to his electoral college victory. The 2010 Census also pointed out that by 2025 Hispanics would become the largest minority group in the United States and that their numbers would increase significantly not only in battleground states but states like Texas that could potentially put it in play in future elections.

The Get-Out-the-Vote operations (also known as GOTV) of both parties resulted in a greater participation by Hispanics. Even though Mitt Romney won the same percentage of white voters as George H. W. Bush in 1988, he still lost the election. The Obama campaign, using social media, door-to-door contacts, and grassroots volunteers, were able to identify pro-Obama voters and more important, got them to the polls. Many of these voters were minority voters who voted for Obama in 2008 and were also first-time voters in 2012.

(c) One law that some states passed that could have decreased minority turnout was photo identification regulations. The law would have forced all voters to show a government-approved identification card before voting. If a voter did not have the card, the voter would not have been able to vote. This law would have reduced minority turnout because that group would have had more difficulty understanding the requirements and it would have also been more difficult for them to obtain the specific card that was approved for identification. Opponents of these laws called it voter suppression and many of them were ruled unconstitutional by the courts.

SCORING GUIDELINES FOR DATA-BASED FREE-RESPONSE QUESTION (6 POINTS)

Part (a) 2 Points

One point is earned for identifying the trend of the share of the white vote compared with the Hispanic vote from 1976 to 2012.

- The white voter turnout has decreased from 89 percent in 1976 to 72 percent in 2012, while the Hispanic voter turnout increased from less than 1 percent in 1976 to 13 percent in 2012.

One point is earned for explaining why this trend was an important factor in determining the winner of the 2012 presidential campaign.

- Because the white vote dropped by 17 points and the Hispanic vote increased by almost 13 percent, Barack Obama was able to overcome the deficit in the overall percentage of white voters who voted for him.
- Another reason this was significant was that many of the Hispanic votes were from key battleground states like Nevada and Colorado.

Part (b) 2 Points

One point is earned for explaining how the 2010 Census contributed to the increase in Hispanic voters and 1 point is earned for explaining how the Get-Out-the-Vote operation increased the Hispanic vote. Acceptable answers include:

- The Hispanic population was the fastest-growing minority group according to the 2010 census and that growth took place in many of the key battleground states that Obama ultimately won contributing to his electoral college victory.
- By 2025 Hispanics would become the largest minority group in the United States and that their numbers would increase significantly not only in battleground states but states like Texas that could potentially put it in play in future elections.
- Even though Mitt Romney won the same percentage of white voters as George H.W. Bush in 1988, he still lost the election.
- The Obama campaign, using social media, door-to-door contacts, and grassroots volunteers, were able to identify pro-Obama voters and more important, got them to the polls.

Part (c) 2 Points

One point is earned for identifying a law that could have decreased minority turnout and 1 point is earned by explaining how that law would have reduced minority turnout. Acceptable answers include:

- Photo identification regulations. The law would have forced all voters to show a government-approved identification card before voting. This law would have reduced minority turnout because that group would have had more difficulty understanding the requirements and it would have also been more difficult for them to obtain the specific card that was approved for identification.
- A change of early voting hours and early voting locations. It would have reduced minority turnout because many minority voters took advantage of early voting opportunities, and if the hours and/or locations were reduced, they would not have found it as easy to vote.

A SUMMARY OF THE FREE-RESPONSE ANSWER SECTION

- Four mandatory answers are worth 50 percent of the examination.
- Strive to write each answer within 25 minutes.
- Data-based answers should make references to the information provided in the stimulus (chart, graph, etc.).
- All answers should give supporting evidence in the form of specific historical or contemporary examples.
- Perform all tasks listed in the question: Define, Identify, Describe, or Explain.
- Questions attack specific issues related to politics and government.
- Read questions carefully and understand the topics tested.
- In some questions, the interrelationship between two subjects may be explored.
- Tasks will vary from question to question. One question may ask you to explain, while another part of a question may ask you to illustrate, describe, discuss, or list.
- If you are asked to list or identify, do so. You can use incomplete sentences, bulleted statements, or phrases in your response.
- The free-response answer requires you to understand the nature of the question, write a response that demonstrates an understanding of the question using specific examples, and develop a logical, coherent response.
- Write neatly so the rater can easily read your response.

PART ONE
Constitutional Underpinnings

The Theory of Modern Government

1

→ **CONSERVATIVE**

→ **DELEGATE MODEL**

→ **DIRECT DEMOCRACY**

→ **ELITE AND CLASS THEORY**

→ **GOVERNMENT**

→ **LIBERAL**

→ **LINKAGE INSTITUTION**

→ **LOOSE CONSTRUCTION**

→ **PLURALISM**

→ **POLICY AGENDA**

→ **POLITICAL PARTIES**

→ **POLITICS**

→ **PUBLIC POLICY**

→ **REPRESENTATIVE DEMOCRACY**

→ **STRICT CONSTRUCTIONISTS**

→ **TRUSTEE MODEL**

CONTEMPORARY CONNECTION

Over $4 billion was spent by candidates, political parties, and special interest groups in the 2014 midterm election—the most in any midterm election. Perhaps that is why many people believe in the elite theory of government, one of the theories of modern government that we explore in this chapter.

When looking at the interrelationship between government and politics, you need to understand the theoretical nature of both concepts. Government has an impact on our everyday lives in many ways. Our federal form of government has a huge effect on the manner in which we are able to function as part of our society—from the manner in which our recycled garbage is picked up to the speed limit on interstate highways. The political decisions that come into play result in these many policy decisions.

A working definition of government is those institutions that create public policy. Constitutionally defined, the formal institutions of government on the national level are the executive branch headed by the president, the legislative branch consisting of the Congress, and the judicial branch made up of the Supreme Court and lower courts. A similar structure exists on the state and local levels. In addition to the defined institutions of government, modern government is also characterized by those agencies that implement public policy—bureaucracies, including regulatory agencies, independent executive agencies, government corporations, and the cabinet. These institutions, sometimes acting independently, sometimes acting in concert, create and implement public policy.

The noted political scientist Harold Laswell, in a famous description, defined politics as "who gets what, when, and how." This definition can be expanded to include why—why politicians are able to succeed or fail in getting elected and why they succeed or fail in the process of creating policy. Politics, unlike government, is not defined constitutionally but evolved from the writings of James Madison, Alexander Hamilton, and John Jay in the Federalist Papers, unwritten traditions and precedents that started with the formation of the first political parties, and the philosophical differences that emerged after candidates were elected to office. Politics is characterized by conflict and resolution, compromise, and the interrelationship of individuals and groups.

**THE LIBERTY BELL HAS LONG BEEN
A SYMBOL OF DEMOCRACY**

Government and politics, thus, can be defined by a formula that combines both concepts and results in an end goal: government plus politics equals the creation of public policy. In other words, what government does through politics results in public policy. In evaluating how successful government and politicians are, you must look at the extent that public policy is achieved. This chapter also explores in detail those forces that come into play in the quest to control the policy agenda on both a theoretical and a practical level.

THE BASIC FUNCTION OF GOVERNMENT

Government is essential because it has an impact on your everyday life.

If you look at the basic function of government as protection through defense and support of individuals through raising revenue, you will clearly see that government influences everybody. It is also clear that not everybody has the same needs, shares the same ideology, or has the same priorities.

PREAMBLE TO THE CONSTITUTION

- the establishment of a more perfect union
- the establishment of justice
- the insurance of domestic tranquility
- the promotion of the general welfare
- the security of individual liberty

Once you consider these principles, you'll see how people can differ on the meaning, interpretation, and implementation of these functions of government. When you look at specific examples of these functions and how they affect us, you will see the scope of government. Such policy areas as universal health care, the nature and size of our armed forces, the welfare system, Social Security and Medicare, and the extent that government should regulate our lives illustrate the expanding role of government and the impact it has on our lives.

The Meaning of Politics

If you define politics as who gets what, when, how, and why, then you have to determine the nature of the process and outcome. Because politics deals with individuals and their needs, values, and attitudes, it stands to reason that people with similar needs, values, and attitudes will band together to form political parties. Once a political party is formed, in order for the needs, values, and attitudes to translate into actual policy, the party must succeed in electing its members to office. Thus individuals running for office must have a base of electoral support, a base of political support (the party), and a base of financial support. Obviously, the issue of incumbency comes into play as those elected officials who are reelected become entrenched in the system and have an advantage over young political mavericks who want to break into the system.

Politics, the means by which individuals and groups get involved, results in the formal election of officials.

The Electorate

The role of the electorate is also crucial in determining the means with which individuals get involved. How the voters perceive the candidate's positions on issues, the way people feel about the party, the comfort level of the voter in relation to the candidate and the party, as well as the influence the media have on the election all come into play in the eventual success or failure of the candidate.

In 2000 the electorate couldn't make up its mind between George W. Bush, who promised to bring "honor and integrity" back to the Oval Office, and the incumbent vice president, Al Gore, who had to separate himself from Bill Clinton's scandals while still identifying himself with the longest period of prosperity in United States history. In the end, Gore narrowly won the popular vote but lost the electoral vote in one of the closest and most disputed elections in history.

George W. Bush campaigned for reelection in 2004 emphasizing that he would "build a safer world and a more hopeful America." His Democratic opponent, Senator John F. Kerry, told the voters that he was the "real deal" and that "America deserves better." The voters decided not to change a commander-in-chief during a time of war and gave the incumbent both a popular and electoral vote majority.

In the first election since 1952 that did not feature an incumbent president or vice president, Barack Obama, the first African-American nominee of a major political party, campaigned using the theme "change we can believe in." His opponent, Arizona senator John McCain, chose "country first," emphasizing his military credentials. The country elected Obama, giving him a majority of the popular vote and more than 350 electoral votes.

In 2012, incumbent president Barack Obama ran for reelection against former Massachusetts governor Mitt Romney. Even though the economic climate favored the challenger, President Obama was able to define Governor Romney as the candidate who identified with the wealthiest Americans. Obama was reelected with 332 electoral votes.

Federalists *vs.* Anti-Federalists

In looking at the Federalist Papers, you can see how the U.S. political system was characterized and created from established groups who had differing attitudes toward how best to form a new government. In Federalist No. 44 James Madison writes in 1787 "We are brought to this undeniable conclusion that no part of the power is unnecessary or improper for accomplishing the necessary objects of the Union. The question, therefore, whether this amount of power shall be granted or not resolves itself into another question, whether or not a government commensurate to the exigencies of the union shall be established; or in other words, whether the Union itself shall be preserved." The Anti-Federalist position found in *The Debates on the Constitution in Letters from*

The U.S. political system evolved from various interest groups vying to implement a policy agenda.

the Federal Farmer, written in 1787, responds by stating that "there appears to me to be not only a premature deposit of some important powers in the general government—but many of those deposited there are undefined, and may be used to good or bad purposes as honest or designing men shall prevail." Even the overall fight over the ratification of the proposed constitution was waged on "party lines." Federalists supported ratification. Anti-Federalists opposed ratification. In this case, the policy agenda was the adoption of a new constitution.

Once the Constitution was ratified, two parties evolved. The Federalist Party, headed by Alexander Hamilton and made up of the country's upper class, supported a strong national government and set a policy agenda that would solve the nation's economic problems. In doing so, the party appealed to business interests such as manufacturing and trade. It believed in a loose construction, or a liberal interpretation, of the Constitution. The opposition party, the Democratic-Republicans, led by Thomas Jefferson after his return from France where he was the United States ambassador, was characterized as the party of the "common man." It believed in a more limited role of the central government and was considered to be strict constructionist, which is characterized by a belief in a conservative interpretation of the Constitution. Its constituency was farmers, merchants, and the middle class of American society. The party was afraid of a powerful president and believed that Congress should be the main cog of government. In the 2010 midterm elections a unique special interest group, the Tea Party, emerged and played a significant role in determining the outcome of the election. The Tea Party's name is derived from the Boston patriots who organized the Boston Tea Party in 1773. The modern-day Tea Party consists of its founders, Republicans who served in the House of Representatives, and a grassroots movement of people who believed in less government, lower taxes, and lower government spending, and has as one of their battle cries, "taking the government back." Even though it is not a formal political party, it influenced the Republican Party by supporting candidates in the primaries and general election. Many of the victorious candidates who won were "Tea Party candidates" and pledged to support the principles of the movement.

Special interest groups played a significant role in the 2012 presidential election and the 2014 midterm election. As a result of the Supreme Court's finance decisions, independent groups raised millions of dollars and ran campaign ads throughout the primary and general campaign.

Linkage Institutions—The Informal Institutions

Public policy is affected by the linkage institutions of political parties, elections, interest groups, and the media.

By definition, a linkage institution is the means by which individuals can express preferences regarding the development of public policy. Examples of linkage institutions are political parties, special interest groups, and the media. Preferences are voiced through the political system, and when specific political issues are resolved, they become the basis for policy. In today's political system, the two major political parties, the Democrats and the Republicans, each have national platforms that outline their position on various public issues. For instance, the Republican Party has stood for less government, whereas today's Democratic Party has supported government programs such as Medicare. In areas of social concern, Republicans have been opposed to abortion on demand, whereas Democrats have been identified as a party favoring choice.

In order to implement these policies, Democrats and Republicans have to be elected to public office. Candidates and political parties must assess the nature of the electorate. Are there a significant number of single-issue groups, those special interests who base their vote on a single issue? Or is the candidate's stand on issues broad enough to attract the mainstream of the voting electorate? The media, through daily newspapers and television newscasts, as well as columnists and editorials, attempt to influence the voters, the party, and the candidate's stand on issues. The media have been accused of simplifying the issues by relying on photo opportunities (photo ops) set up by the candidates and 30-second statements on the evening news shows (sound bites). The interaction of linkage institutions results in the formation of a policy agenda by the candidates running for elected office.

An example of how linkage institutions work is the 2010 midterm elections. As a result of the rise of the grassroots movement that called themselves "the Tea Party" (named after the colonists who dumped tea in Boston Harbor in 1773), many Tea Party members voted Republican in the midterm election resulting in a gain of 63 seats and control of the House of Representatives for the Republicans. The trend continued in 2014 as the Republicans gained 13 seats in the house and took control of the Senate.

Policy-Making Institutions

Even though each branch of government has separate powers, a significant policy-making function is defined by the Constitution. In addition, the development and growth of bureaucracies becomes a fourth branch of government, because it has independent regulatory power and is connected directly and indirectly to the federal government itself.

The formal institutions created by the Constitution— including the presidency, Congress, and the courts and bureaucracies— are the significant and major policy-making institutions.

The president as chief executive proposes to Congress a legislative agenda. Along with this agenda is a budget proposal that defines the extent of government involvement in supporting legislation as well as the size of government. The decision to sign or veto legislation determines the fate of legislation and the resulting public policy. Congress, through its committee system and ultimately its votes, determines the fate of the president's legislative agenda and the proposed budget. Over the past 30 years, the issue of the nation's deficit has been paramount in determining the nature of legislation passed. This changed in 1996 after President Clinton signed a balanced budget. By 2000 the debate shifted away from deficit spending to what the budget surplus should be used for. After September 11, 2001, tax cuts, a recession, and an expanded war on terrorism resulted in the return of large deficits.

President Obama, facing the worst economic crisis since the Great Depression, signed the American Recovery and Reinvestment Act of 2009. This law cost close to $1 trillion and included tax cuts for 95 percent of Americans as well as job stimulus provisions. Obama also announced measures that dealt with the ailing banks, auto industry, and housing market. These acts, along with the 2010 federal budget, resulted in the largest deficits in American history, totaling more than $1 trillion.

The new Republican majority in the House of Representatives threatened not to authorize an increase to the national debt in 2011 unless President Obama agreed to spending cuts. As a result, Congress reached an agreement with the president to postpone the elimination of the so-called Bush tax cuts until 2012 along with major cuts in defense and discretionary spending, called the sequester. Ultimately, the country avoided going over what was called the "fiscal cliff" in January 2013 when the Bush tax cuts were kept for everyone earning under $400,000. The sequester cuts, known as sequestration, took effect in March 2013. The reductions in spending authority were approximately $85.4 billion split between spending cuts in defense and spending cuts in discretionary funds. These cuts were achieved by program cuts as well as federal employee furloughs. As a result of public pressure some agencies such as the Federal Aviation Authority (FAA) were able to shift some of the cuts to avoid air traffic controller furloughs. An effort to come up with a grand budget deal between the president and Congress failed. In 2013, the Bipartisan Budget Act of 2013 was passed that raised budgeting caps but also lowered the projected deficit.

THE SUPREME COURT

The Supreme Court in particular has a direct impact on the public policy through its interpretation of the Constitution and how it relates to specific issues brought before the Court. An activist Court will forge new ground and through such decisions as *Roe v Wade* or *Brown v Board of Education* establish precedents that will force legislative action. A Court that shows judicial restraint will maintain the status quo or mirror what the other branches of government have established as current policy. Decisions that established the legitimacy of state restrictions on abortions such as parental approval, and a narrower interpretation of Miranda Rights (those rights guaranteed to people arrested) were characteristic of a more conservative Rehnquist court in the late 1980s and 1990s.

BUREAUCRACIES

The size of government has increased since World War II as a result of the bureaucracy, which became an integral part of the government. Even though the size of the government workforce has decreased, the influence of the bureaucratic agencies on public policy has been dramatic. In particular, regulatory agencies such as the Food and Drug Administration (FDA) and the Environmental Protection Agency (EPA) have issued directives as a result of congressional legislation. The Clean Air Act resulted in a number of policy statements by the EPA regarding auto pollution in the individual states. The FDA debated the advisability of approving the abortion pill RU486 and gave the go-ahead for a private group to conduct testing. It was approved in 2000, and consumers were able to purchase the drug.

Evolution of Representative Democracy

The development of our representative democracy evolved from other forms of democracies.

From the roots of our political system in ancient Greece, to the writings of Enlightenment thinkers such as Montesquieu and Locke, to the principles outlined in the Declaration of Independence, our representative democracy has emerged as a distinct republican form of government.

The origins of Greek democracy come from the premise that governmental rule should be that of the many rather than the few. In its purest form a direct democracy would have every citizen attending a town meeting and voting on every issue with the majority prevailing. Because of the size of the country, this becomes impractical and works only on a limited scale such as the classic New England town meeting where, for instance, a town's budget is approved.

Enlightenment thinkers proposed that a democracy should rely on the consent of the people. They also felt that there were natural rights that could not be taken away by the government, such as life, liberty, and property. In drafting the Declaration of Independence, Thomas Jefferson felt that these principles of unalienable rights should be incorporated. They were also included in the Constitution. The individual became the central focus of government policy. Such concepts as equality, freedom, and order became the driving forces of our democracy.

ELECTIONS

The measure of democracy became open and free elections. In order for a democracy to succeed, these elections had to be open to all citizens, issues and policy statements of candidates had to be available to the electorate, citizens could form political parties to advocate policies, and elections would be determined by a majority or plurality. Obviously, our constitutional republic in its early days did not meet the criteria. Slaves and women were not given the right to vote. There were property requirements, and the state legislatures determined who would represent the states as senators. Even today, we still have an electoral college, which determines the official outcome of presidential elections based on the vote of electors rather than the direct vote of citizens.

Today, the test to determine whether our democracy is working still relies on the way the individual determines the final fate of who runs the government and how policy is determined. Through linkage institutions and sovereignty, individuals must have a forum and a vote to determine their elected officials. Guarantees of voting equality through "one man, one vote" representation, the recognition that the size and make-up of congressional districts should be as democratic as possible, has achieved this goal. Amendments to the Constitution creating direct elections of senators; voting rights for freed slaves, women, and 18-year-olds; the elimination of poll taxes; and legislation such as the Voting Rights Bill have accomplished this. Participation in government and politics is another indicator. In 2012, many states attempted to pass legislation that would have made voting more difficult by passing voter identification laws and limiting early voting opportunities. Proponents of the legislation claimed these measures would prevent voter fraud. Opponents of these polices viewed it as voter suppression. Ultimately, the courts ruled many of these measures unconstitutional. In 2013, the Supreme Court struck down a key provision of the Voting Rights Act freeing nine southern states to change their election laws without advance federal approval.

ROLE OF GOVERNMENT

Government itself must become responsive. It must respect minority rights even though its elected officials were chosen by majority rule. Individual freedom must be respected and is guaranteed through the Bill of Rights. Court decisions such as *Tinker v Des Moines* have reinforced the concept that the First Amendment is even applicable to high school students. Finally, government itself must operate on the basis of consensus and compromise. Otherwise public policy, the measure of whether government succeeds or fails, will not be implemented. During the Obama administration, the cry of "gridlock" was heard because a Democratic president had difficulty achieving his legislative agenda because there was a divided Congress and then a Republican Congress.

After the Republicans assumed control of Congress in 1994, a divided government again dominated American politics. In 1995, the Republicans tested a weakened president by forcing a government shutdown caused by a budget stalemate. This backfired when public opinion turned against the GOP. A complete turnaround occurred at the conclusion of the 104th Congress prior to the 1996 election when both the president and Congress reached compromises regarding health-care portability, the minimum wage, and welfare reform. At the start of the 105th Congress a bipartisan agreement on a balanced budget was reached.

After the contested 2000 election, newly elected President George W. Bush had to face a divided Congress in 2001 when one of his fellow Republicans became an independent and voted with the Democrats, giving the Democrats a single vote majority in the Senate. This lasted until the 2002 midterm election, when the Republicans again regained control of Congress. In 2006, the Democrats won back Congress as a result of voter discontent with the Iraq War. The Democrats expanded their majorities in both houses in the 2008 election, thus ending divided government.

In 2010, the Republicans regained control of the House of Representatives by winning more than sixty seats. The Republicans also gained six seats in the Senate but failed to win a majority. In 2014, the Republicans took complete control of Congress. Thus, a new era of divided government began with the 114th Congress.

The Importance of Control

If you control the agenda, you will be the one to get the what, when, and how. There are three schools of thought regarding how the agenda is controlled. The first theory, pluralism, involves different groups all vying for control of the policy agenda. No single group emerges, forcing the groups to compromise. A centrist position is achieved, and, although no one group is totally happy, a number of groups, as a result of the bargaining that goes on, agree on mutually acceptable positions.

Elite and class theory revolves around an economic strata of society controlling the policy agenda. An upper class, the wealthy of society, is recognized as the elite and controls the linkage institutions of government. The Majoritarian model of democracy is the purest form of democracy. Its principal tenet relies on direct democracy, with a majority vote characterizing the model. In practical terms, when voters get a proposal on the ballot by the initiative process, they will vote on it directly by using majority rule.

Congressmen and women also rely on contrasting theories that dictate their behavior. The delegate model of representation, also known as the representational view, is characterized by voters electing their representatives as their own delegates representing them for the primary purpose of acting exclusively as their voice in Congress. The trustee model of representation, also known as the attitudinal view, is characterized by voters electing their representatives as their own trustees and giving them the autonomy to act for the good of the constituents enabling the congressmen and women to act out of a conscience even if the majority of voters might disagree.

MERGING OF POLITICAL THEORIES

Our democracy has components of each of these political theories. No one theory is ideal. Each has its own advantages and disadvantages. However, most political analysts would agree that a democracy characterized by a pluralist society working in harmony and achieving compromise through centrist positions usually has a good chance of success.

Historically, when the Federalists became the first party to control the government, it was controlled by the elite. Today, many critics of our system contend that there are too many special interest groups who, through their political action committees, are able to influence key lawmakers. Those officials who are able to achieve consensus seem to have the most success in achieving public policy goals.

The Importance of Goals

Modern government changes as a result of who can best serve the public interest.

In evaluating the success or failure of government and our political system, always analyze whether elected officials are achieving their goals, which translate into public policy. Another way of putting it is whether or not officials are meeting the needs of the public they serve. To make a final judgment, you should ask the following questions about government and politics as you continue reading this text:

- What is the public interest?
- Who determines the parameters of what the public wants?
- How much influence should government have on the lives of its citizens?
- How big should government be?
- How much money should government spend?
- What is the best way to raise money for government spending?
- How should government and its elected officials deal with serious ethical issues such as abortion, euthanasia, and birth control?
- Should candidates campaign negatively in order to get elected?
- How should government and politicians restore the public's confidence in their elected officials and government?

Section 1: Multiple-Choice Questions

1. Which of the following is considered a linkage institution?

   (A) The bureaucracy
   (B) The Congress
   (C) The executive department
   (D) The government
   (E) The media

2. All of the following are characteristics of politics EXCEPT

   (A) individuals with similar ideas banding together to form political parties
   (B) the means through which individuals and groups get involved
   (C) who gets what, when, how, and why
   (D) the passing of laws that serve to further minority rights
   (E) the interrelationship of individuals and groups

3. Which of the following institutions established in the Constitution make public policy?

   (A) The Senate, the president, and political parties
   (B) The Congress, the president, and the courts
   (C) The Congress, the courts, and the military
   (D) The Congress, the president, and the military
   (E) The Congress, the president, and the bureaucracy

4. Which of the following best defines a set of institutions linking government, politics, and public policy?

   (A) An educational system
   (B) A political system
   (C) A social system
   (D) An economic system
   (E) A socioeconomic system

5. Which of the following principles describes a philosophy of the Federalist Party?

   (A) Federalists believed in a loose construction of the Constitution.
   (B) Federalists believed in a strict interpretation of the Constitution.
   (C) Federalists believed in a conservative interpretation of the Constitution.
   (D) Federalists believed that Congress should be the main cog of government.
   (E) Federalists believed that the interests of the common man should be reflected in government.

6. All the following characteristics reflect the reasons why political parties are formed EXCEPT:

   (A) People band together because of similar needs.
   (B) People band together because of similar values.
   (C) People band together because they have similar income.
   (D) People band together because of similar beliefs.
   (E) People band together because they have similar goals.

7. Which of the following groups examines a candidate's record primarily on specific issues?

(A) Single-interest groups
(B) Elite groups
(C) Plurality groups
(D) Democrats
(E) Republicans

8. All of the following are basic principles of our democracy today EXCEPT a belief in

(A) the worth and dignity of the individual
(B) the need for political equality
(C) universal health care
(D) the guarantee of individual freedoms
(E) the need for a balance between freedom and order

9. Which of the following institutions is commonly called the fourth branch of government?

(A) The bureaucracy
(B) Special interest groups
(C) The executive branch
(D) The Congress
(E) The Supreme Court

10. Which of the following principles is most fundamental to democratic theory?

(A) Free elections and universal suffrage
(B) Minority rule
(C) Universal public education
(D) Political parties
(E) A written constitution

11. All of the following factors contribute to an enlightened understanding of the electorate EXCEPT

(A) interest groups
(B) the media
(C) the right to property
(D) political parties
(E) the Internet

12. Which of the following groups believes that bargaining and compromise are essential to a democracy?

(A) Elitists
(B) Pluralists
(C) Independents
(D) Democrats
(E) Republicans

13. Which of the following theories contends that our society is divided along class lines and that a narrow upper-class strata rules regardless of the formal organization of government?

(A) Elite
(B) Pluralist
(C) Communist
(D) Socialist
(E) Egalitarian

Answer Explanations

1. **(E)** Type of Question: Definitional

   The media, along with elections, political parties, and special interest groups, are the linkage institutions. The government represents the formal institutions such as the Congress. The bureaucracy and executive department are institutions created by law.

2. **(D)** Type of Question: Negative

   Choices A, B, C, and E are all characteristics of politics. Choice D is the outcome of the political process.

3. **(B)** Type of Question: Identification and analysis

   The question asks you to identify the formal institutions established by the Constitution that by definition are responsible for creating public policy. The three formal institutions found in the Constitution are the legislative branch represented by the Congress (Article I), the executive branch represented by the president (Article II), and the judicial branch represented by the courts (Article III). Even though the military and bureaucracy may make policies, they are either responsible to a specific branch of government or, as in the case of the bureaucracy, not formally established in the constitution. Political parties are linkage institutions, and even though they make recommendations regarding public policy, they do not have any power to make it.

4. **(B)** Type of Question: Definitional

   A political system by definition is a set of institutions linking government, politics, and public policy. An educational system, social system, economic system, or socioeconomic system may have components of a political system; however, none of them has all the characteristics of a political system.

5. **(A)** Type of Question: Identification and analysis

   Federalists believed in a loose construction of the Constitution, meaning a broad interpretation. Anti-Federalists believed in a strict interpretation, or conservative view, of the Constitution, and they believed that Congress should have more influence than the president. The Anti-Federalists also reflected the interests of the common man.

6. **(C)** Type of Question: Negative

   Even though the Republican Party has been accused of being the party of the rich, and similar income may play some role in determining political preference, it does not apply as much as needs, values, beliefs, and goals as reasons why people join a particular political party.

7. **(A)** Type of Question: Identification and analysis

   Even though a Democrat or Republican may have a strong preference for one issue, by definition a single-interest group such as the National Rifle Association uses guns as the sole criterion in the endorsement of candidates.

8. **(C)** Type of Question: Except/Characteristics

Dignity, political equality, the guarantee of individual freedoms, and a belief in the need for a balance between freedom and order are all characteristics of our democracy. Universal healthcare may be a goal, but it is not a principle of a democracy.

9. **(A)** Type of Question: Identification

Because the bureaucracy can create and implement policy, it is known as the fourth branch of government. Special interest groups may like to consider themselves as being as influential as the formal institutions of government, but by definition they are considered linkage institutions. The other choices are the three branches of government as defined by the Constitution.

10. **(A)** Type of Question: Identification of a characteristic

Though universal public education, political parties, and a written constitution can be features of a democracy, they are not necessary for a democracy to succeed. Free elections and universal suffrage are essential for the establishment of democratic rule.

11. **(C)** Type of Question: Identification/cause and effect

Interest groups, the media, political parties, and the Internet all contribute to an enlightened understanding of the electorate. The right to property is guaranteed by the Constitution but does not directly contribute to an enlightened understanding.

12. **(B)** Type of Question: Definitional

Even though Democrats and Republicans may state that they believe in bargaining and compromise, in reality they do not always practice what they preach. Pluralists fit the definition that the question raises.

13. **(A)** Type of Question: Definitional

Upper-class strata is the clue to the answer. The other groups may accuse the government of being dominated by the elite, but they do not fit the definition in the question.

Section 2: Free-Response Question (6 points)

> **Directions:** You have 25 minutes to answer the following question. This question is based on your knowledge of U.S. government and politics, and it may contain materials from charts, graphs, and tables which you will have to analyze and draw conclusions from. Make sure you provide specific and sufficient information and examples in your answer.
>
> In policymaking, American liberals and conservatives express different policy preferences. These differences can be attributed to the theoretical and practical ideologies held by each.
>
> (a) Identify and explain two ways in which liberals and conservatives differ from each other.
>
> (b) Compare the way liberals and conservatives differ from each other from (a) and apply these differences to two policies.

SAMPLE RESPONSE

(a)   Liberals and conservatives often differ in the way that they would shape public policy. Liberals are usually on one end of the political spectrum, and conservatives are on the other.

There are two main differences between liberal and conservative theory. The first difference relates to the importance each group assigns to freedom and order and the extent to which they value one over the other. Liberals do not want to give up personal freedom in the name of preserving order. They do not think it is the place of government to tell them how to live and what they can and cannot do. Conservative ideology, on the other hand, states that it is the government's primary duty to preserve social order even if certain personal freedoms are sacrificed in the process.

The second difference we've seen arose in the twentieth century. It relates to the balance between freedom and economic equality. Liberals feel that the government has the responsibility to promote economic and social equality among the people. They want to ensure equality of opportunity on both a social and economic level. Conservatives, on the other hand, embrace a policy of personal freedom. They want the individual to decide whether or not to redistribute his own wealth. Thus, they want the government to promote a laissez-faire approach toward business.

(b)   The positions described in (a) translate into major policy differences between liberals and conservatives. The first example is in the area of economic policies. Liberals believe that the government should pass laws that give economic opportunities for the lower and middle classes that provide a safety net. Legislation such as Medicare and the Health Care Reform Act, known as The Patient Protection and Affordable Care Act, and the extension of unemployment insurance are examples of policies that liberals favor. Conservatives, on the other hand, reject these policies as spending policies that will add to the nation's deficit. Conservatives have a different economic philosophy that translates into what has been called "trickle-down" economics. Conservatives believe in reducing government spending while providing tax breaks for all segments of the population. A good example of this was the Bush tax cuts that were passed in 2001.

A second policy on which conservatives and liberals differ is in the area of social policy. Liberals believe that it is the government's responsibility to provide equality of opportunity through affirmative action programs. Civil rights legislation passed during the Great Society is a good example of liberal legislation. Other social policies that liberals favor are equality for gays and women's right to choose whether to have an abortion. Conservatives oppose affirmative action legislation, and they have actively promoted passing state propositions that ban affirmative action programs. Conservatives believe that the government should pass laws restricting abortion and they have backed the passage of the law banning late-term abortions.

SCORING GUIDELINES FOR FREE-RESPONSE QUESTION (6 POINTS)

Part (a) 4 Points

One point is earned for identifying a specific way that liberals differ from conservatives. One point is earned for identifying a specific way that conservatives differ from liberals. Two points are earned for explaining these differences.

- Freedom and order—specific policy areas such as gun control, rights of the accused, abortion, and affirmative action will be accepted.
- Freedom and economic equality—specific policy areas such as tax legislation, affirmative action programs, and government spending will be accepted.

Part (b) 2 Points

Two points will be earned for an explanation of the differences between a liberal and conservative policy area.

- Economic policies such as Medicare, and health care reform
- Social areas such as affirmative action, gay rights, and abortion

Constitutional Foundations

2

- → ANTI-FEDERALISTS
- → ARTICLES OF CONFEDERATION
- → CONNECTICUT COMPROMISE
- → CONSENT OF THE GOVERNED
- → CONSTITUTION
- → DECLARATION OF INDEPENDENCE
- → FEDERALIST PAPERS
- → FEDERALIST PARTY
- → GREAT COMPROMISE

- → LIMITED GOVERNMENT
- → NATURAL RIGHTS
- → NEW JERSEY PLAN
- → *SECOND TREATISE OF CIVIL GOVERNMENT*
- → SHAYS' REBELLION
- → THREE-FIFTHS COMPROMISE
- → UNALIENABLE RIGHTS
- → VIRGINIA PLAN

CONTEMPORARY CONNECTION

Citizens who felt that the "consent of the governed" principle was being violated turned to an alternative. After the 2012 election, hundreds of thousands of Americans from all 50 states signed petitions to secede. Texas is in the lead with the Lone Star State's petition getting more than 100,000 signatures.

The Constitution provides the basic framework of government. It is the supreme law of the land. It evolved from a political philosophy which, although democratic in origin, was cynical and had economic interests in mind when the document was finalized. In order to understand the practical manner in which the Constitution describes the relationship of the branches of government to each other, to the states, and to the individual, you first must look at what preceded its ratification—the history of British rule of the colonies, the American Revolution, and the failed first attempt at creating a workable constitution, the Articles of Confederation. These factors all contribute to the creation of what has been called a living document—the Constitution of the United States.

THE DECLARATION OF INDEPENDENCE

Thomas Jefferson, John Adams, Benjamin Franklin, Roger Sherman, and Robert Livingston included the political ideas from philosophers such as Locke, Rousseau, and Montesquieu in the Declaration of Independence. Looking at Locke's *Second Treatise of Civil Government*, you can't help but notice the similarities between the language Locke used and the phrases used in the Declaration of Independence. Ideas such as natural rights as they relate to life, liberty, and property; the consent of the governed; and the concept of limited government were all borrowed by the authors of the Declaration of Independence. For instance, Locke describes natural rights as "the state of nature

A powerful heritage created a climate that influenced our forefathers to turn toward a rocky and risky road of revolution.

has a law to govern it, which obliges everyone." The Declaration of Independence calls natural law "Laws of Nature and Nature's God." On equality, Locke refers to people as "men being by nature all free, equal and independent," whereas the Declaration of Independence announced that "all men are created equal." In addition, the Declaration of Independence used many of the concepts from English Common Law related to the rights of the accused and the institutions such as representative colonial assemblies as the rationale why the colonists wanted to revolt against Great Britain.

THE DECLARATION OF INDEPENDENCE LAID THE FOUNDATION FOR REPRESENTATIVE GOVERNMENT

Looking at the Declaration of Independence itself, you should be able to summarize the major parts of the document:

- **The Philosophical Basis**—Using Locke's philosophy, the Declaration of Independence establishes "unalienable rights" as the cornerstone of natural rights. As a consequence of these rights, limited governments are formed receiving their powers from "the consent of the governed."

- **The Grievances**—In a lawyerlike dissertation, the second part of the Declaration of Independence makes the case against Great Britain. Taxation without representation, unjust trials, quartering of British soldiers, abolition of colonial assemblies, and a policy of mercantilism created a logic for drastic change.
- **The Statement of Separation**—Announcing to the world that the colonists had no choice but to revolt, Jefferson stated that it is not only the right, but the duty of the colonists to change the government. You should understand how risky the revolution was for the colonists. Like David against Goliath, the outcome of the American Revolution was far from certain. England had superior power, a navy that was supreme, and resources that could support a war effort. The colonists, resorting to guerrilla tactics and a knowledge of their land, had leadership and a desire for freedom.

Called a "conservative revolution," the new leaders tried to create a government based on the idea of the consent of the governed. Individual state governments guaranteed their citizens the rights they had under British rule. Power was not centralized and the new nation made sure that the new constitution, the Articles of Confederation, could not end up as a government with a king.

> **The American Revolution restored to the colonists the rights they had as British subjects and carried out many of the major promises of the Declaration of Independence.**

Even though the Declaration of Independence stated that "all men were created equal," the societal structure did not reflect equality. The unalienable rights of "life, liberty, and the pursuit of happiness" were assumed to apply to male white colonists. The issue of slaves and women having these rights was not addressed. Because the American Revolution was the first attempt at applying these principles, the fact that all segments of society were not initially included was not surprising because those in power did not want a great deal of political and social upheaval. Whether this principle has been realized is still a debatable question. Today, many minority groups would make the argument that they have not been given full equality.

Property as an indicator of wealth and status was also a requirement for political office. The states and individual state legislatures became the dominant force. Economic problems immediately faced the new nation in the form of repayment of war debts to the central government and individuals facing an economic recession caused by the war. Farmers who believed that the new government was not fulfilling the objectives of the Declaration of Independence took up arms. Even though Shays' Rebellion failed, it sent a signal to the newly formed government that it had major problems.

THE ARTICLES OF CONFEDERATION

Although the Articles of Confederation recognized the need for a central government, it relied on the states to make the decisions that would ultimately determine whether the country would survive. Under the Articles of Confederation, the national government had two levels of government—a weak national government with a one-house congress and dominant state governments. Congress was given limited power to declare war, make peace, and sign treaties. The national government could borrow money, but it had no power to tax the individual states. The Articles of Confederation created a national army and navy, but the government had no power to draft soldiers. There was no chief executive or national court system, and legislation had to be passed by a two-thirds majority.

> **The Articles of Confederation were doomed to failure from their onset.**

The states could create economic havoc by imposing tariffs on each other, by creating their own currency in addition to the national currency, by refusing to amend the Articles of Confederation (an amendment needed unanimous approval by the states), and by refusing to recognize treaties made by the national government.

Foreign policy was virtually nonexistent. The Barbary pirates threatened our ships, and our borders were vulnerable to attacks from both English and Spanish interests.

A success of the national government was the Northwest Ordinance, which abolished slavery in the newly acquired Northwest territories.

The most positive aspect of the government was that a new middle class was developing on the state level. Even though the old guard from the colonial era still existed, small farmers began to dominate state politics. This created a broader political base and started the beginning of opposing political parties (Federalists and Anti-Federalists).

By 1787 it was obvious that, at a minimum, the Articles of Confederation had to be revised, and many felt that they should be totally changed to reflect the realities of what a functional government should be.

Constitutional Convention

A diverse delegation, representing varying interests, met in Philadelphia and concluded that a new constitution was needed to replace the Articles of Confederation.

With the exception of Rhode Island, the rest of the states sent 55 delegates to the Constitutional Convention in Philadelphia in 1789. The make-up included merchants, lawyers, farmers, and bankers as well as state government officials. Leaders such as Thomas Jefferson, Thomas Paine, Patrick Henry, John Adams, and John Hancock doubted that abolishing the Articles of Confederation was the answer to the country's problems and did not attend. Those in attendance felt that a revision of the Articles of Confederation would not go far enough. Hamilton, Washington, and Madison led the fight for a new constitution. Benjamin Franklin, at age 81, was one of the oldest delegates attending the convention and the only delegate to have signed both the Declaration of Independence and the Constitution.

Philosophically, the delegates were split on how to reconcile basic differences regarding the organization of a new government. They shared a cynical belief that people could not be given power to govern and that political conflict would naturally occur if there were not built-in checks. Because the delegates came from the newly emerging middle class as well as the traditional rich property owners, they quickly saw that factions would exist both in the government and in society. The Federalist Papers, in Federalist No. 10, pointed out that these factions could ultimately paralyze effective government. Self-interest of the delegates resulted in an agreement that the objective of government should be to protect the property owner. Ultimately a series of checks and balances, outlined in Federalist No. 47, and a structure of government that stressed a separation of powers became the fiber of the new Constitution.

THE CONSTITUTION

The framers of the Constitution believed that inequities of wealth were a principal source of political conflict, but they did not try to eliminate them from the Constitution.

Constitutional historian Charles Beard in his *An Economic Interpretation of the Constitution* (1913) argued that the founding fathers were concerned with protecting the wealth of the property class. He painted a picture of the delegates to the convention as men who were wealthy and who cared about the financial interests of that class.

The compromises reached at the convention included voting, representation, slavery, and trade. Because wealth was such an important consideration, the delegates decided to let the individual states determine the criteria for voting qualifications. Property became the major criterion, and each state was able to determine who was eligible to vote in the national elections for Congress and the president.

A Bicameral Congress

A series of compromises was reached.

The thorny issue of how to create a new Congress split the convention between the larger more populous states and the smaller states. The smaller states, led by New Jersey, insisted that each state should have equal representation. The Virginia Plan argued that a legislature based on population would be more equitable. The Connecticut Compromise, also known as the Great Compromise, resulted in the formation of a bicameral (two-house) Congress—one house is represented equally by the states (the Senate) and the other house is represented by population (the House of Representatives).

Once the structure of the new Congress was agreed upon, the divisive issue of slavery had to be resolved. There was never a doubt that Jefferson's original proposition that "All men are created equal" would never see the light of day in the new Constitution. Nevertheless, the issues of slave trade and slave representation had to be resolved. The South agreed to halt the import of slaves in 1808 if the North agreed to return fugitive slaves. More difficult was the issue of representation. If each slave counted as one person, the South could have easily held the balance of power in the House of Representatives. Thus, the Three-Fifths Compromise was agreed on. Every five slaves would count as three people for representation and tax purposes.

The last major compromise dealt with tariffs. The North wanted to tax Southern exports to Europe and wanted to protect their own manufactured goods. The South did not want to tax European goods so that their own exports would not be taxed. They agreed to tax only imports.

Economic Issues

The delegates also addressed the weaknesses of the Articles of Confederation. Because a primary concern was protection of the property owner, they dealt with economic issues. Congress was given the power to tax, regulate interstate and foreign commerce, create a viable national currency, and, in what later became known as the elastic clause, make "all laws necessary and proper" to carry out the stated powers of Congress.

States were strictly prohibited from duplicating the powers of the federal government that would have an impact on the nation's economy (i.e., denied the power to coin money, regulate interstate and foreign commerce, and interfere with the federal government's ability to collect debts).

The drafters also saw the need for a chief executive and a court system; however, as we will soon see, the relationship between these two branches of government became the benchmark of the new Constitution.

THE BIRTH OF POLITICAL PARTIES

The Federalists, in Federalist Paper No. 10, led by Alexander Hamilton, John Jay, and James Madison, argued that a "tyranny of the majority" could threaten the economic fiber of the nation. They believed that the new Constitution, through its checks and balances and the separation of the three branches of government, would ensure the protection of the minorities. Through a series of articles published as the Federalist Papers and signed by the pseudonym Publius, they outlined the necessity of a government that would be forced to compromise as a result of the separate powers of each branch. They also felt that the Constitution had enough safeguards built in for individuals. The Constitution gave each state "full faith and credit" as well as a "republican" form of government. In addition, as the Federalists were quick to point out, the prohibition of the passage of *ex post facto* laws (laws that were retroactive in nature) and bills of attainder laws

The first political parties were born during the fight to ratify the new Constitution. Because the philosophy of each party reflected an economic base, it became apparent that the issue of individual rights could jeopardize the approval of the new Constitution.

(laws that dictated prison sentences for accused who were not given a trial) and the prohibition of suspending the writ of *habeas corpus* (a guarantee of individual due process rights) gave individuals protection against a tyrannical federal government. Typically, the Federalists represented the upper class, bankers, and rich large-property owners. Their economic philosophy was clearly expressed throughout the Federalist Papers.

The Anti-Federalists, led by the newly emerging middle class, had George Mason and Richard Henry Lee as their chief spokesmen. In a rival publication to the Federalist Papers, *Pennsylvania Packet,* and *Letters from the Federal Farmer,* and through individual essays penned under the name of Brutus, they argued that the principles of the Declaration of Independence would be eroded by the new Constitution. They felt that the Constitution would firmly establish an economic elite and would create the potential for an abusive federal government, especially in the area of protecting individual rights.

The Anti-Federalists insisted that a bill of rights had to be part of the new Constitution. Otherwise, a powerful president supported by the Congress could easily abuse the civil liberties of the individual. Additionally, the sovereignty of the states became a concern even with the guarantees provided. Nowhere was this argument more heated than in New York. The Anti-Federalists prevented the approval of the Constitution until Madison and Hamilton guaranteed that the first Congress would approve a bill of rights. Typically, the Anti-Federalists represented the farmers and the so-called common people. They rejected the elitist base represented by the Federalists.

Section 1: Multiple-Choice Questions

1. John Locke's *Second Treatise of Civil Government* advocates

   (A) a divine monarchy
   (B) rights for the minority
   (C) majority rights
   (D) natural rights
   (E) democratic rule

2. When the Articles of Confederation were adopted, the nation's major concern was dominated by

   (A) slavery
   (B) religious freedom
   (C) equality for women
   (D) political dominance by the central government
   (E) economic issues

3. Which of the following documents represents the first adopted Constitution for the United States?

   (A) Declaration of Independence
   (B) Bill of Rights
   (C) Articles of Confederation
   (D) Virginia Plan
   (E) Connecticut Plan

4. Which of the following statements in the Federalist Papers referred to "the most common and durable source of faction"?

   (A) A new and emerging middle class
   (B) The absence of a strong national government
   (C) The unequal distribution of property
   (D) The abuse of minority rights
   (E) The powers given to the president

5. Madison believed that in order to prevent a "tyranny of the majority" the new government should include all the following EXCEPT

   (A) creating political institutions that could function with the consent of a majority
   (B) limiting the president's term of office
   (C) creating different branches of government with distinctive and separate powers
   (D) creating a system of checks and balances
   (E) limiting the ability of the electorate to vote directly for government officials except members of the House

6. Which of the following documents created a compromise that led to the formation of a bicameral legislature?

(A) Articles of Confederation
(B) Connecticut Compromise
(C) New Jersey Plan
(D) Virginia Plan
(E) Three-Fifths Compromise

7. The Federalists believed that a nation dominated by factions would lead to

(A) a tyranny of the majority
(B) protection of minority rights
(C) a recognition that factions would be in the best interests of the country
(D) another revolution
(E) favorable economic growth

Answer Explanations

1. **(D)** Type of Question: Generalization

You must know the content of Locke's *Treatise* to answer this question. The trick parts of the question are the choices that reflect the consequence of the correct answer. If natural rights are the philosophical basis of government, then it follows that minority rights are protected and there would be democratic rule. If you knew that Locke was a classical philosopher, you might get confused between the concept of natural rights and a divine monarchy.

2. **(E)** Type of Question: Comparing and contrasting concepts and events

Even though slavery and the ineffectiveness of the central government were factors during the critical period, economic issues, specifically a depression facing the country (remember Shays' Rebellion), was the dominant concern. Religious freedom and equality for women were incorrect choices. Slavery and the role of the central government were issues decided by the Constitutional Convention.

3. **(C)** Type of Question: Chronological

Even if you were not sure of the chronology of the documents, only one of the documents is a constitution. The Connecticut Plan, although adopted, was only a part of the Constitution. The Declaration of Independence stated the philosophical basis of government, but its purpose was to outline the colonists' grievances against Great Britain. Even though much of the Declaration of Independence was eventually incorporated into the Constitution and Bill of Rights, it was not a constitution.

4. **(C)** Type of Question: Stimulus-based short quotation

This is an extremely difficult question because factions could be caused by a conflict between classes, the abuse of minority rights, or the absence of a strong national government. You have to understand the substance of the Federalist Papers to choose the unequal distribution of property (also it is an economic factor) as the best answer.

5. **(B)** Type of Question: Definitional

Drawing upon your knowledge of the Federalist Papers, you must choose the one answer that does not support the prevention of a tyranny of the majority. Even though factually, choice B is correct, the president's term was not limited until the Twenty-Second

Amendment was ratified in 1952. Choice A refers to the provisions of the Constitution that provide for a two-thirds vote (i.e., overriding a veto, passing a treaty). Choice D is the foundation of the Federalist viewpoint, and choice E reflects the only branch of government that was voted directly at the time of ratification. The president is elected through the electoral college, and the direct election of senators did not occur until the passage of the Seventeenth Amendment in 1913.

6. **(B)** Type of Question: Stimulus based

   After eliminating the Articles of Confederation, you are left with four choices that all relate to the drafting of the Constitution at Philadelphia. The Three-Fifths Compromise dealt with the issue of slavery. The New Jersey Plan and Virginia Plan both attempted to create a single house, the former based on equality of states and the latter based on population. The Connecticut Compromise incorporated both ideas into a bicameral legislature.

7. **(A)** Type of Question: Cause-and-effect relationships

   If you connected factions to a major aspect of the Federalist Papers and realized that a consequence of factions could well be a tyranny of the majority (again language used in the Federalist Papers), you should be able to eliminate choices B, C, D, and E.

Section 2: Free-Response Question (6 points)

> According to the arguments raised in The Debate on the Constitution, the Constitutional Convention "charted the course of the bloodless revolution that created the government of the United States and the world's oldest working national charter."
>
> Using the Federalist Papers and your knowledge of U.S. politics and government:
>
> (a)   Give two examples of how the authors of the Federalist Papers defined the character of the national government.
>
> (b)   Illustrate the Federalist position regarding the nature and creation of two of the branches of government.

SAMPLE RESPONSE

(a)   Federalist Paper No. 51 stresses the fact that federal government is stronger than a confederacy. It also suggests the proper game plan for the structure of government: the formation of three branches—executive (president), legislative (House of Representatives and Senate), and finally judiciary (Supreme Court). Madison had the idea that each branch would have separate powers. The branches should rely on each other but be able to check each other's power. The government would depend upon the people for their support as well as their input on how the government should be run. Once the federal constitution was put in place, it had the effect of, in some ways, supplanting the state constitutions, making the states conform to the central document. With all these elements coming together, a new republican government replaced the Articles of Confederation.

In Federalist No. 10, James Madison showed how factions caused the downfall of the government under the Articles of Confederation and discussed how similar factions could have a serious impact on the newly formed republic. Madison explained that by setting up republican governments in the individual states of the union, factions based on local levels would be kept from taking control of the national government. He refuted the well-known argument that a republic could be extended only over a certain sphere of territory, which began with the writings of Montesquieu. He said that a large republic has two advantages over a small one: a greater number of worthy candidates for office and a larger electorate, which is more likely to select qualified candidates. This document clearly states that the main problem in government is factions: in a republic those who are most fit to rule do so as elected officials. Madison differentiates between a democracy and a republic. Republics regulate power differently; they also are brought together directly because territory and people are greater in a republic.

Perhaps the most prominent concern of the Anti-Federalists was the issue of a federal government becoming absolutely omnipotent. They favored states' rights above all others. By giving the states the jurisdiction to protect the rights of their citizens and the power to enforce legislature that applied specifically to different regions, the threat of the federal government superseding the rights of the states would be lessened.

(b) In studying both the Constitution and the Federalist Papers, you find many topics related to the executive branch. They also relate to modern-day issues that symbolize the ideas that the framers originally had in mind. Presidential power is a very important part of our country's government. As the Federalist Papers pointed out, a weak and feeble executive who cannot lead will result in a bad execution of presidential powers and the government as a whole. If there is a weak president, then Congress is more influential and powerful. The ideas expressed in the Federalist Papers coincide with those found in the Constitution on many issues concerning the presidency. Through the power of the president as commander in chief, you can see the many characteristics in the Constitution that are derived from the Federalist Papers.

An idea that is covered in both the Constitution and the Federalist Papers is that of a civilian commander in chief being the president. The idea of asking Congress to declare war and develop a viable foreign policy is one of the most important duties carried out by the president. In the Constitution the clause reads, "The president shall be commander in chief of the army and navy of the United States, and of the militia of the several states when called into the actual service of the United States." Similarly, as reported in the Federalist Papers, the Continental Congress voted that the president should have the power to declare war and will act as commander in chief; however, in practice he has to gain approval from the Congress. This process limits the executive power but still allows for a large amount of control by the executive, which is what the Federalists wanted.

SCORING GUIDELINES FOR FREE-RESPONSE QUESTION (6 POINTS)

Part (a) 4 Points

Two points are earned for identifying two Federalist Papers and 2 points are earned for giving an explanation of how the identified Federalist Papers defined the character of the national government:

- Federalist Paper No. 51 defines the structure of the national government—three branches having separate powers
- Federalist Paper No. 10 defines how factions are necessary and could negatively impact the national government, thus making it necessary to create state and local governments
- Federalist Paper No. 47 defines the nature of the separation of powers and checks and balances

Other Federalist Papers can also be used as long as they define a specific aspect of the government.

Part (b) 2 Points

One point is earned for giving two examples of how the author of the Federalist Papers defined the character of the national government, and one point is earned for showing the Federalist position regarding the nature and creation of two branches of the national government:

- The Federalist Papers warned about the creation of a weak and feeble executive stressing the need for a president who is a civilian commander in chief
- The Federalist Papers spoke of a Congress that has the power to declare war
- The Federalist Papers described a judiciary that was independent and had justices holding office for "life," without any term limits

The Constitution

3

→ BICAMERAL LEGISLATURE

→ CHECKS AND BALANCES

→ CONCURRENT POWER

→ ELASTIC CLAUSE

→ ELECTORAL COLLEGE

→ ENUMERATED POWERS

→ *EX POST FACTO* LAWS

→ EXECUTIVE ACTIONS

→ FEDERALISM

→ FULL FAITH AND CREDIT

→ IMPLIED POWER

→ INHERENT POWER

→ JUDICIAL REVIEW

→ PREAMBLE

→ PRIVILEGES AND IMMUNITIES

→ RECESS APPOINTMENT

→ RESERVED POWER AMENDMENT

→ SEPARATION OF POWERS

→ SUPREMACY CLAUSE

→ UNWRITTEN CONSTITUTION

→ WRIT OF *HABEAS CORPUS*

CONTEMPORARY CONNECTION

In June 2014, the U.S. Supreme Court ruled that recess appointments made by President Barack Obama were unconstitutional. The decision illustrated the conflict between the president and the Senate over the principle of advise and consent. This chapter explores the Constitution, its principles, its power sharing among the three branches of government, and the manner in which it has been interpreted and evolved since its ratification.

After the U.S. Constitution was ratified in 1789, the future success of this young new republic hung in the balance. After struggling with the Articles of Confederation, the United States found in the Constitution a new opportunity to demonstrate that its form of limited government could work. By 1791 an additional 10 amendments, the Bill of Rights, were ratified, fulfilling a promise made to the Anti-Federalists at the state ratifying conventions.

This chapter also explores in great detail the Constitution, the supreme law of the land. It will explain how this document is considered the key instrument of government and how it has evolved in its more than 200-year history. It is a practical document as well as a functional document. Each branch of government can lay claim to certain powers unique to its own function. The interrelationship among the branches is also established in the principle of checks and balances. The powers of the national government are defined. State governments are given legitimacy, and the delicate relationship between the states and federal government, known as federalism, is established. The rights of the citizens are clearly outlined in the Bill of Rights as is the ability of the people to exercise the right to vote. Limits are placed on both the federal government and the state governments.

If you look at the Constitution as a road map and drive through its avenues, you will discover that it is laid out in a manner that is clear, concise, and logical. It provides ample opportunity for the driver to take different routes and explore the heart and soul of the basis of government for the United States.

LONGEVITY

Looking at the Constitution, you should be able to picture a document that is laid out simply and directly. From the clarity of purpose in the Preamble, to the organization and structure of the three branches of government, to the amending process, the Constitution provides for orderly and effective government.

The Preamble, starting with "We the People," defines the objectives of the Constitution:

- to form a more perfect union
- to establish justice
- to ensure domestic tranquility
- to provide for the common defense
- to promote the general welfare
- to secure the blessings of liberty

The fact that a reference is made to the longevity of the Constitution to future generations (posterity) indicates that the authors were not looking to make major revisions. They certainly hoped that the document would adapt to changing times.

The major factors creating longevity of the Constitution include

- the separation of powers of each branch of government
- checks and balances including a recognition that a simple majority vote may not be enough of a check
- a built-in elastic clause as part of Congress's power
- a reserved power clause giving states power not delegated to the national government
- rights guaranteed to the citizens
- precedents and traditions creating an unwritten constitution
- judicial review growing out of an interpretation of the power of the Supreme Court
- an amending process, which is flexible enough to allow for change even though it involves more than a majority vote
- the inherent powers of the president

BRANCHES OF GOVERNMENT

The first three articles of the Constitution provide the basis of the organization of the government. Article I broadly defines the legislative powers of Congress. It splits the responsibility between a bicameral (two-house) legislature. The House of Representatives is defined first as the body most directly responsible to the people. The Senate, its makeup based on equal representation, joins in a partnership with the House in passing laws. The rules of impeachment of government officials are also outlined in Article I. It is interesting to note that there are subtle differences (which will be discussed later in this chapter) between the two bodies. The public's view of Congress has continued to deteriorate since the 1970s. In a poll conducted in 2015, 73 percent of the people questioned were critical of the Congress. Yet in the 2014 midterm election, a majority of people indicated that they would vote for their incumbent. Another related issue dealing with the organization of Congress is term limitations. In 1995 the Supreme Court in the case of *Thorton v Arkansas* ruled that state-imposed term limits were unconstitutional, indicating that the only way congressional terms could be altered was through an amendment.

Powers of the Chief Executive

Article II determines the nature of the chief executive, giving responsibility to a president and vice president. Even though powers are not as specifically defined as in the legislative branch, the president's major responsibility is to administer and execute the public policies of the United States. The inherent power of the president, which includes those powers that the president exercises that grow out of the existence of the national government, expands the power of the presidency. By signing congressional legislation into law, the president assumes the responsibility of enforcing the laws of the land. Reference is also made to the president's authority in the area of foreign policy. This article also outlines the mechanics of the electoral college and determines its procedures in the case where a candidate does not receive a majority of the electoral votes. The article refers to executive departments, though it does not specifically mention the president's cabinet or the federal bureaucracy.

Judicial Branch

Article III outlines the nature of the judicial branch. It is interesting to note that unlike the first two articles, this article is the most vague regarding the qualifications of its members. It refers to one Supreme Court and the manner in which cases get there. But it does not give the Supreme Court the broad authority it has assumed. This authority of judicial review was given to the Court in the landmark case of *Marbury v Madison* (1803). The scope of the court system is set in Article III, and the jurisdiction of the court system is defined. This article also defines treason, and provides for a range of penalties, including death, if a person is convicted of the crime. The only time that has happened was when Ethel and Julius Rosenberg were convicted of giving the Soviet Union information concerning the development of the atom bomb. They were tried and convicted of treason and executed after the Supreme Court denied their appeal.

> Specific powers and qualifications granted to Congress guarantee the legislative process as well as create distinctive differences between the two houses of Congress that make the House more representative than the Senate.

By separating the three branches of government, it becomes apparent that the drafters of the Constitution were concerned with the delicate balance of power that would exist among the three branches of government. The Constitution neatly lays out the various powers of each branch of government without any reference to which of the branches should be the lead player.

LEGISLATIVE POWERS

The two houses of Congress created as a result of the 1787 Connecticut Compromise resulted in the establishment of a House of Representatives and a Senate. The House of Representatives is made up of 435 members based on the census taken every 10 years. According to the 2010 census, there is one House seat for approximately every 710,767 people in each state. It also includes "shadow" representatives from the District of Columbia, Guam, Puerto Rico, The Virgin Islands, and American Samoa. Each state has a minimum of two senators and one representative. As a result of the Supreme Court decision *Baker v Carr*, the principle of "one man, one vote" was established. This decision created guidelines for drawing up congressional districts and guaranteed a more equitable system of representation to the citizens of each state. The Supreme Court has been asked to review some districts in the South drawn up to ensure racial representation. In a highly controversial decision, the Court ruled in 1995 that a racially apportioned district in Georgia set up to comply with the Voting Rights Act of 1965 was unconstitutional based on the equal protection clause of the Fourteenth Amendment. The 2014 Supreme Court voting rights decision left the door open for these kinds of districts to be created. In other situations, in order to rectify congressional boundaries, some state legislatures based on political affiliation created districts that favored the political party in power. This action became known as gerrymandering.

House of Representatives

The House of Representatives is considered more representative than the Senate because of its size, term of office, and qualifications for office. The term of office for a representative is two years compared to six years for a senator. A person serving in the House has to be at least 25 years old, an American citizen for seven years, and an inhabitant of the state that the congressman represents. A senator, on the other hand, must be at least 30 years old, nine years a citizen of the United States, and a resident of the state that the senator represents. After states have passed term limitations restricting the number of consecutive terms a representative can serve, in 1995, the Supreme Court ruled that these laws were unconstitutional.

When you look at the specific power of each house, you also can see how the House is "closer to the people." Besides the fact that senators were originally appointed by state legislatures, the House of Representatives is given the responsibility of starting all revenue bills and initiating the process of impeachment. During the impeachment hearings of Richard Nixon and Bill Clinton, the House Judiciary Committee passed impeachment charges. Nixon resigned before the Senate could try him, whereas Clinton was acquitted by the Senate. The Senate must also pass revenue bills and can certainly pass a different version, but it must wait for the House to pass its version of the bill. The Senate tries impeachment cases and, in the only two cases involving a president, after voting on articles of impeachment, failed to convict Andrew Johnson by one vote and acquitted Bill Clinton. The other major difference in the allocation of power between the two bodies is that the Senate has the responsibility of approving presidential appointments and treaties.

Congressional Powers

The common powers of the Congress are listed in Article I Section 8. These are the enumerated or delegated powers of Congress. They include the power to

- collect taxes, pay debts, and provide for the common defense and general welfare
- borrow money
- regulate commerce among the states (interstate commerce) and with foreign countries
- establish uniform laws dealing with immigration and naturalization and bankruptcies
- coin money
- make laws regarding the punishment for counterfeiting
- establish post offices
- make copyright laws
- establish federal courts in addition to the Supreme Court
- define and punish piracy
- declare war
- raise and support armies and a navy
- create a national guard

In this same section, implied powers are defined in the "necessary and proper" clause, which states that Congress has the power to "make all laws necessary and proper for carrying into execution the foregoing powers. . . ." This clause is also known as the elastic clause and is a major and significant power of Congress, granting the Congress the ability to interpret its lawmaking ability in a broad manner. Even though strict interpreters of the Constitution reject the extent of its elasticity, Congress has demonstrated an ability to change with the times. From the creation of the National Bank in the 1800s to the passage of the Brady Bill (establishing a waiting period for handgun purchase), congressional legislation, more often than not, reflects the tenor of the times.

Powers denied to Congress are the denial of the writ of habeas corpus, giving appeal protection to the accused; the passage of bill of attainder laws, which proscribe penalties without due process; and the passage of ex post facto laws, which take effect after the act takes place. In addition, Congress cannot pass export taxes or grant titles of nobility to its citizens.

The issue of how much power the Congress exerts in comparison to the other branches and whether it becomes an imperial Congress is the theme of Chapter 7, The Congress.

EXECUTIVE POWERS

Because of the unique qualities of the presidency, the qualifications for office are the strictest among the three branches. The president must be a natural-born citizen (unlike senators and representatives, who can be naturalized citizens), at least 35 years old, and a resident of the United States for at least 14 years. The source of power of the president comes from the language in Article II Section 1, "The executive power shall be vested in a president of the United States of America." The term of office is four years, limited by constitutional amendment to no more than two terms.

The president becomes a central and unique player in government as a result of the manner in which the definition of chief executive is stated. The only specific powers and duties listed in Article II Sections 2 and 3 include

- the power to act as commander in chief of the armed forces
- the ability to obtain information from members of the executive branch
- the power to grant pardons
- the power to make treaties with the consent of the Senate
- the power to appoint ambassadors, justices, and other officials with the advice and consent of the Senate
- the power to sign legislation or veto legislation
- the duty to give Congress a State of the Union report
- the power to call special sessions of the Congress
- the inherent power of the president

Even though there are far fewer powers and responsibilities listed for the president than for the Congress, because the president can interpret the role of the executive in a broad manner, the power of the president in modern times has increased more than the other branches. From the administration of Franklin Roosevelt and the implementation of his New Deal to the new world order of George Bush, the power of the president has been on the rise. As head of state, the visibility of the president in ceremonial areas far exceeds that of a congressman. The president is also considered the titular head of the political party in power and thus wields a great deal of power in relation to party appointments.

Executive Actions

Executive actions by the president are defined as policy directives that are ordered by the president without any congressional authorization. They differ from executive orders, which are policy directives aimed at federal agencies. Executive orders are legally binding and can be reversed by the Congress and the courts. Executive actions change existing federal policies that are under the

Specific powers and qualifications granted to the executive department guarantee and define the role of the president as a central player in government.

jurisdiction of the federal government. President Obama issued a number of highly controversial executive actions during his presidency. The most controversial actions related to gun control and immigration.

The Vice President

The vice president's responsibility is also listed in Article II. The only stated responsibility of the vice president is to preside over the Senate and be the deciding vote if there is a tie vote. This occurred in President Clinton's first administration when Vice President Al Gore cast the decisive vote to pass the president's budget proposal. It was a key piece of legislation for the new president and set the course of his economic program. The vice president is also next in line to succeed the president in case of death and, as a result of the Twenty-Fifth Amendment, can take over the presidency if the president is disabled.

The Electoral College

Article II also outlines the role of the electoral college, even though it does not use that term, in the election of the president. Simply stated, the electoral college consists of presidential electors in each state. The number of electors is based on the state's population. The states with the greatest population have the most electoral votes. When the voter casts a vote for president, in reality the vote goes to one of the presidential electors designated by the candidate in that state. The number of electors for each state equals the number of senators and representatives that state has in Congress. Thus the number can change based on the census. The candidate who receives the most votes receives all the electoral votes in that state. The candidate with a majority of the electoral votes is elected to office. The electors gather in Washington, D.C., in December and cast their ballots based on the results of the November election. If no candidate receives a majority of the electoral votes, the election of president is determined by the House of Representatives. Specific cases of how the electoral college affected presidential elections will be discussed in Chapter 12, Nominations, Campaigns, and Elections.

More and more attention is paid to the president by the media and the public. Frequent opinion polls track the job approval of the president. The president's personal and public life has been placed under scrutiny. Presidential candidates like Gary Hart and sitting presidents like Richard Nixon, Ronald Reagan, and Bill Clinton have been criticized for personal as well as presidential acts. This microscopic view of the presidency, according to some political scientists, has weakened the institution.

JUDICIAL POWERS

Specific powers and responsibilities granted to the judicial department guarantee and define the role of the courts.

Unlike the legislative and executive departments, the judiciary has no specific qualifications for office. The Constitution in Article III states that judges shall "hold their offices during good behavior." The Supreme Court is the only court established by the Constitution. Lower federal courts are established by the Congress. Even the size of the Supreme Court is not defined. It has remained at nine sitting justices in modern times, although the number has been as low as five. Franklin Roosevelt attempted to pack the Court in 1937 after the Court ruled a number of his New Deal acts unconstitutional. Congress rejected the attempt. Terms of office for Supreme Court justices, by extension of the description of service, is life after appointment. Typically, Supreme Court justices come from other federal judgeships. The appointment process has become more and more difficult as a result of close questioning by the Senate Judiciary Committee. Appointments by Richard Nixon were turned down. One of the most publicized confirmation hearings took place when

George Bush sent Clarence Thomas's name to the Senate and he was accused by Oklahoma law professor Anita Hill of sexual harassment. In addition, nominees are also questioned on their attitudes regarding potential issues the Court may have to rule on, such as abortion. Nominees must tread a very thin line during this process and must not be too specific. They must avoid creating a conflict that would arise if they rule on a case they have already spoken about.

The major power given to the judicial branch is defined as "the judicial power (which) shall extend to all cases, in law and equity, arising under this Constitution, the laws of the United States, and treaties made. . . ." The real power, that of judicial review, has grown in importance throughout the history of the Court. Specific cases and the role of the Court in American life will be discussed in Chapter 9, The Judiciary. The Constitution describes cases through original jurisdiction that the Court can hear directly. The vast majority of cases heard in the Supreme Court are brought on appeal from state and federal courts. This is called appellate jurisdiction. Congressional law as well as presidential actions have also been taken up by the Supreme Court.

It is interesting to note that of the three branches of government, the Supreme Court has no direct responsibility or accountability to the voters. Sitting justices, once confirmed, decide on cases based on their own interpretation of the Constitution. The impact of the Supreme Court on policymaking has increased in modern times. Many Court experts point to the landmark decision of *Brown v Board of Education* (1954) as a turning point in the history of the Court.

BALANCE OF POWER

Based upon the writings of Montesquieu in *The Spirit of Natural Laws* and James Madison in Federalist No. 47, the concept of checks and balances became a central feature in our government. As Madison stated, "It is agreed on all sides, that the powers properly belonging to one of the departments ought not to be directly and completely administered by either of the other departments. It is equally evident, that neither of them ought to possess, directly or indirectly, an overruling influence over the others in the administration of their respective powers."

As a result of the separate powers of the institutions of government, a delicate balance of power exists among the three branches.

Some specific examples of how each branch of government has used its power to check another branch may be useful to illustrate the importance of this feature.

- President Barack Obama has said he would use his veto power if the Republican Congress voted to repeal the Affordable Care Act.
- The Senate changed its rules to increase the number of presidential appointments that required Senate confirmation.
- In 2015, the Supreme Court ruled that Gay Marriage was constitutional opening the door for marriage equality.
- The Congress did not approve a federal budget resulting in a government shutdown in 2013.

As of 2015, there have been more than 2,500 presidential vetoes of congressional bills. Congress overrode more than 100 of them. The Supreme Court has found more than 100 acts of Congress unconstitutional. The Senate has refused to confirm 27 nominees to the Supreme Court and nine cabinet members. Other appointees have withdrawn as a result of sure Senate opposition. There have been several cases of congressional impeachment of federal judges. One way the president can get around Senate opposition to an appointment is through a recess appointment, a temporary appointment of the president's choice made during a congressional recess. This temporary appointment can serve for only one year, at the end of which time the president must resubmit the nominee for Senate confirmation. The Supreme Court ruled that many of the appointments were unconstitutional.

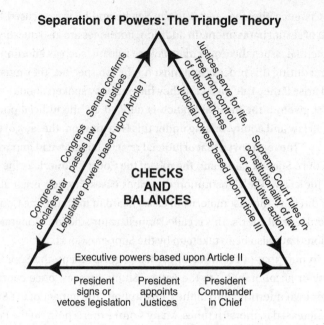

Separation of Powers: The Triangle Theory

CHECKS AND BALANCES

Congress declares war

Congress passes law

Senate confirms Justices

Legislative powers based upon Article I

Justices serve for life, free from control of other branches

Judicial powers based upon Article III

Supreme Court rules on constitutionality of law or executive action

Executive powers based upon Article II

President signs or vetoes legislation

President appoints Justices

President Commander in Chief

The critics of checks and balances point to the potential of a constitutional crisis developing if one branch attempts to challenge the authority of another. For instance, if the president as commander in chief deploys troops in a country for an extended period of time and ignores the provisions of the War Powers Act, an act of Congress that limits presidential authority to send armed forces to another country, there is a good possibility that an unresolvable conflict between the executive and legislative branches could occur. Typically, the Supreme Court does not get involved in adjudicating those kinds of conflicts. In fact, Congress has challenged the president's authority in such foreign policy conflicts in Somalia and Bosnia but has stopped short of placing restrictions on his authority.

Probably the most significant feature of checks and balances is that it consistently proves that our government is limited. Even though many political scientists point to the power of the presidency, even our most dominant presidents had to deal with the interests and concerns of the legislature and judiciary. Other features of our government and political system that have an impact on the size and function of the presidency include

- the role of political parties
- the growth of the federal bureaucracy
- the development and expansion of the information superhighway and the role of media, which puts a great deal of pressure on elected officials
- the emergence of the United States as the last superpower from the cold war, which places a tremendous responsibility on our country's leaders, forcing them to work together to solve major foreign policy problems

FEDERALISM

The organization of the Constitution defines the relationship between the states and the federal government.

Besides establishing a balance of power among the three branches of government, the Constitution also maps out the relationship between the federal government and the states in two articles and one amendment.

In Article IV, the term "full faith and credit" is used to describe the mutual respect and legality of laws, public records, and judicial decisions made by states. In effect, if Nevada has laws establishing rules for marriage and divorce, New York must recognize those laws as valid. Congress passed the Defense of Marriage Act (DOMA), and President Clinton signed it into law in 1996. This law gave states the authority not to recognize gay marriages performed in other states, and it also denied gays who were legally married all the federal benefits given to other married couples. This law was challenged and The Supreme Court ruled in the case of *Windsor v United States* that the section of the Defense of Marriage Act that denied federal benefits to legally married gay couples was unconstitutional, thus enabling legally married gay couples to receive over 1,000 federal benefits. However, states that did not recognize gay marriages were still able to do so though if a legally married gay couple moved to that state the couple would still receive federal benefits. In the case that state laws do conflict with each other, the law within each state is recognized as legal for that state. By extension, Section 2 recognizes that "the citizens of each state shall be entitled to all the privileges and immunities" of citizens in all the states. This provision is significant because it guarantees that the rights of a citizen in one state will be respected by other states. The phrase "privileges and immunities" becomes a significant phrase in the Fourteenth Amendment where states are told they cannot abridge the privileges and immunities of its citizens. States also recognize the legitimate claim to its fugitives through extradition. Finally, in Article IV Section 4, the United States guarantees every state a "republican form of government." The use of the word *republican* is important. It suggests that every state must establish a limited representative government. It also guarantees that the United States will protect every state from outside attacks or internal strife.

State Government

Perhaps the most significant statement that defines the relationship of the federal government to the states is found in Article VI. The supremacy clause states that "the Constitution, and the laws of the United States . . . shall be the supreme law of the land." In effect this clause tells the states that they cannot pass laws or pursue actions that come into conflict with federal actions. It also refers to all state officials pledging their allegiance to the Constitution. The court case *McCulloch v Maryland* in 1819 established this precedent when Maryland was told it could not tax the National Bank.

The principle of limited government is woven into the Constitution.

The concept of federalism, the overall relationship between the federal government and state governments, is defined in the Tenth Amendment of the Constitution. It specifically tells the states that they have reserved powers. Powers not delegated to the government by the Constitution are given to the respective states. The application and interpretation of this relationship will be fully explored in Chapter 4, Federalism.

By including language that gives legitimacy to state governments and establishes a defined relationship among the states and between the federal government and states, a federal system of government is formed.

Limited Government

Throughout the entire document and in the amendments, both the federal government and state governments are told they do not have unlimited power. The three branches are limited through the system of checks and balances. The Congress is told that it cannot deny the writ of habeas corpus, the right of appeal, or pass bills of attainder, predetermined jail sentences imposed before a trial. There are, however, exceptions to some of these limitations. In times of national emergency, the Supreme Court has determined that the federal government can place major restrictions on the civil liberties of its citizens. During the Civil War, Lincoln suspended the writ of habeas corpus in the border states. During World War II, Roosevelt ordered Japanese-American citizens living on the West Coast to internment camps.

In fact the entire rationale for including a Bill of Rights in the Constitution was to reinforce this concept of limited government. From the opening words of the First Amendment, "Congress shall make no law respecting . . . ," to the due process guarantees of the Fifth and Fourteenth Amendments, the government is told that rights of its citizens must be protected. A further examination of this issue will be taken up in Chapter 5, The Bill of Rights and Civil Liberties.

This principle of limited government is the end extension of the philosophy of the Enlightenment thinkers—that government is created by the consent of the governed. If people have natural rights, it must also be assumed that government cannot take these rights away.

PROVISION FOR CHANGES

An enduring document, the Constitution provides for a process in which it can be amended to meet the needs of a changing society.

If you don't count the Bill of Rights and the prohibition amendments, the Constitution has been amended only 15 times. The revisions have been significant and help to strengthen, expand, and explain provisions found in the original document. The amendments can also be classified in five ways:

- creating additional power for the federal government such as the legalization of a progressive income tax (sixteenth)
- limiting power to the state governments such as prohibiting states from making laws that deny equal protection for its citizens (fourteenth)
- adding the right of popular sovereignty to various groups such as former slaves (thirteenth), women (nineteenth), and 18-year-olds (twenty-sixth)
- taking away and adding to the power of the voter to elect public officials (seventeenth, direct election of senators; twenty-second, limiting presidential terms)
- changing the structure of government (twenty-fifth, presidential succession and disability)

There are two methods used to amend the Constitution. The one that has been used the most requires a two-thirds vote in both houses of Congress and ratification in three-fourths of the state legislatures. The second method is when Congress must call for a national constitutional convention after a request is made by two-thirds of the state legislatures; then either three-fourths of the state legislatures must ratify the amendment or three-fourths of ratifying conventions held in the states must approve it. There may also be a time limit placed on the ratification of most amendments passed by Congress. One of the most debated constitutional amendments was the proposed Equal Rights Amendment, which would have guaranteed the equality of rights by the United States and every state based on sex. This amendment was given seven years and then an extension to pass in two-thirds of the state legislatures. It died in 1982, falling short of the necessary votes because of political pressure brought on by groups opposed to public funding of abortion and groups concerned about the effect that affirmative action would have on various labor laws. Other amendments such as the Twenty-Seventh Amendment, which places restrictions on Congress passing pay raises for themselves, took over 200 years to ratify! The vast majority of amendments including the Bill of Rights took less than a year to ratify.

If the Constitution is an enduring document, then one must project that other amendments to the Constitution are a real possibility. Such measures as a balanced budget amendment, a term limits amendment for Congress, the abolition of the electoral college, and a provision for equal rights for women and homosexuals have advocates. However, as was shown after the Supreme Court ruled in *Texas v Johnson* (1989) that flag burning is a legal form of political protest, Congress failed to pass a constitutional amendment supported by President George Bush making it illegal to burn or desecrate the flag.

THE UNWRITTEN CONSTITUTION

The unwritten constitution, as well as the Constitution's elasticity, adds to its viability. Political parties, the president's cabinet, special interest groups, political action committees, and the federal bureaucracy are important examples of traditions, precedent, and practice incorporated into our form of government.

The elastic clause and powers given to the Congress in the Constitution are perhaps the greatest instruments of change that Congress has at its disposal. From the passage of the Judiciary Act of 1789 to the creation of the many executive branch departments, Congress has used its power to expand the size of government. Congress has used the elastic clause to pass civil rights legislation, it has broadly interpreted the meaning of interstate commerce, and has passed a war powers act under its power to declare war.

Neither the Constitution nor any law provides for the establishment of political parties, nominating conventions, primaries, and most of the political system we are used to. Even though the Federalist Papers warned of the danger of political factions and George Washington echoed that point of view, the influence of political parties has become a dominant feature of government. When the Republican Party can unite and not provide a single vote for the president's budget proposal, one can see the importance of party politics. When a party decides to start a filibuster (continuous debate) in the Senate to block the passage of legislation, this becomes an additional check.

The Supreme Court has also gone beyond the constitutional parameters in establishing precedent. From the *Marbury v Madison* (1803) decision establishing judicial review to *Roe v Wade* (1973), which found a way to constitutionally protect the right of a woman to have an abortion, the Court forges new ground based on its interpretation of the Constitution.

Custom and tradition are an integral part of government. After executive departments were established by Congress, Washington announced the formation of cabinet positions. Congress then codified this concept as they approved additional cabinet positions. A two-term president was the accepted tradition until Franklin Roosevelt broke it. After he died, an amendment limiting presidential terms was passed, making the tradition a written component of the Constitution. After John Kennedy was assassinated, the presidential succession amendment was ratified. Little did the country realize that it would be used not as a result of an assassination, but rather because the country's vice president, Spiro Agnew, and, not much later, the president, Richard Nixon, would resign.

This chapter focused on the document that sets the course for American government and politics. An understanding of the Constitution makes your job easier as you look more closely at the specific workings of our government and political system.

The Constitution's flexibility and adaptability enable the creation of new instruments of government.

Section 1: Multiple-Choice Questions

1. The Constitution's writers carefully drafted a document that would create

   (A) strong states and a weak central government
   (B) weakened power in the state and national government
   (C) the ability to adapt to changing times
   (D) a dominant national government with no active participation from the states
   (E) an equal distribution of power between the states and national government

2. Which of the following governmental bodies is most directly responsible to the electorate?

   (A) The House of Representatives
   (B) The Senate
   (C) The executive branch
   (D) The Supreme Court
   (E) The bureaucracy

3. The question of the constitutionality of a term limit for legislators imposed by a state constitution is based on which of the following arguments?

   (A) The state's ability to set time and manner of elections for state office holders
   (B) The fact that the Constitution sets the qualifications for congressmen
   (C) The ability of people to vote directly for senators and representatives
   (D) The ability of voters to create term limits for state office holders
   (E) The fact that the Congress is scheduled to vote for a term limits amendment
       to the Constitution

4. The practice of judicial review was first established by which of the following actions?

   (A) The Constitution gives life terms to Supreme Court justices.
   (B) Justices serve as long as they maintain good behavior.
   (C) The Supreme Court exercises judicial precedent.
   (D) The Supreme Court has appellate jurisdiction.
   (E) The Supreme Court can declare a congressional act unconstitutional.

5. Which of the following resulted after the Supreme Court made a ruling in *Baker v Carr*?

   (A) The principle of "one man, one vote" was established.
   (B) Congressional districts became gerrymandered based on political considerations.
   (C) Congressional districts were created as a result of racial considerations.
   (D) Congress modified existing voting districts for state offices.
   (E) Congress was able to modify congressional districts in states where there was not
       equal representation.

6. All of the following are considered enumerated powers of the Congress EXCEPT

   (A) coining U.S. currency after the Constitution was ratified
   (B) establishing inferior courts in addition to the Supreme Court
   (C) setting up the first National Bank of the United States
   (D) establishing uniform immigration laws
   (E) regulating commerce among the several states

7. The implied power clause in the Constitution has been described as the ability of Congress to take which of the following actions?

   (A) Pass an assault weapons ban
   (B) Withdraw funds allocated to troops in Haiti
   (C) Pass a balanced budget amendment to the Constitution
   (D) Raise the price of stamps to 50 cents
   (E) Pass a law setting quotas for immigrants

8. In addition to the stated constitutional powers of the president, which of the following roles does he take on?

   (A) Acting as head of his political party
   (B) Granting pardons
   (C) Making treaties
   (D) Giving a State of the Union address
   (E) Signing or vetoing legislation

9. Which of the following is the only stated constitutional responsibility of the vice president?

   (A) Attending funerals of foreign dignitaries
   (B) Taking on special tasks assigned by the president
   (C) Presiding over the Senate
   (D) Filling in for the president when he is out of the country
   (E) Presiding over the House of Representatives

10. Which of the following represents a major reason why the electoral college was created?

    (A) It would encourage third-party candidates.
    (B) It would enable a select group of electors to cast the final vote for president and vice president.
    (C) It would encourage greater voter turnout.
    (D) It would give more power to the Congress in determining the outcome of presidential elections.
    (E) It would give the voters in smaller states a greater role in selecting the president and vice president.

11. All of the following represent examples of limited government EXCEPT

    (A) the application of habeas corpus in criminal appeals
    (B) the prohibition of passage of bills of attainder laws
    (C) Congress not being allowed to pass ex post facto laws
    (D) the inability of the president to grant titles of nobility
    (E) the Reserved Power Clause of the Tenth Amendment

12. All of the following represent examples of the use of checks and balances EXCEPT

    (A)   the 35 successful vetoes made by President George Bush

    (B)   the Senate rejection of the 1999 Comprehensive Nuclear Test Ban Treaty

    (C)   the Supreme Court ruling the Flag Desecration Act unconstitutional

    (D)   Congress passing the Crime Bill after a conference committee made changes

    (E)   Congress invoking the provisions of the War Powers Act

13. Which of the following actions increases the power of the president?

    (A)   A greater reliance on the states to solve problems

    (B)   A greater reliance on the federal government to solve problems

    (C)   The president having to work with a majority party in Congress different from his own

    (D)   An increased investigative role by the media

    (E)   The downsizing of the federal bureaucracy

14. The appointment of Supreme Court justices in the 1980s was characterized by

    (A)   quick approval by the Senate of nominees

    (B)   rejection of the majority of appointees

    (C)   limited background checks of the nominees

    (D)   limited input from legal associations and special interest groups

    (E)   bitter confirmation battles over personal and philosophical positions of the nominees

Answer Explanations

1. **(C)** Type of Question: Cause-and-effect relationships
   On the surface, the choices suggest that the correct answer deals with federal-state relationships. Because each of those choices (A, B, D, and E) is factually incorrect and choice C is a correct generalization, you have a broadly defined question with a general statement.

2. **(A)** Type of Question: Comparing and contrasting concepts and events
   Based on the responsibility of the Congress to initiate all appropriations bills, the size of the House compared to the Senate and the fact that the people do not directly vote for the president, Supreme Court justices, or appointments to the bureaucracy, the House is considered to be the one governmental body closest to the voter. Every two years, voters have the chance to change representatives, as they did in the 1994 midterm election.

3. **(B)** Type of Question: Solution to a problem
   Term-limits restrictions were argued before the Supreme Court in 1994, and the Court ruled in 1995 that they violated the Constitution.

4. **(E)** Type of Question: Cause-and-effect relationship
   Judicial review was established as a result of the fact that the Court declared the Judiciary Act of 1789 unconstitutional in the case of *Marbury v Madison.*

5. **(A)** Type of Question: Cause-and-effect relationship
   Baker v Carr established the concept of one man, one vote. The intent of the decision was not to create gerrymandered districts or districts created to satisfy racial considerations. The decision directed state legislatures, not the Congress, to draw up new districts and did not have any impact on voting districts for state offices.

6. **(C)** Type of Question: Definitional

You must know what the term *enumerated* means and then be able to apply the definition to a specific example that does not fit the definition. The classic example of an implied power of Congress arose as a result of the *McCulloch v Maryland* decision when the Court said that the creation of the second National Bank was constitutional based on the elastic clause.

7. **(A)** Type of Question: Definitional

Again, you must know the definition of implied power and then be able to apply it to a specific example. In this case, the passing of an assault weapons ban as part of a crime bill was implied as part of the general-welfare-legislating ability of Congress. The other choices are all examples of delegated powers in Article I Section 8.

8. **(A)** Type of Question: Comparing and contrasting concepts and events

Granting pardons, making treaties, giving a State of the Union address, and signing or vetoing legislation are all specific powers and/or responsibilities of the president listed in Article II of the Constitution. Taking on the role as head of a political party is an assumed responsibility that the president has taken on.

9. **(C)** Type of Question: Identification and analysis

The only constitutional function of the vice president is presiding over the Senate and casting tie-breaking votes. Of course, the vice president is also first in the line of succession if the president dies in office. The president can develop other roles for the vice president. For instance, President Clinton gave Vice President Gore the job of coming up with a report on how to reinvent government.

10. **(B)** Type of Question: Cause-and-effect relationship

The founding fathers doubted that the voters were wise enough to elect the president directly. Instituting an electoral college resulted in presidential electors being given the responsibility of actually voting for the president. These electors were chosen by majority vote, and the number of electors each state had was determined by its population.

11. **(E)** Type of Question: Definitional

In order to answer this question, you must know the definitions of limited government, habeas corpus, bill of attainder laws, ex post facto laws, and titles of nobility. The Reserved Power Clause gives states those powers not delegated to the federal government, thus expanding the power of the states.

12. **(D)** Type of Question: Identification and analysis

After thinking about the definition of checks and balances, you must apply it to the examples given in the question. The only choice that does not involve a direct check is the passage of the Crime Bill after it comes out of conference. The other choices are all excellent examples of checks and balances.

13. **(B)** Type of Question: Cause-and-effect relationships

Choices A, C, D, and E all limit the power of the president in dealing with solutions to different types of problems. If there is a greater reliance on the federal government to solve problems, you can conclude that a by-product would be an increased role on the part of the president.

14. **(E)** Type of Question: Sequencing a series of events

This question requires you to know something about the nomination of Supreme Court justices in the 1980s. Even if you just knew about the Clarence Thomas nomination, you would be able to know through process of elimination that these nominations are characterized by bitter confirmation battles.

Section 2: Free-Response Question (6 points)

Thomas Jefferson wrote, "The Constitution belongs to the living and not to the dead."

(a) Identify and explain one constitutional provision that illustrates Jefferson's statement. Give two examples of how the provision had an impact on public policy.

(b) Describe two ways the Constitution can be amended. Identify a constitutional amendment passed since 1960 and explain how the amendment changed public policy.

SAMPLE RESPONSE

(a) The "necessary and proper," or elastic, clause in the Constitution allows the federal government to take action in areas not specifically delegated to it by the Constitution. This clause is most often invoked in justifying the federal government's action regarding issues not originally considered at the Constitutional Convention. A recent example of this clause's impact on public policy is the Brady Bill. The bill mandated a seven-day waiting period prior to the purchase of a gun, during which the purchaser's record would be checked for prior convictions and arrests. Throughout the nation's 200-year history, the "necessary and proper" clause has given the federal government the authority to do many things that it would have been impossible for it to do because the Constitution never specifically granted the government the authority to act with respect to those areas.

Another example of the application of the elastic clause is the health care debate, which has often centered on whether or not the federal government has the duty to pay for an individual's medical services. If one believes that, in this day and age, sufficient health care is necessary to ensure the welfare of individuals, then there is constitutional precedent stating that the federal government has an obligation and responsibility to fund health care.

(b) The most dramatic way of changing the Constitution is through the formal amending process. This process is outlined in Article V of the Constitution. The amendment process has two stages: proposal and ratification. The first stage can be achieved in one of two ways. The first way is for an amendment to be proposed by a two-thirds vote of both houses of Congress. The second way is for an amendment to be proposed by a national constitutional convention requested by the legislatures of two-thirds of the states. The second stage of the amending process, ratification, can also be achieved in two possible ways. The first way is for an amendment to be ratified by the legislatures of three-fourths of the states. The second way for an amendment to be ratified is by a convention called for that purpose by three-fourths of the states.

The Twenty-Fifth Amendment (1967) to the Constitution is a perfect example of the Constitution's flexibility. When the Constitution was first drafted, it did not have any provisions for presidential disability or a vacancy in the office of the vice president. This amendment established a process whereby if the president becomes disabled, the vice president assumes the responsibilities of that office until the president can resume his duties. This provision has never been fully utilized, although when a president undergoes surgery (as Ronald Reagan did when he was shot), the vice president is technically in charge. The second part of this amendment was utilized after Richard Nixon's vice president, Spiro Agnew, resigned and Nixon appointed Gerald Ford. After Nixon resigned, Ford appointed the Governor of New York, Nelson Rockefeller, vice president with the approval of both houses of Congress.

SCORING GUIDELINES FOR FREE-RESPONSE QUESTION (6 POINTS)

Part (a) 4 Points

Four points are earned for identifying, explaining, and giving two examples of how one constitutional provision shows how the Constitution is flexible:

- The elastic clause—Congress can pass laws that are necessary and proper: the Brady Bill, health care, civil rights legislation
- The amending process—amending the Constitution changes the intent of the original Constitution: voting, civil rights
- The inherent power of the president—expands the power of the president without congressional approval: sending troops to fight without congressional approval, stem cell research
- Judicial review—gives the courts the power to interpret the Constitution and declare laws unconstitutional: abortion, civil rights, rights of the accused

Part (b) 2 Points

Two points are earned for describing the two ways the Constitution can be amended. One point is earned by identifying a constitutional amendment that has passed since 1960 and 1 point is earned for explaining how that amendment changed public policy:

- The Constitution can be amended after a majority of both houses of Congress passes it and three-fourths of state legislatures ratify it.
- An amendment to the Constitution can be passed if two-thirds of the states call for a national convention and three-fourths of the states ratify it.
- Any amendment passed after 1960 will be given credit, and if the amendment is applied to public policy, a second point will be earned.

Federalism

4

- → BLOCK GRANTS
- → CATEGORICAL GRANTS
- → COMMERCE CLAUSE
- → COMPETITIVE FEDERALISM
- → COOPERATIVE FEDERALISM
- → CREATIVE FEDERALISM
- → DEVOLUTION
- → DUAL FEDERALISM

- → FISCAL FEDERALISM
- → FUNDED MANDATES
- → LAYER CAKE FEDERALISM
- → MARBLE CAKE FEDERALISM
- → *MCCULLOCH V MARYLAND*
- → NEW FEDERALISM
- → UNFUNDED MANDATES

CONTEMPORARY CONNECTION

In 2009, the Department of Education announced the "Race to the Top" grant program that states could apply for if they adopted specific testing and teacher evaluation procedures and what was called a "common core" curriculum. Even though a majority of states took part in the program, by 2015 some states decided to opt out of the grant program because they felt that the federal government was becoming too intrusive in what was supposed to be a state run function—education. This chapter looks at the relationship between the states and the federal government, known as federalism.

Federalism, the division of power between the federal government and state governments, has been a central and evolving feature of our system of government. Political scientists also refer to this relationship as one where the federal government is divided among various levels of local government. This chapter also explores the various levels of government, their individual powers, their shared powers, and the historical and constitutional bases of federalism. It will also look at fiscal federalism, the manner in which the federal government offers federal assistance through different kinds of grants to state and local governments.

Advocates of a strong federal system believe that state and local governments do not have the sophistication to deal with the major problems facing the country. They feel that local politicians are provincial in their point of view and would advocate sectional issues that do not take into account the interests of an entire nation. People favoring a strong federal system also point to the inability of state and local governments to support the vast programs without an extensive tax base. They also feel that an elitist group would gain control and ignore the needs of the minority.

Critics of a strong federal system point to the fact that local leaders are most sensitive to the needs of their constituents. They also feel that states have a better ability to develop public policy that can be supported by a broad tax base. And critics point to the many demands made upon local governments by the federal government in order for the states to receive financial aid from the federal government.

Through this debate you can see how important the relationship among levels of government is. It can affect the kind of political participation that exists. It can determine the kind of public policy that is developed and implemented. Such issues as a national drinking age, a national speed limit, and consistent emission standards in every state have emerged in the debate over which level of government is best suited to solve the problems facing the country. Additionally, after the Republicans won back control of Congress in 1994, the issue of devolution of federal power, returning the balance of federal-state responsibilities back to the states, emerged in the name of unfunded mandates, those regulations passed by Congress or issued by regulatory agencies to the states without federal funds to support them.

LOCAL GOVERNMENTS

Federalism organizes a country's government, taking into account the needs of local levels of government.

Compared to other means of dividing power, federalism establishes a unique working relationship with the other levels of government and its people. Neither component can abolish or alter the other single-handedly. On the other hand, a unitary system of government centralizes all the power, and a confederation decentralizes all the power. Most parliamentary governments like Great Britain and France are unitary. Power can be taken away from the local unit by the central authority. The former Soviet Union, after its breakup, formed the Russian Confederation. The United States had a confederation, under the Articles of Confederation, that failed after a few short years in existence. The loosest confederation that exists on the international scene is the United Nations.

The advantage of the federal system over a unitary system and confederations is that there is a distinctive line drawn between what is in the purview of the central government versus what local governments are concerned with. The central government is concerned with broader issues affecting the entire country such as foreign policy, interstate matters, and immigration. Local governments are concerned with matters that have a direct impact on the daily lives of their citizens such as motor vehicle laws, garbage, education, and public health and welfare. Shared interests involve methods of raising revenues and the creation of a criminal justice system as well as common spending programs. Public policy is developed by both state and federal legislation. Yet, at times, the distinction between which policies are federal and which should be developed by the states becomes cloudy.

Schools

Between the operations of the federal government and local governments, our lives are deeply affected by a federal form of government. The sheer number of governments that exist nationwide illustrate the complexity of the federal system. If you are concerned with the education of your child, you must be aware of the local requirements set up by your town's school board, and you have to support the school district through some kind of tax system. The state government may set up minimum graduation requirements and laws affecting the certification of teachers. The national government may offer states and local districts aid if the districts meet national standards.

In 2001 Congress passed the "No Child Left Behind Act." According to the Department of Education, "The NCLB Act incorporates increased accountability for states, school districts, and schools; greater choice for parents and students, particularly those attending low-performing schools; more flexibility for states and local educational agencies in the use of federal education dollars; and a stronger emphasis on reading, especially for our youngest children." Specifically, the provisions of the No Child Left Behind legislation direct the U.S. Department of Education to "hold schools accountable for academic achievement by setting academic standards in each content area for what students should know and be able to do; gather specific, objective data through tests aligned with those standards; use test data to identify strengths and weaknesses in the system; report school condition and progress to parents and communities; empower parents to take action based on school information; celebrate schools that make real progress; and direct changes in schools that need help." In 2009, the Department of Education implemented as part of the American Recovery Act the "race to the top" program that encouraged states through grants to satisfy certain educational policies such as performance-based standards for teachers and principals, complying with nationwide standards, promoting charter schools and privatization of education, and computerization. Part of the standards included a "Common Core" curriculum. By 2015, states began to opt out of the grant program because of the Common Core demands.

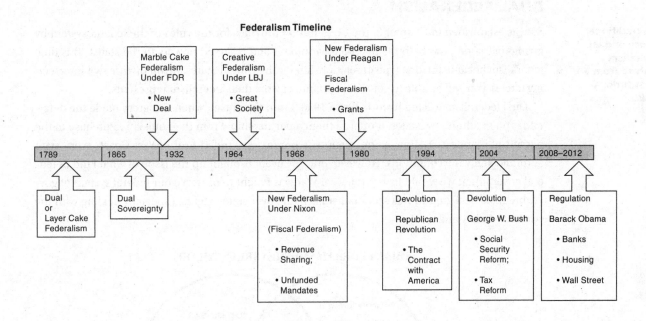

Federalism Timeline

HISTORY OF FEDERALISM

Even before the Constitution was ratified, strong arguments were made by Alexander Hamilton, John Jay, and James Madison in the Federalist Papers urging the inclusion of a federal form of government to replace the failed confederation. In Federalist No. 9 Hamilton states, "This form of government is a convention by which several smaller states agree to become members of a larger one, which they intend to form. It is a kind of assemblage of societies that constitutes a new one, capable of increasing, by means of new associations, until they arrive to such a degree of power as to be able to provide for the security of the united body." Those who feared that the federal government would become too strong were assured by Madison in Federalist No. 14 that "in the first place it is to be remembered that the general government is not to be charged with the whole power of making and administering laws. . . . The subordinate governments, which can extend their care to all those other objects which can be separately provided for, will retain their due authority and activity." These excerpts illustrate the fact that a federal form of government was central to the success of the new Constitution.

The historical foundation of federalism was established through the writings in the Federalist Papers and early Supreme Court decisions.

Court Cases

After the Constitution was ratified and the new federal form of government was formed, the new government established lines of authority defining its power structure. By 1819 the first real challenge to the authority of the United States by individual states took place in the case of *McCulloch v Maryland*. The issue revolved around the right of Maryland to tax paper currency needed by a branch of the U.S. National Bank located in that state. The bank was established by Congress using the elastic clause of the Constitution. In one of a series of landmark decisions, the Supreme Court, under the leadership of John Marshall, ruled unanimously that the "power to tax involves the power to destroy." It reasoned that because the United States had the right to coin and regulate money it also had the right to set up a National Bank to do this under the "necessary and proper" clause. After the bank was created, the laws protecting it were supreme; therefore, Maryland could not tax the federal institution.

DUAL FEDERALISM

The traditional theory of dual federalism evolved from a constitutional basis.

As was established in Chapter 3, the Constitution provides for the rules of the federal system by giving delegated powers to the federal government and reserved powers to the states. This dual federalism became the first type of relationship for the United States. If you picture two intersecting circles, you will be able to get a clear picture of what dual federalism represents.

Dual federalism existed historically to 1930. From the outset, when Congress made the determination to admit new states, it offered them a partnership. From the Louisiana Purchase to the pursuit of Manifest Destiny, as our country's borders expanded to the West Coast, every state admitted knew the conditions. However, one key event brought up the issue of what kind of federal government we would have—the Civil War was fought to preserve our federal system of government. Its background was sectionalism, a battle over states' rights, especially dealing with the issues of slavery and tariffs.

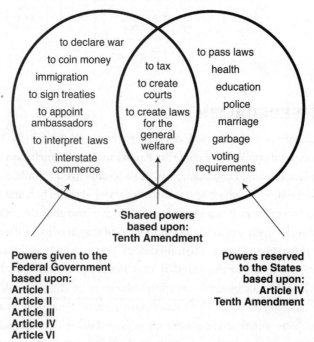

DUAL FEDERALISM: THE CIRCLE THEORY

to declare war
to coin money
immigration
to sign treaties
to appoint ambassadors
to interpret laws
interstate commerce

to tax
to create courts
to create laws for the general welfare

to pass laws
health
education
police
marriage
garbage
voting requirements

Shared powers based upon: Tenth Amendment

Powers given to the Federal Government based upon: Article I Article II Article III Article IV Article VI

Powers reserved to the States based upon: Article IV Tenth Amendment

LAYER CAKE FEDERALISM

An extension of dual federalism developed after the Civil War. It became known, according to political scientist Morton Grodzins, as layer cake federalism. It was a federalism characterized by a national government exercising its power independently from state governments. Following a more traditional approach, layer cake federalism was constitutionally based, and each level of government tried to exercise its own control over its own sphere of influence.

MARBLE CAKE FEDERALISM

If the federal government's relationship with the state governments could be described as a layer cake in the nineteenth and early twentieth centuries, then with the onset of the New Deal, federalism could be classified as a marble cake. Think of the two circles pictured above with bits and pieces of marble. The federal government becomes more intrusive in what had been typically the domain of state governments.

While it may sound contradictory, a cooperative federalism developed during the New Deal and lasted until the Great Society, resulting in greater growth of the federal government. Political scientists compare it to a marble cake.

During the New Deal, President Roosevelt needed drastic action to solve the problems brought on by the Great Depression. Establishing federal relief and recovery programs such as the Agricultural Adjustment Act (AAA) and the National Recovery Act (NRA), and reforming such localized institutions as banks with the Federal Deposit Insurance Corporation (FDIC) resulted in a much greater involvement on the local level by the federal government. Public work programs such as the Civilian Conservation Corps further brought the federal government into cities. Public policy became more of a sharing between the federal and state levels of government. The national government would provide the money; state governments would administer the programs. There were critics of these efforts. New Deal programs such as the AAA were declared unconstitutional by the Supreme Court.

CREATIVE FEDERALISM

The Great Society of Lyndon Johnson provided an even greater reliance on federal programs. Such actions as Medicare, Medicaid, the War on Poverty, and increased civil rights legislation forced the states to rely more heavily on federally funded programs. It also created an era of further cooperation among the many levels of government. The following components describe this creative approach to federalism:

Creative federalism during the Great Society increased the marble cake approach of intergovernmental relations.

- sharing the costs between the national and state governments for programs that typically would fall under the purview of state control,
- guidelines and rules set down by the federal government in order for the states to reap the benefits of federally funded programs,
- providing for the dual administration of programs such as Medicaid, which has a shared approach financially as well as administratively.

COMPETITIVE FEDERALISM

When Richard Nixon proposed a series of measures aimed at decentralizing many of the Great Society programs of Lyndon Johnson, he dubbed his program "the new federalism." This theme was later picked up by Ronald Reagan in 1980 and became the hallmark of his administration.

Competitive federalism under Nixon in the 1970s and Reagan and Bush in the 1980s reversed the marble cake nature, creating a "new federalism," where the states were given more responsibility.

The aim of competitive federalism was to offer states pieces of the marble cake but to have them accept it with conditions and with a promise to develop programs on their own. Federal orders in the Equal Opportunity Act of 1982 mandated compliance by the states under the threat of criminal or civil penalty. A second example was the placement of restrictions on other federal programs if a state did not meet the criteria of a specific program. Over 60 federal programs ranging from civil rights to the environment have this requirement. A third example is crossover requirements. If a state is going to receive federal money, it must agree to do something in return. For instance, under the Emergency Highway Energy Conservation Act of 1974, states had to agree to limit highway speed limits to 55 mph if they wanted to receive funding for highway repair. Additionally, under this competitive new federalism, states were forced to create their own standards of compliance based on federal legislation. The Clean Air Act of 1970 set national standards for air quality but directed the states to implement the law and enforce it.

FISCAL FEDERALISM

> Fiscal federalism, through different grant programs, slices up the marble cake into many different pieces, making it even more difficult to differentiate the functions of the levels of government.

The development of federalism since the New Deal has been fiscal in nature—that is how much funding is appropriated by the federal government to the states, under what conditions, and what the states can do with these funds.

Fiscal federalism can be classified in three major program areas: categorical grants including project and formula grants, block grants, and revenue sharing. They are usually aimed at assisting the states in areas of health, income security, education, employment, and transportation. A categorical grant is defined as federal aid that meets the criteria of a specific category and has specific criteria attached to them. These criteria can range from nondiscriminatory practice to minimum wages.

Grants

The two types of categorical grants that are given are project grants, which are based on competitive applications by states and individuals, and formula grants, which are based on specific formulas developed by Congress. These grants have an impact on such areas as families with dependent children and nutrition programs. Block grants are a form of federal aid with far fewer strings attached. They go to local communities for specific purposes, and the states decide where and how to spend the money. Along with revenue sharing, which gives money directly to the states with no strings attached, these two forms of fiscal federalism were vastly reduced under Ronald Reagan and George H. W. Bush.

An example of the block grant concept implemented during the Clinton administration was welfare reform. After vetoing the Republican-sponsored welfare reform proposal, President Clinton ultimately signed into law a far-reaching welfare reform bill in 1996. This law transferred the responsibility of welfare to the states. The federal government eliminated the entitlement and gave block grants to the states. The states then developed their own programs to move people from welfare to work within a five-year period.

In answering the questions regarding the use of federal grants, you should have a broad understanding of the overall purposes of the grant and mandate programs. The overall objective is to provide the states and localities with money they normally would not get. This would have the effect of reducing the fiscal burden on the states. In return, the federal government is able to achieve national goals they set in specific areas like education or helping minorities. The federal government through these kinds of grants can direct where this money goes and earmark it to those states with a poorer population. The money could also be used by a target audience with experts controlling the allocation of money received. The end result would be the development of many programs by state and local agencies without creating massive government bureaucracy.

DEVOLUTION

After the election of 1992, deficit reduction became a primary goal of President Clinton. After his budget proposal was approved by Congress, it became apparent that fiscal federalism and grant programs would be greatly affected by cutbacks in the federal budget. Even so, the trend seemed to support grants based on specific federal requirements. The move toward national educational standards was supported by a number of federal grants to school districts willing to accept the concept.

The Rhenquist Court has reflected the changing nature of federalism. It has affirmed the ability of the federal government to pass along programs to the states, yet it has also made it clear that, in areas such as abortion and carrying out the death penalty, states can and should act on their own. In one of the most interesting decisions the Court made, *United States v Lopez* in 1995, the Court, in a 5–4 decision, ruled that the Federal Gun Control Act prohibiting the possession of a gun within 1,000 feet of a school was unconstitutional based on a misuse of federal authority. The Court has also limited the power of the federal government to enforce provisions of the Americans with Disabilities Act during the last decade.

After the election of 1994, the Republican Contract with America clearly signaled a return to a more traditional approach now called "devolution." This trend continued as the Republicans maintained their majority in both houses in the 1996 election. Such measures as welfare reform, a balanced budget amendment to the Constitution, and regulatory reform were introduced with the explicit purpose of downsizing government and returning power to the states. Congress passed an Unfunded Mandates Law that placed major restrictions on Congress and the executive branch regarding passing legislation and regulations that had a price tag for the states. In fact states challenged the Motor Voter Act of 1993 as an unfunded mandate placing an unfair fiscal burden on the states. California refused to appropriate the funds necessary to implement it, and the Justice Department brought the state to court. The courts, however, ruled that California must abide by the provisions of the law. Other parts of the contract were passed by one or both of the houses but not signed into law by the president. But the message of the election was clear—federalism was again undergoing a major transformation that will last well into the twenty-first century, and with the election of George W. Bush in 2000, the trend of devolution was high on their agenda.

As it turned out, George W. Bush had a mixed record. Even though he was a proponent of devolution, the federal government grew during his two terms. A Medicare Prescription Drug Act was passed and the federal budget increased every year, resulting in record deficits and one of the worst recessions in the nation's history. After Barack Obama was elected president, many of his proposals to end the recession came into conflict with devolution. Obama favored massive government spending and a return to increased regulation of the banking and housing industries.

After the 2010 midterm elections, the new Republican House majority and the supporters of the Tea Party urged President Obama to reduce federal government spending and the role that the federal government plays in imposing regulations on the states. A new era of increased devolution would be a consequence of these policies. Yet, Congress still passed a bill that President Obama signed that was called The Dodd-Frank Wall Street Reform and Consumer Protection Act. Republicans promised to weaken these measures after their midterm victories in 2010 and 2014.

Since 1944 federalism has been moving toward devolution, the return of power to the states.

Section 1: Multiple-Choice Questions

1. Which of the following represents the theoretical definition of federalism?

   (A) A division of power between the federal government and state governments
   (B) A strict separation of power between the federal government and state governments
   (C) A division of power between the federal government and state governments where the power emanates from the states
   (D) A singular relationship that is characterized by control emanating one way from a central government
   (E) An equally shared power relationship among the branches of government

2. Advocates of a strong federal system believe in all the following EXCEPT

   (A) State and local governments do not have many of the resources necessary to deal with the problems facing the country.
   (B) Local politicians are provincial in their point of view.
   (C) State and local governments cannot support the vast programs necessary to support citizens.
   (D) Local leaders are more suited to solve problems than national leaders.
   (E) Factions would be more likely to gain control in a country dominated by local interests.

3. According to the writings of the Federalist Papers, which of the following reflects a major reason for the support of a federal system?

   (A) Local governments are best suited to meet the needs of the majority interests of the country.
   (B) Local governments will maintain their authority and will be able to care for their citizens.
   (C) The central government is best suited to recognize the needs and interests of local governments.
   (D) There will be a constant clashing of opinions between the interests of the local and federal governments.
   (E) Factions would be strengthened by the formation of a federal system of government.

4. The constitutional basis of dual federalism can be found in

   (A) the "necessary and proper" clause
   (B) the Tenth Amendment
   (C) the elastic clause
   (D) the implied power provision
   (E) the enumerated powers

5. Which general area of policy is generally left up to the states?

   (A) Foreign policy
   (B) Military policy
   (C) Relations among the several states
   (D) Health and welfare
   (E) Immigration

6. Which general area of policy is generally left up to the central government?

   (A) Health
   (B) Interstate commerce
   (C) Education
   (D) Police
   (E) Voting requirements

7. Which kind of federalism best describes an autonomous relationship between the states and national government?

   (A) Cooperative federalism
   (B) Creative federalism
   (C) Layer cake federalism
   (D) Fiscal federalism
   (E) Marble cake federalism

8. All of the following are characteristics of marble cake federalism EXCEPT

   (A) There are mingled responsibilities and blurred distinctions between the levels of government.
   (B) The federal government becomes more intrusive in state affairs.
   (C) There is a greater sharing of responsibilities between the federal and state levels.
   (D) The national government exercises its power independently from state governments.
   (E) There is greater cooperation between the federal and state governments.

9. Which type of federalism is characterized by a pattern of competitive grants?

   (A) Dual federalism
   (B) Cooperative federalism
   (C) Fiscal federalism
   (D) Creative federalism
   (E) Marble cake federalism

10. An alternative developed by the federal government that places the primary fiscal responsibility on the states was

   (A) revenue sharing
   (B) project grants
   (C) formula grants
   (D) unfunded mandates
   (E) reimbursement grants

11. Which of the following laws was challenged by states because they felt that the federal government imposed an unfair unfunded mandate?

   (A) Family and Medical Leave Act of 1993
   (B) Motor Voter Registration Act of 1993
   (C) Clean Air Act of 1970
   (D) Clean Water Act of 1972
   (E) Assault Weapons Ban of 1994

12. Richard Nixon and Ronald Reagan's vision of a new federalism favored

   (A) an increase in the power and authority of the federal government
   (B) a cooperative spirit between the federal and state governments
   (C) an increase in federal mandates
   (D) the downsizing of the federal government
   (E) a decrease in the defense budget

Answer Explanations

1. **(A)** Type of Question: Definitional
   The key word in this question is *theoretical*. As you have seen, there are many types of explanations and examples of federalism. This question is looking for the student to realize that federalism deals with a division of power. Choice B's use of the phrase "separation of power" is misleading and choice C, though using "division of power," gives the wrong explanation. Choice D refers to a unitary form of government.

2. **(D)** Type of Question: Comparing and contrasting concepts and events
   Looking for the one exception, you must recognize that choices A, C, and E are basic arguments developed for a strong federal system. Because choices B and D are opposites, one of the answers provides the solution to this question. Because an advocate of a strong federal system would not want to concede the fact that local leaders are more capable than national leaders, that answer provides a weak argument for a strong federal system.

3. **(B)** Type of Question: Solution to a problem
   The Federalist Papers attempted to provide a rationale not only for the ratification of the Constitution but also for the specific components of the new government including federalism. Even though the Federalist Papers speak of factions and raise the issue of the roles states play, they speak directly to the fact that on the local level governments will still have autonomy regarding local issues.

4. **(B)** Type of Question: Solution to a problem
   The Tenth Amendment encompasses both the enumerated powers of the Congress and the reserve powers of the states. The implied power gives Congress the authority to use the "necessary and proper" clause. Thus the Tenth Amendment provides the constitutional basis of dual federalism.

5. **(D)** Type of Question: Comparing and contrasting concepts and events
   This question and the following question require a knowledge of the differences among enumerated powers, delegated powers, and reserve powers. Using the process of elimination, you should be able to isolate health and welfare as a reserve power of the states.

6. **(B)** Type of Question: Comparing and contrasting concepts and events
   This question asks you to do the opposite from the previous question. Just as in Question 5, you should know that choices A, C, D, and E are reserve powers of the state. The interstate commerce clause gives you a clue that it is an enumerated power.

7. **(C)** Type of Question: Definitional
   Although it is often easier to come up with the name rather than the definition, in this question you can readily become confused over the different types of federalism. Thus you should use a strategy of eliminating obviously wrong answers. Because cooperative

federalism and marble cake federalism are synonymous, you can eliminate them easily. Creative federalism and fiscal federalism both took place during the Johnson and Nixon presidencies. Thus the autonomous relationship was an earlier form of federalism.

8. **(D)** Type of Question: Identification and analysis

Using the definition and visualizing what a marble cake looks like, choice D should jump out as the exception. Choices A, B, C, and E illustrate the mingling of responsibilities between the federal and state governments.

9. **(C)** Type of Question: Identification and analysis

This question is a reversal of the previous question and asks you to relate the predominant feature of competitive federalism—that it is fiscal. Even though there are fiscal components in the other choices, fiscal federalism is directly related to competitive grants.

10. **(D)** Type of Question: Cause-and-effect relationships

This question is very difficult because you must understand the differences between categorical grants, revenue sharing, formula grants, and unfunded mandates. Only unfunded mandates place on the states the primary responsibility to pay for the service provided by the government.

11. **(B)** Type of Question: Cause-and-effect relationships

As a result of the Republican victory in 1994 and motivated by the passage of the Unfunded Mandates Law, many states decided to challenge the implementation of the Motor Voter Registration Act based on the cost factor to the states.

12. **(D)** Type of Question: Solution to a problem

Richard Nixon and Ronald Reagan have been credited with creating the concept of new federalism. In general terms, both presidents favored a downsizing of the federal government. The only exception was in the area of the defense where they believed it was necessary to increase the defense budget. This question becomes difficult if you believe that a decrease in the defense budget was a characteristic of the new federalism approach rather than the general downsizing of the federal government.

Section 2: Free-Response Question (4 Points)

> Since 1980 Congress has proposed legislation that would change the nature of federalism and also served as a blueprint for the completion of President Ronald Reagan's vision of a "new federalism." (4 points)
>
> (a)   Define the term "new federalism."
>
> (b)   Explain how new federalism changed the relationship between the states and the federal government.
>
> (c)   Describe how two of the listed policies passed by Congress since 1980 accomplished the goals of new federalism.
> (1)   Americans with Disabilities Act
> (2)   Unfunded Mandates Act of 1994
> (3)   Welfare Reform Act of 1996

SAMPLE RESPONSE

(a)   This new federalism is the name given to a plan outlined by President Ronald Reagan in his State of the Union message in 1982. According to his plan, a number of federally administered programs would be turned over to the states.

In Reagan's view, the centralization of power in Washington during the twentieth century had diminished the proper constitutional role of the states in the federal system, making government too expensive and removing it from popular control. To remedy this problem, he proposed transferring responsibility for more than 40 health, education, welfare, and transportation programs to the states by 1988. In return, the federal government would assume responsibility for the Medicaid program, distributing $28 billion a year among the states until 1991. Reagan's plan was criticized because it meant that state control would mean reduced benefits for the poor, and the state governments themselves seemed reluctant to take on the burdens it entailed.

The Americans with Disabilities Act 1990

(1)   A landmark law, The Americans with Disabilities Act was signed into law by President George H.W. Bush in 1990. This law provided that people who had physical and mental disabilities could not be discriminated against. It also mandated that employees provide reasonable accommodations for their employees who had disabilities, and mandated that states and businesses provide accessibility for the disabled. This meant that a multi-level business that did not have an elevator had to build one. It also meant that cities had to provide ramps and sidewalk paths to accommodate wheelchairs.

Even though the Tenth Amendment to the Constitution reserves these types of actions to the states, the law mandated that the states and private businesses abide by them. Though the new federalism suggested a reduction in the role the federal government took, the ADA as it was known accomplished the goal of states carrying out the directives of the act rather than the federal government dictating every aspect of the law.

Unfunded Mandates Act of 1994

(b)   (2)   Unfunded mandates became popular during the 1980s and 1990s as Congress ran out of money but not enthusiasm for passing regulations. Congress simply told the lower levels of government that they had to pay for the new programs. During the 1980s Congress passed roughly 27 major statutes with new regulatory burdens for state and local governments.

Federal bureaucrats also got into the act, issuing thousands of pages of directives to accompany each major piece of regulatory legislation, such as the Endangered Species Act and the Clean Water Act. In all, the Congressional Budget Office estimates that regulations imposed on the local governments between 1983 and 1990 cost up to $12.7 billion.

When state and local governments are forced to use money to work on projects that are not pressing issues, they waste money that could be spent on more important concerns. Mayor Richard Daley estimated that Chicago spent at least $160 million on unfunded mandates in 1991; that money could pay for 3,200 police officers. The passage of the Unfunded Mandates Law clearly relates back to Reagan's new federalism.

Welfare Reform Act of 1996

(3) The Republicans' Contract with America set the stage for welfare reform. The proposed Welfare Bill under the Contract eliminated the guiding principle of poverty and food programs, which was that anyone who qualifies for these programs automatically gets them. However, President Clinton vetoed the measure because he believed the food stamp provisions, which would replace food stamps and child nutrition programs with a lump-sum payment to each state, were too extreme.

However, in the closing days of the 104th Congress and during the 1996 election campaign, the Republican Congress again passed a Welfare Bill, the Personal Responsibility and Work Opportunity Reconciliation Act of 1996, which was signed into law by President Clinton. The key provisions of the law included making welfare a transition to work by requiring welfare recipients to find work after two years on assistance. States would receive block grants in lieu of the former Aid to Dependent Children funds and would help support families during the transition into jobs. A maximum five-year term limit for welfare payments was enacted, with each state creating individualized programs. Other provisions included uniform interstate child support laws and a live at home and stay in school requirement aimed at unmarried minor parents who would be required to live with a responsible adult and participate in educational and training activities in order to receive assistance. The law also guaranteed healthcare for poor children, the disabled, pregnant women, the elderly, and people on welfare. The overriding theme of the law was to have states move people into jobs. One controversial aspect of the law was a denial of welfare benefits to legal immigrants. Opponents of this aspect promised that the new Congress would amend the law to soften this requirement.

SCORING GUIDELINES FOR FREE-RESPONSE QUESTION (4 POINTS)

Part (a) 1 Point

One point is earned for the definition of new federalism.

- New federalism is the turning over of federally administered programs to the states.
- The term "devolution" would also be acceptable in defining what new federalism's goal is.

Part (b) 1 Point

One point is earned for a description of how new federalism changed the relationship between the states and the federal government.

- Using Reagan's actions as an example, he proposed transferring health, education, welfare, and transportation programs to the states.
- Actions of other presidents turning over federal programs to the states are also acceptable.

Part (c) 2 Points

Two points are earned for describing how two policies by Congress since 1980 accomplished the goals of new federalism.

- The Americans with Disabilities Act (1990) gave the states the responsibility of providing accessibility and accommodations to the disabled.
- Unfunded Mandates Act of 1994—limited the scope of monetary provisions that Congress could impose on the states.
- Welfare Reform Act of 1996—gave the states the responsibility of making welfare a transition to work by requiring welfare recipients to find work.

PART TWO
Civil Rights and Civil Liberties

The Bill of Rights and Civil Liberties

5

- → BILL OF RIGHTS
- → CIVIL LIBERTIES
- → CLEAR AND PRESENT DANGER DOCTRINE
- → CRUEL AND UNUSUAL PUNISHMENT
- → DOUBLE JEOPARDY
- → ESTABLISHMENT CLAUSE
- → EXCLUSIONARY RULE
- → FIGHTING WORDS DOCTRINE
- → FREE EXERCISE CLAUSE
- → *GITLOW V NEW YORK* (1925)
- → INCORPORATION OF THE FOURTEENTH AMENDMENT

- → INDICTMENT
- → JUDICIAL FEDERALISM
- → LIBEL
- → LIVING WILL
- → MIRANDA RIGHTS
- → PRIOR RESTRAINT
- → PROCEDURAL DUE PROCESS
- → SELECTIVE INCORPORATION
- → SEPARATION OF CHURCH AND STATE
- → SLANDER
- → SUBSTANTIVE DUE PROCESS
- → SYMBOLIC SPEECH
- → WRIT OF HABEAS CORPUS

CONTEMPORARY CONNECTION

After National Security Agency analyst Edward Snowden fled the United States in 2013 and released thousands of documents, it became clear to what extent the government was using surveillance techniques. The release of these documents began a debate on whether the Constitution's Fourth Amendment's privacy protections were violated by the government, or whether national security allowed the government to conduct this program. This chapter explores the origins of the Bill of Rights, their meaning, application and interpretation of them, and how they apply to the states through what is called "selective incorporation." Significant Supreme Court decisions that have been handed down and impact the Bill of Rights are also discussed.

The Bill of Rights, adopted in 1791 by the states two years after the ratification of the Constitution, established the civil liberties for Americans. Viewing the Bill of Rights you will notice a number of "negative" statements:

- "Congress shall make no law . . ." abridging freedom of religion, speech, press, assembly, petition.
- "The right of people to keep and bear arms shall not be infringed."
- "No soldier shall . . . be quartered."

- "The right of the people . . . shall not be violated . . ." regarding unreasonable searches and seizures.
- "No person shall be held . . ." to be a witness against himself, in double jeopardy, or "deprived of life, liberty, or property without due process of law . . . ."
- "Excessive bail shall not be required, nor excessive fines imposed, nor cruel and unusual punishments inflicted."

These excerpts illustrate why the Bill of Rights represents a basic definition of a person's civil liberties—those rights of the people that the government cannot take away. They are guaranteed in the Constitution, in the Bill of Rights, in other amendments passed, as well as through court interpretation. These rights are characterized as substantive, the kind of limits placed on the national government (like the First, Second, and Eighth Amendments) and procedural, outlining how the government is supposed to treat individuals (for instance the Fifth Amendment). Civil liberties differ from civil rights. Civil liberties protect individuals from abuses of the government, whereas civil rights come about as a result of the equal protection under the law. Both civil liberties and civil rights limit the power of government.

This chapter also explores the historical development of the Bill of Rights and gives you a breakdown of the nature of the Bill of Rights and how it protects individuals against the tyranny of the government, as well as highlights key Supreme Court decisions. It also explains how the Bill of Rights through these Court decisions has been extended to the states, creating a form of judicial federalism.

INDIVIDUAL RIGHTS AND THE CONSTITUTION

Historically, the Constitution could not have been ratified without an agreement that a bill of rights would be included.

It became apparent to the Founding Fathers that, without some kind of compromise regarding a statement of the people's rights, the ratification of the Constitution would be in jeopardy. When the original proposal was made by George Mason, a Virginia delegate, to add a bill of rights to the Constitution in 1787, it was turned down by the Federalist forces controlling the convention. However, when the states began the ratification process, it became obvious that the necessary nine states needed to approve the document would not vote to ratify without an agreement to add a series of amendments that would protect people from the potential abuses by the national government. The Federalists argued initially that a bill of rights was not necessary because the states under a federal system would protect their citizens. The Anti-Federalists insisted that these rights be written and included in the proposed Constitution.

States such as Massachusetts, South Carolina, New Hampshire, Virginia, and New York agreed to support a bill of rights immediately after the Constitution was ratified. In the argument over whether or not to include a bill of rights into the original Constitution, James Madison wrote in the Federalist No. 84, "I go further and affirm that bills of rights, in the sense and to the extent in which they are contended for, are not only unnecessary in the proposed Constitution but would even be dangerous." On the other hand, in a *Letter from the Federal Farmer to the Republican* (an Anti-Federalist publication), it was written that "People, and very wisely too, like to be express and explicit about their essential rights, and not to be forced to claim them on the precarious and unascertained tenure of inferences and general principles. . . ." The Anti-Federalist forces prevailed, and the bill of rights was adopted in 1791.

Selective Incorporation

The John Marshall Court of the 1800s was responsible for key decisions that clarified the nature of government. Decisions such as *Marbury v Madison* (1803), *McCulloch v Maryland* (1819), and *Gibbons v Ogden* (1824) defined the power of various components of government. And even though the Court ruled that it had the power to declare state laws unconstitutional, it refused to extend the provisions of the Bill of Rights to the states.

In *Barron v Baltimore* (1833), the Court ruled that the Bill of Rights limited only the national government, not the states. In turning down Barron's argument that the city of Baltimore had deprived him of just compensation of property under the Fifth Amendment, Marshall wrote that "Each state established a constitution for itself, and in that constitution provided such limitations and restrictions on the powers of its particular government as its judgment dictated . . . the fifth amendment must be understood as restraining the power of the general government, not as applicable to the states." This decision established the nature of judicial federalism regarding the extension of the Bill of Rights to the citizens of the states. It created a concept of dual citizenship, wherein a citizen was under the jurisdiction of the national government as well as state governments. After the Fourteenth Amendment was passed in 1868 with its clear statement that "No state shall abridge the privileges and immunities of its citizens . . . ," the people received the complete protection of the Bill of Rights. Southern states passed Jim Crow laws and segregation became an acceptable practice. Chapter 6 discusses the incorporation of civil rights into the Bill of Rights.

The first time the Supreme Court applied a state case to the Bill of Rights, known as the Incorporation Doctrine, occurred in *Gitlow v New York* in 1925. Gitlow was convicted in New York of advocating the forcible overthrow of the government using violent means. The Court ruled that his actions were in violation of a New York statute because his actions created a "bad tendency," which endangered the public welfare. More important was the statement made by the majority that determined that "freedom of speech and of press—which are protected by the First Amendment from abridgment by Congress—are among the fundamental personal rights and 'liberties' *protected by the due process clause of the 14th Amendment from impairment by the States.*" For the first time, the Supreme Court ruled that there was a direct relationship among the Fourteenth Amendment, actions by the states, and the Bill of Rights. This selective incorporation reached its peak under the leadership of Earl Warren in the 1950s and 1960s. Each time the Court made a ruling that incorporated an aspect of the Bill of Rights to the states, the concept of judicial federalism was defined more fully.

As we delve into the specific nature of the Bill of Rights and civil liberties, we will also point out which significant cases contributed to the nationalization of the Bill of Rights.

> **Even after the Bill of Rights was extended to the states as a result of the passage of the Fourteenth Amendment, citizens needed protection against state abuses from the Supreme Court.**

FREEDOM OF RELIGION

"Congress shall make no law respecting an establishment of Religion, or prohibiting the free exercise thereof. . . ."

Called the establishment clause, this component of the First Amendment to the Constitution defines the right of the citizens to practice their religions without governmental interference. It also places a restriction on government, creating a "wall of separation" between church and state. From the settlement of this country by the Pilgrims who sought religious freedom to the belief by the Jehovah's Witnesses that they should not be forced to participate in religious activities in public schools, this clause has been the foundation of religious liberty in this country. However, it is also balanced by what is called governmental accommodation of religion, which is the ability of government to allow certain religious practices possibly including some direct forms of aid to public institutions. The line between government fostering of religious practice in our society and accommodation is the basis of many Supreme Court decisions in this area. Some of the major questions raised in this area follow:

> **The First Amendment's guarantee of free exercise of religion is balanced by the separation of church and state.**

- To what extent does use of the word *God* in public institutions violate the separation of church and state?

- Can states directly support parochial schools with public funds?
- Can states legislate nondenominational prayer, a moment of silence, creationism as a part of the curriculum, and equal access to its facilities to religious groups?
- Can clergy recite a blessing at graduation ceremonies?
- Are seasonal displays at public areas allowable?
- Are vouchers and public monies used for private parochial schools constitutional?

These are just a few of the many questions raised by the establishment clause. The following key Supreme Court decisions have created precedent.

Key Court Cases

***Engle v Vitale* (1962)**—This decision struck down a New York State nondenominational prayer that started with the words "Almighty God, we acknowledge our dependence upon thee . . ."

***Lemon v Kurtzman* (1971)**—The Lemon test, which came out of this case, sets the criteria in determining whether the line of governmental interference is crossed. The three-pronged standard indicates that the purpose of the legislation must be secular, not religious, that its primary effect must neither advance nor inhibit religion, and that it must avoid an "excessive entanglement of government with religion." Even though this case struck down a law that provided governmental aid to private schools, it has been used as a barometer to measure other legislative practices of the state.

***Lee v Weisman* (1992)**—This decision directed school officials not to invite clergy to recite prayers at graduation ceremonies.

FREEDOM OF SPEECH AND THE PRESS

"Congress shall make no law . . . abridging the freedom of speech, or of the press . . . ."

The guarantees of freedom of speech and press are also limited by the interests and well being of the citizens.

The protection of the citizens' right of free expression versus the government's interest of limiting speech and the press for the interests and safety of the country and its citizens is basic to the interpretation of this clause of the First Amendment. From John Peter Zenger's concept of complete freedom of the press on the one hand to Justice Oliver Wendell Holmes's recognition that you cannot yell "Fire" in a darkened movie theater on the other hand, the issue of how much freedom of speech and the press can be allowed has been debated.

Speech can be categorized as symbolic and expressive. It extends to public areas of commercial speech as well as private application. It raises the complex issue of what is acceptable and what is obscene. Government has the role to maintain a balance between order and the ability of its citizens to criticize policy. The issue of what constitutes "fighting words" or a "clear and present danger" goes to the heart of free speech and expression.

Press is characterized by the written word and the ability of a publication to print material without prior review or prior restraint (censorship) by a governmental body. It also raises issues regarding the rights of reporters to pursue a story and what constitutes libel.

Some of the major questions raised in this area follow.

- Can the government limit free speech and press during times of war or other national emergency?
- To what extent can organized "hate groups" such as the Ku Klux Klan and Nazis advocate their views publicly?
- What kinds of actions are considered symbolic speech?

- How do you define speech and expression that is obscene?
- When do libel and slander come into play?

Key Court Cases

***Schenck v United States* (1919)**—Justice Holmes ruled for the majority that Schenck did not have the right to print, speak, and distribute material against United States efforts in World War I because a "clear and present danger" existed.

***Chaplinsky v New Hampshire* (1942)**—In a key incorporation case, a doctrine defining what constitutes "fighting words" was established as a result of spoken words that "by their very utterance inflict injury or tend to incite an immediate breach of peace that governments may constitutionally punish." These words "have a direct tendency to cause acts of violence by the person to whom, individually, the remarks are addressed." However, the Court has also determined that the use of obscenities aimed at governmental policy or worn on clothing as a means of protest do not constitute fighting words in and of themselves.

***New York Times v Sullivan* (1964)**—This decision created a base definition of what constitutes libel—material that is written with malice and a reckless disregard for the truth. Slander criteria are very similar, but much more difficult to prove when charges are made against public officials.

***Tinker v Des Moines* (1969)**—This decision established that students' rights are "not shed at the schoolhouse gates" and defined the students' wearing a black armband in silent protest of the Vietnam War as "a legitimate form of symbolic speech." These rights were later restricted in the student press case *Hazelwood v Kuhlmeier* (1988) when the Court gave school administrators the right to censor a school newspaper.

***New York Times v United States* (1971)**—Known as the Pentagon Papers case, the Supreme Court ruled that the government did not have the right to prevent the *New York Times* from printing information about the history of the country's involvement in the Vietnam War.

***Texas v Johnson* (1988)**—Based on the arrest of Gregory Lee Johnson for burning a flag outside the Republican National Convention in protest of the president's foreign policy, the Supreme Court ruled that this action was a form of symbolic speech protected by the First Amendment. The Supreme Court decisions in this area have tended to tread a thin line.

**THE *TEXAS v JOHNSON* CASE DETERMINED THAT BURNING
A FLAG WAS CONSIDERED SYMBOLIC SPEECH**

McConnell v Federal Election Commission (2003)—The Supreme Court ruled that the major provisions of the McCain-Feingold campaign finance law were constitutional. Specifically, the justices said that the ban on soft money and the restrictions placed on television advertising did not violate free speech.

Citizens United v Federal Election Commission (2010)—This case overturned parts of the *McConnell v Federal Election Commission* (2003), the court ruling that corporate funding of political advertisements that did not specifically endorse a candidate was constitutional under the First Amendment's free speech clause and could not be limited. The court upheld the parts of the 2003 *McConnell* case that required the disclosure of political advertising sponsors and it upheld the ban of direct corporate and union contributions to political candidates. In 2014, the Supreme Court struck down the total amount of money one contributor could give to all candidates, political parties, and PACs combined in federal elections. Known as *McCutcheon v FEC*, the court's ruling almost completely eliminated any soft money restrictions, other than money directly given to one candidate. Candidates could raise money from multiple sources giving individuals the right to donate millions of dollars. The significance of these cases was that in the 2010 and 2014 midterm elections and the 2012 presidential campaign independent expenditures skyrocketed.

FREEDOM OF ASSEMBLY

"Congress shall make no law respecting . . . the right of the people peaceably to assemble, and to petition the Government for a redress of grievances."

> The ability of people to assemble, associate, and petition the government freely may come into conflict with the legitimate interests of the government and individuals.

The rights of people to gather in places they want and express their point of view without government interference, the right of association, and by extension the right to present their point of view to a governmental body are the central themes in the final clause of the First Amendment. These rights must be balanced by restrictions such as the time, manner, and place of assembly. They also must be aware of the protection of the individuals at the scene of assembly. Additionally, the extent to which individuals through their association in political groups can exert pressure on the government must be taken into account.

Some of the major questions raised by the themes of this clause follow.

- What constitutes equitable time, manner, and place restrictions on groups?
- To what extent can these demonstrations take place on public and private property?
- If a group an individual plans to associate with advocates violence, can the government restrict association and the right to petition?

Key Court Case

DeJonge v Oregon (1937)—In a key incorporation case, the Supreme Court ruled that the Fourteenth Amendment's due process clause applies to freedom of assembly. The Court found that DeJonge had the right to organize a Communist Party and speak at its meetings even though the party advocated "industrial or political change or revolution." However, in the 1950s with the fear of communism on the rise the Court ruled in *Dennis v United States* (1951), that Dennis, who was leader of the Communist Party, violated the Smith Act by advocating the forcible overthrow of the United States government.

The issues revolving around freedom of assembly and petition have continued to challenge restrictions placed on groups. In 1994 an anti-abortion group, Operation Rescue, was restricted in the manner in which they could demonstrate against a clinic performing abortions. The Court said that the group had to picket within a minimum distance from the clinic. Cases such as this illustrate how social issues such as abortion get mixed up with First Amendment issues of assembly.

RIGHT TO KEEP AND BEAR ARMS

"The right of the people to keep and bear arms, shall not be infringed."

Although the historical intent of the Second Amendment was the right of each state to maintain an armed militia, it has been interpreted as the right of individuals to own weapons. The National Rifle Association has become a primary interest group in supporting the gun enthusiast and hunter's right to purchase and use arms. With the issue of crime and violence a significant concern of society, laws have been proposed restricting the availability, use, and kinds of weapons. This clash has resulted in a national debate over the meaning of the Second Amendment as shown in the following questions.

- Should registration and a waiting period be required for a person to own recreational guns?
- Should certain types of arms such as assault weapons be banned?

The Second Amendment's provision for the people's right to bear arms has become a rallying call of interest groups as well as a caveat of many segments of society.

Key Court Case

The first Second Amendment case to be heard by the Supreme Court is *United States v Miller* (1939). This case determined that a section of the National Firearms Act of 1934, which made it a crime to ship certain kinds of weapons across states lines unless they were registered, was constitutional because it did not have any link to a state militia. Because this was a federal case, the regulation of arms has been a state matter. This was changed as a result of the passage of the Brady Bill in 1993. Named after President Reagan's press secretary who was seriously injured by a handgun in the attempted assassination of the president, it took more than ten years to obtain congressional approval. The law placed restrictions on handgun registration, setting up a minimum waiting period before purchase. Many states had to change their laws based on this legislation. A 1997 Supreme Court decision did, however, strike down the part of the law forcing local officials to perform instant checks. The National Rifle Association lobbied against its passage, insisting that it would not stop criminals from obtaining weapons. They used the same rationale in arguing against the passage of an assault weapons ban that was part of the Crime Bill passed in 1994.

The first Supreme Court decision that ruled on the question of whether the right to bear arms constitutionally protected individuals came in 2008, when the court announced its decision in *District of Columbia v Heller*. This case challenged a Washington, D.C., gun control law that banned guns in the District and required any legal guns to be unloaded. In a 5–4 decision, the court ruled that the law was unconstitutional and that the Second Amendment protected an individual's right to bear arms. How far-reaching this decision is remains a question, since the decision only applied to Washington, D.C., and federal laws. In 2010, the Supreme Court ruled in *McDonald v Chicago* that the Second Amendment's right to bear arms applies to the states.

RIGHT TO PRIVACY

Quartering of soldiers "in time of peace" shall be illegal "without the consent of the owner."

"The right of the people to be secure in their persons, houses, papers, and effects, against unreasonable searches and seizures, shall not be violated, and no Warrants shall issue, but upon probable cause . . . ."

The first of three amendments that deal with the due process rights of individuals, those procedural rights that protect individuals from governmental interference, are the Third and Fourth Amendments. They deal with such issues as search and seizure and the right of privacy. Included in the Bill of Rights because of abuses in this area by Great Britain when it ruled the colonies, these amendments prevent the unrestricted quartering of soldiers, blanket search warrants, and the unlimited invasion of privacy by the government.

By and large, the only time the Third Amendment has been used by the government was during the Civil War when the North quartered troops in Southern mansions. There have been no Supreme Court cases involving the Third Amendment.

The Fourth Amendment has come under the scrutiny of both the federal and state governments in determining how far they can go in obtaining evidence. The key criterion in determining the legitimacy of the search is probable cause. That becomes the first component of the due process rights of individuals, which also applies to the states as a result of a similar clause in the Fourteenth Amendment. An exception to the probable cause component is the "plain view" characteristic. It allows police to obtain evidence that is in sight of the investigators. Situations such as emergencies, investigations requiring wiretapping, and the extent a police official can search a car are also raised by the Fourth Amendment. Some of the major issues related to the Fourth Amendment follow.

- To what extent can police conduct a search without a warrant and obtain evidence found to prosecute an individual?
- What methods can law officials use to obtain evidence?
- Can the right of privacy extend to social issues such as abortion?
- Can the government use wire taps without a court order?

Key Court Cases

Wolf v Colorado (1938)—In the first incorporation case that dealt with the privacy section of the Fourth Amendment, the Supreme Court held that even though the exclusion of illegally obtained evidence as stipulated by state law was not mandated by the due process section of the Fourteenth Amendment, the court did say that the Fourteenth Amendment's due process clause did apply to the states. They said the states could adopt other measures that would not fall below the minimum standards set forth in that amendment. The decision was overturned by the *Mapp v Ohio* case.

Mapp v Ohio (1961)—A key state incorporation case, *Mapp v Ohio* established the exclusionary rule for states. The exclusionary rule determined that police may obtain only that evidence available through a legitimate search warrant. Other evidence found at the scene of the crime is not admissible in the trial; it must be excluded. This doctrine has been modified by the plain view doctrine. Many people have been critical of the exclusionary rule, suggesting that it handcuffs the police from obtaining legitimate evidence necessary to prosecute a criminal. Since *Mapp v Ohio*, other cases have created further exceptions. In *Nix v Williams* (1984) the Court allowed "inevitable discovery" of tainted evidence, that is, evidence that would have eventually been discovered with a legal warrant. *United States v Leon* (1984) created a "good faith" doctrine, which stated that if the police obtained essential evidence in good faith and did not violate the spirit and intent of the Fourth Amendment, that evidence would be allowed.

Griswold v Connecticut (1965)—The Court struck down a Connecticut law that prohibited the use of contraceptives. It arose after a doctor was arrested for distributing birth control devices. Using the privacy provision of the Fourth Amendment, the Court stated that individuals had the right to privacy in the area of sexual relations.

***Roe v Wade* (1972)**—Using the concept of being "secure in their persons," the Supreme Court ruled that abortions are constitutionally protected. It set up a trimester system allowing unrestricted abortions in the first trimester but regulated abortions during the second trimester and allowed the states to ban abortion during the third trimester unless the mother's or baby's life was endangered. This decision has been most controversial and set the stage for a national debate. We will come back to this issue in the next chapter.

***United States v Leon* (1984)**—In this decision, the Court created a "good faith" exception to the exclusionary rule, allowing the introduction of illegally obtained evidence where police can prove that the evidence was obtained without violating the core principles of *Mapp v Ohio*.

***Planned Parenthood v Casey* (1992)**—The Court upheld a Pennsylvania law requiring minors to wait 24 hours after receiving parental approval before getting an abortion as constitutional. The decision also struck down a provision mandating that women obtain "informed spousal consent" and upheld, in principle, *Roe v Wade*.

RIGHT TO PROCEDURAL DUE PROCESS

"No person shall be held to answer for a capital . . . crime, unless on a presentment or indictment of a Grand Jury . . . nor shall any person be subject for the same offense to be twice put in jeopardy . . . nor shall be compelled . . . to be a witness against himself, nor be deprived of life, liberty, or property without due process of law . . . ."

"In all criminal prosecutions, the accused shall enjoy the right to a speedy and public trial . . . and to be informed of the nature and cause of the accusation; to be confronted with the witnesses against him; to have . . . process for obtaining witnesses . . . and to have the Assistance of Counsel for his defense."

". . . the right of trial by jury shall be preserved . . . ."

Procedural due process can be viewed as a series of steps established by the Fifth, Sixth, and Seventh Amendments that protect the rights of the accused at every step of the investigation and limit how governmental power may be exercised. The following steps represent the steps taken: the manner in which the evidence is gathered (Fourth Amendment), the charges made by the police upon arrest (habeas corpus), the formal indictment and interrogation (allowance made for obtaining lawyers, witnesses), the trial (speedy and public trial, impartial jury, guarantees against self-incrimination, trial by jury), and the right to confront witnesses. Another kind of due process, substantive, places limits on the government as they relate to the content of legislation and the extent government can use its power to enact unreasonable laws.

> The Fifth, Sixth, and Seventh Amendments, which establish procedural due process for the accused, have been viewed by critics as an over-protection of criminal rights and the placement of an undue burden of proof on the government.

Before looking at key cases, you should have a clear understanding of the intent of each of these steps. Habeas corpus, a right that cannot be taken away by government, found in the body of the Constitution in Article I Section 9, has also been called a writ of liberty. It directs the police to show cause why a person may be held for a crime. It has also been used by convicted criminals as a route to appeal their conviction from the state courts to the federal courts based on procedural issues. An indictment is a formal list of charges made by a grand jury. When enough evidence is given to the grand jury, it develops a list of formal charges that is presented to the accused prior to trial. A speedy trial has been defined by law on the federal level as a trial that must take place no more than 100 days after arrest. Each state has laws addressing this issue. A public trial means that it is held in a public courthouse. Depending upon the specific issue, the extent of public viewing and media coverage can be determined by the judge. The right to a jury trial does not necessarily mean that the jurors will be identified by name. In the trial of the World Trade Center bombers, the jury was chosen in this manner. In obtaining an adequate defense, the conditions in which a defendant can obtain a lawyer based on financial considerations and the exact time a lawyer is brought in are not defined. Double jeopardy means that once a verdict is handed down, you cannot be tried twice for the same crime. That does not mean that if you are found innocent of state charges, you cannot be tried for a federal offense dealing with the same issue. That is what happened to the police involved in the beating of Rodney King.

Surveys taken have shown that much of the public is critical of the manner in which courts have interpreted these provisions. Crime and violence have become a national concern. Anti-crime legislation and Supreme Court decisions have responded to the public's concern.

Some of the questions raised by these amendments follow.

- Can due process rights be suspended during times of national emergencies?
- Is live media coverage of trials allowable?
- Does a lawyer have to be assigned to a defendant who cannot afford one?
- At what point does the accused have the right to consult a lawyer?
- To what extent do the police have to advise the accused of their rights?

Key Court Cases

***Escobedo v Illinois* (1964)**—Danny Escobedo requested the assistance of a lawyer after he was arrested for the murder of his brother. The police would not grant the request even though there was a lawyer at the police station. Escobedo made a number of incriminating statements without his lawyer present, which were later used against him at the trial. The Supreme Court ruled Escobedo's due process rights of self-incrimination and right to counsel were violated and he was released from prison.

***Gideon v Wainright* (1964)**—This landmark case established that the accused has the right to an attorney even if he or she cannot afford one. Gideon, accused of a felony in Florida, requested the assistance of a lawyer. The Florida criminal justice system allowed free assistance only in cases that were punishable by death. Gideon defended himself and lost. The Supreme Court ruled that his Sixth Amendment due process rights made applicable by the Fourteenth Amendment were denied.

***Miranda v Arizona* (1966)**—In probably one of the most publicized cases of its kind, Ernesto Miranda, mentally retarded, was accused and convicted of rape and kidnapping. He confessed to the crime under intense interrogation without any mention by the police of his right to obtain a lawyer or what consequences the answers to their questions would have on the outcome of the trial. The Supreme Court, in its landmark ruling, established the Miranda rights. Those rights directed the police to inform the accused upon arrest that he has a constitutional right to remain silent, that any thing said can be used in court, that he has a right to consult with a lawyer at any time during the process, and that a lawyer will be provided if the accused cannot afford one. The accused must be asked if he understands these rights and told that he has the right to remain silent and at any time request a lawyer. Since the *Miranda* ruling, the courts have begun to limit some of the rights established by these cases.

***New York v Quarles* (1984)**—The Court created a "public safety" exception to the *Miranda* warnings allowing the police to arrest an accused criminal without reciting the *Miranda* rights where public safety is threatened.

***Hamdi v Rumsfeld* (2004)**—Enemy combatants held in the United States have due process rights.

EIGHTH AMENDMENT

"Excessive bail shall not be required, nor excessive fines imposed, nor cruel and unusual punishments inflicted."

As part of the procedural due process, an accused has the right to post bail, an amount of money set by the court as a guarantee that the person will return to stand trial. This amount may not be excessive and is imposed based on the nature of the crime and the history of the accused. Critics of the system raise the issue that if the accused cannot afford the bail, even if it is not excessive, then the person is unduly punished prior to the trial.

> The Eighth Amendment completes the due process cycle and raises the issue of the extent a government can impose punishment on convicted criminals.

Excessive fines and cruel and unusual punishment have resulted in some of the most passionate arguments revolving around the nature and extent of government imposed punishment.

Some of the major issues posed by this amendment follow.

- What constitutes excessive bail?
- Is the death penalty cruel and unusual punishment?

Key Court Case

Gregg v Georgia (1976)—The landmark case, which held that "the punishment of death does not invariably violate the Constitution." However it did affirm standards and criteria set down in *Furman v Georgia* (1972), regarding discretion of judges and make-up of juries. Since *Gregg*, other criteria have been established regarding the kinds of cases that can result in the kinds of executions and the manner in which states impose death penalties. The Court has also ruled that other forms of treatment of criminals while they are in prison can also be cruel and unusual. Such penalties as denial of medical assistance or an interpretation that narcotics addiction is a crime rather than an illness that can be treated violated the Eighth and Fourteenth Amendments.

These issues have resulted in a national debate regarding the best way to create a balance between society's needs of protecting its citizens and the rights of the accused. A federal crime bill that created a "three strikes and you're out" feature passed the Congress in 1994 and has been duplicated in many states. This bill mandates that life imprisonment be given for federal crimes if a criminal is convicted of three felonies.

UNDEFINED RIGHTS

"The enumeration in the Constitution, of certain rights, shall not be construed to deny ... others retained by the people."

"The powers not delegated to the United States by the Constitution, nor prohibited by it to the States, are reserved to the States respectively, or to the people."

Called by some the elastic clause of the Bill of Rights, the Ninth Amendment guarantees that those undefined rights not listed anywhere in the Constitution cannot be taken away. Such issues as abortion and the "right to die" have come under the umbrella of this amendment.

> The Ninth and Tenth Amendments to the Constitution further define rights not listed in the Constitution to the people and states.

The Tenth Amendment, discussed in Chapter 4, extends to the states the right to create laws for the best interests of their people. It is the basis of federalism, and when this amendment comes into conflict with the other amendments of the Bill of Rights and the Fourteenth Amendment, the outcome of the dispute further defines the changing nature of federalism. The more the Supreme Court nationalized the Bill of Rights through the application of the Fourteenth Amendment, the more judicial federalism made the Bill of Rights apply directly to the states.

Some of the questions raised by these amendments follow.

- Does an individual have the right to die?
- How do the courts resolve the conflict between state and federal laws and issues raised by the Bill of Rights?

Key Court Cases

United States v Lopez (1995)—The Supreme Court ruled that Congress misused its authority in enacting the Gun-Free School Zone Safety Act, which made the possession of a gun within 1,000 yards of a school a federal crime. The Court held that enforcement of such an act comes under the authority of the states.

Printz, Sheriff/Coroner, Ravalli County, Montana v United States (1997)—Challenging the provision of the Brady Law, which mandated local officials to perform background checks on people purchasing handguns, the Supreme Court ruled that that specific part of the law was unconstitutional.

The discussion involving the relationship of the Bill of Rights to the state's right to develop its own laws and procedures goes to the heart of what the future of federalism will be. There is no doubt that the nationalization of the Bill of Rights through the incorporation of the Fourteenth Amendment has had a significant impact on state laws. From the interpretation of the First Amendment freedoms to the rights of the accused, the states increasingly have to be responsive to the principles of the Bill of Rights. However, decisions reached by the Rehnquist Court have tilted some of the power back to the states.

Gonzales v Oregon (2006)—The Supreme Court ruled that the federal government could not block Oregon's Assisted Suicide Law by moving against physicians who assisted terminally ill patients by giving them medicine that would enable them to commit suicide.

National Federation of Independent Business v Sebelius (2012)—The Supreme Court ruled that the Affordable Care Act (also known as "Obamacare") was constitutional. In a split decision, the court ruled that even though the Congress violated the Tenth Amendment's interstate commerce clause by imposing a penalty on those individuals who did not pay for health insurance, Congress under its power to tax did have the authority to collect a fee if health insurance was not bought.

Section 1: Multiple-Choice Questions

1. Which of the following arguments represents the best reason why a bill of rights was added to the Constitution?

   (A) The Federalists felt that the central government would not protect the citizens.

   (B) The Anti-Federalists believed that the masses needed to know what their rights were.

   (C) Ratification of the Constitution including a bill of rights was supported by both the Federalists and Anti-Federalists.

   (D) Key states insisted on a bill of rights prior to approving the Constitution.

   (E) The Anti-Federalists felt that the Constitution alone protected citizens from abuses of the central government.

2. Which of the following decisions made by Chief Justice John Marshall's Court established the principle that the Bill of Rights only applied to the federal government?

   (A) *Marbury v Madison* (1803)

   (B) *McCulloch v Maryland* (1819)

   (C) *Gibbons v Ogden* (1824)

   (D) *Barron v Baltimore* (1833)

   (E) *Fletcher v Peck* (1810)

3. The Supreme Court decision *Gitlow v New York* established the principle that

   (A) there was no relationship between the Fourteenth Amendment and the Bill of Rights

   (B) free speech was not protected by the Bill of Rights in state cases

   (C) incorporation of the Bill of Rights in state cases was allowed

   (D) there was an indirect relationship between the Fourteenth Amendment and the Bill of Rights

   (E) judicial review could take place in state cases by the Supreme Court

4. The establishment clause of the First Amendment speaks of

   (A) an officially sanctioned nonsectarian religion for the United States

   (B) a wall of separation between church and state

   (C) government not being able to accommodate religion in public places

   (D) government agencies creating watchdog committees to prevent religious infringement in the schools

   (E) the passage of the equal access law

5. Which of the following Supreme Court cases established the "clear and present danger" doctrine?

   (A) *Schenck v United States* (1919)

   (B) *Texas v Johnson* (1989)

   (C) *Chaplinsky v New Hampshire* (1942)

   (D) *Abrams v New York* (1919)

   (E) *Tinker v Des Moines* (1969)

6. The terms *prior review* and *prior restraint* refer to which of the following constitutional principles?

(A) Freedom of the press
(B) Freedom of speech
(C) Freedom of assembly
(D) Due process
(E) Freedom to petition one's grievances

7. The Lemon test is used to determine if

(A) there is unfair government interference regarding free speech
(B) the government is acting properly in due process cases
(C) there are illegal tactics used by PACs
(D) death penalty convictions are fair and reasonable
(E) legislation that deals with religion creates illegal government interference

8. The principle established by the Supreme Court in the case of *Tinker v Des Moines* (1969) states that

(A) schools can act in loco parentis
(B) student rights did not stop at the schoolhouse gates
(C) principals have the right to censor student publications
(D) student symbolic speech may be censored by school officials even if it does not create a disruption
(E) principals have the right to suspend students without a hearing

9. The principle established in the Supreme Court case of *Texas v Johnson* (1989) was based on

(A) religious speech
(B) active speech
(C) symbolic speech
(D) fighting words
(E) government accommodation of speech

10. In the case of *Mapp v Ohio,* (1961) the Supreme Court established

(A) the exclusionary rule of evidence
(B) the fighting words doctrine
(C) the bad tendency doctrine
(D) the prurient interest principle
(E) the stop and frisk rule of evidence

11. Which of the following cases used the Ninth Amendment as a constitutional argument?

(A) *Griswold v Connecticut* (1965)
(B) *Collins v Smith* (1978)
(C) *Cox v New Hampshire* (1941)
(D) *Engle v Vitale* (1962)
(E) *Roe v Wade* (1973)

12. All of the following steps are part of procedural due process EXCEPT

(A) habeas corpus

(B) formal indictment

(C) speedy trial

(D) right to an attorney

(E) a jury made up of different ethnic groups

13. The intent of the decision made in *Miranda v Arizona* (1966) was

(A) the guarantee to accused persons that law enforcement agencies videotape confessions

(B) to tie the hands of the police after they arrest a suspect

(C) to allow the federal government to tighten its criminal laws

(D) to allow state governments to obtain confessions more easily

(E) to guarantee due process rights of the accused

14. The "right to die" is an implicit right found in which part of the Constitution?

(A) The elastic clause

(B) The due process clause

(C) The Fourteenth Amendment

(D) The Ninth Amendment

(E) The Fifth Amendment

Answer Explanations

1. **(D)** Type of Question: Cause-and-effect relationships

This is a relatively difficult question because the answer reflects a political, rather than a philosophical, reason why the Bill of Rights was added to the Constitution. New York, in particular, insisted that a bill of rights be included in the Constitution. In fact their delegation to the ratifying convention was heavily Anti-Federalist. Until the Anti-Federalists received a commitment that a bill of rights would be included, they were ready to vote against adoption. Philosophically, the inclusion of a bill of rights was a means to ensure that the rights of individuals would not be usurped by the federal government.

2. **(D)** Type of Question: Identification and analysis

A number of questions in this chapter have similar characteristics. You are asked to either connect a Court case to a principle or a principle to a Court case. The cases selected are significant, either as landmark precedent cases or as cases that illustrate the incorporation of the Bill of Rights. *Barron v Baltimore* established that the Bill of Rights did not apply to the individual states. For a citizen to argue a deprivation of rights, the state had to also have in its constitution a bill of rights. Most states, in fact, did provide protection for their citizens.

3. **(C)** Type of Question: Identification and analysis

Gitlow became a landmark incorporation case that dealt with the incorporation of a free speech issue to the states in the twentieth century. The Fourteenth Amendment gave the Court the opportunity to use the incorporation principle. But it took the Court until the twentieth century to really begin the process. Such decisions as *Plessy v Ferguson*, in 1896, rejected the incorporation of civil rights, and other civil liberties cases were not addressed until *Gitlow* was decided.

4. **(B)** Type of Question: Definitional

The establishment clause has two parts. The first speaks of Congress not being able to pass a law establishing a religion and the second part guarantees the free exercise of religious beliefs. These two concepts sometimes clash when the state gets involved in the guarantee part. Thus the concept of a wall of separation was developed, which on the one hand set down a test to guarantee noninvolvement by the government, yet allowed accommodation and protected individual rights to practice and follow a religion.

5. **(A)** Type of Question: Identification/principle

The *Schenck* case, which was argued during World War I, established that in times of national emergencies, the government has the right to take away an individual's civil liberties if the action of the individual presents a clear and present danger to the country and its citizens. The other choices, all First Amendment speech cases, established other speech principles such as symbolic speech.

6. **(A)** Type of Question: Definitional

Prior review allows an authority to look over the content of a story before it is published. Prior restraint gives that authority the right to prevent the printing of a story or newspaper. The Courts have generally prevented government from acting as a censor except in the extreme case of national security. Yet in the Pentagon Papers case, the Court clearly decided that the government did not have the right to stop publication of the Pentagon Papers during the Vietnam War. The Court has allowed prior review and prior restraint in student publications (*Hazelwood v Kuhlmeir*).

7. **(E)** Type of Question: Cause-and-effect relationships

The Lemon test, derived from the *Lemon v Kurtzman* case, established a three-pronged test to determine if there is excessive government intrusion in establishing religion. The test included that the purpose of legislation must be secular, not religious; its primary effect must neither advance nor inhibit religion; and it must avoid an "excessive entanglement of government with religion."

8. **(B)** Type of Question: Identification and analysis

The *Tinker* case is the landmark case dealing with Bill of Rights protection for students. It involved symbolic speech, but in the decision the Court expanded the application of the rest of the Bill of Rights to students. Choice A is a correct statement but did not derive from the *Tinker* case. Other cases such as *Goss v Lopez* expanded student due process rights. The other choices all deal with Supreme Court cases that limit student rights and more narrowly apply the *Tinker* decision.

9. **(C)** Type of Question: Identification and analysis

The *Texas v Johnson* case dealt with the right of Johnson to burn an American flag as a symbol of protest against the Reagan administration's foreign policy. The First Amendment clearly addresses the issues of free speech, assembly, and petition, but it does not specifically speak of the concept of symbolic speech. The 5–4 decision stated that Johnson had the right to use the flag as a symbol of political discontent, even if in the process he desecrated it.

10. **(A)** Type of Question: Identification and analysis

Mapp v Ohio is the precedent case that established the exclusionary rule of evidence to state cases. The exclusionary rule prevents police from introducing evidence obtained without a proper search warrant and gives Fourth and Fourteenth Amendment protection to the accused in state cases. It previously existed for federal cases. The other choices reflect principles established by other Supreme Court cases.

11. **(E)** Type of Question: Cause-and-effect relationship

The Ninth Amendment to the Constitution has been rarely used in Supreme Court arguments. The amendment has been referred to as the elastic clause of the Bill of Rights guaranteeing to citizens other rights that are not listed in the Bill of Rights. When *Roe v Wade* was argued, the petitioner used the strategy of applying the Fourth Amendment's "to be secure in their persons" to a woman's right to decide whether or not to have an abortion. The right to make that choice was argued using the Ninth Amendment, and it was accepted by the Court, thereby giving constitutional sanction to the abortion issue.

12. **(E)** Type of Question: Definitional

There are two kinds of due process, procedural and substantive. Procedural deals with the procedures in the Fifth, Sixth, Seventh, and Fourteenth Amendments, which take the accused from arrest to trial. Choices A, B, C, and D are all part of the procedural due process guaranteed by the Constitution. Choice E goes beyond the provision of the Constitution, which guarantees the accused the right to a jury of one's peers. Even though there have been Court decisions that have reversed lower court rulings based on the make-up of juries, it is not a specific part of the procedural due process guarantees.

13. **(E)** Type of Question: Identification and analysis

The common misconception that students have in regard to the *Miranda* decision is that the so-called Miranda rights, which came about because of the decision, were original guarantees provided for by the Fifth Amendment. The other difficult part of this question is that many people feel that *Miranda* had the negative consequence of tying the hands of the police. Even though the more conservative Burger and Rehnquist Courts have narrowed the interpretation of *Miranda*, it is still a key due process guarantee.

14. **(D)** Type of Question: Cause-and-effect relationships

As in an earlier question, the Ninth Amendment's expansion of rights given to individuals suggests clearly that the rights of individuals are not limited to the rights mentioned in the Bill of Rights. The elastic clause aspect of it is implied. Technically, the elastic clause refers to Article I Section 8 and the ability of Congress to make laws that are necessary and proper.

Section 2: Free-Response Question (9 points)

> The Supreme Court has attempted to balance society's needs for protecting its citizens and guaranteeing due process to the accused.
>
> (a) Define what is meant by due process and choose two provisions in the Constitution that illustrate your definition.
>
> (b) Using your definition in (a) and the provisions you chose, describe one Supreme Court case that balanced society's needs for protecting its citizens and guaranteeing due process to the accused. In your answer make sure you give one fact of the case, one constitutional issue, and explain the significance of the case. (For illustrative purposes two cases are given as examples and more than one fact and more than one issue are provided.)

SAMPLE RESPONSE

(a)   Due process is defined as the constitutional guarantees that an individual has from the time of an arrest to the guarantees of not answering questions to the police without an attorney present, the right to call your own witnesses, the right to confront your accusers, and the right to a speedy trial with an attorney provided to defend you. Two provisions of the Constitution that describe due process are the Fifth Amendment's "due process clause," which states that an individual cannot be deprived of life, liberty, or property without due process of law, and the Sixth Amendment's right to a speedy trial.

Mapp v Ohio (1961)

(b)   The exclusionary rule limited the state's ability to use evidence found in unrestricted searches without warrants. It incorporated the finding in the case of *Weeks v United States* in 1914, which had created the same standard for federal crimes, thus applying the Fourteenth Amendment's due process clause to the states. In the case, police officers suspected that Dolleree Mapp was harboring a dangerous and armed criminal in her house and hiding gambling material. They knocked on her door and insisted that they should be able to search the house for the fugitive. Mrs. Mapp did not let the police enter. Shortly thereafter, the police came back waving a piece of paper they claimed was a warrant and forced their entry into the house. During the search they did not find the criminal. They did, however, discover a chest that contained pornographic magazines. Because Ohio law prohibited the possession of this material, they arrested Mrs. Mapp, and she was convicted of possession of obscene materials and sent to prison.

The constitutional issue in the case was whether or not Mrs. Mapp's Fourth and Fourteenth Amendment rights of privacy were violated because the police entered the house without a legitimate search warrant. The state argued that in *Wolf v Colorado,* the Supreme Court established the precedent that in state cases the exclusionary rule of evidence was permissible. Mrs. Mapp's attorney pointed to the federal case and argued that the police acted illegally by taking evidence that was not covered by a search warrant and using that evidence to convict Mrs. Mapp.

The Warren Court wrote that "the prohibition against unreasonable searches would be meaningless unless evidence gained in such search was excluded." The significance of the case is that it limited law enforcement agencies from using illegally obtained tainted evidence called "fruit from the poisonous vine" in state cases. It sent a clear message that protections guaranteed by the Fourth and Fourteenth Amendments applied to the accused, even if it meant that somebody charged with a crime could potentially get off on a "technicality." This rule has been modified by the Rehnquist Court in three ways. First, the Court said that tainted evidence could be used if that evidence "ultimately or inevitably would have been discovered by lawful means." Second, the Court determined a good faith exception to the rule. This meant that, if the police investigation was conducted using good faith, evidence could be used even if there was not a warrant. Third, the Court gave the police greater flexibility in obtaining evidence if they could demonstrate that in the search there had been an "honest mistake." The *Mapp* case clearly illustrates the complexity of how far law enforcement agencies and the state can go to protect the legitimate interests of society.

Gregg v Georgia (1976)

In the case of *Gregg v Georgia,* the Court had the difficult problem of applying a standard it set in a case heard a few years before, *Furman v Georgia.* In that case the Court determined the death penalty to be illegal based on the fact that judges used arbitrary discretion in applying the penalty and that juries were biased based on their racial make-up. It begged the issue of the cruel and unusual punishment provision of the Eighth Amendment. Therefore, when another Georgia case emerged in 1976, the Burger Court decided to look at the entire issue.

Troy Gregg and Floyd Allen were arrested, after being stopped by police for driving a stolen car, for the brutal murder of two men who were shot and found in a ditch near a highway rest stop. Gregg was searched, and the police found a gun that was later identified as the murder weapon. Allen cooperated with the police and informed them that Gregg had shot the men to rob them and steal their car. Gregg claimed self-defense. Georgia tried Gregg for murder and armed robbery.

Based on the *Furman* decision, Georgia changed its trial procedure and Gregg first was found guilty by a jury that was considerably more balanced than in the *Furman* case. After the guilty verdict, the judge gave the jury clearly defined instructions that they could either impose the death penalty under specific circumstances or sentence Gregg to life imprisonment. The jury sentenced Gregg to death.

Gregg's attorneys appealed the case based on the Eighth Amendment's "cruel and unusual punishment" provision. They also invoked the privileges and immunities clause and due process/equal protection clauses of the Fourteenth Amendment, suggesting that racial minorities were being discriminated against by Georgia. Finally, they claimed that Georgia was still violating the *Furman* standard by allowing the jury to impose the death penalty in an arbitrary and capricious manner. Georgia claimed that imposition of the death penalty for capital crimes was appropriate and reasonable to the intent of the Eighth Amendment and that the guidelines the judge used came under the *Furman* doctrine.

The Court ruled definitively that "the punishment of death does not invariably violate the Constitution." Since the decision, the Supreme Court has had to expand the criteria used in determining death penalty legality in such areas as mentally incompetent criminals, criminals under the age of 18, and the manner in which the death penalty is imposed. In addition, the Court has severely limited habeas corpus appeals of death row inmates, going as far as not granting a stay even when there was new evidence in hand that clearly showed the innocence of the person who was going to be put to death by the state.

This case and other decisions by the Rehnquist Court swing the pendulum to the interests of society in the manner in which the state can deal with the criminal elements. Surveys have shown that given a choice between the rights of the accused established in such cases as *Mapp v Ohio* and the ability of the state to deal with criminals and impose a death penalty, the majority of the people polled would favor harsher penalties for the criminals and fewer restrictions placed on the police.

SCORING GUIDELINES FOR FREE-RESPONSE QUESTION (9 POINTS)

Part (a) 3 Points

One point is earned for the definition of due process and 1 point is earned for each of two provisions of the Constitution that are identified. Each point earned must be defined, identified, and include a discussion of what is meant by the definition and how the provision describes due process.

Answers may include, but are not limited to:

- the definition of due process must include the procedures used when an individual is accused of a crime such as . . .
- the Fourth Amendment's protections against unreasonable search and seizure
- the Fifth and Fourteenth Amendments' due process clause
- the Sixth Amendment's right to a speedy trial
- the Sixth Amendment's right to an attorney

Part (b) 6 Points

One point is earned by correctly choosing a Supreme Court due process decision. Two points are earned for correctly applying the constitutional provisions to the case. One point is given for correctly describing a fact of the case. One point is earned for correctly identifying a constitutional issue, and 1 point is earned for correctly explaining the significance of the case.

Examples of Supreme Court cases that could be used include but are not limited to:

- *Mapp v Ohio* (1961)
- *Gregg v Georgia* (1976)
- *Gideon v Wainright* (1964)
- *Miranda v Arizona* (1966)

Civil Rights: Equal Protection Under the Law

6

→ AFFIRMATIVE ACTION

→ AMERICANS WITH DISABILITIES ACT (1991)

→ BRANDEIS BRIEF

→ CIVIL RIGHTS

→ *DE FACTO* SEGREGATION

→ *DE JURE* SEGREGATION

→ DECLARATION OF SENTIMENTS AND RESOLUTIONS

→ EQUAL PROTECTION UNDER THE LAW

→ IMMIGRATION ACT OF 1991

→ JIM CROW LAWS

→ NATIONALIZATION OF THE BILL OF RIGHTS

→ *PLESSY V FERGUSON* (1896)

→ SENECA FALLS CONVENTION

→ SEPARATE BUT EQUAL

→ SUFFRAGE

CONTEMPORARY CONNECTION

The issue of police procedures resulting in the arrests and deaths of African-Americans created a national discussion after the New York City police used "stop and frisk" to search predominantly African-Americans, after an incident in Ferguson Missouri where a police officer shot and killed an African-American, and in New York City after an African-American was choked to death in a routine arrest. This chapter traces the history of how the Fourteenth Amendment to the U.S. Constitution guarantees equal protection under the law.

The history of the civil rights movement parallels the nationalization of the Fourteenth Amendment of the Constitution.

Even though the Civil War solved the problem of slavery and established the legitimacy and dominance of the federal government, the fact remained that many states still passed Jim Crow laws, legislation that legalized segregation even after the adoption of the Fourteenth Amendment. Segregation existed in America, and the Supreme Court in the *Plessy* decision stated "separate but equal" was an acceptable standard. Some inroads were made as civil rights activists pressured the national government to address the issue of racial discrimination. But it took the landmark *Brown v Board of Education* decision for the movement to see results.

Other minority groups such as women, immigrant groups, Native Americans, homosexuals, senior citizens, and the young have faced discrimination. Congressional legislation and Supreme Court decisions have used affirmative action programs as a means of providing equality under the law.

This chapter also explores the constitutional and legislative basis of civil rights for minority groups. It will focus on the issue of affirmative action programs and how government attempts to solve one of the most perplexing problems facing American society.

EQUAL PROTECTION TO ALL

"No State shall make or enforce any law which shall abridge the privileges or immunities of citizens of the United States; nor shall any State deprive any person of life, liberty, or property without due process of law; nor deny to any person within its jurisdiction the equal protection of the laws."

The equal protection clause of the Fourteenth Amendment provides the basis of the civil rights movement.

We previously defined civil rights as the substantive application of equal protection under the law to individuals. Prior to the passage of the Fourteenth Amendment, the Bill of Rights was the only protection citizens had. Even the principles outlined in the Declaration of Independence, natural rights, inalienable rights, and the statement "all men are created equal" suggested that civil rights should be an integral part of our government. But the issue of slavery quickly brought to a stop any fulfillment of these principles. The *Dred Scott* case in 1857 established that slaves were property based on the due process clause of the Fifth Amendment.

Fourteenth Amendment

The significance of the Fourteenth Amendment is that it aimed to nationalize the meaning of civil rights through the Incorporation Doctrine. On the surface it seemed that states could no longer discriminate against their citizens. Yet one of the first key Court cases after the passage of the amendment had a chilling effect on any thought of nationalization of the Bill of Rights. The slaughterhouse cases, in 1873, involved suits by individuals against states, accusing the states of the denial of property rights under the Fifth and Fourteenth Amendments. The Supreme Court dismissed the suits and ruled that the intent of the Fourteenth Amendment was to protect the freed slaves, not incorporate the Bill of Rights. Yet when the Congress passed in 1875 the first civil rights acts since the Civil War, the Supreme Court did not follow the principle set down in the slaughterhouse cases.

When a provision of the civil rights act, which established the legality of access to public accommodations, theaters, hotels, and other public facilities, was challenged, the Supreme Court ruled that aspect of the congressional act unconstitutional. Its logic was that the Fourteenth Amendment applied only to the states "operating under cover of the law." But the definitive action by the Court in *Plessy v Ferguson* in 1896 put the issue to rest. When Homer Plessy challenged the Louisiana state law that created two classes of railroad fares, the Supreme Court, using the fact that the passenger train had only an intrastate route, ruled that separate but equal facilities were constitutional under the equal protection provision of the Fourteenth Amendment.

Even after the Supreme Court case nationalized the Bill of Rights in the *Gitlow* case (described in Chapter 5), it reversed itself in a significant due process case, *Palko v Connecticut* (1937). This case involving the issue of double jeopardy gave Connecticut the right to try an individual a second time. The concept of applying the Fifth and Fourteenth Amendments' due process provisions to citizens who felt their "privileges and immunities" were being violated by the state was rejected. The concept of ordered liberty became the criterion for any incorporation of the Bill of Rights into the Fourteenth Amendment.

Then how did the Fourteenth Amendment finally become the basis of the civil rights movement? It took the Supreme Court over 50 years to finally reverse *Plessy*. *Brown v Board of Education* signaled the beginning of equal protection under the law for African-Americans. There were, however, other significant First Amendment and due process cases before *Brown*, which started the process of incorporation.

Key Court Cases

- *Gitlow v New York* (1925)—freedom of speech
- *Near v Minnesota* (1931)—freedom of the press
- *Powell v Alabama* (1932)—access to a lawyer in capital cases
- *De Jonge v Oregon* (1937)—freedom of assembly
- *Cantwell v Connecticut* (1940)—freedom of religion
- *Wolf v Colorado* (1949)—unreasonable search and seizure

After the *Brown* decision, an activist Supreme Court used the principle of incorporation in many of their decisions to promote Fourteenth Amendment due process rights and equal protection under the law. The criteria they used were threefold:

- reasonable classification, the distinctions drawn between persons and groups;
- the rational basis test, if the legislative intent of a law is reasonable and legitimate and serves the public good; and
- the strict scrutiny test, which places the burden on the states to prove that laws that discriminate fulfill a "compelling governmental interest."

AFRICAN-AMERICANS

Supreme Court Justice Stephen Breyer, at his confirmation hearings, called *Brown v Board of Education* (1954) the most significant Supreme Court decision in the history of the Court. In a unanimous decision written by Chief Justice Earl Warren, the Court redefined the meaning of the Fourteenth Amendment. It said that "in the field of public education the doctrine of 'separate but equal' has no place. . . . Segregation is a denial of the equal protection of the laws." It also called upon states to end segregation practices using "all deliberate speed." Yet in a survey taken on the fiftieth anniversary of the *Brown* decision, many school districts still have not fulfilled the *Brown* vision.

Brown put an end to de jure segregation, segregation by law. States and local municipalities have been able to continue the practice through de facto segregation, segregation of schools and other public facilities through circumstance with no law supporting it. Housing patterns, schools, and other public facilities have existed where they set up segregation as a basic practice. The Congress and Supreme Court have attempted to deal with de facto segregation.

The landmark Civil Rights Act of 1964 made discrimination in public accommodations such as hotels and restaurants illegal. The law was affirmed by the landmark *Heart of Atlanta Motel v United States* in 1964. This case involved an Atlanta motel on an interstate highway that serviced a majority of travelers. The motel discriminated against African-American patrons. It claimed that the Title II provision of the Civil Rights Act of 1964 was unconstitutional. In a unanimous decision, the Court, using the interstate commerce provision of the Constitution, upheld the legality of the law. The Twenty-Fourth Amendment, passed the same year, made any tax related to the voting process illegal. In 1965 the Voting Rights Act was passed. This law protected the right of African-Americans to vote and made provisions for federal assistance in the registration process. The Civil Rights Act of 1968, called the Open Housing Act, made illegal the practice of selling real estate based on race, color, religion, national origin, or sex. The issue of busing to solve racial discrimination practices was resolved in the *Swann v Charlotte-Mecklenberg County Schools* case in 1971. The Court ruled that busing was a legal means of achieving the "all deliberate speed" component of the *Brown* decision. Even though these actions contributed to the civil rights of African-Americans, civil disobedience, racial riots, and stonewalling attempts on the part of public officials hampered the progress of the civil rights movement.

The civil rights era for African-Americans was ushered in by the *Brown* decision, other Supreme Court decisions, and congressional legislation.

In a split, important decision, the Supreme Court in *California Board of Regents v Bakke* in 1978 established two concepts. A majority ruled that Bakke, a white who was denied admission to the medical school, had been the victim of "reverse discrimination" because the school set up a set of racial quotas that violated Bakke's equal protection. However, in the more important part of the ruling, a 5–4 majority also stated that even though race cannot be used as the sole basis for determining admission, the Constitution and Civil Rights Act of 1964 could be used as a criterion for affirmative action programs. President Johnson, using an executive order, directed all federally supported programs to adopt this criterion.

Affirmative Action

The *Bakke* case brought the issue of affirmative action into the forefront of civil rights. Both the Supreme Court and Congress have been sensitive to the issue of job discrimination. Legislation and decisions by the Court have dealt with that issue and more often than not have accepted affirmative action as a basis of determining whether job discrimination exists. The public has been very critical of affirmative action as a means of achieving civil rights for African-Americans and other minority groups. We will deal with it in relation to other groups later in this chapter.

Insofar as it has had an impact on African-Americans, in 1979 the Court again permitted an affirmative action program favoring African-Americans in private industry if the program corrected past injustices (*Weber v Kaiser Aluminum*) (1979). In 1988, Congress passed new civil rights legislation that permitted the federal government to take away federal funds from colleges that discriminate. And in 1991 it passed a Civil Rights Act that placed the burden on the employer to prove that hiring practices are not discriminatory in nature. This 1991 act became a battleground between Congress and President Bush. Bush initially vetoed the piece of legislation calling it a "quota bill." Congress softened the bill to include the hiring provision as well as a provision that placed a responsibility on the employer rather than the worker to determine if any hiring tests were discriminatory. The significance of this act was that Congress, in proposing this legislation, responded to previous Supreme Court decisions that seemed to place the responsibility of initiating antidiscrimination suits on the individual. In addition, it illustrated the heated nature of affirmative action programs.

The nature of affirmative action started evolving in a dramatic form during the Clinton presidency. In a major policy speech, President Clinton indicated that he favored a policy of affirmative action that would "mend it, not end it." However, individual states moved toward ending it. A Texas Federal Appeals Court ruled that the Bakke decision allowing race to be used as a factor for admission did not apply to Texas state colleges. The California State Board of Regents also invalidated race as a factor in admissions in their University system in 1996. California voters also approved in 1996 the California Civil Rights Initiative, also known as Proposition 209. This initiative effectively directed California not to take race or gender into account in government hiring practices. A California appeals court ruled the measure constitutional. The Supreme Court refused to hear the case. Thus, the provisions of the referendum were implemented in California.

Because minority enrollment decreased, California instituted a policy that guaranteed admittance to its university system for the top 10 percent of minority students applying for admission.

In the spring of 2003, a 5–4 Supreme Court ruled in two cases involving the University of Michigan undergraduate school and University of Michigan Law School that the principles laid out in the *Bakke* decision were still valid. Writing for the majority, Justice Sandra Day O'Connor said in the undergraduate case that the school could not use a point system in which race was used as a basis for their admissions system because it was too similar to a quota system. However, in the law school a "critical mass" criteria could be used as a basis for admissions. These cases were significant because they continued the long-standing practice of using race as a basis for admissions. In 2006, voters in Michigan rejected the use of race-based affirmative action programs.

In 2013, the Supreme Court heard arguments concerning the affirmative action admissions policy of the University of Texas at Austin. The case, brought by undergraduate Abigail Fisher in 2008, asks that the Court declare the admissions policy of the University inconsistent with *Grutter v Bollinger*, a 2003 case. Fisher was denied enrollment in the university system because the state had a policy that accepted ten percent of each high school's population. Fisher fell below that standard and was denied entrance even though she had higher scores than minorities who were accepted even though they were also below the ten percent in their graduating classes.

The Supreme Court ruled that the Texas affirmative action program was unconstitutional, sending the case back to the lower courts to review the entire program. However, the court still recognized that race could be used as a factor in college admissions and did not overthrow other college affirmative action programs previously ruled constitutional. In 2014, the court ruled that a Michigan constitutional amendment that banned affirmative action in the state's public universities was legal.

Key Court Cases

***Richmond v Corson* (1989)**—This case created the impetus for Congress to pass the Civil Rights Act of 1991. It established the following five procedures for evaluating the legitimacy of affirmative action programs.

1. A scrutiny test evaluates programs based on racial classification.
2. Congress has more power than the states through the provisions of the Fourteenth Amendment to enforce equal protection provisions.
3. When the state takes action, it must do so based on evidence that past discriminatory practice existed.
4. Affirmative action remedies must be specific and apply to past injustices.
5. States may develop affirmative action programs "narrowly tailored . . . necessary to break down patterns of deliberate exclusion."

***Gratz v Bollinger; Grutter v Bollinger* (2004)**—The University of Michigan undergraduate school's admission practice was unconstitutional (*Gratz*) because it relied too much on a quota system. The University of Michigan's law school's admission system was constitutional (*Grutter*) because it relied on a broad-based policy of using race as a basis for admissions. Both decisions affirmed the *Bakke* case.

WOMEN

Most political scientists point to the Seneca Falls Convention in 1848 as the beginning of the fight for equality. At this convention Elizabeth Cady Stanton led the fight for political suffrage and supported a doctrine very similar in nature to the Declaration of Independence. The Declaration of Sentiments and Resolutions for women's rights stated in part, "The history of mankind is a history of repeated injuries and usurpations on the part of man toward woman. . . ." It listed a series of abuses such as government failing to allow women to vote, the compelling of women to submit to laws in which they had no voice in passing, and the withholding of rights given to other members of society. It took the passage of the Nineteenth Amendment in 1920 for woman to gain the right to vote.

The fight to gain equality for women has been tedious and arduous.

The Age of Feminism

A turning point in the battle for equality was the publication of Betty Friedan's book *The Feminine Mystique* in 1963. The dawn of the age of feminism was born. Groups such as the National Organization for Women (NOW) and the National Women's Political Caucus were formed. They supported a proposed amendment to the Constitution, the Equal Rights Amendment.

Previously described in Chapter 4 in the section dealing with the amending process, it attempted to do for women what the Fourteenth Amendment eventually did for African-Americans. It was ironic that one of the arguments used against its passage was that the amendment was not necessary because the equal protection clause of the Fourteenth Amendment already existed. One of the earliest acts passed was the Equal Pay Act of 1963, which required employers to pay men and women the same wages for doing the same jobs.

The issue of "comparable worth," paying women equally for jobs similar to those held by men, was challenged in 2007 in the Supreme Court case *Ledbetter v Goodyear Tire and Rubber Company*. Lilly Ledbetter sued Goodyear Tire, her longtime employer, after she discovered that her salary was lower than what men received for the same job. However, the suit was brought to court after the expiration of the legal time limit to sue for damages, which is set forth in the Title VII section of the Civil Rights Act of 1964. In a 5–4 decision, the court ruled against Ledbetter, declaring that she did not meet the legal deadline of suing within 180 days of the start of the alleged discrimination, even though she claimed to be unaware of the salary differential for many years. This decision was criticized by labor unions and women, who argued that the result of the case ignored the fact that Goodyear had discriminated against Ledbetter. Congress attempted to rectify this by passing the Lilly Ledbetter Act, which allows suits to be filed after the discovery of discrimination regardless of when that discrimination first occurred. It was vetoed by George W. Bush but passed again by Congress and signed into law by President Obama shortly after he was elected president.

Women's Rights

Women's rights became a reality as a result of many of the acts of Congress and Supreme Court decisions that came about initially to give African-Americans their civil rights. The Civil Rights Act of 1964 had an anti-sex discrimination provision. In 1972 those Title VII provisions were extended by the Education Act of 1972. Title IX of that act made sex discrimination in federally funded education programs illegal. Just prior to that legislation, in 1969, a presidential order directed that equal opportunities for women be considered as national policy. It took a key court case, *Reed v Reed* (1971), which made a state law that favored men over women in the selection of an estate's executor unconstitutional, to establish a legal precedent. Two years later in *Frontiero v Richardson* (1973), the Court spoke definitively, stating that "There can be no doubt that our nation has had a long and unfortunate history of sex discrimination. . . ." A "medium scrutiny" standard was established in 1976 in *Craig v Boren* when the Court ruled that if discrimination was apparent, whether it was aimed at men or women, it would be illegal. The courts have also ruled that certain work-related situations constitute job discrimination. In 1977 in *Dothard v Rawlinson*, the Court struck down an Alabama law forbidding women from serving as prison guards in all-male prisons. In 1992 in *UAW v Johnson Controls*, the Court ruled that Johnson Controls could not prevent women from working in a battery factory, even if the work caused infertility in women.

A related issue, sexual harassment in the workplace, has been raised since the confirmation hearings of Supreme Court Justice Clarence Thomas. Since University of Oklahoma law professor Anita Hill raised those charges, the public's awareness of the issue has been on the rise. President Clinton's appointment of Ruth Bader Ginsburg to the Supreme Court in 1994 sent a signal that job discrimination and sexual harassment would not be tolerated.

Advances in political office also became a feature of the quest for women's rights. From the victory of Connecticut Governor Ella Grasso in 1974, to the appointment of Sandra Day O'Connor as the first woman Supreme Court Justice in 1981, Ruth Bader Ginsburg in 1994, and Sonia Sotomayor, the first Hispanic woman in 2009, Elena Kagan in 2010; in 2014 Janet Yellen was appointed the head of the Federal Reserve; and to the nomination of Geraldine Ferraro as Walter Mondale's running mate in the 1984 presidential election, to the election of Representative Nancy Pelosi as the first Speaker of the House, women have successfully attained significant public positions. In the 1992 elections more women were elected to Congress than ever before, including the first African-American Senator, Carol Moseley Braun. The trend continued in the 2000 election when more women senators were elected, including Hillary Rodham Clinton, who was elected as a senator from New York. She is the first former First Lady elected to public office. She also ran unsuccessfully for president in 2008 and was appointed secretary of state by President Obama. That same year, Sarah Palin became the first woman to run for vice president on the Republican ticket with Senator John McCain.

LGBT COMMUNITY

Attempts by gay activists, including Lesbians, Gays, Bisexuals, the Transgender community, and federal and state legislatures to guarantee equal protection for homosexuals have fallen short. In fact, many initiative referendums, including one in Colorado in 1993, not only rejected gay rights proposals, but also established legal obstacles for gays. Even the Supreme Court was not sympathetic. *Bowers v Hardwick* in 1986 dealt with the issue of the legality of a Georgia antisodomy law. Because the challenge took place by two homosexuals who violated the law, the case was viewed as a test for gay rights. The Supreme Court upheld the validity of the Georgia state law. In 2003, the Court reversed *Bowers* in *Lawrence v Texas*, ruling that a Texas sodomy law was unconstitutional.

> **Gay rights have lagged behind the gains of other minority groups.**

However, in 1992, the people of Colorado adopted a statewide initiative known as Amendment 2. This provision provided that the state could not adopt any laws providing protected status for homosexuals. The referendum was brought to court and reached the Supreme Court in a case entitled *Roemer v Evans*. The Court found Amendment 2 to be unconstitutional based on the fact that "this class of persons was being denied the 'equal protection of the laws' because they were being precluded from seeking protection under the law against discrimination based on their defining characteristic." The decision provided a victory for gay rights supporters.

But in 2000 the Supreme Court, in a narrow 5–4 decision, ruled that a homosexual Boy Scout leader could be barred from that position by the Boy Scouts of America's national organization. The case arose when the Boy Scouts barred New Jersey Scout leader Jim Dale, a homosexual, from his position. The Scouts claimed that they had a right under the First Amendment's freedom of association to decide whom to exclude from membership in their organization. New Jersey claimed that since the Boy Scouts' meetings took place in a public school, the Scouts violated New Jersey's public accommodation laws. The Court ruled in favor of the Boy Scouts. Fallout from the decision was widespread as many schools throughout the country refused to allow the Boy Scouts to meet if homosexuals were barred from participation. In 2013, the Boy Scouts of America announced they were reconsidering their past opposition to allowing gay scouts.

Don't Ask; Don't Tell

In 1992 President Bill Clinton, through an executive order, directed the military to follow a "Don't ask, don't tell, don't pursue" policy. It allowed homosexuals to enlist and serve in the military as long as they did not disclose the fact that they were gay. This policy was criticized by many in Congress, and it had a difficult time being accepted by the military establishment. The order was challenged in federal court, and the Court declared part of the policy unconstitutional based on the First Amendment free speech provision and the Fifth Amendment due process provision. The uneasily-balanced policy did not change during the administration of the next president, George W. Bush. When President Barack Obama was elected in 2008, he signaled his support for the repeal of Don't Ask, Don't Tell. The military leadership was hesitant to advocate a change because the United States was involved in two wars, one in Iraq and the other in Afghanistan. From 2008 to 2010 gay groups and gay servicemen and women who were discharged filed court petitions to find the law unconstitutional. Federal appeal courts sided with these suits and ordered the military to stop the policy. The Obama administration convinced the courts to order a "stay," halting the implementation of the repeal. The Defense Department conducted a review of the policy, and President Obama urged Congress to pass legislation repealing the Don't Ask, Don't Tell policy. Congress passed the repeal in 2010 and President Obama signed the law. The military ceased removing gay soldiers from service, and in 2011 homosexuals were allowed to serve in the military without fear of dismissal.

Although there have been few concrete victories, gay activist groups have been outspoken in their quest for equal protection under the law. They have insisted on marching alongside mainstream groups in parades, and they have made inroads on college campuses.

Gay Marriage

However, the biggest victory for gay rights came in the spring of 2004 when the Massachusetts Supreme Court ruled that gay marriages were legal. A firestorm reaction from opponents of the decision resulted in the drafting of an amendment to the United States Constitution that would define marriage as the union of a man and woman and make illegal any attempt to recognize on a national basis the legality of a gay marriage. Even though Congress passed and Bill Clinton signed the Defense of Marriage Act in 1996, a law that allowed states not to recognize gay marriages from other states and made illegal any federal benefits to states that did allow gay marriages, proponents of the amendment and President George W. Bush felt that its passage would be the only way to protect the institution of marriage. The Senate debated the issue and the amendment never came to a vote because of a Democratic filibuster.

Connecticut became the second state to approve same-sex marriage in 2005. In 2008, the California Supreme Court struck down the state's ban on same-sex marriage, and about 18,000 gay couples were married in California. In 2008, opponents of the decision passed a statewide initiative, Proposition 8, which created a constitutional amendment banning same-sex marriage. The initiative was challenged but was upheld by the California Supreme Court. Same-sex marriages performed prior to the passage of Proposition 8 remained legal. In 2010 a federal appeals court overturned the ban and the proponents of the proposition appealed the ruling. Ultimately, this case, as well as the legality of the 1996 Defense of Marriage Act (a law that prohibited federal benefits to gay couples who were married or recognized by a state), probably ended up before the U.S. Supreme Court. In 2010, California District Court and a federal appeals court overturned the ban and the proponents of the proposition appealed the ruling. State officials refused to defend the case. The Supreme Court ruled that Proposition 8 was unconstitutional because the lower court ruled that way and the Supreme Court said that the party defending the proposition had no "standing" to argue the case. The 1996 Defense of Marriage Act was ruled unconstitutional allowing legally married gay couples to receive federal benefits. Currently 37 states plus the District of Columbia permit gay marriages and 4 states recognize civil unions. The Supreme Court ruled 5–4 in 2015 in *Obergefell v Hodges* that the equal protection clause of the Fourteenth Amendment required that states issue marriage licenses to gay couples. This meant that gay marriage was legal in the United States.

OTHER MINORITY GROUPS

The minority group pie is being cut up into smaller and smaller pieces. Lobbyists and special inter-ests represent almost every segment of the American society. Senior citizens, sometimes known as "gray panthers," have become an activist group, especially since life expectancy has increased tre-mendously. Society and government have become very sensitive to the needs of the handicapped. And with the realization that young people are the future leaders of the country, Congress has passed civil rights legislation especially in areas affecting educational policy that has an impact on the youth.

Senior Citizens

Ever since Social Security became an entitlement as part of Franklin Roosevelt's New Deal program, senior citizens have been recognized as a segment of society that is a responsibility of the government; today, they are one of the fastest grow-ing segments. Anytime there is talk of government cutbacks on Social Security or Medicare, groups such as the American Association of Retired Persons (AARP) lobby against the cuts. Senior citizens care about the issue of age-based job dis-crimination. Even with many seniors retiring voluntarily at age 65, a number of complaints regarding employer discrimination against senior citizens have sur-faced. Age discrimination acts were passed by Congress in 1967, and in 1975 civil rights laws made it illegal for any employer to discriminate against people over 40. In 1978 an amendment to the Age Discrimination in Employment Act raised the compulsory retirement age to 70. However, today there is a growing movement to ban any kind of mandatory retirement age. The issue of healthcare has also been a major concern of senior citizens.

> Senior citizens, the handi-capped, and young people seeking civil rights and equal protection under the law have influenced government, resulting in the creation of public policies.

Disabled Americans

Handicapped Americans make up around 20 percent of the population. They include people with physical, mental, and emotional disabilities. Many of them have been denied support services. It is only in the last 20 years that government has recognized the needs of this group. The exception to this was the recognition that veteran groups needed aid when they returned from World War I and World War II. The GI Bill of Rights was a major piece of legislation passed at the conclusion of World War II. In 1975 the Education of All Handicapped Children Act was passed, giving children the right to an education with appropriate services that meet the needs of specific disabilities. The landmark act passed in 1991, the Americans with Disabilities Act (ADA), required employers, schools, and public buildings to reasonably accommodate the physical needs of handicapped individuals by providing such things as ramps, elevators, and other appropriate facilities. This act also extended into the job market, making it illegal for employers to discriminate against the handicapped. The courts have recognized these acts protecting the rights of disabled Americans. Yet there are issues that may not be as definitive. Does the ADA protect individuals with chronic diseases? The Supreme Court has imposed limits. But in a decision reached in 2001, the Court ruled that a professional golfer, Casey Martin, who had a physical handicap would be able to use a golf cart during tournament play.

In subsequent decisions, the Court using the sovereign immunity provision of the Eleventh Amendment limited individual lawsuits against states under the provisions of the Americans with Disabilities Act.

Age Discrimination

Many of the same problems facing senior citizens or the handicapped also face young people, who have no significant lobby group. How have their civil rights been taken away? Cases like *Hazelwood v Kuhlmeir* (1988), which gives school administrators the right to censor school-sponsored publications and plays; *Bethel School District v Fraser* (1986), which gives school officials the right to discipline students as a result of a speech that was given by a student running for office containing obscenities; and *New Jersey v TLO* (1985), which gives school officials an almost unlimited right to search a student suspected of violating school rules, weaken the *Tinker* doctrine and severely limit the civil rights of young people. In 1995 the Court ruled in *Vernonia v Acton* that random drug testing of student athletes was constitutional. There has been legislation protecting young women and the handicapped.

Title IX of the Civil Rights Act prohibited gender discrimination in such areas as sports and the right to enroll in all classes. The Americans with Disabilities Act applied to students attending school and in fact provided for extensive special education opportunities. State laws also protect young people against child abuse and mandate child support to families who have experienced divorce. Youth today have cried out for protection against violence and drugs in the schools and community. They have expressed the need to have employment opportunities after graduation from high school and college. And they received legislation in 1993 that established a National Service Program, making it easier for high school students to obtain government aid so that they can attend college in return for national service. One of the issues affecting young people that has become very controversial is adoption practices. Cases involving child custody point out the necessity for laws that recognize the needs of the child as well as the natural and adoptive families.

Native Americans

Virtually every segment of American society, including Native Americans and groups who have immigrated to the country and have obtained either citizenship or legal alien status, pursues their right to obtain the "American Dream." In order to accomplish this goal, their quest for civil rights is ongoing and is perhaps even more crucial because these groups have had a very difficult time reaping the benefits of living in this country.

Other minority groups such as Native Americans and "new immigrants" continue to struggle for civil rights.

Native Americans have an official government agency established as part of the Department of Interior. The Bureau of Indian Affairs has the responsibility of seeing that all legislative benefits are administered to Native Americans who by law are American citizens and have the right to vote whether or not they live on reservations. Native Americans living on reservations have a separate status and are recognized by treaty as possessing the full characteristics of sovereign nations. They are immune from state and federal laws, and they have the right to govern their reservations as they see fit. Other Native Americans living outside the reservation have faced severe poverty and must seek the assistance of the states they live in. Militant leaders such as Russell Means and related groups have pressured the government for specific aid packages regarding healthcare, educational opportunities, housing, and jobs.

Immigrants

Immigrant groups such as Hispanics and Asians have grown in numbers as problems facing their home countries have increased. The 2010 Census reported that Hispanics were the fastest-growing minority. Cuban and Haitian immigrants have settled in Miami. Puerto Ricans and Jamaicans have made New York City a second home. Mexicans have fled poor economic conditions and have settled in Texas, Arizona, and California. Asians have fled war in Southeast Asia and have left Korea and Japan. Many have become citizens; others have obtained legal status. Unlike natural-born Americans, they are having an extremely difficult time obtaining civil rights. There is a tremendous resentment on the part of the American people to those groups placing an additional burden on America's welfare system. Even though these groups are increasing in numbers, they have yet to achieve complete political equality. There are an increasing number of Hispanic and Asian representatives in Congress. A Congressional Hispanic Caucus has been formed. Governor Bill Richardson became the first Hispanic-American to run for president in 2008. The courts have recognized the problems facing these groups. In the case of *Lau v Nichols*, in 1974, the Supreme Court ruled that Title VI of the Civil Rights Act of 1964 mandates schools to offer English as a second language to non-English-speaking students. A corollary language problem facing these groups arises when cities pass legislation making English the official language of the municipality. States like California have passed referenda abolishing bilingual education programs.

Just as nativist groups turned against immigrants after the first great influx (1880s–1920), Americans during the 1990s reacted in a strong way against immigrants and illegal aliens. From the efforts of California voters, who passed Proposition 187 in 1994, which attempted to deny illegal aliens social services and education, to the attempts of Republicans to deny welfare for legal immigrants, Americans continued to express concerns about the impact of immigration on the country. In 2006, a debate emerged on what to do about the approximately 12 million illegal immigrants in this country. President George W. Bush proposed a comprehensive immigration bill that would have secured the nation's border while giving illegal immigrants a path to citizenship through a guest worker program. Congress rejected this proposal and voted to build a 700-mile fence to prevent illegal immigrants from coming into the country. The debate over illegal immigration intensified after the 2008 election. In 2010, Arizona passed a very controversial immigration law that gave state authorities the right to stop and check the immigration status of people they felt were illegal immigrants. There was an outcry of opposition from immigration groups, and the Obama administration, through the Department of Justice, challenged the law because the administration claimed that the enforcement of immigration policy is a federal prerogative. The Supreme Court ruled that parts of the law were legal, including the controversial requirement that allows the police to stop and check an immigrant's status. In 2012, President Obama signed an executive order that gave legal status to undocumented children who were brought to the United States before they turned 16 years old, are no older than 30, have been in the United States for at least 5 years, have been convicted of no serious crime, and have a high school diploma, a GED, or a stint in the U.S. military. In the 2012 election, 70 percent of Hispanics voted for President Obama. When Congress was not able to pass comprehensive immigration reform, President Obama then issued a highly controversial executive action in 2014. According to the U.S. Citizenship and Immigration agency the actions:

> cracked down on illegal immigration at the border, prioritized deporting felons not families, and required certain undocumented immigrants to pass a criminal background check and pay taxes in order to temporarily stay in the U.S. without fear of deportation.

These initiatives include:

- Expanding the population eligible for the Deferred Action for Childhood Arrivals (DACA) program to people of any current age who entered the United States before the age of 16 and lived in the United States continuously since January 1, 2010, and extending the period of DACA and work authorization from two years to three years.

- Allowing parents of U.S. citizens and lawful permanent residents to request deferred action and employment authorization for three years, in a new Deferred Action for Parents of Americans and Lawful Permanent Residents* program, provided they have lived in the United States continuously since January 1, 2010, and pass required background checks.

- Expanding the use of provisional waivers of unlawful presence to include the spouses and sons and daughters of lawful permanent residents and the sons and daughters of U.S. citizens.

- Modernizing, improving, and clarifying immigrant and nonimmigrant visa programs to grow our economy and create jobs.

- Promoting citizenship education and public awareness for lawful permanent residents, and providing an option for naturalization applicants to use credit cards to pay the application fee."

The program was highly controversial and was criticized by the Republican leadership in Congress and was challenged by the Republican Congress, the governor of Texas, and other states attorneys general. In 2015, a federal court of appeals ruled that the President's actions were illegal and until final appeal is made to the U.S. Supreme Court, the executive action will not be implemented.

Section 1: Multiple-Choice Questions

1. Which of the following historical events advanced the intent of the Fourteenth Amendment?

    (A) Jim Crow laws
    (B) Black codes
    (C) Grandfather voting laws
    (D) Literacy voting tests
    (E) Civil rights acts

2. Which of the following judicial principles reduced the impact of the Fourteenth Amendment?

    (A) Separate but equal
    (B) All deliberate speed
    (C) Equal protection under the law
    (D) Privileges and immunities of people
    (E) Habeas corpus

3. Which of the following doctrines made the Bill of Rights applicable to the states?

    (A) Incorporation principle
    (B) Clear and present danger
    (C) Separation of powers
    (D) The reserved power clause
    (E) The elastic clause

4. All of the following criteria were used to establish the nationalization of the Fourteenth Amendment EXCEPT

    (A) reasonable classification of race
    (B) the rational basis test
    (C) the strict scrutiny test
    (D) the suspect class test
    (E) the police power of states

5. Which of the following represents a legal difference between de facto and de jure segregation?

    (A) De facto segregation has been made illegal.
    (B) De jure segregation is legal.
    (C) De jure segregation is illegal based on Supreme Court decisions.
    (D) De facto segregation is supported by real estate agents.
    (E) De jure segregation was overturned by the *Plessy v Ferguson* (1896) decision.

6. Which of the following constitutional provisions has been used to strike down discrimination in public accommodations?

   (A) Tenth Amendment's reserve power clause
   (B) Article I Section 8's commerce clause
   (C) First Amendment's right to assemble
   (D) Affirmative action laws
   (E) Fifteenth Amendment's suffrage clause

7. A major impact of the *Bakke* (1978) decision was that

   (A) racial quotas were legal
   (B) racial preferences for minority groups were illegal
   (C) reverse discrimination based on quotas was illegal
   (D) affirmative action programs sponsored by the government were illegal
   (E) affirmative action programs sponsored by the states were illegal

8. All of the following criteria represent procedures used for evaluating the legitimacy of affirmative action programs EXCEPT

   (A) a scrutiny test based on racial classification
   (B) affirmative action programs based strictly on quotas
   (C) states taking action based on evidence that past discriminatory practice existed
   (D) affirmative action remedies must be based on specific remedies
   (E) affirmative action programs must be based on narrowly tailored principles

9. "The history of mankind is a history of repeated injuries and usurpations [in the past] of man toward woman."

   Which of the following documents contained this passage?

   (A) Declaration of Sentiments and Resolutions
   (B) Equal Rights Amendment
   (C) Seventeenth Amendment
   (D) *The Feminine Mystique*
   (E) Title VII of the Civil Rights Act of 1964

10. Which of the following cases helped further civil rights for students?

    (A) *Tinker v Des Moines* (1969)
    (B) *Hazelwood v Kuhlmeir* (1983)
    (C) *New Jersey v TLO* (1985)
    (D) *Bethel v Frasier* (1986)
    (E) *Cleveland Board of Education v Lafleur* (1974)

11. Discrimination in the workplace has been made illegal by all of the following EXCEPT

    (A) Civil Rights Act of 1964
    (B) Supreme Court decision in *Craig v Boren* (1976)
    (C) Supreme Court decision in *Dothard v Rawlinson* (1977)
    (D) Supreme Court decision in *UAW v Johnson Controls* (1991)
    (E) passage of Proposition 187

Answer Explanations

1. **(E)** Type of Question: Cause-and-effect relationships

   Choices A, B, C, and D all weakened the intent of the Fourteenth Amendment. Jim Crow laws and black codes legalized segregation. Grandfather voting laws permitted former Confederate officials to vote even though they were technically not eligible and prevented African-Americans from voting under the Fifteenth Amendment. Literacy tests also made it very difficult for African-Americans to vote. The civil rights acts in the 1880s were the first attempt by Congress to nationalize civil rights. The Supreme Court, however, ruled that the public accommodation sections were unconstitutional.

2. **(A)** Type of Question: Cause-and-effect relationships

   Like the previous question, choices B, C, and D increased the importance of the Fourteenth Amendment. All deliberate speed was a key part of the *Brown v Board of Education* decision; equal protection under the law and privileges and immunities of people are key provisions of the Fourteenth Amendment. Habeas corpus is a civil liberty guarantee. Choice A, separate but equal, was one of the most significant results of the *Plessy v Ferguson* case and institutionalized segregation.

3. **(A)** Type of Question: Definitional

   The incorporation or nationalization of the Bill of Rights began with civil liberty cases in the early part of the twentieth century. It was not until the *Brown* case that this principle began to apply fully to civil rights cases. Clear and present danger came from the *Schenck* case. Separation of powers, the reserved power clause, and the elastic clause are all constitutional principles.

4. **(E)** Type of Question: Negative

   A compelling interest of the state such as the police power tends to weaken the doctrine of nationalization of the Bill of Rights. A major characteristic of incorporation stems from the phrase "No State shall deprive persons. . . ." Choices A through E are all tests the courts apply to equal protection cases.

5. **(C)** Type of Question: Definitional

   By definition, de jure segregation is by law and de facto segregation is by fact or circumstance. After the *Brown* decision, de jure segregation was illegal. Choice D may happen, but if it can be proven, it would be just as illegal as de jure segregation.

6. **(B)** Type of Question: Sequencing a series of events

   If you think of the court case *Heart of Atlanta Motel v United States*, you would conclude that the commerce clause was responsible for the decision that made the Civil Rights Act of 1964 apply to public accommodations located on the interstate highway. Even though choices C, D, and E are related to civil rights issues, they did not directly result in the recognition that discrimination in public accommodations is illegal.

7. **(C)** Type of Question: Cause-and-effect relationships

   The *Bakke* decision had two major components. The first answered the question posed by Bakke. Could he be denied admission to Davis Medical School because of a quota? The Court, using the equal protection clause of the Fourteenth Amendment, said that quotas were illegal. However, the Court also ruled that racial preferences could be used as part of an overall plan when it came to schools or work.

8. **(B)** Type of Question: Generalization

The Courts have ruled that strict racial quotas invalidate affirmative action programs. Choices A, C, D, and E are all standards the Court has used in determining whether there is a sufficient cause to rule that an affirmative action remedy is necessary.

9. **(A)** Type of Question: Chronological

By process of elimination you can probably eliminate choices C, D, and E. A constitutional amendment would not have that kind of language. Neither would a legislative act. *The Feminine Mystique* may have dealt with the issue of feminism, but it was not historical in nature. The Equal Rights Amendment never passed, and it would not contain such an emotional statement. However, just like the Declaration of Independence, the Declaration of Sentiments and Resolutions became the first rallying call for women's suffrage.

10. **(A)** Type of Question: Identification and analysis

Even though choices B, C, and D all deal with students, the outcome and significance of those cases weakened the doctrine established in *Tinker* that student rights are not shed at the schoolhouse gates. *Hazelwood* dealt with student press censorship. *TLO* enabled a school administrator to search a student without a warrant. Frasier's First Amendment rights were limited by the school as a result of the content of a speech he was making. The *Lafleur* case dealt with the issue of maternity leave.

11. **(E)** Type of Question: Negative

This question requires a knowledge of the decisions made in specific cases as well as the content of the Civil Rights Act and Proposition 187. You can probably figure that the Civil Rights Act of 1964 would prohibit discrimination. Because three Supreme Court cases are given, you could possibly eliminate the three of them as similar answers. Proposition 187, a voter initiative, took away state social services for illegal aliens in California.

Section 2: Free-Response Question (4 points)

> The federal government, through executive action, congressional legislation, and Supreme Court decisions, has pursued an active policy of civil rights for minority groups.
>
> (a) Identify and explain a Supreme Court decision that advanced civil rights for African-Americans.
>
> (b) Identify and explain a constitutional amendment that was initiated to advance the cause of equal rights for women.

SAMPLE RESPONSE

(a) Affirmative action is also another area of public policy that is affected by the Supreme Court. Affirmative action is any action taken by the federal government to benefit minorities (sort of like reverse discrimination). Affirmative action can be seen in many aspects of society from quotas in college to minority candidates trying to get a broadcast license. The latter point is the foundation of the case *Metro v FCC*. The FCC uses reverse discrimination when giving out broadcasting licenses and favors minorities intentionally when considering broadcast licenses. The Court ruled that affirmative action was constitutional and the FCC won this case decisively. Judicial activism is used in this case to prove that affirmative action is constitutional by the Supreme Court, and the judges have created a new law separate from the legislative branch. Affirmative action is a concept built up by the courts and is a product of judicial activism. School policy, affirmative action, and civil rights are integral areas of public policy that need to be understood and followed through watching the courts. Judicial activism and restraint are very important ideas to understand because they usually help mold the decisions of many cases and play vital roles in our judicial system. These have been accompanied by much state and local civil rights legislation.

Women

(b) The successes of African-American militants encouraged women activists. Even though the struggle for suffrage had achieved voting rights for U.S. women under the Nineteenth Amendment in 1920, women now sought equal treatment in other social relationships such as employment and property rights. The Equal Rights Amendment (ERA), proposed as the Twenty-Seventh Amendment to the U.S. Constitution and intended to outlaw discrimination based on sex, states that "equality of rights under the law shall not be denied or abridged by the United States nor by any State on account of sex." Originally drafted by Alice Paul of the National Woman's Party and introduced in Congress in 1923, the ERA lay dormant until 1970, when great support was generated for it by the National Organization for Women (NOW). The ERA was approved by the House of Representatives in 1971 and by the Senate in 1972. On June 30, 1982, ratification of the ERA fell three states short of the 38 it needed.

The overriding purpose of the ERA was to give women explicit constitutional protection not afforded by the equal protection clause of the Fourteenth Amendment. The objective was to place sex discrimination within the direct context of violation of constitutional rights, the most serious sanction in the U.S. legal system.

SCORING GUIDELINES FOR FREE-RESPONSE QUESTION (4 POINTS)

Part (a) 2 Points

One point is earned for the identification of a Supreme Court case that advanced civil rights for African-Americans. One point is earned for an explanation of how that Supreme Court case increased civil rights for African-Americans.

Answers may include, but are not limited to:

- *Brown v Board of Education* (1954)—overturned the doctrine of "separate but equal" and ordered the integration of public schools

- *Heart of Atlanta Motel v United States* (1964)—the court ruled that the Civil Rights Act of 1964 was constitutional

- *California Board of Regents v Bakke* (1974)—race can be used as a factor in affirmative action programs, but quotas were illegal

- *Metro v FCC* (1990)—the court ruled that affirmative action programs were legal

Part (b) 2 Points

One point is earned for the identification of a constitutional amendment that was initiated to advance the cause of equal rights for women. One point is earned for explaining how the amendment would have increased the rights of women.

Answers may include, but are not limited to:

- Nineteenth Amendment (1920)—gave women the right to vote

- Equal Rights Amendment (1970)—introduced but never ratified by the states, this amendment would have created a "Fourteenth" amendment for women

PART THREE
The Institutions of Government

The Congress

7

- → *BAKER V CARR*
- → CASE WORK
- → CLOTURE
- → CONFERENCE COMMITTEES
- → CONGRESSIONAL OVERSIGHT
- → CONSTITUENT
- → EARMARKS
- → FILIBUSTER
- → FRANKING
- → GERRYMANDERING
- → GRIDLOCK
- → IMPERIAL CONGRESS
- → INCUMBENTS

- → JOINT COMMITTEE
- → LOGROLLING
- → MAJORITY LEADER
- → MINORITY LEADER
- → PORK BARREL
- → PRESIDENT PRO TEMPORE
- → REAPPORTIONMENT
- → REGULATORY POLICY
- → SELECT COMMITTEES
- → SPEAKER OF THE HOUSE
- → STANDING COMMITTEES
- → WHIPS

CONTEMPORARY CONNECTION

President Obama and the House Republican majority could not agree on extending the budget in 2013. As a result, the government shutdown and non-essential operations ceased. When a continuing resolution for fiscal year 2014 was approved, the shutdown ended. This chapter explores the way the Congress operates, its rules, its practices, and its lawmaking.

The Congress can be viewed as the citizens' direct link to the branch of government that is responsible for forming public policy. It has a number of functions including, but not limited to, representing the interests of constituents, lawmaking through consensus building, oversight of other governmental agencies, policy clarification, and ratification of public policies.

As the focal point of public policy development, the Congress has come under public criticism. Polls have reflected deep voter concern regarding the issues of congressional gridlock, term limits for representatives and senators, and the influence of lobbyists and PACs on representatives. Many newly elected representatives have committed themselves to reforming congressional structure, procedures, and practices.

This chapter also explores these public concerns of the Congress, the advantage of incumbency and the changing face of Congress, the structure of Congress, the lawmaking process, the constituent relationship between the voters and their representatives, the influence of lobbyists, and the attempts at congressional reform. The issue of whether an imperial Congress is threatening our system of government will also be discussed in the sample free-response answer at the end of the chapter.

QUICK CONSTITUTIONAL REVIEW OF CONGRESS

- Basis of constitutional authority is found in Article I.

- A House member must be at least 25 years old, an American citizen for seven years, and an inhabitant of the state the representative represents. Representatives serve two-year terms.

- A senator must be 30 years old, an American citizen for nine years, and a resident of the state the senator represents. Senators serve six-year terms.

- Common powers delegated to Congress, listed in Article I Section 8 include the power to tax, coin money, declare war, and regulate foreign and interstate commerce.

- Implied congressional power comes from the "necessary and proper" clause, which has been referred to as the elastic clause.

- House of Representatives has the power to begin all revenue bills, to select president if there is no electoral college majority, and to initiate impeachment proceedings.

- Senate has the power to approve presidential appointments and treaties and to try impeachment proceedings.

- Congress may overrule a presidential veto by a two-thirds vote of each house.

STRUCTURE

> The organization of the Congress relies on a seniority and party system and the use of a committee system, which facilitates day-to-day operations.

The bicameral (two-house) structure of the Congress made it a necessity to develop an organization that would result in the ability of both houses to conduct their own business, yet be able to accomplish the main function—the passage of legislation.

Each house has a presiding officer. The influence of the Speaker of the House cannot be underestimated. The speaker is selected by the majority party, and even though a House Majority Leader is also part of the unofficial structure of the House, it is the speaker who is really the leader of the majority. In 1993 Speaker Thomas Foley and House Majority Leader Richard Gephardt worked together to pass much of President Clinton's legislative agenda.

After the 1994 midterm elections, the Republicans chose controversial and conservative Representative Newt Gingrich as the new speaker. Promising to deliver on the Republican Contract with America (a description concludes the review portion of this chapter), he immediately consolidated control. He earned a reputation as one of the most powerful speakers since the days of Joe Cannon. His power was diminished after the 1996 elections. Facing serious ethics charges, Gingrich was forced to loosen his grip on committee chairs and Republican representatives who disagreed with him. After the Republicans lost seats in the House in the 1998 midterm elections, Gingrich resigned from the House. Representative Dennis Hastert was elected the new speaker. Hastert became the longest-serving speaker, serving until the Democrats took control of the House of Representatives in 2006. They elected Nancy Pelosi, the first female speaker of the House. In 2015, Speaker Boehner resigned under pressure from insurgent members of his own party. Congressman Paul Ryan, 2012 Republican Vice-Presidential candidate and chairman of the powerful Ways and Means Committee was elected the new Speaker.

The speaker presides over House meetings and is expected to be impartial in the way meetings are run, even though he or she is a member of the majority party. However, in the power to preside and keep order, the speaker wields a great deal of power: recognizing speakers, referring bills to committees, answering procedural questions, and declaring the outcome of votes. The speaker also names members to all select (special) committees and conference committees (a committee that meets with the Senate to resolve differences in legislation). The speaker usually votes only to break a tie and has the power to appoint temporary speakers, called speakers pro tempore, to run meetings. The speaker is also third in line after the vice president to succeed the president.

The presiding officer of the Senate, the president of the Senate, is the vice president of the United States. It is a symbolic office, and more often than not the Senate chooses a temporary presiding officer, the president pro tempore to run the meetings. The only specific power of the vice president in the capacity of Senate presiding officer is to break ties. The president pro tempore does not have the same power or influence as the Speaker of the House. Unlike the House, the real power in the Senate lies with the Senate Majority Leader. In 2014, the Republicans took control of the Senate; and, thus, the Senate majority leader was a Republican.

The Committee System

Committee chairs, those representatives who chair the standing committees of the House and Senate, wield a great deal of power. In fact, most of the work is done through the committee system. Committee chairs are selected as a result of the seniority system, an unwritten custom that established the election of committee chairs as a result of length of service and of which party holds the majority in each house. Four types of committees exist in both houses. Standing committees deal with proposed bills and are permanent, existing from one Congress to the next. Examples of standing committees are Banking, Foreign Affairs, Energy, Governmental Affairs, and Appropriations. Select committees are specially created and conduct special investigations. The Watergate Committee and Iran-Contra investigators were select Senate committees.

Joint committees are committees made up of both houses for the purpose of coordinating investigations or special studies and expedite business between the houses. Conference committees resolve legislative differences between the House and Senate. Such bills as the Crime Bill of 1994 and the Welfare Reform Act of 1996 had to go through a conference committee. Many bills, in fact, must be resolved in this manner. Committee makeup is determined by the percentage of party representation in each house. Representatives attempt to get on influential committees such as the House Ways and Means Committee (which is responsible for appropriations measures), the House Rules Committee (which determines the order in which legislation will reach the floor for a vote), and the Senate Judiciary Committee (which makes a recommendation regarding presidential judicial appointments). Most representatives are members of at least one standing committee or two subcommittees (smaller committees that are organized around specific areas). These committees influence legislation by holding hearings and voting on amendments to legislation that has been referred to their committees. The committees also provide oversight reviewing the actions of the executive branch. In the House, a key oversight committee is the Committee on Oversight and Government Reform. This committee holds hearings that investigate executive branch abuses. Two examples of this were hearings held regarding the attack on the American embassy in Benghazi and Internal Revenue Service overreach. In the Senate, the Senate Intelligence Committee investigated conduct by the Central Intelligence Agency resulting in torture, and in 2014 released a scathing report condemning such practices. After the 1994 elections the Republican majority passed new rules that limited the terms of House committee chairs to no more than six years and reduced the number of committees and their staffs.

Along with the committee system, each house has a party system that organizes and influences the members of Congress regarding policymaking decisions. The majority and minority leaders of both houses organize their members by using whips, or assistant floor leaders, whose job is to check with party members and inform the majority leader of the status and feelings of the membership regarding issues that are going to be voted on. Whips are responsible for keeping party members in line and having an accurate count of who will be voting for or against a particular bill. The party caucus or party conference is a means for each party to develop a strategy or position on a particular issue. The majority and minority party meet privately and determine which bills to support, the type of amendments that would be acceptable, and the official party positions on upcoming business. They also deal with the selection of the party leadership and committee membership.

POLICYMAKING

The avenues taken by Congress to achieve policy-making go beyond the mere passage of legislation.

Besides the legislative power of Congress, it also has nonlegislative responsibilities. Constitutional amendments, election of a president and vice president if there is no electoral college majority, impeachment, approval of executive appointments, and congressional oversight (the power used by Congress to review the operation and budgets of the executive branch) are used by Congress to influence and determine public policy. Congress uses the power of congressional oversight to gather information useful for the formation of legislation, to review the operations and budgets of executive departments and independent regulatory agencies, to conduct investigations through committee hearings, and to bring to the public's attention the need for public policy.

By far the most important function of Congress is the legislative responsibility. Before explaining the different approaches to lawmaking, it is important that you understand the way a bill becomes a law. (See display box below.)

Obviously, this is a simplified version of the process. And if the president vetoes the bill, the Congress must vote separately to determine whether each house has a two-thirds majority to override it.

In a typical congressional session, over 10,000 bills are offered, and fewer than 10 percent of them are enacted.

It's one thing to introduce legislation, and it's another to get it passed into law. Tactics such as the Senate filibuster, an ongoing debate that needs a vote of 60 senators to cut off debate, called cloture, protect minority interests. In 2013, the senate changed its filibuster rules by passing what was called "the Nuclear Option." Instead of requiring 60 votes to approve many presidential appointments, this new rule required a simple majority. The Republican minority was against this procedural change claiming that it weakened the ability of the minority to debate the qualifications of appointees. In an attempt to increase legislative output, Congress can use several techniques to move legislation along. Logrolling (or "I'll vote for your legislation, if you vote for mine") coalitions, consensus building, and pork barrel deals often result in agreement to pass bills. An excellent example of consensus building was the passage of the North American Free Trade Agreement (NAFTA).

Congressional oversight refers to "the review, monitoring, and supervision of federal agencies, programs, activities, and policy implementation. Congress exercises this power largely through its standing committee system."

The same report issued by the service in 2001 stated, "Oversight, as an outgrowth of this principle, ideally serves a number of overlapping objectives and purposes:

- improve the efficiency, economy, and effectiveness of governmental operations;
- evaluate programs and performance;
- detect and prevent poor administration, waste, abuse, arbitrary and capricious behavior, or illegal and unconstitutional conduct;
- protect civil liberties and constitutional rights;
- inform the general public and ensure that executive policies reflect the public interest;
- gather information to develop new legislative proposals or to amend existing statutes;
- ensure administrative compliance with legislative intent; and
- prevent executive encroachment on legislative authority and prerogatives."

In sum, oversight is a way for Congress to check on, and check, the executive branch of government.

HOW A BILL BECOMES A LAW

Bill introduced in House
↓
Bill assigned to committee
↓
Amendments offered
↓
Bill goes to Rules Committee
↓
Bill brought to floor for debate
↓
Amendments offered
↓
Bill voted on
↓
If it fails, no other action until it is introduced again; if it passes and is the same as bill in Senate, it goes to the President.
↓

Bill introduced in Senate
↓
Bill assigned to committee
↓
Amendments offered
↓
Bill assigned for debate
↓
Bill brought to floor for debate
↓
Amendments offered
↓
Bill voted on
↓
If it fails, no other action until it is introduced again; if it passes and is the same as bill in House, it goes to the President.
↓

Different versions passed go to a Senate/House conference committee where differences are ironed out
↓

Bill goes back to full House for vote

Bill goes back to full Senate for vote

→ Bill passes and goes to President ←

CONGRESSIONAL LEGISLATION

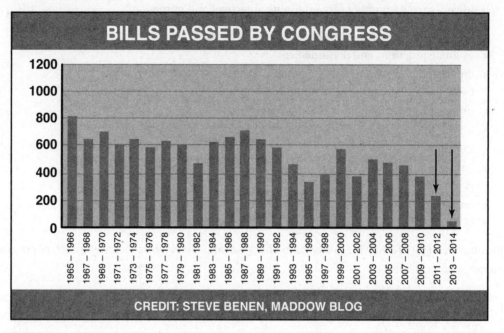

BILLS PASSED BY CONGRESS

CREDIT: STEVE BENEN, MADDOW BLOG

This graph illustrates the number of bills passed by Congress since 1965. Notice that the last Congress, the 113th Congress, passed the fewest bills of any Congress. It's critics called it the "do nothing Congress."

CONSTITUENT SERVICE

Constituency relationships provide essential information and services and are the foundation for reelection.

If the essence of a senator or representative revolves around the issue of representing one's constituency, then the elected official must define the kind of congressperson he or she will be. Once elected through the formal process of an open and free election, the definition must begin. Demographic representation mirrors the desires of the people being represented. Symbolic representation is defined by the style and message of the representative and the manner in which the people perceive the job he or she is doing. How responsive the legislator is to the constituents' wishes is the last characteristic of representation. The manner in which a representative responds to the people who elected him or her is called constituent service. The question of whether the representative should reflect the point of view of his or her constituents or vote his or her own opinion after hearing information on any issue is a long-standing problem for elected officials.

Members of Congress must represent their districts, taking into account individual constituents, organized interests, and the district as a whole. For their individual constituents, representatives set up mobile offices and respond personally to written letters. They contact federal agencies, sponsor appointments to service academies, and provide information and services. For organized groups, they introduce legislation, obtain grants and contracts, give speeches, and attend functions. For the district as a whole, representatives obtain federal projects (sometimes from pork barrel legislation), look for ways of getting legislation that will increase employment or tax benefits, and support policies that will directly benefit the geographic area of the district.

Through such public relations practices as sending out a congressional letter highlighting a reference in the Congressional Record of individuals or the achievements of people in their districts, representatives attempt to get close to the people they represent.

REFORM

Attempts at reforming Congress aim to clean up abuses of the people's branch of government.

Of the three branches of government, the public has given Congress the lowest approval ratings. Yet every election they send a majority of incumbents back to Congress. There seems to be a love/hate relationship between the people and their representatives and senators. Many suggestions have been made to improve and reform the organization and productivity of Congress. The poll pointed out the following beliefs:

- Gridlock is a problem—Congress is seen as inefficient, and because of the complicated legislative process, most bills never see the light of day. Reforms such as streamlining the committee system, improving the coordination of information between the House and the Senate, and requiring some kind of action on all bills proposed have been made.
- Congress does not reflect the views of its constituents. People have suggested that with the growth of the Internet, representatives should interactively get information from their constituents before voting on crucial issues.
- Representatives are so busy running for office, that they become beholden to special interest groups and PACs—The response has been that some states voted to establish term limits. The Supreme Court decided this issue in 1995 and ruled that it was unconstitutional for states to enact term limits for senators and representatives.
- Relations between the Congress and the president have deteriorated when one party is in control of the executive branch and the other party controls one or both houses (divided government). When there is a fiscal crisis, the conflict between the branches increases. The debt ceiling crisis in 2011 when the Republican House fought the president when the debt limit had to be raised and the fiscal cliff crisis at the end of 2012 when the Republican Congress resisted raising taxes for those couples making more than $500,000 were examples of the conflict between the president and the Congress.

Congressional Oversight

Through the process of congressional oversight, agency heads are called before congressional committees to testify about issues related to the workings of the agency. According to the Congressional Research Service, Congressional oversight refers to "the review, monitoring, and supervision of federal agencies, programs, activities, and policy implementation. Congress exercises this power largely through its standing committee system."

The same report issued by the service in 2001 stated, "Oversight, as an outgrowth of this principle, ideally serves a number of overlapping objectives and purposes:

- improve the efficiency, economy, and effectiveness of governmental operations;
- evaluate programs and performance;
- detect and prevent poor administration, waste, abuse, arbitrary and capricious behavior, or illegal and unconstitutional conduct;
- protect civil liberties and constitutional rights;
- inform the general public and ensure that executive policies reflect the public interest;
- gather information to develop new legislative proposals or to amend existing statutes;
- ensure administrative compliance with legislative intent; and
- prevent executive encroachment on legislative authority and prerogatives.

In sum, "oversight is a way for Congress to check on, and check, the executive branch of government."

CONTRACT WITH AMERICA

As mentioned earlier in the chapter, the new Republican majority in the House of Representatives, elected in 1994, campaigned on a platform called the Contract with America. This contract became a blueprint for legislative action in the first 100 days. It promised the American people that the following items would be brought to the floor for a vote:

"In the first 100 days, we're pledging in writing to bring to a vote:

1. A balanced budget amendment and line item veto;
2. A crime bill that funds police and prisons over social programs;
3. Real welfare reform;
4. Family reinforcement measures that strengthen parental rights in education and child support enforcement;
5. Family tax cuts;
6. Stronger national defense;
7. A rise in the Social Security earnings limit to stop penalizing working seniors;
8. Job creation and regulatory reform policies;
9. Common sense legal reforms to stop frivolous lawsuits; and
10. A first-ever vote on term limits for members of Congress."

In a remarkable demonstration of party discipline, the Republican majority succeeded in bringing to a vote every item in the contract. In fact, on the first day of the 104th Congress, in a marathon session that lasted well into the early morning hours of the next day, the House voted to reform itself, cutting down the number of committees and their staffs, restricting the terms of committee chairs, and changing the rules of the House itself, making it easier to offer amendments. In many cases the Senate stymied the House's attempt to achieve legislative success with a significant number of the provisions of the contract defeated or modified in the Senate. A significant bill signed into law by President Clinton was a measure designed to mandate representatives to follow the same laws that Americans must follow such as civil rights legislation and minimum wage laws. The Contract with America hit a responsive chord with the American people as shown by a survey that suggests the approval rating of Congress increased from previous years.

Section 1: Multiple-Choice Questions

1. The qualifications for members of the House of Representatives are found in Article I of the Constitution. All of the following are requirements for a House member EXCEPT

   (A) must be 25 years old
   (B) must be an American citizen for seven years
   (C) must be a resident from the state represented
   (D) can be a naturalized citizen
   (E) cannot serve for more than two consecutive terms

2. Which of the following political theories would claim that many senators and representatives come from the upper middle class or the upper economic class of American society?

   (A) Elite
   (B) Pluralist
   (C) Conservative
   (D) Centrist
   (E) Majoritarian

3. Which of the following factors generates the most significant advantage for a Congressional candidate?

   (A) Being wealthier than the opponent
   (B) Getting the most press coverage
   (C) Being invited to the most town meetings
   (D) Being an incumbent
   (E) Taking positions on key social issues

4. All of the following represent reasons why voters choose congressional candidates EXCEPT

   (A) endorsements by groups who represent different views than the voter
   (B) political advertisements
   (C) the positions the candidates take on key issues
   (D) party affiliation of the voter
   (E) the candidates' positive standing in political polls

5. Which of the following functions of senators and representatives would be the most important to their constituents?

   (A) Attending political fund raisers
   (B) Networking with lobbyists
   (C) Accepting PAC money
   (D) Recommending a high school student to one of the military academies
   (E) Making a speech about national defense that is printed in the Congressional Record

6. Senators and representatives are often criticized for making deals with other legislators or the president in order to get programs, projects, and grants moving along the legislative process. What is this legislation called?

   (A) Constituent laws
   (B) Rider legislation
   (C) Logrolling
   (D) Pork barrel legislation
   (E) Legislative veto

7. Which of the following House committees is responsible for setting the agenda for legislation coming to the floor?

   (A) Rules Committee
   (B) Ways and Means Committee
   (C) Appropriations Committee
   (D) The Policy Committee
   (E) The Armed Services Committee

8. Which of the following individuals presides over the House of Representatives?

   (A) The House Minority Leader
   (B) The House Pro Tem
   (C) The House Majority Leader
   (D) The Speaker of the House
   (E) The House Majority Whip

9. The Speaker of the House has many responsibilities. All of the following reflect roles the speaker plays EXCEPT

   (A) acting as chief presiding officer of the House
   (B) serving as third in line in presidential succession
   (C) making committee assignments for both parties
   (D) playing a key role in appointing committee chairs
   (E) working hand in hand with the president relating to the legislative agenda if they are both from the same party

10. All of the following contribute to the success of incumbent members of Congress in election campaigns EXCEPT

   (A) Incumbents usually raise less campaign funds than do the challengers.
   (B) Incumbents tend to understand national issues better than do their challengers.
   (C) Incumbents are usually better known to voters than are their challengers.
   (D) Incumbents can use staff to perform services for constituents.
   (E) Incumbents often sit on committees that permit them to serve district interests.

11. A member of the House of Representatives who wishes to be influential in the House would most likely seek a place on which of the following committees?

(A) Agriculture
(B) District of Columbia
(C) Public Works and Transportation
(D) Rules
(E) Veterans Affairs

12. All of the following are examples of congressional oversight committees EXCEPT

(A) the Banking Committee holding Whitewater hearings
(B) the Select Committee on Campaign Activities to investigate campaign abuses
(C) the House Judiciary Committee's hearing on the impeachment of President Clinton
(D) the Select Senate Watergate Committee
(E) the Select Iran-Contra Committee

13. Pork barrel legislation helps the reelection chances of a member of Congress because such legislation

(A) gives the member of Congress national standing and coverage on national television news
(B) helps earn the member of Congress a reputation for service to his or her district
(C) attracts campaign contributions from ideological political action committees
(D) prevents other candidates from claiming that the member of Congress is too liberal for his or her district
(E) requires the member of Congress to travel extensively

Answer Explanations

1. **(E)** Type of Question: Negative

   Choices A, B, and C are all listed in Article I as criteria for qualifications for members of the House. Remember that the qualifications for the Senate and the president are different. Only the president cannot be naturalized. A term limit is not mentioned in the Constitution, although over 20 states have imposed this qualification.

2. **(A)** Type of Question: Hypothetical

   The clue in this question is found in the description that senators and representatives come from the upper middle class or upper economic class. From Chapter 1, you should be able to identify that characteristic as elite. A pluralistic approach would suggest that candidates come from a broader spectrum. A conservative approach would suggest that a candidate wants less government. Centrist and majoritarian are positions taken after the election.

3. **(D)** Type of Question: Cause-and-effect relationships

   Even though choices A, B, C, and E are all factors that can create electoral advantages, by far incumbency plays the most important role in determining an inherent advantage. In fact, sometimes press coverage and taking positions on key social issues can result in negative publicity, and the mere appearance at town meetings does not necessarily translate into votes. Finally, wealth can be countered by PAC donations.

4. **(A)** Type of Question: Comparing and contrasting concepts and events

   Political advertisements, the stand a candidate takes, party affiliations, and the candidate's standing (either positive or negative) in polls all have an impact on voters. Even though endorsements play a role, if the endorsement is by a group or a paper the voter does not agree with, it does not play a role in why a voter would support a particular candidate.

5. **(D)** Type of Question: Solution to a problem

   The problem is to determine which function a senator or representative plays is most important to his or her constituents. Even though choices A, B, C, and E are all functions of elected officials, the most important role a senator or representative can have is constituent service such as recommending a voter's child to a service academy.

6. **(C)** Type of Question: Sequencing a series of events

   Logrolling is a deal-making process that fits the definition. Pork barrel legislation benefits constituents and can be added as riders to other pieces of legislation.

7. **(A)** Type of Question: Identification and analysis

   By definition the Rules Committee is responsible for determining the order of action on proposed legislation. The Ways and Means Committee reviews bills dealing with appropriations. The Appropriations Committee is a Senate committee. There is no Policy Committee, and the Armed Services Committee deals with the military.

8. **(D)** Type of Question: Definitional

   By definition, the Speaker of the House presides over meetings of the House of Representatives. There is no House pro tem, only a Senate pro tem. The House Majority Leader and Majority Whip play specific functions dealing with party unity and delivering on the legislative agenda set forth by the majority party.

9. **(C)** Type of Question: Sequencing a series of events

The Speaker of the House has many functions. Even though the speaker has significant input in the committee assignments of members, it is up to each party to select specific committees for their members. The speaker has direct input in the selection of all committee chairs.

10. **(A)** Type of Question: Cause-and-effect relationships

The understanding of the issue of incumbency in the election of senators and representatives is essential to your understanding of the institution. Incumbents usually have a significant advantage over challengers in every area of the campaign. In fact, studies have indicated that because of the factors mentioned in choices B, C, D, and E, incumbents are more often than not elected. This does not occur in a midterm election where the president's popularity is low.

11. **(D)** Type of Question: Cause-and-effect relationships

Any representative who gets a position on the Rules Committee has an inherent advantage over representatives who have positions on the other committees listed. The Rules Committee determines the order of all pending legislation and House policy, whereas the other committees only review legislation germane to a particular area.

12. **(C)** Type of Question: Definitional

By definition, an oversight committee is a watchdog committee. It may be a select committee like the Watergate or Iran-Contra Committee. Or it could be a standing committee like the Banking Committee. The House Judiciary Committee had a constitutional responsibility to hear impeachment evidence.

13. **(B)** Type of Question: Definitional

By definition, pork barrel legislation is done so that a particular district gets the benefit of congressional representation. Voters perceive their representatives and senators as providers for their districts and, therefore, owe a debt of thanks to them. Even though elected representatives and senators can get national coverage and PAC donations and may travel extensively, it is the constituent aspect that helps the reelection chances of a representative or senator who can successfully deliver the pork.

Section 2: Data-Based Free-Response Question

Member of Congress—Selected Characteristics: 1995 to 2009

[As of the beginning of the first session of each Congress, except as noted. Figures for Representatives exclude vacancies]

Members of Congress and year	Male	Female	Black[1]	API[2]	Hispanic[3]	Age[4] (in years)					Seniority[5,6]				
						Under 40	40 to 49	50 to 59	60 to 69	70 and over	Less than 2 yrs.	2 to 9 yrs.	10 to 19 yrs.	20 to 29 yrs.	30 yrs. Or more
REPRESENTATIVES															
104th Cong., 1995...	388	47	[7]40	7	17	53	155	135	79	13	92	188	110	36	9
106th Cong., 1999...	379	56	[7]39	6	19	23	116	173	87	35	41	236	104	46	7
107th Cong., 2001...	376	59	[7]39	7	19	14	97	167	117	35	44	155	158	63	14
108th Cong., 2003...	376	59	[7]39	5	22	19	86	174	121	32	54	178	140	48	13
109th Cong., 2005...	369	65	[7]42	4	23	22	96	175	113	28	37	173	158	48	18
110th Cong., 2007...	361	74	[7]42	4	23	20	91	172	118	34	62	159	160	37	17
111th Cong., 2009...	366	72	[7]41	8	(N/A)	24	84	156	126	44	66	166	142	42	18
SENATORS															
104th Cong., 1995...	92	8	1	2	—	1	14	41	27	17	12	38	30	15	5
106th Cong., 1999...	91	9	—	2	—	—	14	38	35	13	8	39	33	14	6
107th Cong., 2001...	87	13	—	2	—	—	8	39	33	18	11	34	30	14	9
108th Cong., 2003...	86	14	—	2	—	1	12	29	34	24	9	42	29	13	7
109th Cong., 2005...	86	14	1	2	2	—	17	29	33	21	9	41	29	14	7
110th Cong., 2007...	94	16	1	2	3	—	11	31	34	24	12	42	24	13	9
111th Cong., 2009[8]...	83	17	1	1	(N/A)	—	7	31	38	22	9	34	28	17	10

–Represents zero. NA Not available. [1]Source: Joint Center for Political and Economic Studies, Washington, DC, *Black Elected Officials: Statistical Summary*, annual (copyright). [2]Asian and Pacific Islanders. Source: Prior to 2005, Library of Congress, Congressional Research Service, "Asian Pacific Americans in the United States Congress," Report 94-767 GOV; starting 2005, U.S. House of Representatives, "House Press Gallery," <http://www.house.gov/daily/> (as of May 25, 2009) and U.S. Senate, "Minorities in the Senate," <http://www.senate.gov/artandhistory/history/common/briefing/minority_senators.htm> (August 30, 2010). [3]Source: National Association of Latino Elected and Appointed Officials, Washington, DC, *National Roster of Hispanic Elected Officials*, annual. [4]Some members do not provide date of birth. [5]Represents consecutive years of service. [6]Some members do not provide years of service. [7]Includes District of Columbia and Virgin Islands delegate. [8]Excludes vacancies.

Source: Except as noted, compiled by U.S. Census Bureau from data published in *Congressional Directory*, biennial.
See also <http://www.gpoaccess.gov/cdirectory/browse.html>.

This table shows selected characteristics of the members of Congress from 1995 to 2009. From this information and your knowledge of U.S. politics:

(a) identify three characteristics indicated in the table.

(b) for one characteristic chosen, describe the changes in the makeup of Congress during the time period indicated.

(c) explain the impact that two characteristics have had on Congress.

SAMPLE RESPONSE TO QUESTION (8 POINTS)

(a)   After analyzing the table "Members of Congress—Selected Characteristics: 1995–2009," a number of dramatic features are portrayed:

- More than any other category, the increase of female representatives and senators has been dramatic.
- More representatives and senators are between 40 and 60 years old.
- More representatives have served between two and nine terms; more senators have served between one and three terms.

(b)   These statistics have created changes for Congress. Without a doubt, the dramatic increase in female representatives (more than double the number of representatives and triple the number of senators since 1980) was due to gender politics. In 1992 when four women were elected to the Senate and nineteen were elected to the House, it was called the year of the woman in politics. The impact that this had on the Congress was an increase in making woman-related issues part of the public agenda. Many of these issues are economic and social in nature. The response of these newly elected representatives to single mothers' concerns, to abortion rights, and to protection by the government of "safety net" issues has become a priority. Even with the increase in women representatives, statistically they are still only a small percentage of the entire House and Senate.

(c)   The age and seniority of representatives has a direct impact on Congress in the manner in which it develops its own rules and agenda. The 1994 congressional election was an important turning point that illustrates how age and seniority issues affect the institution. The House freshman class of 1994, 104th Congress, though younger and more inexperienced than their counterparts, had a significant impact on the House. Realizing that this core group represented the hopes of the conservative Republican revolution, newly elected Speaker of the House Newt Gingrich pushed major reforms through the House with the support of these newly elected congressmen. The reforms included term limits for committee chairs and rules that would make it easier for less senior members to become directly involved in the legislative process. The Republicans were able to push through a good part of their Contract With America in the first 100 days of the 104th Congress because of the support of these new representatives. Ironically, the power given to these inexperienced congressmen also contributed to the unsuccessful budget battle waged against President Clinton, which resulted in two government shutdowns.

SCORING GUIDELINES FOR FREE-RESPONSE QUESTION (8 POINTS)

Part (a) 3 Points

One point is earned for each characteristic identified from the table.

Answers may include, but are not limited to:

- increase of female representatives and senators
- more representatives and senators are between 40 and 60 years old
- more representatives have served between one and ten terms
- more senators have served between one and three terms
- there has been an increase in the number of Hispanic representatives

Part (b) 3 Points

One point is earned for each of three characteristics discussed. These explanations must include a description of the change on Congress.

Answers may include, but are not limited to:

- women—their issues became part of the congressional legislative agenda
- seniority—increased seniority creates a more stable body and more influence in the committees representatives serve on
- African-Americans—increased number of minorities creates a greater awareness of minority issues

Part (c) 2 Points

One point is earned for the impact each of two characteristics have had on Congress.

Answers may include, but are not limited to:

- age—freshman congressmen in 1994 were younger and more inexperienced and followed the lead of the newly elected Speaker Newt Gingrich
- seniority—term limits were imposed on committee chairs

The Presidency

8

- → APPOINTMENT POWER
- → BULLY PULPIT
- → CABINET
- → CHIEF EXECUTIVE
- → COMMANDER-IN-CHIEF
- → COUNCIL OF ECONOMIC ADVISORS
- → EXECUTIVE OFFICE OF THE PRESIDENT
- → EXECUTIVE ORDER
- → EXECUTIVE PRIVILEGE
- → IMPEACHMENT
- → IMPERIAL PRESIDENCY
- → LINE ITEM VETO

- → NATIONAL SECURITY COUNCIL
- → OFFICE OF MANAGEMENT AND BUDGET
- → PARDON POWER
- → POCKET VETO
- → RIDERS
- → STATE OF THE UNION ADDRESS
- → TRIAL BALLOONS
- → TWENTY-FIFTH AMENDMENT
- → VETO
- → WAR POWERS RESOLUTION
- → WHITE HOUSE STAFF

CONTEMPORARY CONNECTION

In 2015, President Obama issued an executive order that changed our diplomatic relationship with Cuba. The order reestablished diplomatic relations with the country, allowed American citizens to travel to Cuba, and allowed more trade between the United States and Cuba. This order was an example of an inherent power of the president to shape foreign policy. This chapter explores the presidency, the make-up of the executive branch, and the many roles the president plays in shaping policy.

The second of four institutions to be covered, the presidency has evolved into the focal point of politics and government in America. It is the political plum for those seeking elected office. The institution plays a predominant role in government having formal and informal relationships with the legislative and judicial branches and the bureaucracy. Other roles that make the president involved more than any other individual or institution in politics and government will be evaluated. Potential conflicts and the reasons why the institution has been criticized for having an arrogance of power are important areas to explore.

This chapter also focuses on the factors that create a successful presidency. It illustrates how, historically, the institution has grown in importance. The constitutional basis of power as well as the manner in which the president has used executive agencies such as the cabinet, the executive office, and the White House staff demonstrates this growth. Additionally, the shared legislative relationship that the president has with the Congress points to the complex issue of whether the institution has developed into an imperial presidency, a presidency that dominates the political agenda.

Whether or not the president succeeds, to a large extent, depends on the nature of the agenda that is set. The interrelated manner in which the president is able to communicate the agenda with the public, the way the media reports the agenda, and the approval rating of the electorate are factors that define the presidency. As Harry Truman said about the office, "the buck stops here."

QUICK CONSTITUTIONAL REVIEW OF THE PRESIDENCY

- Basis of constitutional power found in Article II
- Must be 35 years old, a natural-born citizen, and a resident of the United States for 14 years
- Chief Executive
- Commander in Chief of the armed forces
- Power to grant pardons
- Power to make treaties
- Power to appoint ambassadors, justices, and other officials
- Power to sign legislation or veto legislation
- Duty to give a State of the Union report
- Election by electoral college
- Definition of term limits, order of succession, and procedures to follow during presidential disability through constitutional amendments
- Informal power based on precedent, custom, and tradition in issuing executive orders, interpreting executive privilege, and creating executive agencies

---

PRESIDENTIAL SUCCESSION

Presidential disability and succession are defined by the Twenty-Fifth Amendment. It allows the vice president to become acting president after the president's cabinet confirms that the president is disabled. This happened for a short period when Ronald Reagan was undergoing surgery after an assassination attempt.

The amendment also outlines the procedures for selecting a new vice president when that office becomes vacant. When a vacancy occurs, the president nominates a new vice president. Unlike other presidential appointments, both the Senate and House must approve the appointment by a majority vote in each house. This occurred after Nixon's vice president, Spiro Agnew, resigned in 1973. Nixon appointed congressman Gerald Ford as vice president, and both houses of Congress approved his selection. When Nixon resigned in 1974, Ford appointed former Governor of New York, Nelson Rockefeller, and both houses of Congress followed the same procedure and approved Rockefeller as vice president.

Nine presidents have not completed their term of office. By law, after the vice president, the Speaker of the House and the Senate president pro-tempore are next in line. Eight presidents have died in office, and one, Nixon, resigned. After Franklin Roosevelt died, in 1945, a constitutional amendment limiting the term of office to no more than two terms or a maximum of ten years was passed. There has been a growing movement to further limit presidential terms to one six-year term to reduce the amount of time and energy devoted to raising campaign funds and the time it takes to campaign for office.

THE BULLY PULPIT

If you think of the presidents who have been powerful and influential and who have demonstrated leadership, they all have one thing in common. These presidents, such as Theodore Roosevelt, Franklin Roosevelt, John F. Kennedy, and Ronald Reagan, all used the "bully pulpit" to advance their policies and communicate with the American people. The term was coined by Theodore Roosevelt who saw the White House as his bully pulpit to advance his agenda. The bully pulpit is used by presidents to:

- manage a crisis,
- demonstrate leadership,
- announce the appointment of cabinet members and Supreme Court justices,
- set and clarify the national agenda,
- achieve a legislative agenda, and
- announce foreign policy initiatives.

Especially with the 24/7 news cycle covered by the media and social media, a president who knows how to use the bully pulpit has a powerful tool to advance the goals of the administration.

The power and influence of the president have evolved and increased as the United States has grown as a world leader.

The growth of the executive departments has also contributed to the increase of presidential power.

THE CABINET

The cabinet was instituted by George Washington; every administration since his has had one. There have also been unofficial advisors such as Andrew Jackson's so-called Kitchen Cabinet. Cabinet appointees need Senate confirmation and play an extremely influential role in government. There are currently 19 cabinet level positions. Creation or abolition of these agencies needs congressional approval. There have been cabinet name changes such as the change from Secretary of War to Secretary of Defense. Cabinet agencies have been created because national issues such as the environment, energy, and education are placed high on the national agenda. Cabinet-level positions have been expanded to include the Office of Management and Budget, the Director of the Environmental Protection Agency, the Vice President, the United States Trade Representative, the Ambassador to the United Nations, and the Chair of the Council of Economic Advisors. In 2002, the cabinet was expanded to include the Director of Homeland Security. The vice president is a permanent member of the cabinet, too. Cabinet officials have come from all walks of life. They are lawyers, government officials, educators, and business executives. Many cabinet officials are friends and personal associates of the president. Only one, Robert Kennedy, was a relative of the president. That practice was stopped by law. Presidents have used cabinet officials in other capacities. Nixon used his Attorney General as campaign manager. Cabinets are scrutinized by the American public to see whether they represent a cross section of the population. It was only recently that full minority representation in the cabinet became a common practice. To put this issue in perspective, the first woman, Frances Hopkins, was appointed to the cabinet in Franklin Roosevelt's administration. Cabinet nominees have been turned down by the Senate. George Bush's appointment of Texas Senator John Tower was defeated by the Senate as a result of accusations that Tower was a womanizer, had drinking problems, and had potential conflict of interest problems with defense contractors. During his term, President Clinton had trouble gaining approval of cabinet appointees. Zöe Baird was nominated as the first woman Attorney General. However, because of allegations that Baird hired an illegal alien as a nanny, Clinton was forced to withdraw the nomination. The event became known as "Nannygate." Issues facing a president are how much reliance should be placed on the cabinet, whether a cabinet should be permitted to offer differing points of view, and how frequently cabinet meetings should be held. Each cabinet member does administer a bureaucratic agency and is responsible for implementing policy within each area.

After Barack Obama was elected president, he established new "vetting" procedures (reviewing of one's credentials) for his appointees. This procedure included a provision that no former lobbyist could serve in an office that the lobbyist had earlier tried to influence. President Obama's first-term cabinet appointment reflected a "team of rivals" in key positions. He appointed his primary opponent Hillary Clinton as secretary of state and kept Republican Robert Gates as the defense secretary. The rest of the cabinet reflected ethnic and gender diversity. In his second term, some of President Obama's appointments were confirmed with significant Republican opposition. For the first time in Senate history, the secretary of defense appointee was filibustered before gaining Senate approval.

THE EXECUTIVE OFFICE OF THE PRESIDENT

Separate from the cabinet is the executive office of the president. It was created by Franklin Roosevelt in 1939. Today it has four major policymaking bodies:

1. the National Security Council;
2. the Council of Economic Advisors;
3. the Office of Management and Budget; and
4. the Office of National Drug Control Policy.

The National Security Council, chaired by the president, is the lead advisory board in the area of national and international security. The other members of the council include the vice president and secretaries of state and defense as well as the director of the Central Intelligence Agency and the chairman of the Joint Chiefs of Staff. The president's national security advisor is the direct liaison. Even though the function of the council is advisory, under Presidents George W. Bush and Barack Obama, it conducted the warrantless wiretapping program that was very controversial.

The Council of Economic Advisors consists of individuals who are recognized as leading economists. They are approved by the Senate and help the president prepare the annual Economic Report to Congress. This report outlines the economic state of the nation.

The Office of Management and Budget (OMB) is the largest agency in the executive office. Its director, appointed with the consent of the Senate, is responsible for the preparation of the massive federal budget, which must be submitted to the Congress in January each year. Besides formulating the budget, the OMB oversees congressional appropriations. It is a key agency because it has tremendous policymaking ability based on its budget recommendations. The department is also the president's direct link to other agencies and helps prepare executive orders and presidential budget policy.

The Office of National Drug Control Policy is a recent addition to the executive office. It is chaired by a director appointed by the president with the consent of the Senate. The head of the agency has been dubbed the nation's drug czar. The responsibility of the agency is to prepare recommendations on how to combat the problem of drug abuse. It also coordinates the policies of other federal agencies in this area. Other departments that exist in the executive office are the Office of Policy Development, the Office of Science and Technology Policy, the Council on Environmental Quality, the Office of Administration, and the Office of the United States Trade Representative.

The Office of Homeland Security is the latest addition to the cabinet. Created after the terrorist attacks of September 11, 2001, the Office of Homeland Security is responsible for protecting the United States against future attacks. Each agency is responsible directly to the president and makes policy recommendations appropriate to each area.

In the summer of 2004, the 9/11 presidential commission held hearings and issued a report that recommended the creation of a new National Counterterrorism Center headed by the director of

The Executive Departments

The White House and the Executive Office of the President

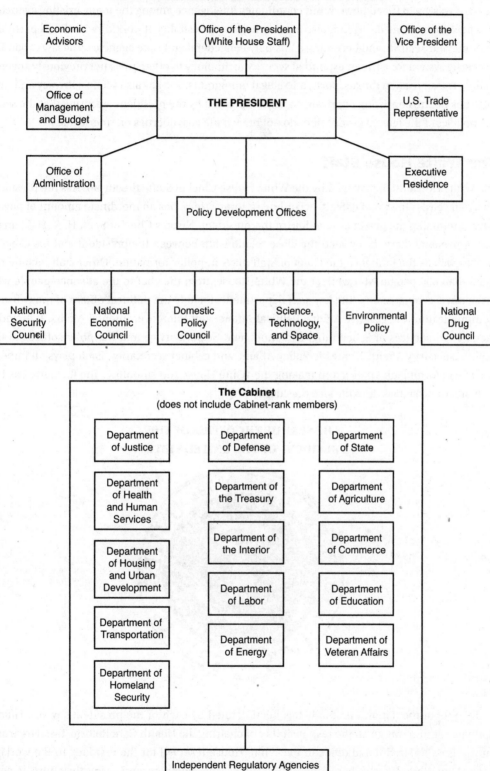

Economic Advisors

Office of the President (White House Staff)

Office of the Vice President

Office of Management and Budget

THE PRESIDENT

U.S. Trade Representative

Office of Administration

Executive Residence

Policy Development Offices

National Security Council

National Economic Council

Domestic Policy Council

Science, Technology, and Space

Environmental Policy

National Drug Council

The Cabinet
(does not include Cabinet-rank members)

Department of Justice

Department of Defense

Department of State

Department of Health and Human Services

Department of the Treasury

Department of Agriculture

Department of Housing and Urban Development

Department of the Interior

Department of Commerce

Department of Transportation

Department of Labor

Department of Education

Department of Homeland Security

Department of Energy

Department of Veteran Affairs

Independent Regulatory Agencies

national intelligence. After much political in-fighting in the Republican-controlled House of Representatives, the bill, which was supported by a majority of Democrats, passed both houses in a lame-duck session of Congress. The law signed by President George W. Bush created a new counterterrorism center with a director appointed by the president and confirmed by the Senate. This director was given broad powers and coordinates intelligence among the many existing agencies. This new director and the agency also has the major responsibility of working with the Department of Homeland Security and becoming a link between federal and state agencies. The law expanded a security system for airlines, expanded security technology to other areas not previously covered such as transportation threats, ports, and illegal immigrants. The law also set up a Privacy and Civil Liberties Board, consisting of private citizens appointed by the president, ensuring that the security policies of the federal government do not breach the civil liberties of Americans.

The White House Staff

The White House staff, managed by the White House Chief of Staff, directly advises the president on a daily basis. The Chief of Staff, according to some critics, has an inordinate amount of power, often controlling the personal schedule of the president. Nixon's Chief of Staff, H. R. Haldeman, kept a personal diary. It revealed the close relationship between the president and his Chief of Staff as well as the influence the Chief of Staff plays in policy formation. Other staff include the more than 600 people who work at the White House, from the chef to the advance people who make travel arrangements. The key staff departments include the political offices of the Office of Communications, Legislative Affairs, Political Affairs, and Intergovernmental Affairs. It includes the support services of Scheduling, Personnel, and Secret Service and the policy offices of the National Security Affairs, Domestic Policy Affairs, and cabinet secretaries. Each plays an important role in formulating policy and making the White House run smoothly. The first lady has her own office and staff as does the vice president.

**THE SEAL OF THE OFFICE OF THE
PRESIDENT OF THE UNITED STATES**

The role of the nation's first lady has been defined by each of the president's wives. Hillary Rodham Clinton was given the responsibility of chairing the Health Care Reform Task Force and moved from the traditional office in the White House reserved for the first lady to the working wing of the White House where other White House staff members work. After the efforts to get a comprehensive health care bill failed, Mrs. Clinton took on a more traditional role as the country's first lady. This role continued during Clinton's second administration. During the Whitewater investigation, Mrs. Clinton testified before a Grand Jury. Charges were not brought against her. Using the theme of her book *It Takes a Village to Raise a Child*, Mrs. Clinton continued to be an advocate for children's causes. Mrs. Clinton also became the only first lady to seek elective office. She was elected to the Senate in 2000 by the voters of New York and was a presidential candidate in 2008 and 2016.

First Lady Michelle Obama followed Laura Bush's model and used her influence by taking up the causes of preventing childhood obesity and working with veterans and their families.

PRESIDENTIAL POWERS

Besides the constitutional authority delegated to the president, the nation's chief executive also has indirect roles. These duties such as chief legislator, head of party, chief of state, and chief diplomat truly define the scope of the presidency. Depending upon the skills of the person in office, the power of the presidency will increase or decrease. Each role has a direct relationship with either a political institution or governmental policymaking body. The skills and ability to use these roles result in a shared power relationship.

> The president not only has separate powers and inherent powers but also has shared powers with the other government and political institutions.

The president as chief legislator develops legislative skills and a shared relationship with Congress. In developing a legislative agenda, the president sets priorities and works closely with members of Congress. Three contrasting presidents—Johnson, Carter, and Clinton—developed different styles in this area. Johnson, having the experience as Senate Majority Leader, already had the skills of working with Congress when he assumed the office after Kennedy's assassination. He was able to achieve a great deal of success with his Great Society programs. Carter, coming from the Georgia governorship, was unable to work with congressional leaders and did not implement his agenda. Clinton, although a former governor, used his support staff and developed a working relationship with his own party leaders who held a majority in each house. For the first three years of his presidency, he was able to push through significant legislation including the Family and Medical Leave Act, a National Service Program, Americorp, and the Crime Bill. The fact that Democrats held a majority was a key factor in whether the president's legislative agenda was completed. George H. W. Bush, who as a Republican, had to work with the Democratic majority, and used a veto 45 times successfully.

When George W. Bush was elected president in 2000, he initially had to work with a divided Congress. After the 2002 midterm election, the Republicans controlled both houses of Congress, and Bush was able to push his legislative agenda through Congress and pursue his foreign policy goals in Iraq and Afghanistan. Bush, working with the Democrats, signed a major tax bill decreasing the tax rates; he also passed the No Child Left Behind legislation that helped reform the nation's schools. After the 2006 midterm election, Bush had to deal with Democratic majorities in the House and Senate. Legislative victories decreased and he faced mounting criticism for the Iraq War. When Barack Obama was elected in 2008, he was able to use his political capital to pass a historic bill reforming the nation's healthcare system.

The Veto

The veto is a primary tool used by the president to influence Congress to meet his agenda priorities. Historically there have been over 1,454 regular vetoes and fewer than 200 have been overridden by Congress. The presidents who have exercised the most vetoes were Franklin Roosevelt (372), Grover Cleveland (304), and Harry Truman (180).

Pocket Veto

Another form of veto a president can use is the pocket veto. This occurs if the president does not sign a bill within ten days and the Congress adjourns within the ten days. This tactic has been used over a thousand times. One of the reasons why the pocket veto is used is that very often there is a rush to pass legislation at the time of planned recesses. One of the issues surrounding the veto is the attempt by some presidents to obtain a line item veto. Many times Congress will attach riders or amendments to bills. These riders, often in the form of appropriations, sometimes have nothing to do with the intent of the bill itself and are often considered to be pork barrel legislation. It becomes a means of forcing the president to accept legislation he would normally veto.

Appointments

According to the Congressional Research Service, "The responsibility for populating top positions in the executive and judicial branches of government is one the Senate and the President share. The President nominates an individual, the Senate may confirm him, and the President would then present him with a signed commission. The Constitution divided the responsibility for choosing those who would run the federal government by granting the President the power of appointment and the Senate the power of advice and consent." When the Senate refuses to act on a presidential appointment, presidents have waited for the Senate to adjourn for three days or more. The president would then use what is called a "recess appointment," which bypasses the Senate for one year. This method has been challenged, and the Supreme Court ruled that recess appointments made by the president are unconstitutional, even if the Senate only convenes in a pro forma session—opening and adjourning without doing any other business. Members of the president's White House staff such as the chief of staff and press secretary do not have to go through the confirmation process.

Legislative Vetoes

Attempts at legislative vetoes of presidential actions have been declared unconstitutional by the Supreme Court. In *INS v Chadha* (1983) the Court ruled that "we have not yet found a better way to preserve freedom than by making the exercise of power subject to the carefully crafted restraints spelled out in the Constitution." Congress does have oversight responsibilities over the intelligence agencies through committee hearings.

In 1994 both houses of Congress passed a line item veto law, which President Clinton signed. Taking effect in 1997, the purpose of the line item veto was to let the president strike individual items from the 13 major appropriations bills submitted by Congress that he considered wasteful spending. The goal of the law was to prevent Congress from increasing appropriations with pork. The law was brought to the Supreme Court and was declared unconstitutional as an illegal expansion of the president's veto power.

Party Leader

As party leader, the president is the only nationally-elected official. Other party leaders such as the Speaker of the House and the majority and minority leaders of the Senate and House are elected by their own parties. In this role, the president has much influence in setting his agenda, especially if he is a member of the majority party. Many times the president will make the argument to the congressional party leaders that their support will "make or break" the presidency. This kind of pressure was put on the Democratic Party when Bill Clinton lobbied for the passage of his first budget. Another key action the president can take to send a message to Congress is to impound funds. By this act the president refuses to release appropriated funds to executive agencies. President Nixon used this practice to curb congressional spending. Congress retaliated by passing the 1974 Congressional Budget and Impoundment Act, which set limits on this practice and set up an independent Congressional Budget Office. This act was significant in shifting the checks and balances scale to Congress. Even though he does not directly have the power to appoint congressmen to committees, the president certainly can influence a party member by promising to support pet legislation of the congressman in return for voting in favor of legislation supported by the president.

Executive Privilege

The president has interpreted the Constitution to allow for executive privilege, the ability of the president to protect personal material. Because the definition of executive privilege is not written, President Nixon in trying to apply this to his Watergate tapes did not succeed in protecting the tapes from a congressional committee investigating potential obstruction of justice charges.

Inherent Power

Besides the delegated powers listed at the beginning of the chapter, the president has an implied power unique to the three branches—an inherent power to make policy without the approval of Congress. This power is derived from the chief-executive clause in the Constitution and the defined power of the president as commander-in-chief. The policy directives can come in the form of executive orders and executive actions, as well as making foreign policy decisions that involve the commitment of troops and weapons to foreign countries. Congress has pushed back on these powers by taking the president to court and passing the War Powers Act.

National Security

Another area of potential conflict between the president and Congress is that of national security. As chief diplomat, the president has the delegated constitutional authority of commander in chief of the armed forces, the person who can make treaties with other nations and appoint ambassadors to nations that are recognized. With treaties and appointments, Congress has a built in check—the Senate must approve treaties by a two-thirds margin and approve presidential appointments by a majority vote. Such significant treaties as the 1962 Nuclear Test Ban Treaty and the 2010 Strategic Arms Limitation Treaty are good examples of the president working closely with the Congress.

Foreign Policy

Who are the players and participants in this aspect of public policy? Constitutionally we have already identified the key players:

- President—in Article II, as commander in chief of the armed forces and chief diplomat, having the power to appoint ambassadors and negotiate treaties.
- Congress—in Article I, having the power to declare war, support and maintain an armed force through appropriations, as well as approve foreign aid allocations; the Senate has the power to approve appointments and must ratify treaties.

Through the bureaucratic agencies of the executive branch and the oversight responsibilities of Congress, specific policy is made. The president relies on two key cabinet departments for advice—the State Department and the Defense Department, both of which are run by civilians. He also relies on the National Security Advisor (a staff position), and the Directors of the National Intelligence, CIA, FBI, and Homeland Security. The secretary of defense, formerly called the secretary of war, is second to the president in directing military affairs. The agency is directly in charge of the massive defense budget and the three major branches of the military. Direct military command is under the leadership of the joint chiefs of staff. It is made up of representatives of each of the military services and chaired by a presidential appointee, also a member of the military. During the Gulf War, General Colin Powell was a visible key player giving valuable advice to President George H. W. Bush and Secretary of Defense Dick Cheney. In 1995, after his autobiography, *My American Journey*, was published, he was urged to run for president as a result of his leadership during the Gulf War.

The secretary of state heads the diplomatic arm of the executive branch and supervises a department with well over 24,000 people, including 8,000 foreign service officers. There are specialists in such areas as Middle East affairs, and the department includes the many ambassadors who are the country's chief spokesmen abroad. Presidents appoint to the position of secretary of state someone on whom they can closely rely and who can map out a successful foreign policy. Some, like John Foster Dulles, Eisenhower's secretary of state, have played a major role. Dulles endorsed the policy of brinkmanship—going close to the edge of an all-out war in order to contain communism. President Clinton appointed the first woman Secretary of State, Madeline Albright, at the start of his second term.

The National Security Act of 1947 established the National Security Council as an executive-level department. It created as its head the national security advisor. One of the most notable people to head the agency was Henry Kissinger, who served under Presidents Nixon and Ford. Kissinger laid the foundation of Nixon's policy to end the Vietnam War and handled the delicate negotiations that led to Nixon's historic visit to China. Condoleezza Rice became a key national security advisor to George W. Bush during his administration. She was appointed and confirmed as the first African-American woman to serve as Secretary of State during Bush's second term. Barack Obama appointed Hillary Clinton, the former First Lady, as his first Secretary of State.

Other agencies that are an integral part of the foreign policy arena include:

- The Immigration and Naturalization Service—deals with those people trying to seek residence in the United States from other countries. It is the agency charged with enforcing immigration policy. At times, it becomes embroiled in controversial issues such as when they had to enforce the executive order made by President Obama allowing children of undocumented immigrants to achieve status.
- The Central Intelligence Agency—created by Congress in 1947 and works under the direction of the National Security Council. Its director has the responsibility of:
  - coordinating the gathering of information related to foreign affairs and national defense for the other federal agencies
  - analyzing and evaluating this information
  - reporting to the president and National Security Council

Besides information reporting, the agency has also conducted covert activities abroad and at times has been criticized for some of its actions. When the Iran-Contra affair was investigated by Congress, it became apparent that the CIA helped coordinate the illegal arms for hostages negotiations.:

- The United States Arms Control and Disarmament Agency—maintains responsibility for negotiations, participation, and implementation of treaties dealing with disarmament. It has focused its attention on monitoring nuclear test ban treaties, the Strategic Arms Reduction Treaty (START), and the Strategic Arms Limitation Talks (SALT), which resulted in the Intermediate Range Nuclear Force (INF) Treaty in 1988. It also has oversight regarding the Chemical Weapons Treaty ratified by the Senate in 1997.

■ The Selective Service System—maintains responsibility for coordinating and raising an army. Even though the draft has been used since the Civil War, the first national draft occurred in 1917 as a result of the Selective Service Act and was renewed again in 1940, prior to the United States' entry into World War II. During the Vietnam War it was a source of controversy. Its critics maintained that draft policy favored those who could gain a deferment by attending college, resulting in many lower- and middle-class young men being sent to Vietnam. Since President Nixon established an all-volunteer military, the Selective Service has existed on a standby basis, administering a registration requirement that takes effect when young men reach the age of 18.

DEFENSE POLICY

The defense budget has a tremendous impact on the economy of the United States. Many times in our history Congress has debated "guns versus butter." And now that the Cold War is over and the country is facing such a large deficit, the pressure to reduce the size of the military establishment is even greater. The proponents of a scaled-down defense point to the fact that we don't need to deploy as many forces throughout the world as we did in the past. They claim that retraining military personnel could be accomplished and that many industries that are defense-oriented could redirect their resources to other areas. Critics argue that, because the United States is the last remaining superpower, we must maintain a strong defense posture. They also doubt that defense industries can easily move away from defense if contracts are cut. This, they argue, would increase the unemployment rate.

Defense policies are closely tied to the foreign policy goals of the nation. Thus national security and vital national interests are two of the overriding objectives in developing a defense budget and operation. As the country saw during the Gulf War, weaponry is an important part of the defense strategy. Both conventional and nuclear weapons for offensive and deterrent purposes play a significant part in the overall defense budget. In the past 25 years, it has also become obvious that as we develop and maintain weapons, we have also entered into agreements to destroy a good part of our nuclear arsenal.

> The defense policy of the United States is caught between the past practice of developing a powerful nuclear deterrence and an uncertain future of budgetary reductions. And yet, providing for the common defense is a primary goal of the government.

The question of how much is enough has always been part of the policy agenda debate. The so-called military-industrial complex has argued that a strong defense will ensure the future security of the United States. On the other hand, the pressure to adjust to a non-cold-war world has resulted in a serious effort to reduce the scope of the defense budget.

War Powers Act

However, it is the war-making power of the president that has caused the most problems. Since the Vietnam War, Congress has become concerned with the president's unilateral commitment of American troops. The Congress responded by passing the War Powers Act in 1973, overriding a Nixon veto. This act states that a president can commit the military only after a declaration of war by the Congress or by specific authorization by Congress, if there is a national emergency or if the use of force is in the national interest of the United States. Once troops are sent, the president is required to keep the Congress informed about the action within 48 hours and must stop the commitment of troops after 60 days. Congress has the leverage of withholding military funding to force the president to comply. This act has been compared to a legislative veto. The proponents of this measure point to such military action as Reagan's invasion of Grenada, Bush's Panama invasion, and Clinton's Somalia and Bosnia policies as examples of why it is necessary for Congress to have authority. Opponents of this measure point to the fact that only the president has the complete knowledge of what foreign policy actions can really have an impact on the national security of the United States. The issue has never been resolved by the courts, and the legislation remains on the books.

Pardon Power

The president's influence over the judiciary comes from his power to appoint Supreme Court justices and grant pardons and reprieves. Most judicial appointments are made after checking the appointment with the Senator of the state the appointee comes from. This kind of "senatorial courtesy" often guarantees the acceptance of the appointment. The difference between a pardon and a reprieve is that a reprieve is a postponement of a sentence and a pardon forgives the crime and frees the person from legal culpability. One of the most controversial pardons came in 1974 when Gerald Ford pardoned Richard Nixon, who had been named as an unindicted co-conspirator in the Watergate scandal. An instance when the Court told the president he went too far was the Supreme Court decision in *Nixon v United States* (1974). The Court told Richard Nixon he must turn over the Watergate tapes and rejected his argument of executive privilege. An extension of the pardoning power is the power of amnesty. For instance, in 1977 Jimmy Carter granted a blanket amnesty to Vietnam War draft evaders who fled to Canada. President Clinton was criticized after announcing over 100 pardons in the last hours of his presidency.

Taken in total, the scope of presidential power raises the issue of whether the office has turned into what historian Arthur M. Schlesinger characterized as the imperial presidency. Looking at the manner in which Johnson and Nixon used presidential power, Schlesinger concluded that "power was so expanded and misused by 1972 that it threatened our Constitutional system." Even if one assumes that a president must use his power, especially in wartime, the question still remains how much power of the president should go unchecked by the other branches of government. It is a question that is still being debated today. In fact, there are proponents of the imperial presidency who feel that the president must exercise both delegated and inferred powers with the cooperation of the other institutions of government for the best interests of the country.

Section 1: Multiple-Choice Questions

1. The Constitution stated that the requirements for being president are all of the following EXCEPT

   (A) obtaining a majority of the electoral votes
   (B) having resided in the United States for at least 14 years
   (C) being a natural-born citizen
   (D) being at least 35 years old
   (E) being a member of a political party

2. Examples of people on the White House staff include all of the following EXCEPT

   (A) the Chief of Staff
   (B) the White House cook
   (C) the National Security Advisor
   (D) the vice president
   (E) the press secretary

3. After Congress passes an appropriations bill, the president may do all of the following EXCEPT

   (A) sign it into law
   (B) send it directly to the Supreme Court for judicial review
   (C) veto it, sending it back to Congress with the reasons for rejecting it
   (D) let it become law after ten working days by not doing anything to it
   (E) not sign it after Congress adjourns, exercising a pocket veto

4. Using the bully pulpit refers to a president

   (A) using the power and influence of his office to exert pressure
   (B) calling upon members of his cabinet to influence legislation
   (C) using his veto power to reject legislation
   (D) signing a piece of legislation into law
   (E) taking a trip to a foreign country to sign a treaty

5. Which of the following is responsible for the preparation of executive spending proposals submitted to Congress?

   (A) Treasury Department
   (B) Council of Economic Advisors
   (C) Federal Trade Commission
   (D) Department of Commerce
   (E) Office of Management and Budget

6. All of the following are formal or informal sources of presidential power EXCEPT

   (A) presidential authority to raise revenue
   (B) presidential access to the media
   (C) precedents set during previous administrations
   (D) public support
   (E) the Constitution

7. The President uses which of the following methods to persuade reluctant members of Congress to vote for a particular bill?

(A) Transfers members who oppose the bill to unpopular committees.

(B) Denies campaign funds to members who oppose the bill.

(C) Threatens to deny renomination to members who oppose the bill.

(D) Threatens to veto a different bill that enjoys bipartisan support in Congress.

(E) Makes a direct appeal to the public.

8. Invocation of the War Powers Act of 1973 would be most important in determining

(A) the nature of the commitment of the U.S. Marines to a peacekeeping role in Bosnia

(B) the amount of financial aid to the Contras of Nicaragua

(C) the timing of naval maneuvers off the coast of Libya

(D) the appointment of the Joint Chiefs of Staff

(E) the legality of extraditing foreign agents responsible for acts of terrorism

9. The usefulness to the president of having cabinet members as political advisers is undermined by the fact that

(A) the president has little latitude in choosing cabinet members

(B) cabinet members have little political support independent of the president

(C) cabinet members are usually drawn from Congress and retain loyalties to Congress

(D) the loyalties of cabinet members are often divided between loyalty to the president and loyalty to their own executive departments

(E) the cabinet operates as a collective unit and individual members have limited access to the president

Answer Explanations

1. **(E)** Type of Question: Negative

At the time of the adoption of the Constitution, the issue of citizenship was very important. The authors of the Constitution created citizenship requirements for elective office. The only elective office that required a person seeking office to be a natural-born citizen was the presidency. Choice E is the correct answer because nowhere in the document is a political party even mentioned. It is part of the unwritten Constitution.

2. **(D)** Type of Question: Negative

The vice president of the United States, although a member of the president's team, is still an elected official. The Chief of Staff, the White House cook, the National Security Advisor, and the president's press secretary are all members of the White House staff.

3. **(B)** Type of Question: Identification/except

The president has other options as outlined in choices A, C, D, and E. Choice B is the correct answer because only the Supreme Court can decide to hear a case dealing with a bill signed into law.

4. **(A)** Type of Question: Definitional

Even though the president has many different tools at his disposal, the bully pulpit of the office is quite effective in gaining public support or giving a message to the Congress, the media, and the public. Through the proper timing of a speech, the president can clearly indicate whether he will be supporting a particular position.

5. **(E)** Type of Question: Identification and analysis

This is a factually based question. The major difficulty is discerning whether the Treasury Department, the Council of Economic Advisors, or the OMB has primary responsibility. By law it is the Office of Management and Budget, although there certainly is input from other agencies in this process.

6. **(A)** Type of Question: Negative

This question requires that you have knowledge of both formal and informal sources of presidential authority. All formal powers are listed in the Constitution (choice E). Choices B, C, and D are sources of informal authority. The president's access to the media furthers an agenda. The support of the people can be used as leverage, and precedents are as significant as written law. Raising revenue, choice A, is a power delegated to Congress.

7. **(E)** Type of Question: Identification and analysis

The president has limited actual powers in taking action against members of Congress who don't agree with him. He may have some influence regarding committee appointments. He has more influence with the chairman of the national committee, but it does not extend to denying campaign funds or renomination. And threatening to veto a popular bill would not accomplish any positive results. Sometimes a direct appeal to the public or using his bully pulpit can succeed.

8. **(A)** Type of Question: Cause-and-effect relationships

The passage of the War Powers Act over President Nixon's veto was prompted by the United States' involvement in Vietnam. The act has never been recognized by a sitting president nor has it been declared unconstitutional by the courts. Since its passage, Congress has threatened to use it when forces were committed to Grenada, Panama, and the Persian Gulf. The president was able to justify those actions. Choices B, C, D, and E are all actions within the legal purview of the president. Committing troops to Bosnia over an extended period of time could be challenged.

9. **(D)** Type of Question: Cause-and-effect relationships

Even though a cabinet member has a primary loyalty to the president, because there is also a huge responsibility to administer a large agency, the secretary also has a loyalty to that department. The president has a wide latitude in choosing cabinet members and many times selects a secretary who was a close political ally. Even if a cabinet member is drawn from Congress, once sworn in, the official's first loyalty is to the president. Cabinet members do have other sources of political support and certainly have more than limited access to the president.

Section 2: Data-Based Free-Response Question (6 points)

Look at the following table based on generally reported press releases:

Event	Approval of President's Actions (%)
Bay of Pigs Invasion	Preevent: 73 Postevent: 83
Cuban Missile Crisis	Preevent: 61 Postevent: 74
Nixon's Trip to China	Preevent: 49 Postevent: 56
Camp David Meeting on the Middle East	Preevent: 42 Postevent: 56
Terrorist Bombing of Marines in Lebanon	Preevent: 48 Postevent: 56
Welfare Reform Legislation Signed	Preevent: 39 Postevent: 58

(a) List three factors that influence presidential job approval ratings.

(b) Using the above chart, choose three events and explain the relationship between that event and the president's approval ratings.

SAMPLE RESPONSE

(a)   The major factors influencing public opinion polls based on this chart include:

- pre- and post-election upswings—most presidents, even those with negative ratings, usually have a jump in the ratings prior to and immediately following elections
- the ability of a president to handle foreign policy crisis—such issues as ending wars, getting embroiled in unpopular wars, and responding quickly to foreign crisis have a dramatic impact on public opinion
- the condition of the economy—inflation, economic recessions, periods of economic recovery, and taxing policies influence the public's viewpoint

(b)   Three events from the chart that influenced the president's approval ratings were the Cuban Missile Crisis, the Camp David Meeting on the Middle East, and Welfare Reform Legislation signed. John Kennedy's approval prior to the Cuban Missile Crisis was around 60 percent. After the crisis was successfully concluded his ratings rose to almost 75 percent. This reflects how the public reacts after a foreign policy crisis. The reverse is also true. If a president doesn't succeed in achieving a foreign policy goal, his approval ratings plummet like George W. Bush's did during the Iraq War. Even though Jimmy Carter's approval ratings were in the low 40s, after the Camp David Accords were signed, the public responded and his approval ratings rose to 56 percent. This reflects how the public reacts to a foreign policy accomplishment. The third example is when President Bill Clinton signed Welfare Reform legislation. Prior to the passage of the bill, his approval rating was under 40 percent. After he signed the bill, the public approval rose to over 55 percent. This reflects leadership shown during a legislative battle between the Congress and the president.

SCORING GUIDELINES FOR FREE-RESPONSE QUESTION (6 POINTS)

Part (a) 3 Points

One point each is earned for listing three factors that influence presidential job approval ratings.

Answers may include, but are not limited to:

- pre- and postelection upswings
- the ability of a president to handle foreign policy
- the condition of the economy
- leadership shown during a domestic crisis
- the ability of a president to get programs through Congress

Part (b) 3 Points

One point each is earned for an analysis of three events from the chart of the relationship between the event and the approval ratings.

Answers may include, but are not limited to:

- Bay of Pigs Invasion—Kennedy's approval rating rose after the event even though it was not successful because he admitted he made a mistake
- Cuban Missile Crisis—Kennedy's approval rating rose after the crisis because Kennedy was able to successfully stop Russia from placing missiles in Cuba
- Nixon's trip to China—Nixon's ratings rose because it was a major foreign policy accomplishment
- Camp David meeting—Carter's approval ratings rose because of the signing of the Camp David Accords
- Terrorist bombing of Marines in Lebanon—Reagan's approval rating rose even though over 300 Marines were killed because of the way he handled the crisis
- Welfare Reform Legislation signed—Clinton's approval ratings rose because the public likes bipartisanship and supported the legislation

The Judiciary

9

- → AMICUS CURIAE
- → APPELLATE JURISDICTION
- → BURGER COURT
- → CONCURRING OPINION
- → CONSTITUTIONAL COURTS
- → CRIMINAL LAW
- → DISSENTING OPINION
- → *GIBBONS V OGDEN* (1824)
- → JUDICIAL ACTIVISM
- → JUDICIAL RESTRAINT
- → JUDICIARY COMMITTEE
- → LITIGATION
- → MAJORITY OPINION

- → MARSHALL COURT
- → *MCCULLOCH V MARYLAND* (1819)
- → MINORITY OPINION
- → ORAL ARGUMENT
- → ORIGINAL JURISDICTION
- → PRECEDENT
- → REHNQUIST COURT
- → SENATE CONFIRMATION
- → SPECIAL COURTS
- → STARE DECIS
- → UNANIMOUS OPINION
- → WARREN COURT
- → WRIT OF CERTIORARI

CONTEMPORARY CONNECTION

The Supreme Court run by Chief Justice John Roberts has turned into what has been described as more conservative than its predecessors. The court's critics describe this type of conservatism as judicial activism. The court's supporters disagree and describe the court's actions as judicial restraint. This chapter explores the Judiciary, its evolution, how it makes decisions regarding constitutional issues, and the ideological battles between the liberal and conservative members of the court. The terms "judicial activism" and "judicial restraint" are also explained in the context of the past and today's court.

One of the more dramatic changes incorporated into the new Constitution was the creation of the judicial branch of government. Realizing that a separate branch was needed to adjudicate legal issues, the Founding Fathers set up a court system that had at its top a Supreme Court holding the final power of constitutional review. In addition to a federal judiciary, consistent with the federal system, states set up their own court systems.

This chapter will explore the nature of the judicial branch of government. It will look at how the court system is organized, how justices are appointed, and the background of judges. A central issue that will be discussed is the policy-making function of the Supreme Court. How cases get to the Supreme Court and how they are decided directly relates to this issue. By looking at the history of the Court, you will also be able to understand the impact the Court has had on American society. Finally, we will look at the ongoing debate regarding the issue of whether the Court's policymaking function should be activist or whether justices should show judicial restraint.

Unlike the other two constitutionally established institutions of government, the judiciary, to many, is the most distant from the average citizen. There is a lack of understanding regarding the powers and function of the Court, and since federal justices serve for life, they are not directly responsible to the electorate. Yet the judiciary helps to maintain a delicate balance between order and liberty. It has a major impact on the average citizen. If you trace the influence of the Supreme Court from the Marshall Court to the Rehnquist Court, you will see how public policy is affected.

QUICK CONSTITUTIONAL REVIEW OF THE JUDICIARY

- Basis of constitutional power found in Article III.
- Judges are appointed by the president with the consent of the Senate and serve for life based on good behavior.
- Judicial power extends to issues dealing with common law, equity, civil law, criminal law, and public law.
- Cases are decided through original jurisdiction or appellate jurisdiction.
- Chief Justice of the Supreme Court presides over impeachment trials.
- Congress creates courts "inferior" to the Supreme Court.

DUAL COURT SYSTEM

The American judicial system has a duality that is consistent with our federal system of government.

The dual nature of the court system reflects the shared power of the national and state governments. According to the Constitution, the Congress can establish lower federal courts. It also permits the states to develop their own criminal justice system and courts to support it. Although they are independent from the federal courts, the state courts are linked by an appeals process that enables individuals to challenge state statutes in federal court. On the federal level Congress has created two kinds of courts—constitutional courts and special courts. Constitutional courts were formed to carry out the direction in the Constitution for the courts to exercise judicial power. Special courts were created by Congress to deal with cases deriving from the delegated powers of Congress such as military appeals, tax appeals, and veteran appeals.

The jurisdictions of federal and state courts depend upon the nature of the cases. The Constitution specifically assigns federal courts jurisdiction in cases dealing with laws arising from the Constitution, treaties, all cases dealing with ambassadors, cases dealing with admiralty and maritime issues, cases in which the United States is involved with two or more states, or cases between citizens of different states. The Supreme Court has original jurisdiction only in those "cases affecting ambassadors, other public ministers and consuls, and those in which a State shall be a party." Exclusive state court jurisdiction involves those cases deriving from state laws. However, through the appeals process, many of those cases could eventually end up in federal court.

STRUCTURE

The structure of the federal court system facilitates the judicial process.

The Constitution allows the establishment of "inferior" courts or lower courts. The first major organizational act of Congress occurred in 1789 with the Judiciary Act creating district courts. Congress has also responded by creating specialized or legislative courts and courts of appeal.

District courts, of which there are currently 94, handle 80 percent of the federal cases brought to them. Each state has at least one federal judicial district. The district court is the court of first hearing for cases involving federal crimes, civil suits involving federal laws, bankruptcy proceedings, admiralty and maritime cases, and immigration cases. United States attorneys are appointed by the president and confirmed by the Senate. They are responsible for bringing cases to the district courts.

The courts of appeal were established by Congress in 1891. They were created to set up an intermediate level of appeal before cases got to the Supreme Court. There are 13 courts of appeal and a Supreme Court Justice is assigned to act as liaison. These courts are responsible to review decisions of district courts and special courts. They review and enforce decisions of federal regulatory agencies and review cases on appeal from state supreme courts. The Supreme Court is the last final court of appeals, and it will be looked at as a separate topic later in this chapter.

SELECTION OF JUSTICES

The other two branches of government, the executive and legislative, are linked in the process of selecting federal justices. In addition, special interests such as the American Bar Association give their input. The result is a process that sometimes gets embroiled in political controversy. The president must get the approval of the Senate for all federal judgeships. In addition, the tradition of senatorial courtesy, the prior approval of the senators from the state from which the judge comes, has been part of the appointment process. This courtesy does not apply to Supreme Court justice nominations. Once nominated, the judicial candidate must appear before the Senate Judiciary Committee and is given a complete background check by the Department of Justice. Usually, lower court justices are not hand-picked by the president. They come from recommendations of other officials. Many lower court judgeships are given as a result of prior political support of the president or political party. From the administration of Franklin Roosevelt to the administration of Barack Obama, with the exception of Gerald Ford, every president has appointed over 90 percent of lower federal court judges from his own political party. There have been an increasing number of minority judges appointed, especially women, African-Americans, and Hispanics.

> The appointment of federal justices has as much to do with partisanship as ideology and is another example of the relationship among government branches and institutions.

Supreme Court Nominations

The consideration of judicial ideology has become increasingly important in the selection of Supreme Court justices. When a Supreme Court nominee appears before the Senate Judiciary Committee, issues such as constitutional precedent, judicial activism, legal writings, and past judicial decisions come under scrutiny. Other issues such as feelings of interest groups, public opinion, media opinion, and ethical and moral private actions of the nominee have been part of the selection process. Let's look at four recent nominees to illustrate this point.

When Justice Lewis Powell left the Court in 1987, President Reagan nominated Robert Bork. Bork had been an assistant attorney general in the Justice Department and was part of the "Saturday Night Massacre" when Nixon fired Attorney General Elliot Richardson. Bork was third in line and carried out Nixon's order to fire the special prosecutor, Archibald Cox, who was investigating the Watergate break-in. Bork was a conservative jurist and believed in judicial restraint. Many of his writings were questioned, as well as a number of his views regarding minorities and affirmative action. He was rejected by the Senate.

After his defeat, the term "Borked" was coined. It refers to a presidential appointee who does not get approved by the senate because of ideological reasons.

Douglas Ginsburg was nominated by Reagan after Bork's rejection. He was also considered extremely conservative. Under intense Senate questioning, conflict of interest issues surfaced as well as allegations that Ginsburg had used marijuana when he was a professor in law school. Reagan withdrew his nomination and finally succeeded in getting unanimous Senate approval for the more moderate Anthony Kennedy.

The most heated debate over confirmation occurred when President Bush nominated Clarence Thomas in 1991 to replace the first African-American Justice, Thurgood Marshall. This nomination brought to national attention the actions of the male-dominated Judiciary Committee when it came to questioning both Thomas and Anita Hill. Thomas was narrowly confirmed by a vote of 52–48. The confirmation process brought to the forefront the conflict between the president's constitutional authority to nominate the person he feels is best qualified and the responsibility of the Senate to approve the nominee. The partisanship of the committee as well as the leaks leading to the testimony of Hill added to the controversy.

When Clinton became president, his first two nominees, Ruth Bader Ginsburg and Stephen Breyer, reflected an attempt on his part to depoliticize the process. Both nominees received easy Senate approval.

The second term of George W. Bush brought about a major change in the makeup of the Supreme Court. Sandra Day O'Connor, the Court's first female appointee resigned. President Bush nominated Judge John G. Roberts, Jr. to replace her. Judge Roberts clerked for William Rehnquist in 1980 when Rehnquest was an associate justice. Roberts went on to serve on the U.S. Court of Appeals for the D.C. Circuit in 1992. He had previously argued 39 cases before the Supreme Court. Roberts described himself as a "strict constructionist" who relied heavily on precedent in determining the outcome of cases that came before him.

Before the confirmation process began, Chief Justice William Rehnquist died and President Bush decided to nominate Roberts as Chief Justice leaving O'Connor's replacement vacant until Roberts was confirmed. After the confirmation hearings were completed, the Senate voted to confirm Roberts as the seventeenth Chief Justice of the Supreme Court. Roberts became the youngest Chief Justice since John Marshall. Bush's nominee to replace O'Connor was federal appeals Judge Samuel Alito, who was confirmed by the Senate.

The death of William Rehnquist ended an era of judicial restraint and conservative activism. Rehnquist's legacy will be far reaching. Decisions in the areas of federalism and the rights of the accused turned the Court to the right. O'Connor's legacy as a swing vote on the Court was also significant. In 2009, Justice David Souter retired. President Obama nominated the first Hispanic-American judge, Sonia Sotomayor, to the Supreme Court. President Obama appointed Solicitor General Elena Kagan to the court after Justice John Stevens retired.

LIMITED NUMBER OF CASES

Even though the Supreme Court receives thousands of cases to review, it chooses only between 75 and 100 cases each session from state courts, courts of appeals, and district courts. Critics claim that the limited number of cases accepted limits the Court's ability to make public policy.

Based on "the rule of four" (a minimum of four justices agreeing to review a case), the Supreme Court's docket is taken up by a combination of appeals cases ranging from the legality of the death penalty to copyright infringement.

Prior to 2000, the court released audiotapes of cases argued on a delayed basis. The Court released audiotapes for the first time in 2000, immediately following the disputed 2000 presidential election and the legal challenges that followed. The tapes were released to the media and were played over the Internet. They continued this practice during subsequent terms whenever there was a case that evoked a large amount of public interest, such as the University of Michigan affirmative action case, the Guantanamo Bay detainee case, and the gay marriage cases.

The process it takes for a writ of certiorari (Latin for "to be made more certain") to be heard is based on five criteria:

- If a court has made a decision that conflicts with precedent.
- If a court has come up with a new question.
- If one court of appeals has made a decision that conflicts with another.
- If there are other inconsistencies between courts of different states.
- If there is a split decision in the court of appeals.

If a writ is granted, the lower court sends to the Supreme Court the transcript of the case that has been appealed. Lawyers arguing for the petitioner and respondent must submit to the Court written briefs outlining their positions on the case. The briefs must be a specified length, must be on a certain color of paper, and must be sent to the Court within a specified period of time. Additional amicus curiae, "friend of the court," briefs may be sent to support the position of one side or the other. Once the case has been placed on the docket, the lawyers are notified, and they begin preparing for the grueling process of oral arguments before the Court. Attorneys are often grilled by the sitting justices for 30 minutes. Often, the Solicitor General of the United States represents the government in cases brought against it. Although these arguments do not usually change the position of the judges, they offer the public an insight into the legal and constitutional issues of the case. After the case is heard, the nine justices meet in conference. A determination is made whether a majority of the justices have an opinion on the outcome of the appeal.

Once a majority is established, sometimes after much jockeying, the Chief Justice assigns a justice to write the majority decision. Opposing justices may write dissenting opinions and if the majority has a different opinion regarding certain components of the majority opinion, they may write concurring opinions. The decision of the case is announced months after it has been reached. Sometimes, when the case is significant, the decision is read by the Chief Justice. At other times a pur curiam decision, a decision without explanation, is handed down. Once a decision is handed down, it becomes public policy. The job of implementing the decision may fall on the executive branch, legislature, or regulatory agencies, or it may require states to change their laws.

Probably one of the most far-reaching cases was *Roe v Wade* (previously discussed), which invalidated a number of state laws. However, a number of cases attempted to redefine the *Roe* doctrine. The fact that the number of cases decided decreased during the Rehnquist years illustrates the restraint of that Court in tampering with Court precedent. Another route of appeal used by people convicted of a crime has been through the writ of habeas corpus. Claiming that their constitutional rights were violated procedurally, criminals appeal their case to the federal courts. In *Herrera v Collins* (1993) the Supreme Court rejected the appeal of a Texas man on death row who claimed that he had new evidence that proved his innocence. The Court ruled that the writ was not in their jurisdiction and sent a clear message to other states that they should handle these appeals.

EFFECT ON PUBLIC POLICY

From the landmark *Marbury v Madison* ruling, to the *Miranda* decision, to the controversies surrounding the separation of church and state, the Supreme Court has had a significant impact on public policy. By looking at the history of the Court, you will be able to see how various chief justices have been identified as contributing to the importance of the Court in the public policy arena.

John Marshall has been given credit for setting the course of the young Supreme Court. When the issue of federal judgeships came to him in the *Marbury* case, Marshall had to find legal rationale to rule that the Judiciary Act of 1789 was unconstitutional. The case revolved around the arguments made by William Marbury, who had been appointed to a minor judgeship by outgoing Federalist President John Adams at the midnight hour of his administration. The incoming

The history of the Supreme Court illustrates its impact on public policy.

Secretary of State, James Madison, refused to deliver the commissions, and Marbury asked the Supreme Court to issue a writ of mandamus directing the executive branch to make the appointments. The argument was made directly to the Supreme Court, using the route of original jurisdiction prescribed by the Judiciary Act. Marshall, who was originally the Secretary of State under Adams responsible for delivering the commissions, was in a real bind. He convinced the rest of the Court that even though Madison was wrong not to deliver the commissions, the Judiciary Act of 1789 was unconstitutional because it did not meet the requirements outlined in the Constitution related to original jurisdiction. The principle of judicial review was established, and the Supreme Court began making crucial policy decisions. Other cases, previously described, such as *Gibbons v Ogden* (1824) and *McCulloch v Maryland* (1819), further strengthened the power of the Marshall Court. The modern court began with the court run by Chief Justice Earl Warren in 1952.

Perhaps the most activist Court in the history of the Supreme Court, the Warren Court (1953–1969) faced the question of determining the future of the civil rights movement. Appointed by President Eisenhower in 1954, Chief Justice Earl Warren convinced a split court that it was essential to overturn the separate but equal doctrine established by *Plessy v Ferguson* (1896). The Court also expanded the rights of the accused and ordered states to reapportion their legislatures (see Chapters 6 and 8).

When Warren retired in 1969, President Nixon had an opportunity to change the face of the Court. He appointed Warren E. Burger, a conservative jurist. He also filled another vacancy by appointing Harry Blackmun to the Court. The Court, however, continued to make rulings that irked those strict constructionists. Even though more conservative than the Warren Court, it continued to break down segregation by ordering bussing to end segregation patterns. It upheld affirmative action programs, and even though it limited aspects of the *Miranda* decision, it continued to recognize the rights of the accused. The Burger Court will be remembered most for the *Roe v Wade* decision. Blackmun also emerged as the Court's liberal spokesperson. Ironically, Burger had to write the majority decision in *United States v Nixon* (1974), which rejected Nixon's claim of executive privilege in not turning over the Watergate tapes.

In 1986, after Republican appointments made by Ford and Reagan, William Rehnquist became the nation's 17th Chief Justice. Along with Sandra Day O'Connor, Anthony Kennedy, and Antonin Scalia, this Court was the most conservative in American history. It began to reverse many of the earlier Warren and Burger rulings. When George Herbert Walker Bush was elected president in 1988, he added to the Court's conservative majority by appointing David Souter and Clarence Thomas. However, Souter took more of a middle-of-the-road approach and emerged as a crucial swing vote in many cases. After Clinton was elected in 1992, he had the opportunity to start the process of reversing the conservatism of the Court by appointing appointees Sonia Sotomayor and Elena Kagan and maintained the liberal minority on the court. The future of the Supreme Court will depend to a large extent on the new coalitions formed and on the outcome of presidential elections. One thing has certainly become evident: a majority may vote one way on one issue, and on another issue an entirely new majority may emerge. In many of these cases, Justices Sandra Day O'Connor and Anthony Kennedy became the important swing votes.

Some of these decisions have been characterized as a new form of judicial activism "conservative activism." The cases that overturned federal laws sent a signal that the federal government was using too much of its inherent powers to create law. In the first four terms that Chief Justice John Roberts has presided over the Supreme Court, the court's majority has been more conservative in their decisions. Along with Justice Alito, Justices Scalia and Thomas—with Kennedy as the swing vote—have tilted the court more to the right.

JUDICIAL PHILOSOPHY

In the early days of the republic, arguments revolving around strict constructionist versus loose constructionist interpretation of the Constitution abounded. Today, we see people arguing whether the Court should be activist or demonstrate judicial restraint. All Supreme Court nominees are asked to describe their judicial philosophy.

The critics of judicial activism make the argument that it is not the Court's responsibility to set policy in areas such as abortion, affirmative action, educational policy, and state criminal law. They feel that the civil liberty decisions have created a society without a moral fiber. The fact that judges are political appointees, are not directly accountable to the electorate, and hold life terms makes an activist court even more unpalatable to some.

On the other hand, proponents of an activist court point to the responsibility of the justices to protect the rights of the accused and minority interests. They point to how long it took for the doctrine of separate but equal to be overturned. And they point to how many states attempt to circumvent court decisions and national law through laws of their own. Proponents of judicial activism also make the argument that you need the Supreme Court to be a watchdog and fulfill its constitutional responsibility of maintaining checks and balances. As Alexander Hamilton wrote in Federalist No. 78, "Laws are dead letters without courts to expound and define their true meaning and operation."

The critics of judicial restraint feel that the interests of government are not realized by a court that refuses to make crucial decisions. They suggest that the federal system will be weakened by a court that allows state laws that may conflict with the Constitution to go unchallenged. Proponents of judicial restraint point to the fact that it is the role of the Congress to make policy and the role of the president to carry it out. They feel that the Court should facilitate that process rather than initiate it. They point to the fact that in many cases the Constitution does not justify decisions in areas where there are no references. The right to an assisted suicide, for instance, became an issue that advocates of judicial restraint urged the Court to reject on the grounds that it was not a relevant federal issue to hear on appeal. The Rehnquist court, in fact, ruled against a group of physicians arguing for the constitutional right to assisted suicide.

One of the ironies in the debate is that those favoring judicial restraint would like to see precedent be the guiding light. However, in declaring congressional laws unconstitutional and creating new precedent, those advocating restraint have themselves become activists.

The debate on whether the Supreme Court should reflect an activist position or exhibit judicial restraint has not been resolved.

Section 1: Multiple-Choice Questions

1. Which of the following represents the best example of a case dealing with original jurisdiction?

   (A) A review of New York and New Jersey arguing over property rights related to Ellis Island
   (B) An appeal by a convict on death row
   (C) A review of the constitutionality of a school district allowing prayer at a graduation ceremony
   (D) A review of President Nixon's decision not to turn over the Watergate tapes to Congress
   (E) A review of a federal law mandating affirmative action in industries that have contracts with the government

2. Which of the following actions requires senatorial courtesy?

   (A) A bill introduced by a senator from one state must get agreement from the other senator in that state.
   (B) Members of the same party agree on the order of legislation.
   (C) Senators from the state in which a judicial appointment is being made by the president are informed of who the candidate is prior to the actual appointment.
   (D) The majority leader of the Senate informs the minority leader who he is appointing as committee chairman.
   (E) The president informs the chairman of the Judiciary Committee of a Supreme Court nominee prior to the announcement.

3. Which of the following committees is responsible for reviewing Supreme Court nominees?

   (A) House Judiciary
   (B) Senate Judiciary
   (C) House Rules
   (D) Senate Appropriations
   (E) House Ways and Means

4. Acceptance of a writ of certiorari is based on all of the following criteria EXCEPT

   (A) a vote by three Supreme Court justices
   (B) a court decision that conflicts with precedent
   (C) a court of appeals decision that conflicts with another court of appeals decision
   (D) inconsistencies between courts of different states
   (E) a split decision in the court of appeals

5. Which represents a major reason for the submission of an amicus curiae brief?

   (A) The Court must rely on precedent cases.
   (B) A friend of the court wishes to provide additional information to the Court.
   (C) Lower courts must provide transcripts of its decisions.
   (D) The Supreme Court requires related interests in the case to submit briefs.
   (E) The brief from the petitioner provides amended information about the case.

6. The Court of which of the following Chief Justices handed down the most activist decisions?

   (A) Salmon Chase
   (B) William Rehnquist
   (C) Earl Warren
   (D) Roger Taney
   (E) Warren Burger

7. An example of a decision that would be classified as activist is

   (A) *San Antonio v Rodriguez* (1973)
   (B) *Dred Scott v Sanford* (1857)
   (C) *Plessy v Ferguson* (1896)
   (D) *Brown v Board of Education* (1954)
   (E) *New Jersey v TLO* (1985)

8. Critics of judicial activism would favor a Supreme Court that would

   (A) give greater protection to the accused
   (B) expand civil rights
   (C) act as a watchdog over the other branches of government
   (D) increase the power of the federal government
   (E) allow the president to influence the opinion of the Court

9. Critics of judicial restraint would favor a Supreme Court that would

   (A) create new precedent
   (B) decrease the power of the federal government
   (C) decrease the power of the state governments
   (D) only agree to hear a limited number of cases
   (E) uphold precedent

Answer Explanations

1. **(A)** Type of Question: Cause-and-effect relationships

   The Constitution defines original jurisdiction as those cases that involve disputes between or among the states. In such instances the case must go directly to the Supreme Court. Most cases get to the Supreme Court on appeal. Thus the only situation that applies to the definition is choice A. Choices B, C, and E are appeals from the state level, and choice D is an appeal based on the constitutionality of executive privilege.

2. **(C)** Type of Question: Sequencing a series of events

   The concept of senatorial courtesy is a tradition that facilitates all judicial appointments to federal courts (not including the Supreme Court). When the president is ready to make the appointment, usually made according to party lines, the president informs and consults with the senators from the state of the appointee. Usually the senators help in the confirmation process.

3. **(B)** Type of Question: Identification and analysis

   According to Article I of the Constitution, the Senate is responsible for "advising and consenting" to presidential appointees to the Supreme Court and other cabinet positions.

The specific Senate committee that makes the initial recommendation to the full Senate is the Senate Judiciary Committee. During the Clarence Thomas hearings, this committee came under much criticism.

4. **(A)** Type of Question: Negative

Choices B, C, D, and E are situations that over the years have become criteria for accepting appeals cases. There is no absolute requirement that states that, if the conditions met in those examples exist, the Court must review the case. However, these examples have become the guiding principles of accepting cases for review. Choice A is incorrect because it is required that four justices agree to hear a case.

5. **(B)** Type of Question: Definitional

If you knew that the definition of amicus curiae is friend of the court, you certainly could pick out the right answer immediately. If you didn't, you could probably proceed to eliminate choice A because, even though it is a truthful statement, it has no relation to the submission of additional briefs. Choice C is also accurate but again does not provide new information. Choice D is a false statement, and briefs do not change information about a case. They make constitutional arguments about the case.

6. **(C)** Type of Question: Chronological

Even though other justices throughout history may have been involved in decisions that have been considered activist, the Chief Justice best known as the leader of an activist court was Earl Warren. Burger's Court continued some of Warren's activism, but it was certainly the intent of Nixon in appointing him to modify the Court's direction.

7. **(D)** Type of Question: Identification and analysis

The classic example of an activist decision is the *Brown* case. The San Antonio case resulted in a decision that affirmed the state's right to fund schools even if it meant that poorer districts did not spend the same amount of money for its students. *Dred Scott* established that slaves were property. *Plessy* affirmed the state's right to allow separate but equal. And New Jersey was able to search TLO without a warrant. These cases are all considered to uphold the principle of judicial restraint.

8. **(C)** Type of Question: Cause-and-effect relationships

Choices A, B, and D are all examples of what proponents of judicial activism would favor. Choice E is the weakest answer since neither activists nor those favoring restraint would want a president to influence Court decisions. Choice C is the correct answer because critics of judicial activism favor a Supreme Court that acts as a watchdog over the other branches of government, ensuring that they do not overstep their authority.

9. **(A)** Type of Question: Cause-and-effect relationships

If the theory behind judicial activism is that courts should break new ground, then Choice A is the correct answer because creating new precedent allows the Court to test new ground. If you think about the Warren Court, that is what it did in cases such as *Brown v Board of Education*, *Miranda v Arizona*, and *Mapp v Ohio*. Choices B, C, D, and E are all characteristics of judicial restraint.

Section 2: Free-Response Question (4 points)

> Depending upon the philosophy of the Supreme Court justices, historically the Court has pursued a policy of judicial activism or judicial restraint.
>
> (a)   Define the terms "judicial activism" and "judicial restraint."
>
> (b)   Choose two of the following and describe one case that can be described as judicial activism and one case that can be described as judicial restraint. Use your definitions from (a) to support your answer.
>
> - rights of the accused
> - affirmative action
> - civil rights

SAMPLE RESPONSE

(a)   Judicial activism and judicial restraint are the two main philosophies that have played major roles in influencing the Supreme Court justices' decisions. Judicial activism is when the judicial branch creates law by overturning precedent, almost doing what the legislative branch in fact does. The Supreme Court is considered to be very strong and sets precedents down for future cases. Judicial restraint occurs when the judicial branch defines and strengthens the law that the legislative branch creates. The Supreme Court in these cases simply upholds legislation. These ideas are present among many areas of public policy and can be outlined in specific cases. These areas include rights of the accused, civil rights, school policy, and affirmative action.

Rights of the Accused

(b)   In the area of the rights of the accused, there has been a pattern of judicial activism. In the matter of *Miranda v Arizona* (1966), the overturned conviction compelled law enforcement officials to carefully inform all suspected persons of their constitutional rights. The Fifth Amendment provides that no person "shall be compelled in any criminal case to be a witness against himself." Miranda was thought to be a prime suspect in the kidnapping/rape of an 18-year-old girl. Miranda was selected by the victim in a police lineup and subsequently questioned for two hours. During the period of his questioning, he was not informed of his constitutional rights against self-incrimination or the right to counsel and proceeded to say enough information that would eventually lead to his conviction. The matter was brought before the Supreme Court and decided in favor of Miranda. This case was also decided under the activist Warren Court as a means of protecting the defendant's rights.

Affirmative Action

In the case of the *Regents of the University of California v Bakke* (1978), the issues of affirmative action and reverse discrimination were dealt with. Allan Bakke, a 32-year-old white male, had applied to the medical school of the University of California at Davis and been flat-out rejected for two years. In place of his acceptance, students with lesser qualifications and minority backgrounds were being admitted over Bakke. The first decision was in favor of Bakke and ordered UC-Davis to admit Bakke into their freshman class. UC-Davis, losing in the California courts, took the matter to the U.S. Supreme Court. The second decision was in concurrence with the first, although leaving the Court badly divided. The decision was rendered under the Burger Court, with the majority opinion coming from Chief Justice

Burger and Justices Powell, Stewart, Rehnquist, and Stevens. The Burger Court did not play a totally activist role because it did not go as far as proponents of affirmative action would have preferred. The Burger Court was more or less settled in a middle ground that enabled it to appease proponents from both sides of the spectrum.

SCORING GUIDELINES FOR FREE-RESPONSE QUESTION (4 POINTS)

Part (a) 2 Points

One point is earned for the definition of judicial activism and one point is earned for the definition of judicial restraint:

- Judicial activism—a court that overturns precedent
- Judicial restraint—a court that believes in "stare decisis," abiding by precedent

Part (b) 2 Points

One point is earned for describing an activist case dealing with either the rights of the accused, affirmative action, or civil rights. One point is earned for describing a case that results in judicial restraint dealing with either the rights of the accused, affirmative action, or civil rights.

Answers may include but are not limited to:

- rights of the accused activist case—***Miranda v Arizona*** (**1966**)—the court established a new set of requirements for police when they detain suspects
- rights of the accused restraint case—***Nix v Williams*** (**1984**)—created an exception to the exclusionary rule
- affirmative action activist case/restraint case—***Regents of the University of California v Bakke*** (**1978**)—activist because it recognized that affirmative action could be used in school admission but restraint because the court outlawed quotas
- civil rights activist case—***Brown v Board of Education*** (**1954**)—overturned the doctrine of separate but equal
- civil rights restraint case—***Heart of Atlanta Hotel v United States*** (**1964**)—the court upheld the constitutionality of the Civil Rights Act of 1964

The Bureaucracy

10

- → BUREAUCRACIES
- → CABINET-LEVEL DEPARTMENT
- → CIVIL SERVICE REFORM
- → DIVISION OF LABOR
- → GOVERNMENT CORPORATION
- → HATCH ACT
- → INDEPENDENT EXECUTIVE AGENCY
- → INDEPENDENT REGULATORY AGENCIES

- → IRON TRIANGLE NETWORK
- → MONOPOLISTIC BUREAUCRACIES
- → PENDLETON ACT
- → QUASI JUDICIAL
- → QUASI LEGISLATIVE
- → RED TAPE
- → REGULATORY POLICY
- → SPOILS SYSTEM

CONTEMPORARY CONNECTION

The total size of the federal work force that makes up the entire federal bureaucracy has decreased over the past 20 years. (See chart on next page.) This chapter explores the organization, function and oversight, and policymaking characteristics of the federal bureaucracy.

When you think about bureaucracies, one of the first things that probably comes to mind is the red tape roadblocks you may have to deal with. However, modern bureaucracies play an important linkage role in government. They are primarily responsible for implementing policy of the branches of government. Some bureaucracies also make policy as a result of regulations they issue.

This chapter also focuses on four types of governmental bureaucratic agencies—the cabinet, regulatory agencies, government corporations, and independent executive agencies. We will also look at the different theories regarding how bureaucracies function. By tracing the history of civil service, you will be able to understand the role patronage has played in the development of government bureaucracies. You will also see how the permanent government agencies became policy implementers and how they must function in relation with the executive branch, legislative branch, and judicial branch.

There have been many attempts to reorganize government to make it more responsive, more efficient, and more effective. The last part of this chapter focuses on the latest efforts to "reinvent" government. Partly a budgetary reform to reduce the deficit and partly an attempt to streamline government, the Clinton administration's efforts in this area have received mixed reviews.

Year	Executive Branch Civilians (Thousands)	Uniformed Military Personnel (Thousands)	Legislative and Judicial Branch Personnel (Thousands)	Total Federal Personnel (Thousands)
1991	3,048	2,040	64	5,152
1992	3,017	1,848	66	4,931
1993	2,947	1,744	66	4,758
1994	2,908	1,648	63	4,620
1995	2,858	1,555	62	4,475
1996	2,786	1,507	61	4,354
1997	2,725	1,439	62	4,226
1998	2,727	1,407	62	4,196
1999	2,687	1,386	63	4,135
2000	2,639	1,426	63	4,129
2001	2,640	1,428	64	4,132
2002	2,630	1,456	66	4,152
2003	2,666	1,478	65	4,210
2004	2,650	1,473	64	4,187
2005	2,636	1,436	65	4,138
2006	2,637	1,432	63	4,133
2007	2,636	1,427	63	4,127
2008	2,692	1,450	64	4,206
2009	2,774	1,591	66	4,430
2010	2,776	1,602	64	4,443
2011	2,756	1,583	64	4,403
2012	2,697	1,551	64	4,312
2013	2,668	1,500	63	4,231

QUICK CONSTITUTIONAL REVIEW OF BUREAUCRACIES

- Constitutional basis found in Article II of the Constitution in the reference to the creation of executive departments.

- Bureaucracies developed as a result of custom, tradition, and precedent.

FUNCTIONS OF BUREAUCRACIES

The United States has turned to bureaucratic agencies as the best way to organize and operate the federal government.

Bureaucracies are defined as large administrative agencies and have their derivation from the French word *bureau*, which refers to the desk of a government worker, and the suffix -*cracy* representing a form of government. Bureaucracies have similar characteristics. They reflect a hierarchical authority, there is job specialization, and there are rules and regulations that drive them.

Approximately four million government workers make up today's federal bureaucracy. The number is even greater if you consider the number of state and local government workers. A little more than 10 percent of the federal employees actually work in Washington, D.C. The majority work in regional offices throughout the country. For instance, each state has many offices dealing with Social Security. About a third of the federal employees work for the armed forces or defense agencies. The number of workers employed by entitlement agencies is relatively small—only about 15-20 percent. The background of federal employees is a mix of ethnic, gender, and religious groups. They are hired as a result of civil service regulations and through political patronage. Even though many people feel bureaucracies are growing, they are in reality decreasing in size.

Workers in federal bureaucracies have different ways of being held accountable. They must respond to

- the Constitution of the United States,
- federal laws,
- the dictates of the three branches of government,
- their superiors,
- the "public interest," and
- interest groups.

Even with the characteristics described, federal workers are complex individuals who are extremely professional in the jobs they are doing.

The federal government is organized by departments, which are given that title to distinguish them from the cabinet. Agencies and administration refer to governmental bodies that are headed by a single administrator and have a status similar to the cabinet. Commissions are names given to agencies that regulate certain aspects of the private sector. They may be investigative, advisory, or reporting bodies. Corporations are agencies headed by a board of directors and have chairmen as heads.

EXECUTIVE-LEVEL DEPARTMENTS

The federal government is organized around the following executive-level departments:

> The formal organization of the federal bureaucracy has a goal of creating an efficient manner of running the government.

- **The cabinet**—There are 15 cabinet departments headed by a secretary (except for the Justice Department, which is headed by the attorney general). The secretaries are appointed by the president with the consent of the Senate. Each department also has undersecretaries, deputies, and assistants. They manage specific policy areas, and each has its own budget and staff.

- **The regulatory agencies**—Known as independent regulatory agencies because they are quasi legislative (they act in a manner that is legislative when issuing regulations) and quasi judicial (they act in a manner that is judicial when enforcing penalties for violations of their regulations) in nature, they are also known as the alphabet agencies. Some examples are:
  - Interstate Commerce Commission (ICC), 1887—The first created independent agency, the ICC regulates specific areas of interstate relations. Historically, it determined which businesses were in violation of the Sherman Antitrust Act.
  - Federal Trade Commission (FTC), 1914—The FTC regulates fair trade, encourages competition, and is responsible for evaluating unfair or deceptive advertising or products that may be unsafe.
  - Food and Drug Administration (FDA), 1931—The FDA regulates the contents, marketing, and labeling of food and drugs.
  - Federal Communications Commission (FCC), 1934—The FCC regulates the television and radio industry and grants licenses to television and radio stations.

- Securities and Exchange Commission (SEC), 1934—Established during the New Deal, it regulates the sale of securities and the stock markets, preventing such abuses as insider trading.
- Environmental Protection Agency (EPA), 1970—Responding to the energy crisis, the EPA implements laws such as the Clean Air Act.
- Occupational Safety and Health Administration (OSHA), 1972—OSHA sets safety and health standards for the work place.
- Consumer Product Safety Commission (CPSC), 1972—CPSC tests and reports about products that may injure the public and issues warnings for those products deemed unsafe.
- Federal Election Commission (FEC), 1975—Created by the Federal Election Campaign Act of 1971, and made even more important as a result of the election abuses uncovered by Watergate, this agency is responsible for monitoring campaign contributions and provides some funding to presidential candidates through matching grants.

- **Government corporations** such as the Tennessee Valley Authority, created during the New Deal, and the Resolution Trust Corporation, created to deal with bankruptcies and the many bank failures of the 1980s—Other corporations are created to take over a failed industry or bail out an essential private industry such as Chrysler.
- **Independent executive agencies** such as the General Services Administration (GSA), which handles government purchasing; the National Science Foundation, which supports scientific research and development; and the National Aeronautics and Space Administration (NASA), which coordinates the country's efforts in outer space.

These agencies each have specific responsibilities that facilitate the day to day operation of the government.

In reality, policy administration of federal bureaucracies has been limited by a number of checks such as

- the legislative power of Congress through legislative intent, congressional oversight, and restrictions on appropriations to agencies;
- the Administrative Procedure Act of 1946, which defines administrative policy and directs agencies to publicize their procedures;
- a built-in review process, either internal or through the court system, for appeal of agency decisions;
- the oversight function of agencies such as the Office of Management and Budget and the General Accounting Office;
- political checks such as pressure brought on by interest groups, political parties, and the private sector that modify bureaucratic behavior.

RELATIONS WITH OTHER GOVERNMENT BRANCHES

> Bureaucracies are linked, but are not subordinate to the other branches of government. They must also be sensitive to interest groups, the media, and public opinion.

Although having an independent nature, bureaucracies are linked to the president by appointment and direction and to Congress through oversight. Agency operations are highly publicized through the media when they have an impact on the public. Interest groups and public opinion try to influence the actions of the agencies.

Bureaucracies are inherently part of the executive branch. Even though the regulatory agencies are quasi independent, they, too, must be sensitive to the president. The president influences bureaucracies through the appointment process.

Knowing that their agency heads are appointed by the president makes them respond to his direction at times. Such agencies as the Environmental Protection Agency (EPA) and the Food and Drug Administration (FDA) have come under executive scrutiny in the 1990s and 2000s. Presidents also issue executive orders that agencies must abide by. The Veteran's Administration (VA) came under close scrutiny in 2014 after a whistle blower revealed lax procedures and fake information regarding care for veterans. The Office of Management and Budget can recommend increases and decreases in proposing new fiscal year budgets. The budgetary process provides the impetus for agency growth. Finally, the president has the power to reorganize federal departments. President Reagan attempted to abolish the Departments of Energy and Education but failed to get the approval of Congress. Congress uses similar tactics to control federal bureaucracies. Because the Senate must approve both presidential appointments and agency budgets, they become sensitive to the issues on Congress's agenda. Through the process of congressional oversight, agency heads are called before congressional committees to testify about issues related to the workings of the agency.

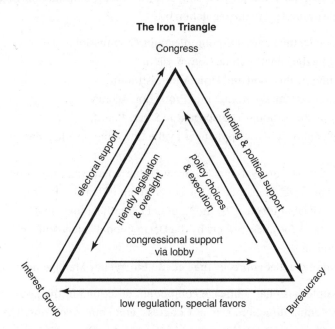

The Iron Triangle

Congress

electoral support

funding & political support

friendly legislation & oversight

policy choices & execution

congressional support via lobby

Interest Group

Bureaucracy

low regulation, special favors

The best example of the interrelationship among bureaucracies, the government, interest groups, and the public is the iron triangle concept. The iron triangle network is a pattern of relationships between an agency in the executive branch, Congress, and special interest groups lobbying that agency. An example of this kind of relationship was the often-criticized military-industrial complex. During the height of the Vietnam War, this relationship between defense-related government agencies and private industry that profited from the war became the antiwar rallying cry of governmental misuse of funds. The close dependence of agencies on interest groups and Congress often results in criticism of that particular agency. If the Environmental Protection Agency has too close a relationship with the industry heads of factories that they are regulating, the potential for abuse certainly exists. If you review the Department of Health and Human Services, you can visualize the iron triangle concept. Their budget is reviewed; legislation that is passed and related to health must be explained to the public; various congressional committees and interest groups such as insurance groups, senior citizen groups, and the medical community review the status of the implementation of law.

PUBLIC POLICY

Bureaucracies implement policy and act as policy regulators.

The major impact of the federal bureaucracy has been in the area of public policy—its implementation and regulation. The independent regulatory agencies, in particular, have had a significant impact in this area.

The Supreme Court decision of *Munn v Illinois* in 1877 is one of the landmark regulatory cases. The case involved a dispute over whether Illinois had the power to regulate the railroad haulage rates of grain. Illinois passed Grange laws that forced the railroad to abide by state rates. The Court determined that because it was in the public interest, the state had the right to regulate this private industry. This ruling influenced the passage of the Interstate Commerce Act and establishment of the Interstate Commerce Commission in 1887. It is ironic that in 1994 this agency came under fire by Congress and was defended by the same interests who were critical of its creation. The railroad and trucking industry were critical of Congress's budget cutbacks of the first independent agency to be created.

You have to only go as far as tracing your daily routine to see how influential regulatory agencies have become. Some examples are the regulation of

- cable television by the Federal Communications Commission,
- food labeling by the Federal Trade Commission,
- meat inspection by the Food and Drug Administration,
- pollution control by the Environmental Protection Agency,
- airline safety by the National Transportation Safety Board,
- safety and reliability of home appliances by the Consumer Product Safety Commission,
- seat belt mandates by the National Highway Traffic Safety Administration,
- gas mileage standards developed by the Department of Transportation,
- the mediation of labor disputes by the National Labor Relations Board,
- factory inspections for worker safety by the Occupational Safety and Health Administration, and
- the coordination of relief efforts by the Federal Emergency Management Agency.

Each of these examples also has a linkage component described in the last section. They were motivated by presidential direction, acts of Congress, and court decisions. The public, interest groups, and the media have reacted to the regulatory and policymaking process. Even though many of these regulations and policies are in the public interest, critics of regulation point to the fact that the costs far exceed the benefits of the entire regulation process. The fear of an overregulated society is one of the issues that is still being debated.

Section 1: Multiple-Choice Questions

1. An advantage that bureaucrats in federal government have over the president in the policymaking process is that bureaucrats

   (A) control the budgetary process
   (B) have an independence from the president that is guaranteed by the Constitution
   (C) find it easier to gather public support than does the president
   (D) usually have a continuity of service in the executive branch that the president lacks
   (E) usually have better access to the media than does the president

2. All of the following influence the Department of Defense's yearly budget EXCEPT

   (A) the desire of the chairman of the Senate Armed Services Committee
   (B) the budget recommendations of the Joint Chiefs of Staff
   (C) the rate of increase of the size of the armed forces
   (D) the number of bases being closed
   (E) the budget request made by the minority party in the House of Representatives

3. Cabinet-level agencies are responsible to

   (A) Congress
   (B) the president
   (C) the courts
   (D) the White House staff
   (E) the executive office of the president

4. Many contemporary politicians have come to see bureaucracies as agencies

   (A) that aim to make realistic recommendations that may result in lower budgets than the year before
   (B) whose main objective is to seek profits
   (C) whose major goal is to cut back on their powers
   (D) who strive to maximize their budgets and powers
   (E) who work more closely with the judiciary

5. According to some political scientists, which policymaking group is largely responsible for the growth of modern governments?

   (A) Bureaucracies
   (B) Congress
   (C) The president
   (D) Private business
   (E) The courts

6. All of the following are characteristics of the independent regulatory agency EXCEPT

   (A) It has responsibility for some sector of the economy.
   (B) It makes rules designed to protect the public interest.
   (C) It enforces rules designed to protect the public interest.
   (D) Its powers are so great that it is often called the "fourth branch of the government."
   (E) It is exempt from court rulings.

7. All of the following are examples of independent regulatory agencies EXCEPT

   (A) the Interstate Commerce Commission (ICC)
   (B) the Federal Communications Commission (FCC)
   (C) the Federal Reserve Board (FRB)
   (D) the Securities and Exchange Commission (SEC)
   (E) the Central Intelligence Agency (CIA)

8. Bureaucratic policy implementation includes all of the following elements EXCEPT

   (A) the ability to abolish a nonfunctioning department in another agency
   (B) the ability to create new operating procedures within its own agency
   (C) the ability to assign new responsibilities within its own agency
   (D) the ability to translate policy goals into operational rules for its own personnel
   (E) the ability to coordinate its own resources and personnel to achieve intended goals

9. Administrative regulations contain all of the following elements EXCEPT

   (A) a grant of power and a set of directions from Congress
   (B) a set of rules and guidelines by the regulatory agency itself
   (C) power granted to the Justice Department to enforce heavy sanctions, including abolishing the agency
   (D) a means of enforcing compliance with congressional goals and agency regulations
   (E) a set of penalties for noncompliance

10. When a president tries to control a bureaucratic agency, all of the following methods are available to him EXCEPT

    (A) appointing the right people to head the agency
    (B) reducing the agency's budget
    (C) issuing executive orders
    (D) recommending a reduction of the agency's following year's budget
    (E) using his office to influence agency direction

11. Which of the following results from an iron triangle relationship?

    (A) Each policy being made independently from the others
    (B) Policies being made that are contradictory from others
    (C) A lack of an integrated, coherent approach to broad policy problems
    (D) A cooperative relationship among a special interest group, a bureaucratic agency, and Congress
    (E) A hostile relationship among the bureaucratic agencies making policy

12. In recent years presidential policy with respect to the federal bureaucracy has been to

   (A) favor an increase in the number of workers to cope with the complexity of federal programs
   (B) favor significant budget increases to fund new programs
   (C) favor a downsizing and reorganization of the work force
   (D) request the creation of new agencies to regulate the transportation industry
   (E) request the elimination of the Central Intelligence Agency

Answer Explanations

1. **(D)** Type of Question: Cause-and-effect relationships
   Using process of elimination, you can come up with the answer to this question. Congress controls the budgetary process of bureaucratic agencies. Even though some bureaucratic agencies have an independence from the president (mostly the independent regulatory agencies), this independence stems from laws passed by Congress. Choice C is incorrect because bureaucrats usually distance themselves from the public and do not usually have close contact with the media. Because many bureaucrats are appointed for longer terms than the president or have civil service appointments, they have a continuity of service.

2. **(E)** Type of Question: Negative
   The question aims at making the student recognize the many different ways that a department budget can be influenced. Choices A, B, C, and D would all contribute to a potential increase in the Defense Department's budget. Choice E, though having a minimal impact, would not be a significant influence since the minority party does not control the agenda.

3. **(B)** Type of Question: Identification and analysis
   Because cabinet heads are appointed by the president, you can argue that these agencies are responsible to the person actually making the appointments. Therefore, the agency is ultimately responsible to the president. Congress does have some control through the budgetary process and using congressional oversight.

4. **(D)** Type of Question: Hypothetical
   Because bureaucracies have developed the reputation of wanting to create so-called empires of power, many politicians have become skeptical. In fact, there have been calls to abolish the Departments of Education and Energy. Therefore, choice D represents what many legislators see as a drawback of the modern bureaucracy.

5. **(A)** Type of Question: Cause-and-effect relationships
   Even though Congress and the president have a direct relationship in creating bureaucracies, it is the bureaucracies themselves that have been criticized for being responsible for the growth of government. That is why President Clinton and Vice President Gore came out with REGO, or reinventing government, by downsizing the federal government.

6. **(E)** Type of Question: Negative
   Choices A, B, C, and D are all characteristics of an independent regulatory agency. Think of examples of these agencies such as the Food and Drug Administration or Environmental Protection Agency, and you will be able to make the connections. Court rulings can negate regulations from these agencies.

7. **(E)** Type of Question: Negative

The characteristics listed in Question 6 all must apply to these agencies. The Central Intelligence Agency may want to act independently at times in the name of national security. However, it is directly responsible to the president. The other agencies in the question all have independent status.

8. **(A)** Type of Question: Negative

The point of this question is that bureaucratic policies are carried out within the department. Choices B, C, D, and E reflect that issue. Choice A goes beyond the parameter suggesting that policy implementation includes the abolition of a nonfunctioning department in another agency. That is not within the authority of a bureaucracy.

9. **(C)** Type of Question: Negative

The enforcement of sanctions and the ability to abolish an agency is given to the executive and legislative branches of government. Choices A, B, D, and E are administrative responsibilities given to bureaucratic agencies themselves.

10. **(B)** Type of Question: Negative

The budgets of bureaucratic agencies are determined by legislative action only. The president can appoint chairs of agencies, can issue an executive order that may negate an agency directive, can recommend a reduction or increase in the budgets of these agencies, and can try to use a bully pulpit to influence the direction of an agency.

11. **(D)** Type of Question: Cause-and-effect relationships

Thinking of a specific example like the military-industrial complex during the Vietnam War gives you the answer to this question. By definition, an iron triangle relationship exists when a bureaucratic agency, special interest group, and legislative arm work hand in hand to develop policies.

12. **(C)** Type of Question: Generalization

With the implementation of the reinventing government program of the Clinton administration, the trend of both the executive and legislative branches has been to downsize and reorganize the federal work force. This has led to a return of many programs to the states where they too had to deal with the issue of the size of their agencies.

Section 2: Free-Response Question (6 points)

> Bureaucratic agencies have the authority to impose regulations on states and local governments even if it means that the legislation imposes unfunded mandates on them. Since the 1990s, there has been opposition to agencies having this type of power and laws passed imposing unfunded mandates.
>
> (a) Define the term unfunded mandate and explain why states have opposed them.
>
> (b) Identify one bureaucratic agency that has quasi-legislative power and give one example of a law that agency regulated that imposed unfunded mandates on the state.
>
> (c) Explain how the unfunded mandate described in (b) impacted the states.

SAMPLE RESPONSE

(a) Unfunded mandates are policies imposed on the states by the federal government. These policies can be in the form of laws or quasi-legislative directives from bureaucratic agencies. They are called unfunded mandates because the states are required to implement the policies and also pay for them, regardless of whether the states support the objective of the policy.

(b) A bureaucratic agency that has quasi-legislative power is the Environmental Protection Agency, known as the EPA. It has the authority to regulate and implement laws passed by Congress that impact the environment. One such law the EPA regulated that imposed unfunded mandates on the state was the 1972 Clean Air Act.

   (Please note: Other laws passed by Congress, such as the Clean Water Act, can also be used to answer the question.)

(c) The impact of this mandate on the states is far reaching. The unfunded mandate imposed by the EPA, as part of the 1972 Clean Air Act, required states to establish guidelines to control pollutants. The EPA is responsible for developing specific air-quality standards as a way to achieve the goals set forth by the act. It executes the provisions of law by establishing national pollution limitations, such as requiring automobiles to meet emission standards and factories to establish pollutant controls. The EPA also established penalties for violators of the law. It conducted investigations based on complaints and instituted lawsuits to enforce its environmental regulations. An outgrowth of the law is an oversight process established as part of the law. It enables Congress to hold hearings in order to monitor how well the law is working. As a result, other laws, including updated versions of the Clean Air Act, the Clean Water Act, and the establishment of a Superfund were passed. With each new law, the EPA was given more responsibility to implement the law. A specific example of how the EPA created a regulation that impacted on the states was the imposition of centralized emission control stations to replace local service stations doing smog tests in those states that had higher than normal pollution problems. Many of the affected states were not prepared to implement the directive and had to ask for a waiver. Thus, the process of law to regulation sometimes results in the regulation not always being implemented.

SCORING GUIDELINES FOR FREE-RESPONSE QUESTION (6 POINTS)

Part (a) 2 Points

One point is earned for the definition of unfunded mandates and one point is earned for explaining why they are called unfunded mandates:

- an unfunded mandate is a policy that is imposed on the states by the federal government.
- they are called unfunded mandates because the states must pay for them

Part (b) 2 Points

One point is earned for identifying an agency, and one point is earned for giving an example of a law that agency regulated.

Answers may include but are not limited to:

- The Environmental Protection Agency—Clean Air Act, Clean Water Act
- The Occupational Safety and Health Administration—Workplace laws
- Food and Drug Administration—labeling of food and drug laws

Part (c) 2 Points

One point is earned for giving a legislative example of how the Unfunded Mandates Act impacted the states and one point is earned for giving a legislative example of how the Unfunded Mandates Act impacted the federal government.

Answers may include but are not limited to:

- impact on the states—the Clean Air and Clean Water Act established a Superfund
- impact on the federal government—the Environmental Protection Agency had to issue regulations
- impact on the states—the Americans with Disabilities Act forced state governments to fund handicap-accessible improvements in all state facilities
- impact on the federal government—Americans with Disabilities Act—the Department of Justice monitors complaints regarding enforcement of the act

Political Parties, Elections, Political Beliefs, the Media, and Special Interest Groups

PART FOUR

Political Parties, Elections, Political Beliefs, the Media and Social Interest Groups

Political Parties and Political Action

11

→ DEMOCRATIC PARTY

→ DIVIDED GOVERNMENT

→ LINKAGE INSTITUTION

→ MCGOVERN-FRASIER COMMISSION

→ NATIONAL COMMITTEE

→ NATIONAL NOMINATING CONVENTIONS

→ NEW DEMOCRAT

→ PARTY DEALIGNMENT

→ PARTY ERA

→ PARTY IDENTIFICATION

→ PARTY MACHINE

→ PARTY PLATFORMS

→ PARTY REALIGNMENT

→ POLITICAL PARTICIPATION

→ POLITICAL PARTY

→ POLITICAL SOCIALIZATION

→ REAGAN DEMOCRATS

→ REFORM PARTY

→ RELIGIOUS RIGHT

→ REPUBLICAN PARTY

→ SUPERDELEGATES

→ TEA PARTY

→ THIRD POLITICAL PARTIES

→ TWO-PARTY SYSTEM

CONTEMPORARY CONNECTION

Divided government, where one party controls the executive branch, while the opposition party controls one or both houses of Congress, was favored by a majority of the American people in the 2014 midterm election. That election, when the Republicans gained control of the House of Representatives and the Senate, brought divided government to both houses of Congress. This chapter explores the nature, function, and organization of political parties and how and why people identify with a particular party. The chapter also looks at how individuals can get involved in the political process through political participation and political action.

The four main linkage institutions are political parties, elections, the media, and interest groups. To fully understand the function of these informal institutions of government, you should view them as input agents that result in output from the policymaking institutions covered in the last section.

The first linkage institution, political parties and the manner in which they influence policy-making through political action, will be developed in this chapter. It will cover the major tasks, organization, and components of political parties. We will contrast the party organization with its actual influence on the policymakers in government. Then we will look at the history of the party system in America, evaluating the major party eras. The impact of third parties on the two-party system will also be discussed.

We will also analyze the ideology of the two major parties by looking at their platforms versus the liberal/conservative alliances that have developed. These coalitions may be the first step in the breakdown of the two-party system as we know it.

The last part of the chapter focuses on the political participation of the average citizen ranging from conventional means of influencing government to more radical, unconventional tools that have influenced our elected officials.

THE TWO-PARTY SYSTEM

Political parties have various functions and serve as one of the primary linkage institutions to government.

If the definition of politics is "who gets when, what, how, and why," then political parties are the means to achieve that end. The nature of the party system in America can be viewed as competitive. Since the development of our first parties, the Federalists and Democratic-Republicans, different philosophies and different approaches to the development and implementation of public policy have determined which party and which leaders control the government. Our system has been one of the few two-party systems existing in democracies; however, the influence of third-party candidates cannot be underestimated. Parliamentary democracies have multiparty governments.

Because the aim of a political party is to influence public policy, in order to succeed, parties must draw enough of the electorate into their organization and ultimately must get enough votes to elect candidates to public office. You can, therefore, look at a political party in three ways:

- the party as an organization,
- the party's relationship with the electorate, and
- the party's role in government.

In order to achieve their goals, all political parties have common functions:

- nominating candidates who can develop public policy,
- running successful campaigns,
- developing a positive image,
- raising money,
- articulating these issues during the campaign so that the electorate will identify with a particular party or candidate,
- coordinating in the governing process the implementation of the policies they supported, and
- maintaining a watchdog function if they do not succeed in electing their candidates.

The completion of each of these tasks depends on how effective the party's organization is, the extent the party establishes its relationship with the electorate, and how it controls the institutions of government. A complete discussion of these components and functions will take place in other parts of the chapter.

Party Eras

The first party era (1828–1860) was characterized by the Democrats dominating the presidency and Congress. The second period (1860–1932) could be viewed as the Republican era. The third era (1932–1968) gave birth to the success of the New Deal and was dominated by the Democrats. The fourth period (1968 to present) has been called the era of divided government. It has been characterized by the election of a president from one party having to deal with an opposition party in one or both houses of Congress.

A new party era may have been ushered in, signaled by the Republican takeover of Congress in 1994. The Republican takeover and the reelection of President Clinton suggests that the era of divided government may be long lasting. In the 2000 election, divided government became the theme. First, in the presidential election, Vice President Al Gore received more popular votes than George W. Bush but still lost the electoral vote. Congress initially remained Republican, but was closely divided. Then in 2001, the Democrats gained a majority in the Senate after a Republican senator left the party. After the midterm election in 2002, the Republicans again solidified their majority, retaking control of the Senate and increasing their majority in the House of Representatives. The 2004 election may have signaled a return of a Republican majority as George W. Bush was reelected by a popular vote majority for the first time since his father won in 1988, and the Republicans increased their majorities in both the House and Senate. In 2006, the midterm election—dominated by the Iraq war, what some called the Bush administration's "culture of corruption," and dissatisfaction with President Bush's job performance—resulted in a Democratic takeover of Congress. The Democrat incumbents did not lose a single seat and gained 29 seats in the House and six seats in the Senate. The results of this election could be attributed to an unpopular president and a war that had lost public support. One thing is certain. Republican gains in the once-Democratic South suggest a continuation of the party realignment in that area of the country.

The 2008 presidential election was a short-lived start of a new party era—one party majority rule. Barack Obama had the largest congressional majority since Lyndon Johnson, who enjoyed a large Democratic majority in both houses of Congress. The era of divided government has shifted to this new era of one party dominance of the executive and legislative branches. This changed after the 2010 midterm election when Republicans regained control of the House of Representatives. In 2014, the GOP also gained more seats in the House and a majority in the Senate, strengthening their hand in policy debates with the president. Many political scientists question the strength of party eras because of the weakening of political parties as illustrated by the increasing number of independent voters, and the rise of the Tea Party. The 2000s can be described as a time where one party had majority rule until a "wave" election brought divided government.

Party Realignment

Party realignment, the shift of party loyalty, occurred in 1932 after the country experienced the Great Depression. Fed up with the trickle-down economic theories of Herbert Hoover, the public turned to the New Deal policies of Franklin Roosevelt. A new coalition of voters supported FDR's New Deal. They included city dwellers, blue collar workers, labor union activists, the poor, Catholics, Jews, the South, and African-Americans where they could vote. An unusual alliance of Northern liberals and Southern conservatives elected Roosevelt to an unprecedented four terms. This coalition, with the exception of Eisenhower's election, held control of the White House and Congress until 1968. A direct comparison can be made among Roosevelt's New Deal, Kennedy's New Frontier, and Johnson's Great Society philosophy and election coalition. The growth of the federal government and the growth of social programs became part of the Democratic platform. However, a party realignment began as Johnson fought for civil rights legislation. The Democratic "solid south" turned increasingly Republican both on the state and national level as white voters rejected the Democratic support for civil rights. In 1980, the so-called Reagan Democrats, blue-collar workers, signaled a new party realignment to the Republican Party.

Period of Divided Government

The Vietnam War and the issue of how this country would fight communism brought the Republicans back to power in 1968. Since then, they have won six of eight presidential elections but were unable to control Congress until 1994. That is why this modern period has been called the period of divided government. The Watergate scandal and Nixon's resignation in 1974 saw a weakened GOP and the eventual loss by Gerald Ford to Jimmy Carter in 1976. That election signaled a new Southern strategy, which Ronald Reagan was able to capitalize on in 1980. Pulling what has been labeled as "Reagan Democrats," Reagan attracted a traditional Democratic base of middle-class workers to his candidacy. It became even more divided from 1981 to 1986 when the Republicans were able to control the Senate. Divided government also existed on the state level with a minority of states controlling both the governorship and state legislatures. Besides being divided on party lines, government became divided on ideological lines. Political scientists began referring to the nation as divided into the "blue states" won by the Democrats and the "red states" won by the Republicans after the 2000 election.

With the election of Bill Clinton in 1992 and his reelection in 1996, the emergence of an ideological party era seemed to be on the horizon. Even though Clinton had a Democratic majority in both houses during his first term, much of his legislative agenda was embroiled in an ideological battle among liberals, moderates, and conservatives who did not always vote along party lines. The rise of the so-called religious right, an evangelical conglomeration of ultraconservative political activists joining the Republican Party, has contributed to this rise of an ideological party era. The attempt at bipartisanship has been replaced by temporary coalitions depending upon the issue of the day.

After the 2000 election, coalitions became even more important since the House was so closely divided and the Democrats had a one-vote majority in the Senate. A good example of the development of a moderate coalition was the one that formed to pass a major tax reduction package and the "No Child Left Behind" education law in 2001.

After the 2006 midterm election, the Democrats regained control of both houses of Congress, and divided government was once again the rule. President George W. Bush faced a hostile House of Representatives, locking horns with Speaker Nancy Pelosi over the direction of the Iraq War. In the Senate the Democrats held a narrow majority, and because major pieces of legislation required a 60-vote majority, Bush was able to block most of the Democratic agenda. Bush did not veto a single piece of legislation during his first term. However, in his second term, facing a Democratic majority, he vetoed 12 pieces of legislation, including legislation dealing with stem cell research, troop funding, and children's health insurance. The Democrats were not able to override any of these vetoes. After Barack Obama was elected in 2008 the Democrats had a majority in both houses until the 2010 and 2014 midterm elections when the Republican Party gained control of the House of Representatives and in 2014 the Senate in what was called "wave election(s)," an election where one party replaces the majority party with a new majority.

THIRD PARTIES

Third political parties, also called minor parties, have played a major role in influencing the outcome of elections and the political platforms of the Democrats and Republicans. Even though these smaller parties and their leaders realize that they have virtually no chance to win, they still wage a vocal campaign. These third political parties can be described as ideological, single-issue oriented, economically motivated, and personality driven. They have been called Socialist, Libertarian, Right to Life, Populist, Bull Moose, and United We Stand. But they all have one thing in common—an effort to influence the outcome and direction of an election. Let's look at some of the more successful third-party attempts.

The modern third-party impact has revolved around a political leader who could not get the nomination from his party. George Wallace's American Independent Party of 1968 opposed the integration policies of the Democratic Party, and he received 13 percent of the vote and 46 electoral votes, contributing to Hubert Humphrey's defeat in a very close election. John Anderson's defection from the Republican Party in 1980 and his decision to run as a third-party candidate had a negligible effect on the outcome of that election.

The announcement by Texas billionaire H. Ross Perot that he was entering the 1992 presidential race, and using his own money to wage the campaign, changed the nature of that race. He announced his intention to run on CNN's *Larry King Show* and said that if his supporters could get his name on the ballot in all 50 states he would officially enter the race. A political novice, he decided to drop out of the race the day Bill Clinton was nominated. He then reentered the heated contest in October, appeared in the presidential debates, and struck a chord with close to 20 percent of the electorate. His folksy style and call for reducing the nation's deficit played a significant role in the campaign. He did not win a single electoral vote, but won almost 20% of the popular vote. Third parties became less important in the 2000s. Ralph Nader running as the Green Party candidate hurt Al Gore's chance in the contested 2000 election.

PARTY DEALIGNMENT

If party realignment signifies the shifts in the history of party eras, then people gradually moving away from their parties has become more of a trend in today's view of party loyalty. This shift to a more neutral and ideological view of party identification has been called party dealignment. Party dealignment is also characterized by voters who are fed up with both parties and register as independents. This trend has been on the rise, and in party identification surveys more than one third of voters identify themselves as independents. In fact those people who are strong party loyalists are so because they believe that the party matches their ideology. The shift of traditional Southern Democrats to the Republican Party came about because many voters perceived the Republicans as a more conservative party than the Democrats. Women activists, civil rights supporters, and people who believe in abortion make up the Democratic coalition because the Democratic Party has supported these issues in their national platform. Party organization and party support have remained stronger than party identification because of the ability of the parties to raise funds and motivate their workers.

Democrats and Republicans have been viewed as having few differences between them. Ideology has become more important than party identification.

Although considered unimportant by many, party platforms are perhaps a better barometer of party identification than traditional measurements. If you look at the 2012 national party platform of the Democratic and Republican Parties, you can see the effect ideological differences had on voter support. A few examples are on the next page.

Even though the party positions differ significantly, it is interesting to note that, when actual legislation is proposed, there is very rarely bloc voting on these issues.

Then how do you determine what constitutes a liberal or conservative ideology? Political labels are deceptive. You may be a social liberal or a civil libertarian but be a conservative when it comes to the role of government in regulating business. If you have a single issue like abortion that is most important, it will make very little difference whether a candidate is a Democrat or Republican. In 2014 a widely reported poll asked people to classify themselves as liberal, moderate, or conservative. Forty-two percent identified themselves as Independent, thirty-one percent as Democrat, and twenty-five percent as Republican. In another poll, when asked what it is meant to be labeled a liberal, people responded in terms of

- accepting change,
- supporting programs that increase spending,
- favoring social programs, and
- believing in the rights of all people.

When asked what it is meant to be a conservative they responded with the following descriptions:

- resistant to change,
- thrifty,
- traditional, and
- narrow-minded.

SYMBOL OF THE DEMOCRATIC PARTY

SYMBOL OF THE REPUBLICAN PARTY

In 2012, the Democratic and Republican parties stressed economic issues and national security issues. The stands on social issues remained the same as the 2008 platforms. Health care was a major plank of both platforms. The Democrats supported the president's Affordable Care Act, which the Supreme Court affirmed, while the Republicans supported a repeal of what they called Obamacare. The Republican platform indicted President Obama for his failure to reduce the unemployment rate to under 8%, while the Democrats pointed to the number of jobs that were created since the president took office in 2009. There were also significant differences in the areas of support of labor unions (Democrats supporting them; Republicans critical) and repeal of the so-called Bush era tax cuts (the Democrats favoring repeal for those who made more than $250,000 while Republicans were against repeal.)

Liberals and Conservatives

These general areas translate into specific liberal/conservative differences when applied to actual issues. For instance, on foreign policy, liberals favor defense cuts. Conservatives, on the other hand, favor government spending on defense over social welfare programs. On social issues liberals favor freedom of choice for abortions, whereas conservatives favor the right to life. Liberals are opposed to school prayer of any kind; conservatives favor moments of silent prayer. Liberals generally view the government as a means of dealing with the problems facing society, whereas conservatives favor a more laissez-faire position. Liberals have been more sympathetic to the rights of the accused, and conservatives have been critical of many of the Warren Court decisions. Yet when you apply these standards to specific bills, there is a clouding up of which party is liberal and which party is conservative.

The term *New Democrat* was applied to President Clinton. Whether this was a public relations gimmick to make Clinton and the Democrats appear to be more conservative, or whether the traditional New Deal liberalism of the party was being modified, is still not clear. Serious differences do exist between the parties. Part of the differences derive from the fact that one party is in power and controls the agenda and that the party out of power must fight to keep their ideas alive. And there are still constituencies that are attracted to the two parties—for instance big business to the Republicans and labor unions to the Democrats.

The Tea Party

Defying liberal and conservative labels, a new party emerged prior to the 2010 midterm election. The Tea Party, named after the colonists who protested against taxes imposed by the British Crown in 1773, was organized by a combination of grassroots Americans and former leaders of the Republican Party. Even though they did not officially petition to get on state ballots, they held a party convention and endorsed many congressional candidates in primary races, successfully defeating a number of Republican Senators and Congressmen and women. After the primaries, the party also endorsed Republican gubernatorial and congressional candidates, many of whom won. Former Alaska governor and 2008 vice-presidential candidate Sarah Palin embraced the movement and became one of their biggest supporters.

The Tea Party's slogan "take back America," refers to its philosophy that a government is best when it governs the least. The Tea Party opposes government spending without cuts in other government programs, favors tax cuts and a balanced budget, and points to the Declaration of Independence and a strict interpretation of the Constitution and the Bill of Rights as their guiding principles.

The Tea Party movement was a big factor in the 2010 midterm elections supporting insurgent candidates to run against Republicans in primaries. They were not successful in opposing President Obama's reelection, and in 2014 they failed to get any of their candidates elected in Republican Senate primaries. They were able to defeat the House majority leader in a primary.

ORGANIZATION

Political parties exist on both the national and local levels. Their organization is hierarchical. Grass roots politics on the local level involves door-to-door campaigns to get signatures on petitions, campaigns run through precinct and ward organizations, county committees, and state committees headed by a state chairman. Local party bosses like Boss Tweed or party machines like the Democratic Tammany machine in New York City or the Daley machine in Chicago have lessened in influence. The national political scene is dominated by the outcome of national conventions, which give direction to the national chairperson, the spokesperson of the party, and the person who heads the national committee. The party machine exists on the local level and uses patronage (rewarding loyal party members with jobs) as the means to keep the party members in line.

> The organization of national political parties helps maintain party discipline. However, local party organizations and their party machines have a major influence on the outcome of elections.

The nominating process drives the organization of the national political party. This procedure has evolved, and, even though the national nominating convention (more on this in the next chapter) still selects presidential candidates, the role of the party caucus and party primary has grown in importance. The role of the national convention is one of publicizing the party's position. It also adopts party rules and procedures. Sometimes this plays an important part in the restructuring of a political party. After the disastrous 1968 Democratic Convention, with rioting in the streets and calls for party reform, the McGovern-Frasier Commission brought significant representation changes to the party. It made future conventions more democratic. Delegate selection procedures aimed to include more minority representation. In 1982 another commission further reformed the representation of the Democratic convention by establishing 15 percent of the delegates as superdelegates (party leaders and elected party officials). These delegates helped Walter Mondale achieve his nomination in 1984 and enabled Al Gore to defeat Bill Bradley easily in 2000. Superdelegates played a significant role in the 2008 Democratic primaries. Primary elections were completed in June, and neither Barack Obama nor Hillary Clinton had a majority of the delegates.

Ultimately, the superdelegates turned to Obama, giving him a majority and enabling him to clinch the nomination. There has been some criticism that these delegates have reduced the democratic reforms of the McGovern Commission.

On the other hand, the Republicans were more concerned about regenerating party identification after the Watergate debacle. They were not interested in reform as much as making the Republican Party more efficient. Their conventions are well run and highly planned. There was, however, some negative publicity at their 1992 convention, which critics said was dominated by the conservative faction of the party. The lesson was learned. In 1996, 2000, 2004, 2008, and 2012 both the Republican and Democratic Conventions were so highly scripted that political scientists concluded that it would be virtually impossible to make a similar mistake.

The National Committee

The national committee, made up of a combination of state and national party leaders, is the governing body of the political party. It has limited power and responds to the direction of the national chairperson. The chairperson is selected by the presidential candidates nominated at the convention. In fact, the real party leader of the party in power is the president himself. The chairperson is recognized as the chief strategist and often takes the credit or blame if gains or losses occur in midterm elections. Some of the primary duties of the national chairperson are fundraising, fostering party unity, recruiting new voters and candidates, and preparing strategy for the next election. Also, congressional campaign committees in both parties work with their respective national committees to win Senate and House seats that are considered up for grabs.

POLITICAL PARTICIPATION

The future of political parties depends on the extent of positive political participation of the electorate and the ability to succeed in creating and implementing public policy.

Participation in the political process is the key gauge of how successful political parties are in involving the average citizen. If you develop the actual vote as the key criteria, the future is certainly not bright. Unlike many foreign countries, the American electorate has not turned out in droves in local or national elections. The reasons why people vote depend on a number of factors including family income, age, education, party identification, and race. Then what does the future hold for the Democrats and Republicans? To answer this question, you must look at the continuum of political involvement.

There is no doubt that statistically the majority of the electorate participates in the political process in conventional ways. From those areas that the majority of people participate to those areas that a minority participate, the population as a whole generally is involved in one or more of the following:

- discussing politics;
- registering to vote;
- voting in local, state, and national elections;
- joining a specific political party;
- making contact with politicians either by letter or phone;
- attending political meetings;
- contributing to political campaigns;
- working in a campaign;
- soliciting funds; and
- running for office.

Yet one of the ironies of conventional political participation is that less than half of those who are eligible actually vote in most elections.

Unconventional participation involves protest and civil disobedience. Activists such as Dr. Martin Luther King, Jr. have influenced the political process through mass meetings such as the March on Washington in 1963. Elected officials responded by passing the Civil Rights Act of 1964.

The future of political parties depends on how closely associated the voters remain with the party. The future is not bright for traditional party politics. There is a sharp decline in party enrollment and an increase in the affiliation of voters calling themselves independents. More and more ticket splitting (where voters cast their ballots not on party lines, but rather based upon each individual candidate running for a particular office) has taken place. The impact of the media on the campaign has weakened the ability of the party to get its message out. Finally, the impact of special-interest groups and PACs has reduced the need for elected officials to use traditional party resources.

Suggestions have been made to strengthen voter identification with the party by presenting

- clearly defined programs on how to govern the nation once their candidates are elected,
- candidates who are committed to the ideology of the party and who are willing to carry out the program once elected, and
- alternative views if it is the party out of power.

The winning party must take on the responsibility of governing the country if elected and accepting the consequences if it fails. This responsible party model would go a long way in redefining the importance of political parties in America. Even though there is a recognized decline in the importance of political parties, it is highly doubtful that our two-party system will change to a multiparty or ideological party system in the future.

Section 1: Multiple-Choice Questions

1. Which of the following defines a team of men (and women) banding together seeking to control the governing apparatus by gaining office in a duly constituted election?

    (A) Political party
    (B) Political opportunism
    (C) Political constituency
    (D) Political agenda
    (E) Political policy

2. All of the following are characteristics of politics EXCEPT

    (A) individuals with similar ideas banding together to form political parties
    (B) the means by which individuals and groups get involved
    (C) who gets what, when, how, and why
    (D) the passage of laws that serve to further minority rights
    (E) the interrelationship of individuals and groups

3. Relationships among which of the following exist in political parties?

    (A) The party and the electorate
    (B) The party and the individual
    (C) The party and the government
    (D) The party and the candidate
    (E) The party and the courts

4. Which of the following translate inputs from the public into outputs from the policymakers?

    (A) Linkage institutions
    (B) Bureaucratic institutions
    (C) Agenda setters
    (D) Policy setters
    (E) Policy coordinators

5. Which of the following philosophies is reflected by the majority of the American electorate?

    (A) A middle-of-the-road philosophy
    (B) Extremely liberal philosophy
    (C) Extremely conservative philosophy
    (D) Radical philosophy
    (E) Reactionary philosophy

6. In the long history of the American party system, successful parties rarely stray from

    (A) supporting big government
    (B) a liberal point of view
    (C) a conservative point of view
    (D) the midpoint of public opinion
    (E) a reactionary point of view

7. Which of the following best describes the history of American political parties?

   (A) America has had a one-party system with two branches.
   (B) America has always responded to a multi-partied system.
   (C) America has had two parties that have consistently dominated the political arena.
   (D) America has always had a three-party system.
   (E) Third political parties have rarely had an impact on the two major parties.

8. Which of the following results after a critical election occurs?

   (A) Redistricting
   (B) Party realignment
   (C) Party dealignment
   (D) Gerrymandering
   (E) Coalition division

9. Which of the following terms means that people are gradually moving away from both parties?

   (A) Dealignment
   (B) Realignment
   (C) Gerrymandering
   (D) Reevaluation
   (E) Criticism

10. Which characteristic reflects party politics of the 1990s?

   (A) Southern liberals and Southern conservatives alike vote with the Republican Party.
   (B) The Republican Party's base is in the Northeast.
   (C) Conservative Southerners shy away from the Republican label.
   (D) The Democrats' Solid South no longer exists in national elections.
   (E) The religious right favors Democratic candidates.

11. Which of the following molds the values a person develops?

   (A) Personal ideology
   (B) Party identification
   (C) Political socialization
   (D) Party dealignment
   (E) Party realignment

12. Which of the following determines the party platform?

   (A) The national convention
   (B) The presidential candidate
   (C) The party bosses
   (D) The local party
   (E) The state party

13. Which of the following time periods reflects a change from the dominance of the Republicans as the nation's majority party?

(A) The Great Depression
(B) The Roaring Twenties
(C) World War I
(D) World War II
(E) The Cold War

14. In which of the following institutions have the Republicans consistently been the minority party from 1968 to 1994?

(A) House of Representatives
(B) Senate
(C) Elected judgeships
(D) State legislatures
(E) Presidency

15. All of the following actions represent the conventional manner people usually participate in the political process EXCEPT

(A) registering to vote
(B) participating in civil disobedience to achieve political goals
(C) joining a specific political party
(D) attending political meetings
(E) voting in elections

Answer Explanations

1. **(A)** Type of Question: Identification/definitional
   The statement is a straight definition of a political party. The process includes the manner in which the nomination is obtained. The constituency involves those who support the party. The agenda is what the party supports. A policy is the result of actions taken by legislators.

2. **(D)** Type of Question: Negative
   Choices A, B, C, and E are all characteristics of politics. Choice D is the correct answer because one of the outcomes of government is the making of public policy.

3. **(E)** Type of Question: Identification/sequencing a series of events
   Choice E, the relationship between the party and the courts, is an external relationship that goes beyond the organizational characteristics of political parties.

4. **(A)** Type of Question: Solution to a problem
   Because a political party is one of the linkage institutions, you should be able to apply the function of a political party to the statement describing the general meaning of a linkage institution.

5. **(A)** Type of Question: Identification and analysis
   By process of elimination and realizing that a centrist position is the predominant philosophy of the electorate, you should pick middle of the road as the only reasonable answer.

6. **(D)** Type of Question: Identification and analysis/cause-and-effect relationships
   Similar to Question 5, you are asked to come up with a conclusion based on the statement that a successful political party usually does not move too far from the center of public opinion.

7. **(C)** Type of Question: Identification and analysis/description
   This is a difficult question. Even though many political parties appear on the ballot, the United States has always been dominated by a two-party system. There have been times that a third party has been influential, but this has not been a consistent feature of the American party system. Choice D does not describe the overall nature of the two-party system.

8. **(B)** Type of Question: Cause-and-effect relationships
   You must know the difference between realignment and dealignment to answer this question. The hint in the question is the phrase *critical election*. This should evoke the image of the start of a party era, which occurs with party realignment.

9. **(A)** Type of Question: Cause-and-effect relationships
   Like Question 8, you must know the difference between realignment and dealignment. The clue here is that people are moving away from both parties. The other choices may be part of the political process but do not result from the situation described.

10. **(D)** Type of Question: Identification and analysis/relationship
    Choice A is incorrect because Southern liberals also vote Democratic. Choice B is incorrect because the Democrats' base is in the Northeast. Choice C is wrong because Southern conservatives strongly identify with the Republican Party. Choice E is incorrect because the religious right favors Republican candidates. Choice D is the correct answer because the Republicans dominate Southern politics.

11. **(C)** Type of Question: Identification and analysis/cause-and-effect relationships
    Choice C, political socialization, molds a person's ideology and a person's party identification. Choices D and E have nothing to do with personal values. They are the results of people moving away from the major parties or moving away from one of the major parties to the other.

12. **(A)** Type of Question: Identification and analysis
    The presidential candidate has a major influence on the platform. Party bosses molded the platform in the era before national conventions became more democratic. The local and state parties send delegates who become part of the process of determining the platform. The delegates to the national convention are the people who actually vote on the party platform.

13. **(A)** Type of Question: Chronological
    The question is asking you to find a critical election period. The Great Depression and Franklin Roosevelt's election represents a change from Republican to Democratic dominance.

14. **(A)** Type of Question: Chronological/sequencing a series of events
    By process of elimination, you should be able to reduce your choices to A and B. If you knew that during the Reagan administration Republicans controlled the Senate, then you would be able to pick A as the correct choice.

15. **(B)** Type of Question: Cause-and-effect relationships

Although each of the choices are ways in which people participate in the political process, civil disobedience is considered an *un*conventional choice, whereas the others are conventional.

Section 2: Free-Response Question (6 points)

> Party realignment and party dealignment have influenced presidential, congressional, and state elections since 1980.
>
> (a)   Define the terms "party realignment" and "party dealignment."
>
> (b)   Explain how realignment and party dealignment have impacted the following elections:
>
> ■   The presidential election of 1980
>
> ■   The congressional election of 1994

SAMPLE RESPONSE

(a)   The issues of party realignment and party dealignment have become more and more prevalent in America's political arena since the election of Ronald Reagan in 1980. Party realignment is defined as the displacement of the majority party by the minority party during a critical election period. Party dealignment is defined as the gradual disengagement of people and politicians from the major political parties.

(b)   In 1980, Ronald Reagan defeated Jimmy Carter, the Republicans took control of the Senate, and "Reagan Democrats" were born. These Democrats, who had become disillusioned with the economic policies of Carter and were upset over the hostage situation in Iran, represented a traditional base of the Democratic Party. Many of them were "blue collar" workers who had suffered the most under the economic policies of Jimmy Carter. Another indicator of the realignment taking place was that even in the South, Jimmy Carter's base, a majority of the electorate voted for Reagan.

In the 1994 midterm elections, the Republicans took control of the Senate for the first time since 1986. They also took control of the House of Representatives for the first time in 40 years. Using the "Contract With America" as a campaign slogan and successfully drawing national attention to the election, voters defeated more incumbents that year than in any other previous election. This event once more reflected the party realignment of the 1992 "Solid South," as it again switched allegiance and voted Republican. Traditional Democratic voters had left their party and elected Republican majorities in both houses of Congress.

SCORING GUIDELINES FOR FREE-RESPONSE QUESTION 2 (6 POINTS)

Part (a) 2 Points

One point is earned for the correct definition of party realignment, and one point is earned for the correct definition of party dealignment:

- Party realignment is the displacement of the majority party by the minority party during a critical election period.
- Party dealignment is the gradual disengagement of people from the major political parties with a shift toward registering as an Independent.

Part (b) 4 Points

One point is earned for an example, and one point is earned for explaining how realignment or dealignment had an impact on the 1980 presidential election. One point is earned for an example, and one point is earned for explaining how realignment or dealignment had an impact on the 1994 midterm election:

- 1980 presidential election—Reagan Democrats caused a realignment
- 1984 congressional election—Republican takeover of Congress resulted in a realignment

Nominations, Campaigns, and Elections 12

- → BATTLEGROUND STATES
- → BELLWETHER STATES
- → CAUCUS
- → COATTAILS
- → CONVENTION BUMP
- → DIRECT PRIMARY
- → DUAL PRIMARY
- → FAVORITE SON
- → FRONT LOADING
- → FRONT-RUNNER
- → GENDER GAP
- → HIGH-TECH CAMPAIGN
- → INFOMERCIALS
- → INVISIBLE PRIMARY
- → KEYNOTE ADDRESS
- → MATCHING FUNDS

- → MCGOVERN-FRASER COMMISSION
- → NONPREFERENTIAL PRIMARY
- → PARTY CAUCUS
- → PARTY REGULARS
- → POLITICAL ACTION COMMITTEE
- → PREFERENTIAL PRIMARY
- → PRESIDENTIAL PRIMARY
- → SOCCER MOM
- → SPIN DOCTORS
- → SUPER TUESDAY
- → SUPERDELEGATE
- → THIRTY-SECOND SPOTS
- → TICKET SPLITTING
- → TRACKING POLL
- → VOTER TURNOUT

CONTEMPORARY CONNECTION

The 2016 primary calendar was changed to reflect the problems caused by the "front-loading" primaries in 2008 and 2012. Both the Republican and Democratic national committees approved later dates for the first caucus and primary states. The Iowa caucus and New Hampshire primaries will take place in early February 2016 followed by the Nevada caucus and South Carolina primary. Super Tuesday was moved back to March. This chapter explores the presidential nominating process: the primary system, political conventions, and strategies used to get elected president.

"Throwing your hat in the ring" marks the traditional announcement by a political candidate running for office. Today's campaign and election resembles more of a "war room" atmosphere than the old-style "whistle stop" rallies. This chapter traces the characteristics of the nominating process and election campaign. In fact, the nominating process has turned into a campaign itself. Thus many of the strategies used to receive a party's nomination are the same as those used to convince the electorate to vote for a particular candidate.

Specifically, we will focus our attention on the campaign to receive the nomination for president, including the primary route, the party caucus, and the nominating convention. We will trace the process a candidate uses, once given the nod, to organize an election campaign including the money requirements, the fundraising techniques used, the restrictions placed on the candidate by federal election laws, and the different strategies used to reach the voter. We will also explore the role of the media in the high-tech campaign waged to get nominated and elected.

As we play the nomination and election game, we will also point to the various reforms being discussed in relation to the length of campaigns, to the primary system, and to the revision of campaign election laws, especially in the area of contributions by special interest groups.

POPULAR *VS.* ELECTORAL VOTES

The vast majority of presidents have reached the office through prescribed methods, and only eleven have served two or more terms.

Once nominated, the outcome of the election is generally determined by whoever receives the most electoral votes. The potential for a third-party candidate drawing enough votes to throw the election into the House of Representatives exists. When Ross Perot received almost 20 percent of the popular vote in 1992 and established his own political party, many political scientists predicted that in a future presidential election no candidate would receive a majority of the electoral votes. Two factors contribute to this threat. First, the rules of the electoral college system dictate that the winner takes all the electoral votes of a state even if one candidate wins 51 percent of the vote and the losing candidate gets 49 percent. Second, the allocation of electoral votes does not always reflect true population and voter patterns.

On four occasions in American history, presidential candidates have lost the election even though they received the most popular votes. In 1824 Andrew Jackson received a plurality of popular votes and electoral votes, over 40 percent of the popular votes to 31 percent of the vote obtained by John Quincy Adams. Yet, Jackson did not receive a majority of the electoral votes; Adams received a majority of the votes from the House and was elected president. In 1876 Republican Rutherford B. Hayes lost the popular vote by a little more than 275,000 votes. Called the "stolen election" by historians, Hayes received an electoral majority after an electoral commission was set up by Congress to investigate electoral irregularities in Florida, Louisiana, South Carolina, and Oregon. The commission voted on party lines, and Hayes was officially elected president. In 1888 Grover Cleveland won the popular vote but lost the electoral majority to Benjamin Harrison. In the 2000 election, Vice President Al Gore received more popular votes than George W. Bush. Bush, however, won the majority of the electoral votes and became our 43rd president. If third-party candidate Ralph Nader had not run, Gore would have won enough electoral votes to have won the election.

Even though this has occurred only four times, there have been extremely close elections, such as the 1960 election between Kennedy and Nixon and the 1976 election between Carter and Ford, where a small shift in one state could have changed the outcome of the election. There is also a potential constitutional problem if a designated presidential elector decides not to vote for the candidate he was committed to support. They are called faithless electors. That happened on nine occasions without having an impact on the outcome. The third anomaly of the system could take place if the House and Senate must determine the outcome of the election. The Twelfth Amendment to the Constitution outlines this procedure, and even though it has happened only once, strong third-party candidates make this a distinct possibility in the future. Elections in 1968 (the American Independent Party candidacy of George Wallace), and the recent candidacy of Ross Perot all influenced campaign strategy.

Two proposed constitutional amendments have been offered to make the system fairer. The first one would create a proportional system so that a candidate gets the proportional number of electoral votes based on the size of the popular vote received in the state. In 2011, individual states such as Pennsylvania considered passing legislation that would split their electoral votes proportionally in the 2012 election. A second plan offered would simply abolish the electoral college and allow the election to be determined by the popular vote with perhaps a 40 percent minimum margin established. Any multiparty race resulting in a victory with less than 40 percent would create a run-off.

INVISIBLE PRIMARY

When you calculate the time it takes between a candidate's announcement that he or she is running to the actual convention, it could easily be two years from start to end. Add to that the actual campaign for president, and you can tack on an additional three to four months.

The road to victory is actually a three-round fight involving a dual campaign to get nominated and elected, each involving a complex strategy.

The "invisible primary," the period between a candidate's announcement that he or she is running for president and the day the first primary votes are cast, will heavily influence the outcome of the primary season. After the candidate declares, the candidate starts building an organization, actively seeking funds—the current start-up fee for presidential races has been estimated at $100 million—and developing an overall strategy to win the nomination. Before the first primary or caucus, the candidate vies for endorsements from party leaders and attempts to raise the public's interest by visiting key states with early primaries such as Iowa and New Hampshire. Debates are also held among the candidates and political ads are shown in the early primary states. Since 1976, when little-known Georgia governor Jimmy Carter threw his hat in the ring, the invisible primary has created a perceived front runner. Front-runner status during the invisible primary has been defined as the candidate who raised the most money. This pattern was broken in 2004, when Vermont Governor Howard Dean raised more money than any other Democrat. His candidacy also pioneered using the Internet to raise a record amount of funds. However, after Dean lost the Iowa caucus, his candidacy imploded. In the election of 2008, Hillary Clinton narrowly led Barack Obama in fundraising prior to the Iowa caucus. Republican Rudy Giuliani led the Republican field, with the eventual nominee John McCain lagging behind in fourth place. The Iowa caucus and New Hampshire primary changed the dynamics of the race. Both Obama and McCain captured their party's nomination, increasing their fundraising as the campaign progressed. The Republican field in 2012 held a series of candidate debates prior to the Iowa Caucus and the New Hampshire primary. Even though former Massachusetts governor Mitt Romney had a fund-raising advantage and was perceived as the best candidate to defeat President Obama, his candidacy suffered a series of setbacks as one candidate after another gained front-runner status. Romney ultimately surged ahead during the primaries.

The invisible primary winner is the candidate who raises the most money before the first caucus.

PRIMARIES AND CAUCUSES

The second stage of the campaign is the primary season. By the time the first caucus in Iowa and the first primary in New Hampshire are held in January, the campaign for the party's nomination is well underway—some 10 months before election day. By the time these early primary votes are completed, many candidates will have dropped out of the race. Prior to 2004, there was a break between the Iowa and New Hampshire votes and other primaries. But in 2004, the Democrats created a primary calendar that characterized as "front-loading," where each week different primaries are held. This is the third phase of the campaign. And in February and March key regional primaries are held on what has been called "Super Tuesday." After Super Tuesday, one candidate usually has enough delegates pledged to him that he becomes the presumptive nominee. This did not happen in 2008, as the Democratic candidates fought until the last primary was completed. In 2012, Governor Romney was able to defeat the rest of the Republican field during the primary season and wrapped up the nomination shortly after Super Tuesday. But his image was damaged during the primary campaign as he was attacked not only by his Republican opponents but also by the incumbent president.

Primaries

> Winning delegate support takes place as a result of a high-tech campaign to convince party regulars that a particular candidate is best suited to run the country.

Without a doubt, the presidential primary has become the decisive way a candidate gains delegate support. It has taken on such importance that key primary states such as New York and California have changed their primary dates so that their primaries take on much greater importance. Today, 30 states have presidential primaries. The others use caucuses or party conventions. Presidential primaries can be binding or nonbinding. They can ask the voter to express a preference for a presidential candidate or delegates who are pledged to support a candidate at the convention. Primaries are used in many ways:

- Proportional representation where delegates are selected based on the percentage of the vote the candidate received in the election.
- Winner takes all, where, as in the actual election, the candidate receiving a plurality receives all the delegates. The Republicans use this method in California. Democratic rules have banned the use of this system since 1976.
- Nonpreferential primary where voters choose delegates who are not bound to vote for the winning primary candidate.
- A primary vote where all the voters, including cross-over voters from other political parties, can express a preference but do not actually select delegates.
- A dual primary vote where presidential candidates are selected and a separate slate of delegates is also voted on. New Hampshire uses this type of primary.

Pre-Convention Strategy

The third stage of the campaign takes place between the time both parties have a presumptive candidate and the conventions where the candidates are officially nominated. In 2004, Massachusetts senator John Kerry won the majority of the Democratic primaries and had enough delegates pledged to him that by March he became the Democratic Party's presumptive nominee. Incumbent Republican president George W. Bush also began his campaign in earnest in March

2004 with a television blitz of more than $60 million. In 2008, Republican senator John McCain wrapped up his party's nomination months before Democratic senator Barack Obama. This gave McCain an opportunity to unify the Republican Party, define his candidacy, and continue to raise funds for the general campaign. Obama seemingly was at a disadvantage, because he finally became the presumptive nominee in June and had a much more difficult time unifying the Democratic Party. In 2012, Governor Romney spent almost all of his resources during the primaries and was not able to draw on his general campaign funds until after he was officially nominated. This put him at a disadvantage because President Obama was able to use all his resources to campaign against the presumptive nominee.

THE PARTY CONVENTION

The fourth stage of the campaign is the nominating convention held by each party. Traditionally, the party out of power holds its convention first. The conventions are highly scripted. The conventions are like a pep rally for the party's base. The key components of the convention are the adoption of the party platform, the keynote speech, the nominating speeches, and the acceptance speeches of the vice-presidential and presidential candidates. After the conventions, each presidential candidate is expected to get a "convention bounce" (a sometimes-temporary increase in positive polling results) in the polls. In 2008, both parties delayed their conventions because they did not want to have a conflict with the Summer Olympics. The conventions were held in successive weeks. The Democrats met first, and Barack Obama's acceptance speech was held in Denver's Invesco Field before the largest audience ever to watch an acceptance speech. The Democrat received a modest poll bounce, which was quickly erased after John McCain announced his choice for vice president, Alaska governor Sarah Palin, prior to the opening of his convention. In 2012 because the Republican and Democratic conventions were held back to back neither candidate received a bounce in the polls.

National conventions date back to the 1830s, when the first "open" party convention was held by Jacksonian Democrats. Historically, conventions have provided excitement, hoopla, and ultimately the nomination of the party's candidates for president and vice president. The 1924 Democratic Convention took 103 ballots to determine the winner. Backroom deals were cut and strange political bedfellows emerged, creating a truly national ticket. Since 1952, both parties have selected their standard bearers on the first ballot. Even though this has been the case, convention coverage by the media guarantees a national audience. Key convention proceedings such as rules and credentials debates, keynote speeches, platform debates, nomination of the presidential candidates, selection of a running mate, and acceptance speeches pique the interest of the electorate. Even the location of the convention can play a role in affecting the party's choice and creating a positive or negative public impression. In 1952, Governor Adlai Stevenson, Illinois's "favorite son" (the candidate backed by the home state), gave the welcoming address, and many political observers felt that it contributed to his nomination that year. In 1968 the riots in Chicago played to a national audience, who came away with the feeling that the Democratic Party was not unified. The close results of the 1968 general election, according to some, would have been different if there had not been riots.

Presidential nominations play an important role in giving the candidate and the party national exposure.

The McGovern-Fraser Commission

The McGovern-Fraser Commission was formed after the disastrous 1968 Democratic Convention. The commission's purpose was to revise the rules of delegate representation that would be adopted for the 1972 Democratic Convention. The report recommended uniformity to the delegate selection process with an emphasis on minority, women, and youth representation. The commission's recommendations were approved and as a result there was a dramatic increase in minority and women delegates. Because these changes were made, the days of smoke-filled rooms where party leaders picked the presidential candidate came to an end as states moved to holding primaries as the means of delegate selection. The commission also created a category known as superdelegates (those delegates, elected party officials, who automatically were able to vote at the convention. In 2008, Barack Obama was able to get the nomination because he convinced these superdelegates he could win in the general election. The Republican Party does not have the same rules and the make-up of the delegates to their convention is not as diverse. The Republicans do not have superdelegates, though elected party officials do attend the convention without having to run in a primary.

Selecting the Vice President

Wheeling and dealing often comes about in the selection of the vice presidential running mate. Since 1940, the political precedent of having the presidential nominees choose their running mates has been established. The philosophy of the presidential nominees in picking a vice presidential candidate has ranged from attempts at "balancing the ticket" to paying off a political debt. The classic choices of Lyndon Johnson as John Kennedy's running mate in 1960, Walter Mondale as Jimmy Carter's selection in 1976, and Lloyd Bentsen's addition to the Dukakis ticket in 1988 illustrate this balancing principle. When George McGovern selected Senator Thomas Eagleton in 1972 in a rushed decision, he soon regretted the choice. The media uncovered Eagleton's history of mental illness, and he was forced to leave the ticket. There sometimes is a sense of history in the elevation of a person to the ticket. Mondale's choice of Geraldine Ferraro of New York was historic, signaling the willingness of the Democratic Party to recognize that a woman had the capability to become president.

That the vice president must be qualified to be president in the event of a president dying in office has been a source of controversy when presidential candidates select running mates. George H. W. Bush's selection of Dan Quayle and the questions regarding Quayle's qualifications hurt Bush's campaign. On the other hand, when a politician breaks the rules, it sometimes helps the image of his candidacy. Clinton's choice of fellow southerner Al Gore violated every previous rule. But the strategy worked, as this baby boomer ticket caught the fancy of the American public. Vice President Gore surprised the pundits by choosing Connecticut senator Joseph Lieberman, the first Jewish candidate for vice president. George W. Bush selected former Secretary of Defense Richard Cheney as his running mate. In 2008, Barack Obama selected one of his rivals for the presidency, Delaware senator Joseph Biden. Biden, who chaired both the Senate Judiciary and Foreign Relations committees, brought experience to the ticket. John McCain surprised the country, choosing a relatively unknown governor from Alaska, Sarah Palin. It was the first time the Republicans chose a woman for vice president. Palin helped unify the Republican Party, but ultimately hurt the ticket because of her inexperience. In 2012, Mitt Romney selected the chairman of the Budget Committee, Paul Ryan, to appeal to the conservative base of the Republican Party.

THE GENERAL CAMPAIGN

The election campaign seems like a 100-yard dash compared to the nominating process. Even though there are similarities to the campaign for nomination in terms of organization and strategy, once the candidate has the official party designation, the fall campaign turns into a fight to the finish. In 1960 Richard Nixon decided to be the first candidate to campaign actively in all 50 states, and some analysts believe it cost him the election. In the 2000 campaign, Al Gore campaigned for a continuation of the Clinton accomplishments while trying to separate himself from the scandals that President Clinton faced—most notably his impeachment. He selected a Clinton critic, Connecticut senator Joseph Lieberman, the first Jewish candidate for the office of vice president. Governor George W. Bush of Texas campaigned as a Washington outsider. He selected a Washington insider, former George H. W. Bush defense secretary Dick Cheney, to be his vice presidential running mate. In 2004, Bush ran as an incumbent, while Democratic senator John Kerry challenged the sitting president's Iraq policies. The 2008 campaign was characterized by a number of firsts. It was the first time there was no incumbent running for president from the previous administration since 1928; the first time an African-American was nominated; and the first time the Republican Party nominated a woman for vice president. In the 2012 campaign, President Obama faced a difficult reelection landscape. The economy still had not recovered from the 2008 recession and unemployment hovered around 8%. The Obama campaign developed a strategy of defining Mitt Romney early as "out of touch." Romney reinforced that image when he was caught on tape at a fund-raiser criticizing 47% of Americans who did not pay income taxes. The first debate energized the challenger but ultimately Obama's ground game provided the margin for victory.

The general campaign begins after the nominating conventions. Labor Day has become the unofficial kickoff of the general campaign. Both candidates must develop an electoral strategy that will ultimately result in winning 270 electoral votes. Since 1990, states have been described as "blue or red" states, blue for Democrats and red for Republicans. Candidates have a base of electoral support and must win the so-called swing states, also known as battleground states that will determine the outcome of the election. In 2000, Florida became the ultimate swing state as its electoral votes were contested until the Supreme Court ruled that a recount could not take place in the case *Bush v Gore*. In 2012, there were nine swing states that Obama targeted and he won all of them except North Carolina giving him a majority of electoral votes.

CAMPAIGN STRATEGY

Campaign strategists develop the day-to-day messaging for each campaign. They make decisions where the money should be spent for political ads, where the candidates should go, the strategy for the presidential debates, and the Get-Out-the-Vote operation. With the rise of social media, the presidential candidates utilize e-mail, create apps, and have Facebook pages and Twitter accounts. There is a 24-hour news cycle and there are often gaffes that the candidates make that dominate the news.

Successful presidential campaigns develop successful campaign strategies.

The presidential and vice presidential debates draw the largest audience. They are run by the Presidential Debate Commission, a nonpartisan organization that comes up with the dates, location, and format of the debates. Typically, there are three presidential debates, with one dealing with domestic issues, one with foreign policy, and one that is a town hall format where questions are asked by undecided voters. These debates can impact the campaigns and can give the challenger the advantage. The first debate held in 1960 between Senator John F. Kennedy and Vice President Richard Nixon was a turning point in that campaign. Incumbents have had difficulty in their first debates. In 2012, President Obama's lackluster performance resulted in a tightening of the race.

One of the most important factors in the general campaign is money. The candidate who is able to raise the most money has a clear advantage. Presidential campaigns from 1976 to 2008 were characterized by presidential candidates using matching funds provided by law to limit the amount of money spent in a presidential campaign. In 2008, Barack Obama decided to raise more than the limit and had a significant spending advantage over his opponent. In 2012, both candidates raised more than a billion dollars, making it the most expensive campaign in presidential history. As a result of the *Citizens United* Supreme Court case, independent groups were able to raise an unlimited amount adding to the total cost of the election.

Issues do make a difference in the campaign. An unpopular war or economic collapse will contribute to the success or failure of a presidential candidate. In 1968, Lyndon Johnson withdrew from the race because of the unpopularity of the Vietnam War. In 2004, George W. Bush was reelected because the country did not want a change while the United States was fighting a war. It was a close election because that war was unpopular. In 2008, the voters punished the Republican Party and its candidate because of the economic problems the country was facing. In 2012, President Obama was able to convince the electorate that the country was making economic progress.

Gaining the support of the party's base is crucial for candidates running for president. Factors such as ethnic, religious, gender, and minority support are crucial for success in a campaign. Traditionally, the Democratic Party's base includes organized labor, African-Americans, women, Jews, and Hispanics. The Republican Party's base includes white men, evangelicals, people who earn more than $100,000, senior citizens, and those living in rural areas. Once the base is solidified, the last piece of the puzzle is getting out the vote. A major change that has occurred in the Get-Out-the-Vote efforts is early voting. Thirty-three states allow early voting and a candidate who establishes a lead can win that state. More than 30 percent of the voters in those states vote either by mail or in person prior to Election Day. Pollsters release daily tracking polls that reflect both national and state polls. The 2004, 2008, and 2012 elections were impacted by both early voting and the ability of the winning candidate to get out the vote. Voter turnout in presidential elections since 1960 is between 50 and 60 percent.

REELECTION

The history of Congress reflects long-standing traditions. The first meetings in both houses established the committee system, which still exists today. Even though the Senate was originally selected by state legislatures (corrected by the Seventeenth Amendment in 1913), both houses fulfilled their lawmaking responsibility. The reelection rate of the Congress in its early days was low. In the first ten years, over one-third of the senators resigned before the end of their terms. In the House a large number of representatives served only one or two terms.

As political parties began to develop, the congressional reelection rate began to increase. By the time of the Civil War, many election victories resulted from party affiliation and incumbency. After the Seventeenth Amendment, the entire political structure of the Congress changed. By the time of the modern-day presidents (Kennedy, Johnson, Nixon, Ford, George H. W. Bush, Clinton, George W. Bush, and Barack Obama), it became evident that influential senators and representatives could use their office as an entrée to the presidency.

Other factors that changed the nature of congressional elections were the make-up of congressional districts, the primary system for nominating candidates, the importance of party politics, and the resulting election of most incumbents.

Election of Incumbents

Primaries and party politics have resulted in the election of incumbents through the 1980s and 2000s. However, a trend that began in 2010 resulted in some Republican incumbents being defeated in primaries when the Tea Party supported more conservative candidates. Many of these

Even though congressional elections have favored incumbency, a new face of Congress has evolved.

candidates were defeated by Democrats in the general campaign. Even though the success of Senate incumbents lags behind the House, it is obvious that once elected a sitting representative has a distinct advantage. The exception to the rule is if there is a scandal involving a representative or if a sitting president is unpopular at the midterm, a smaller percentage of incumbents are reelected. When it became known in 1992 that House members were abusing their checking and post office privileges, many incumbents either decided not to seek reelection or were defeated. Midterm elections in 1994 reflected the public's disapproval of President Clinton's job performance. For the first time in 40 years, the Republicans captured control of both the House and the Senate. In fact, not a single Republican incumbent was defeated in what has been described as an electoral revolution. The Republicans maintained control of Congress after the 1996 presidential election. The 1998 midterm election maintained Republican control, though the margins were cut in both the House and the Senate. After the 2006 midterm elections, the Democrats retook control of the Congress, gaining 29 seats in the House. After the 2008 election, Democrats increased their majorities in the House and Senate achieving a filibuster-proof Senate after a Republican senator switched parties. This 60-seat majority did not last long as the Republicans gained back a seat after they won a victory in Massachusetts in a special election held after the "lion of the Senate" Ted Kennedy died. In the 2010 midterm election, Republicans gained 6 seats in the Senate reducing the Democratic majority to 53 seats. The Republicans kept control of the House. In 2012, the Democrats gained seats in both the Senate and the House but the Republicans kept control in the House.

From 2000 to 2014 House reelection rates ranged from a high of 99 percent in 2000 and 2004 to a low of 85 percent in 2010. In 2014, reelection rates for House incumbents jumped back to 96 percent. Senate reelection rates are lower for the same time period averaging around 80 percent except in 2004 when over 95 percent of Senate incumbents were reelected. Why do incumbents have this advantage? Incumbents are highly visible. The cable network C-SPAN routinely broadcasts proceedings of the House and Senate. Representatives have free franking (sending of mail) privileges, they do case work for their constituents, and most pride themselves in establishing close constituent relationships. They also make sure to co-sponsor legislation. Representatives are quick to take credit for obtaining funds through legislation that favors their home districts called earmarks. This practice is called pork barrel legislation and has been criticized by such political watchdog groups as Common Cause. As a result of campaign fund raising and contributions made by political action committees, incumbents also have a built-in money advantage over their challengers. This advantage results in many weak opponents being nominated. They are compared to cannon fodder and frequently lose by more than 60 percent of the vote.

The 114th Congress is the most diverse in the nation's history, containing more women and minorities than any previous congress. Between both chambers, 96 racial minority members and 104 women from both parties are serving in Congress as of February 2015. However, the House is still 80 percent white, and the Senate is 94 percent white. Congressmen have an average age of 57. The Senate is older than the House, with an average age of 61.

THE MONEY GAME

A California politician once said, "money is the milk of all politics." This has become increasingly evident in light of the amount of money raised and spent by congressional and presidential candidates and the impact of Supreme Court decisions on campaign finance laws. To put this in perspective, look at the following chart from the Open Secrets website.

Cycle	Total Cost of Election	Congressional Races	Presidential Race
2012	$6,285,557,223	$3,664,141,430	$2,621,415,792
2010	$3,631,712,836	$3,631,712,836	N/A
2008	$5,285,680,883	$2,485,952,737	$2,799,728,146
2006	$2,852,658,140	$2,852,658,140	N/A
2004	$4,147,304,003	$2,237,073,141	$1,910,230,862
2002	$2,181,682,066	$2,181,682,066	N/A
2000	$3,082,340,937	$1,669,224,553	$1,413,116,384
1998	$1,618,936,265	$1,618,936,265	N/A

Even though there is federal matching funds for presidential candidates, since 2012 candidates from both major parties rejected those funds so they could raise as much as they could. It is interesting to note that spending for presidential elections has skyrocketed from a little over $5 million dollars in 1952 to over $2 billion dollars in 2012.

Federal Election Laws

Three major pieces of legislation were passed to regulate federal campaign spending:

- The 1971 Federal Election Campaign Act (FECA) set up restrictions on the amount of advertising, created disclosure of contributions over $100 (later changed to $250), and limited the amount of personal contributions candidates and their relatives could make on their own behalf.

- The 1974 Federal Election Campaign Act, passed in response to the Watergate scandal abuses, established a six-person Federal Election Commission whose responsibility it would be to enforce the provisions of the law and established matching federal funds for presidential candidates. In order to receive those funds, a candidate had to raise at least $5,000 in at least 20 states. The candidate would then be eligible for the funds as long as the candidate agreed to disclose campaign contributions and not exceed the limit of the funds.

- The McCain-Feingold Campaign Finance Reform Act of 2000—This act banned what was called "soft money, which was donations to candidates; political parties and Political Action Committees (PACs) that went beyond campaign donations that had limits, called "hard money." The law also increased hard money limits and established a ban on special interest political ads paid for by soft money that would be shown prior to a primary and general election. In 2002, the Supreme Court initially upheld the law, and candidates increased the amount of hard money raised. Special interest groups got around the ban on soft money donations by forming what was called "527" independent groups that were able to give additional funds based on the tax code. These groups also ran ads that represented the interests of those groups.

Supreme Court Decisions

- *Federal Election Commission* (FEC) *v Wisconsin Right to Life* (2007) —The Court ruled that a law regulating certain issue ads that targeted candidates could be made as long as the ad was clear that it was made by the special interest group.

- *Citizen's United v FEC* (2010)—This case changed the entire dynaminic of campaign finance law. Overturning the 2002 case and parts of the McCain-Feingold Act, the Court ruled that based on the First Amendment's free speech clause, unlimited independent expenditures and political advocacy ads could be used by outside groups including corporations, labor unions, and special interest groups as long as the money was not donated directly to a candidate's campaign and disclosure rules were followed. As a result, there was a fivefold increase in the amount of money special interest groups spent in the 2010 and 2014 midterm elections and the 2012 presidential campaign.

- ■ **American Tradition Partnership v Bullock (2012)**—The Court upheld Citizen's United and struck down a ban on corporate political spending. The effect of this case was that the court's ruling made it clear that any future efforts to regulate outside money at the state level would be rejected.

- ■ **McCutcheon v FEC (2014)**—Next to Citizen's United, this case allowed candidates and political parties to collect substantially larger sums from individual donors, thus weakening the hard money limits established in 1974. By striking down so called "aggregate contribution limits," the amount a single individual could give in federal elections to all candidates, political parties, and PACs combined, the Court rules that the federal contribution limits were unconstitutional.

The overall significance of these rulings was to water down existing law that campaign donations were dominated by outside groups, and because aggregate limits no longer existed, even individuals could give millions of dollars to candidates, national parties, local parties, and PACs in an election cycle.

The public funding of presidential campaigns has had a significant impact on the election process since it was instituted in 1971. Money has been given to candidates during the primary campaign, to the parties to help fund national conventions, and to candidates in the general election campaign. In 1988 candidates received more than $65 million in federal matching funds. The two parties got over $9 million for their 1988 national conventions, and George H. W. Bush and Michael Dukakis received over $46 million in public funds. In 2004, candidates received $75 million in federal matching funds. In 2008, McCain received $84 million in matching funds.

	To Each Candidate or Candidate Committee Per Elections	To National Party Committee Per Calendar Year	To State, District, and Local Party Committees Per Calendar Year	To Any Political Committee Per Calendar Year[1]	Special Limits
Individual May Give	$2,600*	$32,400*	$10,000 (combined limit)	$5,000	No limit
National Party Committee May Give	$5,000	No limit	No limit	$5,000	$45,400* to Senate candidate per campaign[2]
State, District, and Local Party Committee May Give	$5,000 (combined limit)	No limit	No limit	$5,000 (combined limit)	No limit
PAC (multicandidate)[3] May Give	$5,000	$15,000	$5,000 (combined limit)	$5,000	No limit
PAC (non-multicandidate) May Give	$2,600*	$32,400*	$10,000 (combined limit)	$5,000	No limit
Authorized Campaign Committee May Give	$2,000[4]	No limit	No limit	$5,000	No limit

* These contribution limits are increased for inflation in odd-numbered years.

[1] A contribution earmarked for a candidate through a political committee counts against the original contributor's limit for that candidate. In certain circumstances, the contribution may also count against the contributor's limit to the PAC.

[2] This limit is shared by the national committee and the Senate campaign committee.

[3] A multicandidate committee is a political committee with more than 50 contributors that has been registered for at least 6 months and, with the exception of state party committees, has made contributions to 5 or more candidates for federal office.

[4] A federal candidate's authorized committee(s) may contribute no more than $2,000 per election to another federal candidate's authorized committee(s).

Section 1: Multiple-Choice Questions

1. Which of the following terms represents the official designation of a person running for office?

    (A) Party nomination
    (B) Voter referendum
    (C) Plebiscite
    (D) Endorsement
    (E) Recall

2. The manner in which candidates attempt to effectively use money and media attention in order to achieve the nomination is called campaign

    (A) gambling
    (B) risk taking
    (C) apathy
    (D) manipulation
    (E) strategy

3. Political "spin" means

    (A) the attempts of handlers to present a favorable account of events
    (B) the whirlwind trips that candidates must make during a campaign
    (C) a candidate's flip-flopping of his opinions
    (D) the news media's coverage of political events
    (E) newspaper editorials taking a stand on an issue

4. The goal of the nominating game is to win a majority of delegates' support at which of the following stages of the campaign?

    (A) Invisible primary
    (B) General election
    (C) Straw ballot convention
    (D) Post convention
    (E) National party convention

5. Before primaries existed, state parties selected their delegates to the national convention through which of the following processes?

    (A) Caucus
    (B) Referendum
    (C) Roundtable discussion
    (D) Blanket primary
    (E) Open primary

6. With the exception of Bill Clinton, George W. Bush, and Barack Obama, no one has been elected president since 1952 without first having won which presidential primary?

(A) Iowa
(B) New Hampshire
(C) Maine
(D) New York
(E) California

7. Criticisms of the election process include all of the following EXCEPT

(A) Disproportionate attention goes to the early caucuses.
(B) Disproportionate attention goes to the early primaries.
(C) Money plays too big a role.
(D) The system allows little room for media involvement.
(E) Participation in the primaries is low and not representative of the entire electorate.

8. In order to organize their presidential campaigns effectively, candidates must do all of the following EXCEPT

(A) Line up a campaign manager who is skilled.
(B) Get a fundraiser that raises significant money.
(C) Hire a pollster who knows how to choose focus groups.
(D) Announce their choice for vice president during the primaries.
(E) Get positive media exposure.

9. If presidential candidates accept federal support in the form of matching campaign financing, then they

(A) are no longer required to disclose their contributions
(B) agree to limit their campaign expenditures to an amount prescribed by federal law
(C) no longer have any limit to their campaign expenditures
(D) are no longer required to disclose how they spend their money
(E) no longer can accept PAC money

10. Presidential candidates must file periodic reports with the Federal Election Commission, listing who contributed money and how it was spent

(A) if they receive matching federal funding
(B) if they did not receive matching federal funding
(C) regardless of whether or not they receive matching federal funding
(D) only if their contributions top $1 million
(E) if they receive any kind of PAC money

11. Few developments since the Watergate crisis have generated as much cynicism about government as the

(A) explosive growth of special interest groups and PACs
(B) lack of qualified presidential candidates
(C) high turnover rate in the House of Representatives
(D) high turnover rate in the Senate
(E) difficulty of getting the Senate to approve Supreme Court justices

12. Which of the following concerns most bothers politicians about the rising costs of campaigning?

    (A) They are forced to accept money from PACs that they may not agree with.

    (B) They are involved with fundraising, which takes up much of their time.

    (C) They don't feel that they are getting their money's worth from high-priced media consultants.

    (D) They don't believe that high-tech campaigns achieve results.

    (E) They don't feel that political advertisements achieve results.

13. Which of the following campaign financing reforms has been adopted?

    (A) Increasing the amount of PAC contributions a candidate can accept

    (B) Abolishing soft money contributions

    (C) Decreasing government subsidies to congressional campaigns

    (D) Allowing more lobbyist gifts to candidates

    (E) Eliminating federal matching funds for presidential campaigns

14. Television news coverage of a candidate generally focuses on all of the following EXCEPT

    (A) where the candidate appeared

    (B) how big the crowds were

    (C) a candidate's explanation of a complex policy statement

    (D) sound bites from the candidate's speech

    (E) photo opportunities staged by the candidate

15. Four decades of research on political campaigns lead to the following conclusion that

    (A) campaigns typically convert voter preferences

    (B) campaigns mostly reinforce and activate, only rarely do they convert

    (C) campaigns have no effect on voter preference

    (D) money has little or no effect on the outcome of an election

    (E) the media coverage of a candidate has little to do with the outcome of an election

16. All of the following factors tend to weaken a candidate's chances for election EXCEPT

    (A) challenging an incumbent

    (B) not using political advertisements

    (C) recognizing that voters have a remarkable capacity for selective perception

    (D) recognizing that party identification has a major influence on voting behavior

    (E) raising large amounts of money

17. Which of the following provides voters the chance to directly approve or disapprove a legislative proposition?

    (A) A recall petition

    (B) A secondary primary

    (C) A referendum

    (D) A run-off primary

    (E) An indirect primary

18. The first time a candidate attempts to effectively use money and media attention in order to achieve name recognition is the

   (A) invisible primary
   (B) the general campaign
   (C) the primary
   (D) the debates
   (E) the caucus

19. Which of the following reforms took place as a result of the McGovern-Fraser Commission?

   (A) The elimination of "pseudo" delegates
   (B) The development of "shadow" delegates
   (C) The creation of special interest delegates
   (D) The use of caucus delegates
   (E) The incorporation of minority delegates

20. All of the following statements about campaign strategy are true EXCEPT

   (A) The candidate must target the campaign.
   (B) The candidate must take advantage of political assets.
   (C) The candidate must campaign in all 50 states.
   (D) The candidate must use issues and events to his or her advantage.
   (E) The candidate must use the campaign organization.

Answer Explanations

1. **(A)** Type of Question: Definitional
   The key words in the question are "official designation." The only other answer that could possibly fit the question is an endorsement. However, an endorsement does not represent the designation of a candidate.

2. **(E)** Type of Question: Definitional
   Again, you need to fill in the definition, looking at the key words "achieve the nomination." There may be gambling, risk taking, or manipulation, but the use of money and media is part of an overall campaign strategy.

3. **(A)** Type of Question: Definitional
   Political spin is a term that came into use during the Clinton administration. His political advisers (handlers) were adept at putting the best face on issues with which Clinton was involved. Choices B, C, D, and E are incorrect because they don't apply to the concept of spin.

4. **(E)** Type of Question: Cause-and-effect relationships
   If you win the majority of the delegates at the national party convention, then you get the party's nomination.

5. **(A)** Type of Question: Sequencing a series of events
   You must know that the development of the primary system evolved from the caucus system.

6. **(B)** Type of Question: Chronological
   Even though you probably do not know the chronology of every primary winner since 1952, because Clinton broke the pattern of having to win the New Hampshire primary

and being called "the comeback kid" despite his loss, you should be able to easily identify which primary the question was talking about. Bush lost the primary in 2000 but went on to beat John McCain. In 2008, Hillary Clinton defeated Barack Obama. Obama went on to win the nomination.

7. **(D)** Type of Question: Solution to a problem
You should be looking for criticism of the election process and then determine the one choice that does not support the premise—there is an increasing role of the media in the election process, from the high-tech campaign to election coverage.

8. **(D)** Type of Question: Hypothetical
Again, look for things candidates must do to organize their campaigns effectively and find the one thing that does not contribute to the effectiveness of a campaign. In this case, you should realize that it is not essential and sometimes can hurt a candidate to announce the choice of the vice president prior to the convention.

9. **(B)** Type of Question: Cause-and-effect relationships
You must know the components of the Federal Election Campaign Act and understand that the key characteristic is the limitation of campaign expenditures as a result of accepting federal matching funds.

10. **(C)** Type of Question: Cause-and-effect relationships
Just like Question 9, you must know that a requirement of the Federal Election Commission is financial disclosure once a candidate decides to accept matching funds.

11. **(A)** Type of Question: Cause-and-effect relationships
Watergate is the key to answering this question. What happened after Watergate in the area of cynicism about government? Even though you may feel that there was a lack of qualified presidential candidates and even though there have been Supreme Court justice nominations that have had problems, the proliferation of PACs has been the dominant criticism post-Watergate.

12. **(B)** Type of Question: Generalization
This question requires your understanding of the nature of the political campaign. It is similar to an EXCEPT question because the answer is negative. Even though the other choices are negative, they are not accurate.

13. **(B)** Type of Question: Solution to a problem
The problem is campaign finance reform. The solution is lowering the amount of PAC contributions. Although the other choices are viable, they have not been offered as possible reforms.

14. **(C)** Type of Question: Generalization
Thinking about television coverage of campaigns and the fact that it focuses on superficial coverage should give away the answer that complex policy statements are rarely covered.

15. **(B)** Type of Question: Chronological
We are looking for a generalization that describes the nature of political campaigns. Through the process of elimination, choice B is the best choice. You can eliminate choices D and E because they are false. Choice A is incorrect because most campaigns do not convert voter preferences, whereas choice C is incorrect because voter preference is reinforced.

16. **(E)** Type of Question: Cause-and-effect relationships

In this question you are looking for a factor that will strengthen a candidate's chance. The only choice that fits that criterion is the raising of large sums of money. Choice C will be chosen by those students who do not understand what selective perception is.

17. **(C)** Type of Question: Identification and analysis

The question describes the characteristics of a referendum. Although recall petitions are also voter initiated, they do not result in the approval of any kind of legislation. Primary votes result in the selection of candidates.

18. **(A)** Type of Question: Sequencing a series of events

Though candidates need to use money effectively and gain media attention throughout the entire campaign, the first time this occurs is during the invisible primary, Choice A. The invisible primary is the period when a candidate, after throwing the proverbial hat into the ring, begins the process of seeking major donations and attempts to gain front-runner status so that the media gives his campaign coverage.

19. **(E)** Type of Question: Identification and analysis/cause-and-effect relationships

To answer this question, you must know the circumstances under which the McGovern-Frasier Commission was created. As described in the chapter, the Commission was formed after the debacle that took place at the 1968 Democratic convention in Chicago where Mayor Daley almost single-handedly prevented minority delegate representation.

20. **(C)** Type of Question: Generalization

This question deals with the nature of campaign strategy. Choices A, B, D, and E are all valid characteristics of campaigning. Choice C was a mistake that Richard Nixon made in the 1960 presidential campaign.

Section 2: Free-Response Question (7 points)

The data in the table on the next page show demographic election trends in recent presidential elections. From this information and your knowledge of United States politics, perform the following tasks:

(a) Identify three demographic characteristics that have played a role in presidential elections.

(b) Explain how these features contributed to the election of those U.S. presidents elected during the time periods detailed in the chart.

(c) Discuss the importance of demographics on presidential politics.

Voter Exit Polls in Presidential Elections 2000–2008			
Characteristic	2000	2004	2008
Percentage of all voters voting for			
Democratic candidate	48	48	53
Republican candidate	48	51	45
Third-party candidates	4	1	2
Percentage of men voting for			
Democratic candidate	43	44	49
Republican candidate	54	55	48
Third-party candidates	3	1	3
Percentage of women voting for			
Democratic candidate	54	51	56
Republican candidate	43	48	43
Third-party candidates	3	1	1
Percentage of whites voting for			
Democratic candidate	55	41	43
Republican candidate	42	58	55
Third-party candidates	3	1	2
Percentage of African-Americans voting for			
Democratic candidate	90	88	95
Republican candidate	9	11	4
Third-party candidates	3	3	2
Percentage of Hispanics voting for			
Democratic candidate	62	53	67
Republican candidate	35	44	31
Third-party candidates	3	3	2
Percentage of 18- to 29-year-olds voting for			
Democratic candidate	48	54	66
Republican candidate	47	45	32
Third-party candidates	5	1	2
Percentage of 65 and over voting for			
Democratic candidate	51	47	45
Republican candidate	47	52	53
Third-party candidates	2	1	2
Percentage of voters from the East voting for			
Democratic candidate	56	56	59
Republican candidate	40	44	40
Third-party candidates	4	–	1
Percentage of voters from the Midwest voting for			
Democratic candidate	48	48	54
Republican candidate	49	51	44
Third-party candidates	3	1	2
Percentage of voters from the South voting for			
Democratic candidate	43	42	45
Republican candidate	56	58	54
Third-party candidates	1	–	1
Percentage of voters from the West voting for			
Democratic candidate	49	50	57
Republican candidate	47	49	40
Third-party candidates	4	1	3

SAMPLE RESPONSE

(a) Three demographic characteristics that have played a significant role in recent presidential elections are gender, age, and race.

(b) Gender is one of the most significant demographic features in presidential elections. The 2000, 2004, and 2008 elections all reflect a gender gap in the way men and women vote. In the 2000 election there was an 11-point gap between women and men, with more women voting for Al Gore and more men voting for George W. Bush. The trend continued in 2004 and became very large again in 2008. Age also is a factor in the way people vote in presidential elections. In the three presidential elections displayed in the chart 18- to 29-year-olds voted Democratic by a much larger percentage than Republican, and in 2004 and 2008 the percentage of 65 and over voted Republican. Race is the most significant factor. In all three presidential elections listed, African-Americans voted heavily Democratic and a majority of white voters voted Republican.

(c) The importance of demographics on presidential politics cannot be underplayed. By examining the chart, it is clear that demographic trends are highly consistent and where they vary, it is usually by a very small percentage. Parties and candidates target groups that have traditionally supported them. That's why the Democrats have gone after the African-American vote, whereas the Republicans seek the votes of white voters. Once the party's base is secured, the candidates go after the so-called swing voters, the voters who are usually more Independent. Swing voters can be found in the suburbs and that is why geography plays such an important role. In 2000, 2004, and 2008 the Midwest suburbs became a battleground for the presidential candidates.

SCORING GUIDELINES FOR FREE-RESPONSE QUESTION (7 POINTS)

Part (a) 3 Points

One point is earned for each demographic characteristic identified from the chart. Acceptable answers are:

- gender
- age
- race and ethnicity
- region of country where you vote

Part (b) 3 Points

One point is earned for explaining how the demographic features chosen in (a) impacted presidential elections in 2000, 2004, or 2008. Acceptable answers are:

- Gender—gender gap between men and women
- Age—young people age 18–29 voting more Democratic than Republican
- Race and ethnicity—African-Americans voting more Democratic than Republican

Part (c) 1 Point

One point is earned for explaining how demographics are an important factor in presidential elections. Acceptable answers include but are not limited to:

- Parties and candidates target groups that traditionally support them.
- The candidates through voting patterns can identify and go after so-called swing voters.
- Candidates using regional voting trends map out a campaign strategy that solidifies their base and go after the states with the most electoral votes.

Political Beliefs and the Media

13

→ CIVIL RIGHTS ACT OF 1964

→ FAIRNESS DOCTRINE

→ INFORMATION SUPERHIGHWAY

→ LITERACY LAWS

→ MASS MEDIA

→ MEDIA BIAS

→ MOTOR VOTER ACT OF 1993

→ PARTY IDENTIFICATION

→ PHOTO OPS

→ POLITICAL SOCIALIZATION

→ POLL TAX

→ PUBLIC OPINION POLLS

→ SAMPLING ERROR

→ SIMPSON-MARZZOLI ACT (1987)

→ SOCIAL MEDIA

→ SOLID SOUTH

→ SOUND BITES

→ SUFFRAGE

→ TALKING HEADS

→ VOTER SUPPRESSION

→ VOTING RIGHTS ACT OF 1965

→ WAVE ELECTION

CONTEMPORARY CONNECTION

A new trend in reporting public opinion in presidential elections called aggregate polling (polls that report trends by taking the average of more than one poll of voters representing different polling outlets along with other factors) was used extensively to predict the outcome of the 2012 presidential election. This chapter explores the linkage institutions of voting and the media. What factors influence voting behavior and party identification? How does the media influence public opinion and political discourse? These questions are answered in this chapter.

Ever since Harry Truman held up a front page of the *Chicago Tribune* that declared "Dewey Defeats Truman," politicians have stopped taking voters for granted. They also view polling and the media with skepticism and rely on their own pollsters and media advisers. If elections prove the legitimacy of a candidate's campaign, the task of the politician is to find the way to influence the citizen to vote for him or her.

This chapter also explores why people either vote or why they stay home on Election Day. By looking at the demographics of America, you will be able to understand voter trends. Even though Americans are notorious in the manner in which they exercise this essential quality of a democracy, recent elections have provided optimism that voter turnout is on the increase. When you view the constitutional basis of voting and its history, you should see how long it has taken for all suffrage to be obtained by every citizen.

In recent elections, public opinion, measured through polls, became a primary barometer of how and why the voter behaved. Political polls were conducted to gauge the feelings and attitudes of the electorate. We will evaluate how polls are conducted, how candidates rely on polls and the media, and the impact of exit polls and the media.

The role of the media, including its historical development and its impact on public opinion and the political agenda, will be the focus in the last section of the chapter. Topics such as the limits placed on the media, the bias in the media, and the future importance of the information superhighway will be discussed.

QUICK REVIEW OF THE CONSTITUTIONAL AND LEGAL BASIS OF SUFFRAGE

- Article I Section 2 Clause (1) required each state to allow those qualified to vote for their own legislatures as well as the House of Representatives.
- Article II Section 1 Clause (2) provided for presidential electors to be chosen in each state with the manner determined by state legislatures.
- The Reserve Power clause of the Tenth Amendment gave the states the right to determine voting procedures.
- The Fifteenth Amendment gave freed slaves the right to vote.
- The Seventeenth Amendment changed the meaning of Article I Section 2 to allow eligible voters to elect senators directly.
- The Nineteenth Amendment made it illegal for the states to discriminate against men or women in establishing voting qualifications.
- The Twenty-Fourth Amendment outlawed the poll tax as a requirement for voting.
- The Twenty-Sixth Amendment prohibited the federal government and state governments from denying the right of 18-year-olds to vote in both state and federal elections.
- The Voting Rights Acts of 1957, 1960, and 1965 increased the opportunities for minorities to register and allowed the attorney general to prevent state interference in the voting process.
- The Supreme Court decision in *Baker v Carr* (1962) established the one man, one vote principle.
- Supreme Court decisions in the 1990s established that gerrymandering resulting in "majority-minority" districts was unconstitutional.

VOTING PATTERNS

Demographics, the type of election, socioeconomic status, religious background, and extent of party identification are some of the factors that influence voting patterns.

In order to understand why people vote, you must look first at the potential make-up of the American electorate. Demographic patterns are determined every ten years when the census is conducted. Besides establishing representation patterns, the census also provides important information related to the population's

- age
- socioeconomic make-up
- place of residence and shifting population movement
- ethnicity
- gender

The 2010 Census

Key aspects of the 2010 census reflect an increase in the aging America, a population shift to the sunbelt, and a decrease in those who would be classified as earning an income close to or below the poverty level. The 2010 U.S. census results released by the Census Bureau indicated big changes in the population of the United States and population shifts from big industrial states to the sunbelt states of the south and southwest. Specifically:

- The official U.S. population count is 308,745,538. In 2000 the population was 281,421,906. That is a growth rate of 9.7 percent, the lowest growth rate since the Great Depression.
- Minorities, especially Hispanics, make up a growing share of the U.S. population and are the largest ethnic group.
- Children are much more likely to be racial/ethnic minorities than adults.
- The fastest-growing states are in the South and West.
- Southern and western states gained seats in the U.S. House of Representatives, while northeastern and midwestern states lost seats.
- Metropolitan areas with the fastest rates of growth are mostly in the South and West; the fastest rates of decline tend to be in the Northeast and Midwest.
- Most U.S. population growth during the past century has taken place in suburbs, rather than central cities.
- The states of Illinois, Iowa, Louisiana, Massachusetts, Michigan, Missouri, New Jersey, New York, Ohio, and Pennsylvania lost congressional seats. New York and Ohio lost two seats.
- The states that gained seats were Arizona, Florida, Georgia, Nevada, South Carolina, Texas, Utah, and Washington. Texas will gain four seats. Florida will gain two seats.

Immigrant patterns and these factors have public policy consequences and are therefore important to the political process.

Political Socialization

Political socialization is the factor that determines voting behavior. There is growing interest in how people actually develop their political orientation, thus making it more likely they will vote. Studies have determined that these attitudes are determined by the family, the media, and public schools. Party identification, the voter's evaluation of the candidates, and policy voting, the actual decision to vote for a particular candidate based on these factors, all come into play in evaluating the overall voting process.

What are the factors, then, that make people decide to cast their vote for a particular candidate? They can be classified in two major categories, sociological and psychological. Sociological factors include:

- income and occupation
- education
- sex and age
- religious and ethnic background
- region of the country where you live
- family make-up

Psychological factors include

- party affiliation and identification
- perception of candidate's policies and/or image
- the feeling that your vote will make a statement

Based on these factors we can make the following statements about who votes, what party those who vote lean toward, and who doesn't vote:

- Voters who are in the lower income brackets and laborers tend to vote Democratic. Those upper-middle to upper-income level voters, many of whom are business and professional white-collar workers, tend to vote Republican. Yet when you compare voting rates of both groups, you will see that citizens with higher incomes and greater education vote in greater numbers than those with lower incomes and less education. This is the number one factor in what determines voter turnout. This pattern held true in the 1976–2012 presidential elections.

- Voting patterns do not usually correlate strongly with gender. Analysts suggest there is a gender gap in national politics, a significant deviation between the way men and women vote. In addition, there is no guarantee that even if a woman ran for national office, she would get the women's vote. With Geraldine Ferraro on the 1984 Democratic ticket, more women voted for the Reagan-Bush ticket, proving that women did not vote just because there was a woman running for vice president. However, since 1988 a trend has developed where women vote for Democratic candidates in greater percentages than men vote. This was particularly true in the 1994 midterm election when polls showed that "angry white" voters heavily supported Republican candidates, whereas women still supported Democratic candidates. Yet in 1996, because for the first time the male vote was split almost 50–50 between Clinton and Dole, women voted for Clinton by more than 10 percent. As stated in the previous chapter, the soccer mom became a new term illustrating why certain women voters favored Clinton so heavily. This trend repeated itself in 2000. In 2004, both campaigns went after the so-called NASCAR dad. President George W. Bush even opened up a NASCAR event with the traditional "Gentlemen, start your engines." John Kerry went goose hunting hoping to siphon the gun owners' vote. But the most significant change that occurred in 2004 was a new gender gap described in Chapter 12, the gap between single and married women. In the elections of 2008 and 2012, Barack Obama continued to attract women to the Democratic ticket, resulting in a gender gap and both a greater percentage of women turning out and voting for him.

- The youth vote is undergoing a major change. Ever since the Twenty-Sixth Amendment was passed, political parties have wanted to capture the young voter. Even though they seem to vote more Democratic than Republican (with the exception of youth supporting Reagan and Bush), the fact remains that they have voted in much lower numbers than other groups. From 1976 to 1988, for instance, the turnout among the youngest voters, those 18–20 years old, was less than 40 percent of the eligible voters. From 1992–2012, MTV ran a "Choose or Lose" campaign, resulting in increased registration and turnout of young voters. In the 2008 and 2012 elections, 18–24-year-olds voted in large numbers for Barack Obama. In the 2010 and 2014 midterms, the youth vote turnout declined significantly from the presidential election years of 2008 and 2012.

**THE YOUTH VOTE HAS BEEN GREATLY INFLUENCED
BY MTV'S ROCK THE VOTE CAMPAIGN**

- Religious and ethnic background highly influences voter choice and voter turnout. Dating back to the early days of immigration, Catholics and Jews tend to vote Democratic (Republicans traditionally supported anti-immigration legislation), whereas northern Protestants tend to vote Republican. Strongly affiliated religious groups also tend to vote more often in general elections, compared to those people who don't identify themselves as being closely connected to a religion. Minority groups, although voting heavily for Democratic candidates, do not turn out as much as white voters. Jesse Jackson and his Rainbow Coalition, minority groups of "color" rallying around causes espoused by Jackson, have been attempting to increase minority registration and voter turnout. Minority groups are a fertile field for political parties to pursue. After the 2000 election, a religious gap became evident. Those people who were regular churchgoers tended to vote Republican, while those who did not attend religious services regularly tended to vote Democratic. This trend continued from 2004–2012.

- Historically, geography has dictated a voter preference. The South voted solidly Democratic after the Civil War. However, the solid South has become much more conservative. They vote Republican more on the national level and continue to vote Democratic in local elections, but it is sometimes hard to tell the difference because of ideology. Comparing voter turnout, proportionally, Northerners vote in greater numbers than Southerners. This difference is explained by a large number of minority voters who are still not registered. New England and sunbelt voters tend to vote Republican, whereas the big industrial states, especially in the big cities, lean to the Democrats but are considered toss-ups in close presidential elections.

- The 2012 election was characterized by a Democratic coalition of 18–30-year-olds, Hispanics, African-Americans, Asians, and women. Governor Romney won almost 60 percent of the white vote. But their share of the electorate has been falling steadily: 20 years ago whites were 87 percent of the electorate; in 2012 they were 72 percent.

- Even though party identification plays a key role in determining voter choice and voter turnout, more and more people are registering Independent. There is a greater overall Democratic registration, but voters tend to respond more to the individual candidate and issues, along with the sociological factors, than just party identification alone.

PARTY IDENTIFICATION

If we assume party identification is a key factor in determining voter turnout and voter preference, then we would assume the Democrats would have the edge. This was definitely true in Congress, where Democrats dominated both houses from World War II until 1994, when the Republicans gained control of the House as well as the Senate. When you look at presidential elections, personality and issues rather than party have been a conclusive factor in determining the outcome of the election. In many elections, ticket-splitting occurred more than straight party line voting. This was especially evident in 1996, 2010, and 2014 when the voters kept in office the Democratic president and a Republican Congress. In order to vote, you must be registered. Historically, this was an important factor explaining why voter turnout was low.

Voting patterns vary from election to election and reached a peak in the 1960s presidential elections.

Voter Declines

Even though it is easier for people to vote and a greater number of people have registered, there has been a consistent downward trend from 1968–2014. The number of people of voting age has more than doubled since 1932. Yet after reaching a high in 1960, the percentage of eligible voters who voted actually declined (except for a small increase in 1984 and 1992). Because of the increase in young voters and successful efforts to enroll minorities and get them to vote, there was a significant increase in the 1992 election when close to 55 percent of the registered voters turned out. In 1996, because of negative voter reaction to the campaign issues raised by President Clinton and Senator Dole, the voter turnout was again below 50 percent. In 2000 the percentage rose to a little above 50 percent. In 2004, there was a record voter turnout that translated into a 60 percent turnout. The 2008 presidential election saw an increase in voter registration and voter turnout. A little more than 62 percent of eligible voters turned out. In 2012, the turnout was 58 percent. Since 1932 the highest presidential turnouts (60 percent or more) were in the three elections that took place in the 1960s. National and international events, as well as new legislation that increased voting opportunities for minorities, were probably responsible for the higher numbers. After Watergate the percentage of voters dropped dramatically. It is interesting to note that in off-year congressional elections, voter turnout is significantly lower. From 1974 to 2014 turnout in midterm congressional elections averaged around 40 percent.

There is a real inconsistency between voter participation and the amount and type of election coverage provided in the campaigns. Everything from presidential debates to town meetings and an increased use of the mass media should result in an increased voter turnout. But because of a decline in party identification and a distrust of politicians, it seems that many eligible voters would rather sit out elections.

THE RIGHT TO VOTE

The history of suffrage reflects increased opportunities to vote.

The country has seen a tremendous change in the legal right to vote. When the Constitution was ratified, franchise was given to white male property owners only. Today there is a potential for over 234 million people who are at least 18 years old to vote. It has been a long struggle to obtain suffrage for individuals who were held back by such considerations as property ownership, race, religious background, literacy, ability to pay poll taxes, and sex. In addition, many state restrictions lessened the impact of federal law and constitutional amendments.

**THE HISTORY OF SUFFRAGE HAS BEEN CHARACTERIZED BY
MINORITY GROUPS FIGHTING FOR THEIR RIGHT TO VOTE**

By the 1800s all religious qualifications were eliminated from voting requirements. Property considerations also were legislated out of existence by most states in the middle of the nineteenth century. The aftermath of the Civil War provided a major attempt to franchise the freed race.

However, the passage of the Fifteenth Amendment was countered by the passage of literacy laws and poll taxes by most Southern states. The progressive era of the early twentieth century saw the passage of two key amendments, the direct election of senators and the granting of voting rights to women. After the *Brown* decision in 1954, Congress began formulating voting rights legislation such as the Voting Rights Act of 1965, and these changes were backed by the passage of the Twenty-Fourth Amendment, eliminating the poll tax (or any other voting tax). The final groups to receive the vote were Washington, D.C., voters, as a result of the Twenty-Third Amendment in 1961 and the 18-year-old as a result of the passage of the Twenty-Sixth Amendment in 1971. In 1992 Jesse Jackson's Rainbow Coalition increased minority voter registration. To make voter registration easier for all groups, the Motor Voter Act of 1993 was signed into law by President Clinton. This law enabled people to register to vote at motor vehicle departments. In fact, it has not been since the Voting Rights Act of 1965 that so many new voters registered. More than 600,000 voters became eligible to vote.

Even though these trends resulted in an increase in the potential pool of voters, it was still left up to the individual states to regulate specific voting requirements. Such issues as residency, registration procedures, age, and voting times affect the ability of people to vote. However, federal law and Supreme Court decisions have created more and more consistency in these areas. This was especially apparent in the 2000 election when the Supreme Court intervened in the Florida recount and decided to stop the recount in *Bush v Gore*. For instance, the Supreme Court has ruled that a 30-day period is ample time for residency. The Motor Voter Act does provide for the centralization of voter registration along with local registration regulations. Some states have permitted 17-year-olds to vote in some primary elections. Literacy tests have been outlawed in every state as a result of the Voting Rights Act Amendments of 1970 and Supreme Court decisions.

Important Legislation

The two significant pieces of modern legislation increasing voting opportunities were the Civil Rights Act of 1964 and the Voting Rights Act of 1965. The Civil Rights Act prohibited the use of any registration requirement that resulted in discrimination and paved the way for the involvement of the federal government to enforce the law. The Voting Rights Act of 1965 finally made the Fifteenth Amendment a reality. It was reinforced by other amendments in 1970, 1975, and 1982. As a result of this act, the poll tax and literacy requirements were addressed. The act gave the attorney general the power to determine which states were in violation of the law and led to the passage of the constitutional amendments after the Supreme Court ruled on the legality of the law. The act also prohibited states from passing their own restrictive voting laws without "preclearance" from the Department of Justice. The Supreme Court ruled in 2013 that the section of the Voting Rights Act of 1965 mandating preclearance by some states before those states could change their voting procedures was unconstitutional. The Court told Congress that if it wanted to reestablish preclearance as a practice, the Congress would have to pass new legislation. Immediately following the decision states that had been required to preclear new procedures started moving toward new voter identification laws.

In the 2012 election, several states attempted to pass legislation that would have lowered voter turnout. States that allowed early voting enacted laws that shortened the early voting period. As a result in Florida, some voters had to wait over eight hours to vote. Other states passed laws that required a photo ID in order to vote. Proponents of this argued that these laws would prevent voter fraud. Opponents called the laws voter suppression because the groups that were impacted were minorities who typically voted Democratic. Courts found that some of the legislation violated the Voting Rights Act of 1965.

There are some cases where restrictions can exist on a person's right to vote. People in mental institutions, the homeless, convicted felons, and dishonorably discharged soldiers have been denied the right to vote in some states. Many states have increasingly passed different kinds of voter identification laws to ensure voter integrity. Opponents of these laws claim that the real reason these laws were passed was to reduce voter minority turnout and other groups who traditionally vote Democratic. The Justice Department has stepped in, and many of these laws have been ruled unconstitutional. Although the impact on presidential elections has been negligible, laws that are implemented could potentially reduce turnout in future elections.

PUBLIC OPINION

Public opinion is molded through a combination of factors at a very early age.

Public opinion can be defined as the attitudes, perceptions, and viewpoints individuals hold about politics and government. Some political scientists view this process as one of political socialization. It is interesting to see the parallels between the factors that influence voting patterns and the factors that mold public opinion and political socialization. They include:

- the family
- the schools
- the church
- molders of public opinion
- the mass media

People internalize viewpoints at a very early age and act on them as they grow older. "Family values" has become an overused phrase but, in fact, is the primary source of the formulation of political opinions. When Vice President Dan Quayle made family values an election issue in 1992, he touched a chord that set off a debate. The reality is that children internalize what they hear and see within their family unit. If a child lives with a single parent, that child will certainly have strong attitudes about child support. If parents tend to speak about party identification, most children will tend to register and vote for the same party as their parents. Schools and the church play a secondary role in the formation of political views. There is no doubt that the Catholic Church's position on abortion has had a tremendous impact on Catholics taking a stand for the "right to life." However, the family unit reinforces the viewpoint.

Schools and teachers inculcate the meaning of citizenship at very early ages. Children recite the Pledge of Allegiance and sing the national anthem. Depending upon how open the educational system is, students will also learn how to question the role of government.

People who are in the public spotlight—whether they are politicians, union officials, successful businessmen and women, spiritual leaders, or your personal doctors, lawyers, or accountants—play an impressive role in molding public opinion. People holding important offices command respect and use different techniques to influence the public. The mass media (covered in the last part of this chapter) is playing an increasingly important role in the formation of people's political attitudes. TV talk shows, interactive technology, and the print media comment on every aspect of our lives. Surveys have shown that the average household watches television more than seven hours a day.

The translation of public opinion into public policy takes place when policymakers truly understand opinion trends. This is one of the most difficult aspects of policymakers. They rely on such things as polls, letters, and personal input from constituents. The next section will discuss polling techniques.

Opinion Polls

In recent years, poll-taking has increased in scope and importance. Pollsters want to determine what the American public is thinking. The results are widely reported in the media, and in a number of cases polls themselves are newsworthy. The qualities that are measured in polls include:

Public opinion polls take the pulse of America regarding many different issues. They also are predictors of the outcome of elections.

- How intense people are in their beliefs and attitudes
- The real wants and needs of individuals that can be translated into policy
- Whether public opinion on any given issue is constant or changing
- The extent to which the public is polarized or has a consensus on any given issue. Issues such as the Vietnam War and healthcare are two examples of the public displaying either polarization or consensus

Using scientific methodology and computer technology, professional pollsters such as Gallup, CNN, and daily newspapers have mastered the art of measuring public opinion. In presidential election years, pollsters aggregate (take the average) all the tracking polls. When looking at political polls, these pollsters consider:

- Who conducts the poll—there is a real difference between a candidate who reports polling results and a neutral organization that conducts a poll
- The sample size—make sure that a random sample was obtained
- If a clear distinction is made regarding the population sample
- When the poll was conducted
- The poll methodology
- The sampling error, which gives the poll statistical validity—±3 percent is usually an acceptable standard
- How clearly the questions were worded

During recent presidential campaigns, CNN and other media outlets took daily tracking polls of both likely voters and those voters who were eligible to vote. The results differed significantly. In 1996, the increased popularity of the Internet contributed to the proliferation of daily tracking polls. On any given day, one could find as many as a dozen polls broken down nationally and by state, by registered voter, by likely voters, by electoral vote, by popular vote, and by over a three-day period as well as over a one-day period. The result was conflicting data. By 2008, polling techniques became so sophisticated that some websites were able to accurately predict both the popular vote and electoral vote margins that Barack Obama received. In 2012, a *New York Times* blogger correctly predicted the electoral result using an aggregate of the tracking polls.

Public opinion polls have become so sophisticated that the use of exit polls in carefully selected precincts can accurately predict the outcome of an election minutes after the polls close. In addition, these polls can give valuable information regarding why people voted the way they did. A serious question has been raised regarding the prediction of elections using exit polls in presidential elections. If the East Coast results are reported right after the polls close, will it influence West Coast voters to stay home? There have even been attempts to legislate restrictions on the use of exit polls.

In the 2000 presidential election polling organizations came under fire. The Voter News Service, a conglomerate of the major media organizations pooling their resources to provide exit poll information, gave inaccurate statistics to the networks regarding the results of the Florida vote. This caused the networks to first call the election for Vice President Gore. Then, when additional information was evaluated, the networks pulled back their initial projection and the state remained in the "too close to call" column until the networks again, based on faulty information, gave the state to George W. Bush in the early hours of the next morning. Based on this, Gore called Bush and conceded the election until it became clear that the real results were so close that a recount of Florida's votes was required. Voter News Service took responsibility for the poor methodology used and, along with the networks, implemented new procedures for the 2004 election.

THE OLD MEDIA *VS.* THE NEW MEDIA

The impact of the information superhighway on the political and public agenda has far-reaching consequences.

As the media continues to try to quench Americans' thirst for information, different kinds of media conglomerates form, and new kinds of technologies are made available. This has led to the growth of the information superhighway. This "thruway" of information has many different exits. Media conglomerates and the Internet are two of the major characteristics of the information superhighway. The media concentration that exists gives the public access to the highway. The structure can be viewed as a three-tiered structure—an inner, middle, and outer tier. The inner tier consists of the three major networks, cable news channels, the national news magazines (*Time*, *Newsweek*, and *U.S. News and World Report*), and the four national newspapers (*The New York Times*, *Washington Post*, *Wall Street Journal*, and *Los Angeles Times*), as well as the national wire service the Associated Press. The middle tier embraces other national newspapers including *USA Today*, *Chicago Tribune*, the *Christian Science Monitor*, and other news services as well as magazines with a strong political slant (*New Republic* and *National Review*). The outer tier consists of local newspapers and local television and radio stations. Crossing these tiers is a concentration of power among major media conglomerates such as Gannett and Time Warner, Disney, and General Electric. The impact of so-called right-wing radio and television commentators such as Rush Limbaugh and Glenn Beck, and Fox News cannot be underestimated.

As the Internet has grown, a new media called the social media has emerged. The social media include e-mail, personal opinion pages called "blogs," Facebook, and Twitter, and other sites that promote personal interaction. The net result is a greater impact on the political agenda. Starting in 1996, every major political candidate had a "website" on the Internet. Candidates also use the Internet for fundraising. In the 2000 election Senator John McCain raised over $1 million using his website. In 2003, presidential candidate Howard Dean set an Internet fund-raising record. Sites such as *moveon.org* and *meetup.org* have changed the political landscape. Political "blogs" (web logs) and video sites such as *youtube.com* have had a major impact on voting behavior. As the public has more and more access to information, the media has the potential to influence the way the public thinks. For instance, having the capability to react immediately to an issue raised by using voice mail enables instant polling to take place. Barack Obama notified his supporters of his choice of Senator Joseph Biden as his vice presidential running mate by text message and e-mail. The Obama campaign utilized the e-mail and cell phone base throughout the 2008 campaign. In 2012, the Obama campaign used social media more effectively than the Romney campaign as a tool to get out their vote. This became a contributing factor in Obama's victory over Governor Romney.

The media, by selecting the events that are covered, also influences what the public perceives as being important. This capability also applies to political leaders. Knowing that they are being broadcast live on C-SPAN certainly encourages House and Senate members to play to a sophisticated TV audience. The White House Office of Communications monitors the media on a daily basis.

The media has also been blamed for the decline of party identification and party politics. Why should an individual get involved with a political party when the interactive media makes it easy to not only access information but also influence office holders? Candidates and office holders also use the media to get their message out in their high-tech campaigns. They use selective leaks, known as trial balloons, to test the political waters. They become "talking heads," with the media focusing on the face of politicians during speeches and talk shows often ending up as sound bites. The information superhighway, thus, certainly is growing in importance, but it may be a double-edged sword. The faster it grows, the less direct control policymakers may have on the average citizen.

MEDIA COVERAGE

Virtually all candidates and every president feel that the media is unfair in the manner in which they cover a campaign or administration. They attempt to control and manipulate the media, creating media events and photo opportunities. Presidents such as Ronald Reagan have even developed successful strategies to control media access by planning the event, staying on the offensive, controlling the flow of information, limiting access by the media, talking only about the issues the administration wants to talk about, speaking in one voice as an administration, and constantly repeating the same message. This worked for Reagan, but when Clinton attempted to move the White House press out of their briefing room, there was a hostile reaction, forcing the president to back down.

The irony of Clinton's lack of success with the media is that during the campaign, many felt that he was their fair-haired boy. However, statistical studies indicated that on balance, the media covered both Bush and Clinton, praising and criticizing them whenever events dictated. The 2008 presidential campaign raised questions about media coverage of major candidates during the primary and general election. Charges of media bias by the Hillary Clinton campaign during the primaries were echoed by John McCain's campaign during the general election. A study, "Winning the Media Campaign: How the Press Reported the 2008 General Election," was conducted by the Pew Research Center's Project for Excellence in Journalism. Their key findings were that even though Obama's coverage started negatively after his nomination, the media's coverage was much more positive as Obama's poll numbers increased. McCain's coverage became increasingly negative after McCain suspended his campaign at the start of the economic crisis. Another finding reflected the nature of media coverage being driven by the so-called "horse race," that is, which candidate was up, and which candidate was down. Overall, the study found that the "press treatment of Obama had been somewhat more positive than negative, but not markedly so." However, media coverage of McCain was described in the study as "heavily unfavorable." In the 2012 presidential election, the mainstream media covered Governor Romney and President Obama in a fairer manner than social media.

Media Bias

The key questions raised regarding coverage are: is it fair and balanced and, if there is an editorial stand, does it make a difference? The question of media bias is answered by the media when they point to what they call the canons of good journalism—objectivity and responsible reporting. There has never been any correlation between newspaper endorsements of a political candidate and the candidate winning the election because of it. In addition, legal restraints such as slander and libel as well as legislative direction from the FCC force the media to abide by standards. During the campaign, the FCC sets down equal-time provisions, which give equal time to all candidates who seek the same office. The Fairness Doctrine, scrapped in 1987, provided that the media air opposing opinions of the same issue. The FCC decided that this provision violated the First Amendment and that, with the proliferation of cable television and the number of talk radio programs, there was a diversity of opinions aired. As a result of the mistakes the media made

The media is both blamed and praised for the type of coverage it provides.

in reporting the results of the 2000 election, the networks and Congress pledged to review alternatives to exit polls. Suggestions such as a standard time to close the polls nationwide have been discussed.

Investigative and Adversarial Reporting

The rise of investigative reporting and adversarial reporting gave rise to complaints that the media was going after politicians and government officials. News magazines such as *60 Minutes* added fuel to the fire.

The turning point of investigative journalism came when Bob Woodward and Carl Bernstein of the *Washington Post* "followed the money," which led to the president's reelection committee and ultimately to President Nixon himself. During the 1980s the press pursued the Iran-Contra dealings of Oliver North and took up Gary Hart's challenge when Hart stated that there was no monkey business in his personal life. The press shot pictures of Hart and Donna Rice on a boat called *Monkey Business* and his presidential aspirations ended.

During the 1988 campaign President Bush literally told *Nightline* correspondent Ted Koppel that he overstepped his bounds as an impartial moderator. The press also went after the personal indiscretions of cabinet nominee John Tower in 1989 and Supreme Court nominee Clarence Thomas in 1991. Bill Clinton was able to defuse the Gennifer Flowers allegation in a post-Super Bowl broadcast of *60 Minutes*. And, in 1996, the financial scandals of President Clinton's campaign were deflected by the Democrats.

Government has had to open up its records to the public as a result of such laws as the 1974 Freedom of Information Act and a number of other sunshine laws. These acts opened up meetings and made records of the government available to the public and media. In the end, a balance must be reached between the needs of the candidate or the government and the legitimate interests of the media in providing accurate, relevant information to the public.

The Internet has also played a key investigative role. In 1998 Internet gossip columnist Matt Drudge broke the story of Bill Clinton's affair with a White House intern on his website before any other traditional media outlet. In ten years time, the Internet and the 24/7 news cycle have resulted in one continuous media watch during political campaigns. Blogs have broken news stories, and campaigns have had to react to videos uploaded to YouTube. In 2006, Senator George Allen's campaign was never the same after he referred to somebody filming his speech as "Macaca," a racial slur. The clip was viewed on YouTube millions of times, and Allen lost the election in a very close contest. In 2012, an anonymous person videotaped presidential candidate Mitt Romney at a private fund-raising event closed to the press. *Mother Jones* magazine, a liberal publication, found the video on YouTube and got permission to release it. On the recording, Romney spoke about how 47 percent of Americans did not pay federal income taxes, how they were looking for government handouts, and that this group would never vote for him. These revelations were very harmful to Romney's campaign.

RELATIONSHIP WITH THE MEDIA

The president's association with the media can be characterized as a love/hate relationship.

From the time John Kennedy instituted televised press conferences, to the challenge by Gary Hart to find some personal indiscretion in his private life, to the limited number of press conferences Ronald Reagan wanted, the role of the press has been a double-edged sword for the president. However, suffice it to say that modern presidents depend and rely on the media to tell the story of the president's agenda. The president uses his press secretary and the office of communications to deal directly with the press corps. He has a great deal of access to television, making prime time speeches for his State of the Union address. He also makes a weekly radio address talking directly to the public on any issue he wants to raise. Using the "bully pulpit," the president is sometimes able to dominate the news cycle.

The press feels that they must establish an adversarial relationship with the White House in order for them to maintain their independence and integrity. Ever since the Woodward-Bernstein investigative reporting that helped bring down the Nixon presidency, presidents have tried to control the media.

There has been the often-described "inside the beltway" coverage of presidential politics, versus what the rest of the country views on the evening news. The White House attempts to manipulate the media. Presidential appearances are designed to maximize his message. A public relations strategy by the White House of blaming the media for the nation's problems has been countered by the press, who claim that they are merely the messengers. Yet the president needs the media to get his message to the American people. The press secretary holds daily press briefings. Reporters are given special invitations to have exclusive interviews with the president.

The relationship between the press and the White House has always raised questions on how the press covers the president. Since 1960, when John Kennedy initiated televised press conferences, the White House press corps have had a "love-hate" relationship with the sitting president. Public polls reflect the sentiment that at times the press is biased against the president, while other polls indicate that the press does not ask the tough questions. Most political scientists find a balance. When the story calls for an investigation, the press usually leads the way. The growth of the "blogosphere" has added to the 24/7 coverage of the presidency. Ever since Watergate, the name *gate* has been attached to presidential coverage—Iran–Contragate, Travelgate, and Nannygate are just a few scandals. The press was relentless in covering the scandal leading to Bill Clinton's impeachment. This type of coverage has been described as a "media frenzy."

THE IMPEACHMENT OF BILL CLINTON

In one of the most bitter and partisan political clashes in American history, the House of Representatives passed two articles of impeachment on December 19, 1998. The events leading to the first elected American president's impeachment read like a sordid novel. Special Prosecutor Kenneth Starr had been investigating President Clinton's role in the Whitewater land acquisition and other alleged White House abuses including the dismissal of travel office personnel and illegally obtained FBI tapes. President Clinton had also been fighting other legal battles. Paula Jones, an Arkansas government official, accused the president of sexual misconduct when Clinton was governor of Arkansas. Clinton denied the charges, and Jones sued the president. The Supreme Court ruled unanimously that Jones's civil suit could proceed while Clinton was still in office. Clinton testified and denied the charges as well as charges that he had been involved sexually with a White House intern. When this relationship with Monica Lewinsky was reported over the Internet in January 1998, Starr began investigating the president to determine whether Clinton lied during his testimony in the Jones suit. Clinton publicly denied any sexual misconduct with Lewinsky; Starr's inquiry took seven months to complete.

The investigation culminated with the unprecedented testimony of the president appearing before a grand jury on video. Clinton again denied any legal wrongdoing, but admitted publicly that he misled the American people and, indeed, had a relationship with the young intern. Starr completed his report in August 1998 and concluded that there was "credible" evidence that Clinton may have committed impeachable offenses. The House Judiciary committee voted on four articles of impeachment. The full House rejected two of the articles and submitted to the Senate the final articles accusing the president of high crimes and misdemeanors as a result of grand jury perjury and obstruction of justice.

The Senate convened in January 1999 and, following the same rules that were in place when Andrew Johnson's impeachment trial took place more than a century earlier, met for nearly two months. The Chief Justice of the Supreme Court, William Rehnquist, delivered the final roll call vote on both counts. The Senate voted 55-45 for acquittal on the perjury charges with 10 Republicans joining with all 45 Democrats. On the count of obstruction of justice, the Senators voted 50-50. Neither of the charges received the necessary two-thirds majority required, and President Clinton was acquitted.

Public opinion played an important part in the impeachment of the president. Throughout the entire investigation, Clinton's job approval ratings were over 60 percent, the highest ratings of any second-term president. His personal approval ratings, however, were well under 40 percent. The public was suggesting that the president's private life should be separated from his public duties. One of the consequences resulting from the public's perception of the impeachment inquiry was that the Democrats gained seats in the November midterm election. This was very unusual since, historically, the party in power usually loses seats. As a result of the election, Speaker of the House Newt Gingrich resigned from the House, forcing the Republican majority to select a new speaker.

As much as the press tries to gain access, the president in the end can control to a certain extent the nature of the coverage. For instance, when the marines landed in Somalia for a humanitarian purpose, the Bush administration gave full disclosure, and there was live coverage of the event. On the other hand, during the Gulf War, the media complained that the administration was preventing the press from doing its job.

PUBLIC APPROVAL

The president must obtain public support for his agenda to be completed.

Public approval and mobilizing public support are crucial for the president to achieve his policy agenda. Public opinion polls are constant barometers of the public mood. From periodic job approval polls to specific polls on how the public feels about public policy proposals, the president's program is constantly being evaluated. The average approval rating of presidents who have finished their term is only around 50 percent. Job approval, when a president is serving, fluctuates greatly. When the Gulf War ended, George H. W. Bush had an approval rating of close to 90 percent. At the closing days of his presidency, it was under 40 percent. After September 11, 2001, George W. Bush also had a 90 percent approval rating. During the presidential campaign in 2004, his job approval hovered around 50 percent. During the 2006 midterm election campaign, Bush's approval rating dropped below 40 percent. By the end of his presidency, Bush's approval reached record lows. From 2010–2014, President Obama's approval rating averaged in the mid-40s reflecting a diminished view of public opinion since his first elecion. Public approval is dependent on party affiliation, age, education, and religious affiliation as well as how a specific event influences the public perception of a president's leadership ability. Specific areas such as the economy, foreign policy crisis, scandals, and legislative successes can influence approval ratings.

Every president wants to believe he has a mandate from the American people. Whether an election was won by a slim majority or a landslide, every president coming into office talks about a "mandate for change." Presidents have used their bully pulpits—the ability to use the office of the presidency to promote a particular program—to influence Congress to accept legislative proposals. Such techniques as Roosevelt's fireside chats and Clinton's town meetings have been successful in getting the president's message out to the public. Once support is obtained, the president must use it as a wedge to get Congress to approve his agenda. Staged events such as bill signings solidify the support so that the next agenda item can be addressed.

Section 1: Multiple-Choice Questions

1. Which of the following conclusions can be made about voting behavior?

   (A) Young people turn out more than any other age group.
   (B) Minorities generally support Republican candidates.
   (C) Southerners vote more than Northerners.
   (D) Voting is a class-based activity.
   (E) Women vote more for Republican candidates than men.

2. Which section of the country has the lowest voter turnout?

   (A) The South
   (B) The Northeast
   (C) The Midwest
   (D) The West
   (E) The Southwest

3. Which class of people has the highest percentage of voter turnout?

   (A) Middle class
   (B) Lower class
   (C) Upper class
   (D) Upper-middle class
   (E) Voter turnout has no relationship to class

4. Which of the following definitions reflects the idea that the victorious party should carry out its proposed agenda?

   (A) Constituent service by the elected representatives
   (B) The integrity of the political party
   (C) The party's platform
   (D) Voter referendums
   (E) The mandate theory of elections

5. Which of the following is a major result of media-centered politics?

   (A) A greater interest in the election
   (B) A greater loyalty to political parties
   (C) An increase in voter turnout
   (D) A decrease in voter turnout
   (E) An increase in the analysis of issues by the media

6. Which of the following represents the most effective way for a president to manage news coverage?

   (A) Controlling the flow of information
   (B) Staying on the defensive
   (C) Having different staff members speak to the press
   (D) Explaining a policy issue multiple times
   (E) Giving reporters unlimited access to his daily routine

7. All of the following are criticisms aimed at the media EXCEPT

(A) The media defines the campaign agenda rather than the candidate.
(B) The media accepts too many negative advertisements.
(C) The media relies too much on polling.
(D) The media's investigations of politicians usually emphasize serious issues.
(E) Talk radio places an unfair emphasis on conservative issues.

8. Which of the following groups represents the audience the media aims to develop stories for?

(A) The college-educated
(B) The upper class
(C) The masses
(D) The lower class
(E) People looking for in-depth analysis of issues

9. All of the following reflect the constitutional basis of suffrage EXCEPT

(A) states determining the time, manner, and place of elections
(B) term limits on United States senators and representatives passed by individual states
(C) the Fifteenth Amendment to the Constitution
(D) the Seventeenth Amendment to the Constitution
(E) the Nineteenth Amendment to the Constitution

10. All of the following statements best explain why people vote EXCEPT

(A) religious views
(B) political socialization
(C) gender politics
(D) the economic class to which they belong
(E) political surveys

11. Which of the following trends most closely reflects the last 40 years of American electoral history?

(A) An increase in suffrage opportunities
(B) A consistent increase in voter turnout
(C) Third-party victories
(D) Campaign finance reform affecting congressional races
(E) Congressional incumbents losing elections

12. All of the following conclusions are true about voting behavior EXCEPT

(A) Voting is a class-based activity.
(B) Young people have the highest turnout rate.
(C) Whites vote with greater frequency than members of minority groups.
(D) Southerners vote in smaller numbers than Northerners.
(E) Women voters tend to support candidates with views similar to their own regardless of whether the candidate is a man or woman.

13. The Motor Voter Act signed by President Clinton makes it easier than ever to vote. All of the following provisions accomplish the goals of the act EXCEPT

    (A) It provides for automatic registration of eligible citizens when they fill out an application for a driver's license.
    (B) It requires that states periodically review their voter lists for accuracy.
    (C) It authorizes $50 million to help cover implementation costs.
    (D) It purges people from voter rolls because they didn't vote in the previous election.
    (E) It provides for automatic registration of eligible voters as a result of license renewal.

14. In a presidential election, if no candidate receives an electoral college majority

    (A) the winner of the popular election becomes president
    (B) a run-off election is held with a new slate of electors
    (C) the election is thrown into the House of Representatives
    (D) the election is thrown into the full Congress
    (E) the Supreme Court determines the winner

15. It has been shown in recent elections that during times of severe economic troubles, the electorate

    (A) do not vote as often as they do during good times
    (B) tend to vote out incumbents
    (C) tend to vote incumbents back in
    (D) are more likely to vote in congressional races than the presidential race
    (E) register in large numbers

16. Which of the following statements is true about the effect of ethnic groups on voter choice during the presidential elections of the 2000s?

    (A) Catholics tend to vote Republican.
    (B) Northern Protestants tend to vote Democratic.
    (C) Jews tend to vote Democratic.
    (D) The religious right tends to vote Democratic.
    (E) Hispanics tend to vote Republican.

17. The validity of a poll is best determined by

    (A) a sample that represents more than half of the people in a population polled
    (B) a large gap between the time the poll is taken and the time the results are released
    (C) partisan groups taking and reporting the results of the poll
    (D) complex questions to be answered by the people being polled
    (E) a sampling error of those polled under 5 percent

18. Which of the following represents what media watchers would portray as the benchmark of investigative journalism?

(A) Tabloid papers reporting accusations by Gennifer Flowers

(B) Magazine articles using anonymous sources accusing President Clinton of a secret rendezvous with Paula Jones

(C) The media stalking Gary Hart looking for evidence of indiscretion during his 1984 presidential campaign

(D) The efforts of Woodward and Bernstein in uncovering the Watergate cover-up

(E) The press going after personal indiscretions of cabinet nominee John Tower

19. Which of the following represents an effect of the passage of the Freedom of Information Act?

(A) More meetings were opened to the public.

(B) It became more difficult to obtain documents from governmental organizations.

(C) Government operations were held in executive session.

(D) Stricter regulations governed the shredding of documents.

(E) The government was forced to open up top secret military documents.

Answer Explanations

1. **(D)** Type of Question: Solution to a problem

The question asks you to identify the characteristics of voting behavior. Through the process of elimination, you should be able to pick choice D as the only factually correct answer. The other choices provide reverse solutions. Young people turn out less than any other age group, Northerners vote more than Southerners, minorities generally support Democrats, and women usually vote for Democrats.

2. **(A)** Type of Question: Identification and analysis

This is a factually based question that requires you to know something about voting patterns. If you thought of the fact that many African-Americans are still not registered in the South, you would have chosen A as the correct answer.

3. **(C)** Type of Question: Definitional

If you knew the definition of political efficacy, those groups who are most aware who they are voting for and why they are voting, it would stand to reason that the upper class would best represent that group.

4. **(E)** Type of Question: Definitional

If the electorate speaks loudly and clearly for a candidate or a party, the election is interpreted as a mandate or direction for change. The other choices reflect different characteristics of parties, candidates, and voters.

5. **(D)** Type of Question: Cause-and-effect relationships/definitional

To answer this question, you must know the definition and implications of media-centered politics. Once you determine that the phrase relates to how the media dominates political campaigns through its coverage of the candidates, you should be able to reach the conclusion that the electorate has become disillusioned with the election process and, therefore, there has been a decrease in voter turnout since 1960. Choice A is the opposite of the correct answer. Choices B and C contradict the impact of media-centered politics. Choice E is also incorrect as in-depth analysis of the issues has decreased over time.

6. **(A)** Type of Question: Sequencing a series of events

Using the Ronald Reagan model, the question asks you to identify how a president controls news coverage. Choice A gets to the heart of the solution, whereas the other choices would hurt the management of news by a president.

7. **(D)** Type of Question: Solution to a problem

If you think of specific examples, you will find it easiest to select D as the correct choice. A criticism of the media is that it investigates the personal lives of politicians rather than the serious issues of the campaign. The other choices have been talked about by media critics as being negative characteristics of the media.

8. **(C)** Type of Question: Generalization

If you have ever heard the phrase "mass media" you know the correct answer to this question. College educated, the upper class, and people looking for in-depth analysis are groups that represent a minority audience. Even though the lower class may be large in number, they also represent only a segment of the society.

9. **(B)** Type of Question: Identification and analysis

If you know the provisions of the Fifteenth, Seventeenth, and Nineteenth Amendments, you would know they all deal with suffrage. Choice A is part of the Reserved Power clause of the Tenth Amendment. Choice B was ruled unconstitutional by the Supreme Court.

10. **(E)** Type of Question: Generalization

Gender and class are reasons why people vote, as well as religion and the process of political socialization. Surveys have no direct impact on why people vote.

11. **(A)** Type of Question: Solution to a problem

Choices B, C, D, and E are all incorrect conclusions relating to the electoral history of the past forty years. Voter turnout has been on the decline; third parties have never won significant electoral victories; campaign finance reform has had an impact on presidential races, and congressional incumbents win the vast majority of the time. Even though there has not been a consistent increase in actual voter turnout, there has been an increase in the opportunity to register and vote.

12. **(B)** Type of Question: Generalization

Young people, even with greater opportunity to register and vote, still lag behind all other age groups. Perhaps one of the reasons is because many young people fail to obtain absentee ballots when they go to college.

13. **(D)** Type of Question: Cause-and-effect relationships

If you did not know the specific provisions of the Motor Voter Act, you should be able to guess that states can't purge names if people don't vote in just one election. If there is a process, odds are that it would take a number of elections before individuals would have to reregister.

14. **(C)** Type of Question: Cause-and-effect relationships

You must know the way the electoral college works (if a candidate does not receive a majority of electoral votes, the election is thrown into the House of Representatives) to answer this question. If you know of any historical examples, you could probably eliminate the other choices. It is interesting to note that the other choices may have seemed correct because the electoral college has been criticized.

15. **(B)** Type of Question: Sequencing a series of events

If you think of the Depression or Clinton's victory in 1992, you should be able to reach the conclusion that incumbents are voted out during times of economic hardship.

16. **(C)** Type of Question: Identification and analysis

Traditionally, the one ethnic group most closely identified with a political party has been Jews. Ever since the Great Depression, Democrats could count on Jewish voters for support. Catholics tend to vote Democratic because of the support given to them when they were immigrants. Northern Protestants tend to support Republicans. The religious right have supported the Republican Party. Hispanics, with the exception of those living in Florida, tend to vote Democratic.

17. **(E)** Type of Question: Cause-and-effect relationships

Polling has been used more and more to determine attitudes and trends. If you do not construct a poll with a sampling error of under 5 percent, you risk the opportunity of reaching invalid conclusions.

18. **(D)** Type of Question: Comparing and contrasting concepts and events

You are being asked to compare and contrast and evaluate the nature of investigative journalism. Each of the examples given has some merit to the way the media acted. However, Woodward and Bernstein have been given the credit for cracking Watergate, the mother of investigative journalism. Thus, that choice is the only correct answer. The other choices all focus on the personal lives of the politicians.

19. **(A)** Type of Question: Identification and analysis

In this relatively simple question, you must know the provisions and intent of sunshine laws. The impact has been to open up governmental meetings based on the public. Even though the government has been forced to release documents, top secret national security documents have been protected. Certain government operations are still able to be held in secret session, but there has to be a legal reason for that action to take place.

Section 2: Data-Based Free-Response Question

Using the following headline and your knowledge of United States politics, answer the following.

UNDER NEW MANAGEMENT

(cont'd)

The 1994, 2006, and 2010 midterm elections have been characterized as "wave elections." Candidates running for office look for issues that will motivate voter turnout and attempt to frame issues that place blame on the party in power.

(a) Define what is meant by a midterm wave election.

(b) Using the above illustration, explain why the Congress was "under new management."

(c) Identify three characteristics that described voter preferences in a wave election.

(d) Explain how the Republicans used the Pledge to America to frame their issues and place "blame" on President Obama.

SAMPLE RESPONSE

(a)   A midterm wave election is defined as an election where the party in power increases their majorities in either one house or both houses of Congress or the party out of power regains control of either one house or both houses of Congress.

(b)   The picture is pointing out the consequences of the fact that voters in 1994 were unhappy with the performance of Democratic members of Congress. They wanted change. That is why the headline "Under New Management" is superimposed over the Capitol. Because Congress had a Democratic majority in both houses, the sign represents the fact that Democrats were no longer in power. The picture also suggests that the vote reflects a revolution of sorts. The Republican takeover has revolutionary consequences, especially if the Contract with America that the Republicans supported is carried out. The voters' discontent is aimed particularly at the Democratic incumbent. Implicit in the headline is the fact that the new Republican majority will also change the way government operates by implementing the provisions of the Pledge to America.

(c)   Characteristics that describe the 2010 voter preference include:

- Voters are sick of government and want change. The Republicans represent the party that will reduce the size and function of the federal government.
- The voters feel that the Democrats are not getting the job done. Even though there were legislative victories, the fight over health reform and the crime bill convinced the electorate that the Democrats could not carry out their 1992 promises.
- Therefore, the voters rejected only Democratic incumbents and, in a majority of open seats, elected Republicans, which resulted in a turnover in both houses of Congress.

(d)   The Republicans used their Pledge to America as the focal point of the campaign. Even though many voters were not aware of the specifics, they felt that the Republicans would do better in such areas as taxes, the role of government, and healthcare. Even though the economy had been improving under the Clinton administration, for the most part many voters believed that the Republicans would in the end do a better job. The Pledge was a set of specific proposals that gave the American people an agenda of items that would be voted on during the first 100 days of the new Congress. The strategy was simple: nationalize the election and make it a referendum on Barack Obama.

SCORING GUIDELINES FOR FREE-RESPONSE QUESTION (7 POINTS)

Part (a) 2 Points

Two points are earned for defining the phrase "midterm wave election":

- as an election where the party in power increases its majorities in either one house or both houses of Congress
- the party out of power regains control of either one house or both houses of Congress

Part (b) 1 Point

One point is earned for explaining what the caption "under new management" meant.

Answers may include:

- the takeover of Congress by the Republicans in 1994
- the takeover of Congress by the Democrats in 2006
- the takeover of the House of Representatives by the Republicans in 2010

Part (c) 3 Points

One point is earned for identifying each of three voting characteristics in either the 1994, 2006, or 2010 midterm election.

Answers may include:

- voters seeking change
- voters feeling the party in power is to blame for the nation's problems
- rejection of incumbents

Part (d) 1 Point

One point is earned for explaining how the Republicans used the Pledge to America to frame the issues.

Answers may include:

- lower taxes
- repeal of "Obamacare"
- the role of government
- the national debt

Special Interest Groups— Lobbyists and PACs

14

→ **CAMPAIGN FINANCE REFORM**

→ **ELITE AND CLASS THEORY**

→ **FACTION**

→ **FREEDOM OF INFORMATION ACT**

→ **HARD MONEY**

→ **INTEREST GROUP**

→ **LOBBYISTS**

→ **POLITICAL ACTION COMMITTEES (PACs)**

→ **SOFT MONEY**

CONTEMPORARY CONNECTION

The National Rifle Association (NRA) has successfully lobbied against legislation that would reinstate the Assault Weapons Ban and laws that would establish stricter background checks when buying guns. They also are active fighting for gun rights on the state level. This chapter explores the nature and evolution of the last linkage institution, special interest groups, and how they act as advocates in the legislative process and campaigns.

Special interest groups, including their lobbyists and political action committees, have been one of the most criticized components of the political process. This chapter will explore the reasons why special interest groups exist, how they developed, and the roles they play in the political process.

We will also apply the group theory that we introduced in Chapter 1 illustrating how special interests operate in the context of a pluralist, hyperpluralist, and elite society. These interest groups all reflect specialized characteristics and can be classified by categories such as economic, occupational, environmental, and minority. The main role of these groups is to influence public policy and the policymakers through lobbying efforts, the formation of political action committees, and legal action.

We will look at the successes and failures of these groups through case studies. When you look at the money spent in the efforts to get senators and representatives to vote for a particular bill and the perks given to them as well as the contributions made to reelection committees, you will understand why citizen groups are calling for major legislative reforms. We conclude the chapter by taking a look at these reform efforts and evaluating future trends.

CHARACTERISTICS

For the purposes of establishing a common understanding, the definition of an interest group is a linkage group that is a public or private organization, affiliation, or committee that has as its goal the dissemination of its membership's viewpoint. The result will be persuading public policy-makers to respond to the group's perspective. The interest groups' goals are carried out by special interests in the form of lobbyists and political action committees. They can take on an affiliation based on specialized memberships such as unions, associations, leagues, and committees.

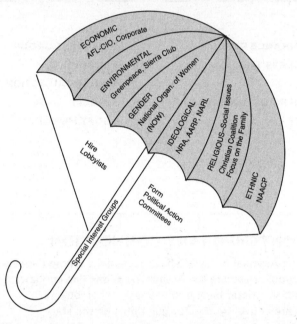

Interest groups and political parties are both characterized by group identification and group affiliation. However, they differ in the fact that interest groups do not nominate candidates for political office. Their function is to influence officeholders rather than end up as elected officials, and they are responsible only to a very narrow constituency. Interest groups can also make up their own by-laws, which govern the manner in which they run their organizations. Because the major function of these groups is the advocacy or opposition of specific public policies, they can attract members from a large geographic area. The only criterion is that the person joining the group has the same interests and attitudes toward the goals of the organization.

In trying to persuade elected officials to a group's position, these groups also provide a great deal of specialized information to legislators. Group advocates also claim they provide an additional check and balance to the legislative system. Critics of the growth of specialized groups claim they are partly responsible for gridlock in government. In addition, critics point to the manner in which groups gain access to elected officials as a tradeoff for political contributions.

Once a specialized group is formed, it also has internal functions such as attracting and keeping a viable membership. Groups accomplish this by making promises to their membership that they will be able to succeed in their political goals, which in the end will benefit the political, economic, or social needs of the members. For example, if people want stricter laws against drunk driving and join Mothers Against Drunk Driving (MADD), they feel a political and social sense of accomplishment when federal law dictates a national minimum drinking age in return for federal aid to states for highway construction. For these groups to succeed, they also must have an adequate financial base to establish effective lobbying efforts or create separate political action committees. Dues may be charged or fundraisers might be held. The internal organization will certainly have elected officers responsible to their membership.

Group Theory

The nature of group membership is not representative of the population as a whole; consequently, the importance of group theory will help explain the context in which special interest groups develop. It is interesting to note that many groups have as their members people with higher than average income and education levels and people who are white-collar workers. However, this is balanced by the number of groups that have proliferated and represent the interests of union members and blue-collar workers. Therefore, when we look again at the group theory described in Chapter 1, you will have a better understanding of group dynamics.

The group theory of modern government encourages the development of special interest groups.

As discussed earlier, there are three potential kinds of group activity—pluralist, majoritarian, and elite. Pluralism suggests that a centrist position results because there is a more far-reaching and balancing group representation. Elite theory defines group behavior as deriving from an upper class. Even though we can make the argument that many interest groups are elitist in nature because of the socioeconomic characteristics of their membership and that there are so many competing groups that can cause gridlock in government, these groups often compete with each other in a manner consistent with pluralism.

Let's support this assertion by briefly describing the characteristics of each of these theories as they relate to special interest groups. Pluralists maintain that

- competing groups are healthy because they provide a political connection to government, offering government officials a choice;
- the competition often clarifies information and prevents any one group from dominating government; and
- competing groups have each developed political strategies to achieve their goals and that eventually the resources of one group will independently affect governmental policy.

Critics of elitist group theory maintain that

- power is concentrated by the largest and richest organizations;
- the unequal nature of the power of groups negates the fact that groups are proliferating; and
- ultimately money talks, and these large groups will have the most influence.

Critics of the majoritarian model of government maintain that:

- direct democracy that relies on majority rule defeats the idea of a representative form of government.
- this model can result in a violation of minority rights since all decisions are made by majority rule.
- a majority rule approach to government can only work on a limited basis such as in a "town meeting" setting.

HISTORICAL BACKGROUND

James Madison wrote in Federalist Paper No. 10, "By a faction, I understand a number of citizens, whether amounting to a majority or minority of the whole, who are united . . . by some common . . . interest, adverse to the rights of other citizens, or to the permanent and aggregate interests of the community." He even went as far as saying that "the regulation of these various and interfering interests forms of the principal task of modern Legislation. . . ."

The fear and deep suspicion of special interest groups goes back to the early days of the republic.

Madison's view was that the development of factions was an inevitable feature of society. Even though he was fearful of their potential, he did not make the argument that they should be abolished. He felt that the separation of powers of the three branches of government and the division of government between the national and local governments would, in the end, provide enough government protection and regulation of these interests. In addition the formation of political parties became an additional balance to the formation of private interest groups, many of which were economically based during the early stages of our country's existence.

One of the first examples of why Madison felt factions could be potentially dangerous was Shays' Rebellion. Daniel Shays organized a group of unhappy farmers attempting to help them forestall foreclosure of their land. Frustrated in their attempts to get government relief, they took up arms. Shays was arrested, and the revolt failed.

Once the Constitution was ratified and the Bill of Rights was added, the First Amendment seemed to give legitimacy to the formation of special interest groups. Their right of free assembly, free speech, and free press and the right to petition seemed to create a validity for group formation. Taken together, groups felt they could associate with each other, free from government interference, disseminate the issues that they believe in to their membership and to government officials, and attempt to influence the course of public policy.

MODE OF OPERATION

Interest groups are categorized according to their function. They all have one common goal—to make their viewpoints part of the political agenda.

As interest groups have grown in number and size, they have also become specialized, representing various concerns. The following represents a cross section of the different kinds of interest groups that have organizations:

- Economic and occupational including business and labor groups, trade associations, agricultural groups, and professional associations
  - National Association of Manufacturers
  - Airline Pilots Association
  - AFL-CIO
  - American Farm Bureau
  - United States Chamber of Commerce
- Energy and environmental
  - American Petroleum Institute
  - Sierra Club
- Religious, racial, gender, and ethnic
  - National Organization for Women
  - National Association for the Advancement of Colored People
  - National Urban League
- Political, professional, and ideological
  - Common Cause
  - American Medical Association
  - Veterans of Foreign Wars
  - National Rifle Association

The majority of these groups have headquarters in Washington, D.C., and they all have operating budgets and staffs. Most have hired lobbyists who make contacts with senators and representatives as well as the executive branch. Many have separate political action committees with well-financed budgets. They place their views on the political agenda through the following techniques:

- testifying at congressional hearings
- contacting government officials directly
- providing officials with research information

- sending letters to their own membership
- trying to influence the press to present their point of view
- suggesting and supporting legislation
- hiring lobbyists
- giving senators and representatives feedback from their constituents
- making contributions through PACs to campaign committees
- taking congressmen on trips or to dinner
- endorsing candidates
- working on the campaigns

All these groups and techniques have the potential of helping the legislative process because they do help inform office holders. They also provide elected officials with a viable strategy and a base of support. These groups also have the expertise to give elected officials an additional slant to a problem. Unlike other constituents who have hidden agendas, special interest groups place their goals on the table, up front.

LOBBYISTS

Lobbyists are the primary instruments for fostering a special interest group's goals to the policymakers. The term comes from people who literally wait in the lobbies of legislative bodies for senators and representatives to go to and from the floor of the legislatures. Manuals have been published for lobbyists outlining the best ways for a lobbyist to be successful. Some of the techniques include:

Lobbyists provide interest groups with specialists to advance their causes and influence policymaking.

- knowing as much as you can about the political situation and the people involved
- understanding the goals of the group and determining who you want to see
- being truthful in the way you deal with people
- working closely with the interest group that hired you
- keeping the people you are trying to convince in your corner by telling them of the support they will receive if they agree to the position of the group
- following up on all meetings, making sure the results you want do not change

Recently, the image of lobbyists has taken a blow because they have attracted negative publicity. Former government officials who become lobbyists have been criticized because they can take unfair advantage of contacts they developed when they were in office. An additional accusation has been made against government appointees who were former lobbyists but still maintain a relationship with the special interest group they worked for before getting the position. In 2006, lobbyist Jack Abramoff was convicted of illegal lobbying practices. As a result, Congress became embroiled in a scandal that revealed what many called a "culture of corruption."

On the other hand, lobbyists also play a positive role as specialists. When tax reform was being considered in the 1980s and 1990s, lobbyists provided an expertise to congressional committees considering the bills. Sometimes lobby coalitions are formed when extremely important and far-reaching legislation, such as healthcare reform, is under consideration. Lobbyists may also take legal action on behalf of the interest group. They file friend of the court (amicus curiae) briefs or may be part of a class action suit. Cases such as *Brown v Board of Education*, *Roe v Wade*, and *Regents of California v Bakke* attracted a great deal of attention and numerous third-party briefs. Lobbyists may also provide ratings of officials. Groups such as Americans for Democratic Action and the American Conservative Union give annual ratings based on their political ideologies. Lobbyists and special interest groups also use the media to push their viewpoint. During the energy crisis, lobbyists for Mobil ran ads that resembled columns, explaining its point of view.

POLITICAL ACTION COMMITTEES (PACs)

Political action committees (PACs) raise money from special interest constituents and donate hard and soft money to political parties and candidates.

When an interest group gets involved directly in the political process, it forms separate political action committees. These PACs raise money from the special interest group's constituents and make contributions to political campaigns on behalf of the special interest. The amount of money contributed over the last few elections has been staggering. PACs such as the National Rifle Association (NRA), labor's "Vote Cope," American Bankers Association (BANKPAC), PAC of the National Automobile Dealers Association, Black Political Action Committees (BlackPAC), and Council for a Strong National Defense have made major contributions to political campaigns and have had a tremendous impact on local and national elections.

The amount of contributions to congressional campaigns by PACs has skyrocketed from 1981 to 2012. From 1981 to 1982, $83.7 million was contributed to candidates for the House and Senate, as compared with over $285 million contributed to candidates running for the House and Senate in 2011–2012.

Top 20 PAC Contributors to Candidates, 2013-2014			
PAC Name	Total Amount	Democratic Percent	Republican Percent
National Association of Realtors	$3,804,455	48%	51%
National Beer Wholesalers Association	$3,017,000	43%	57%
National Auto Dealers Association	$2,795,350	29%	71%
Honeywell International	$2,705,373	43%	57%
Lockheed Martin	$2,632,750	42%	58%
American Bankers Association	$2,533,875	24%	76%
AT&T Inc.	$2,504,250	40%	60%
International Brotherhood of Electrical Workers	$2,467,214	97%	3%
Credit Union National Association	$2,381,500	49%	51%
Operating Engineers Union	$2,361,742	80%	20%
Northrop Grumman	$2,346,750	43%	57%
National Association of Insurance & Financial Advisors	$2,341,500	38%	62%
Blue Cross/Blue Shield	$2,297,300	39%	61%
American Association for Justice	$2,203,500	96%	4%
Boeing Co.	$2,141,500	43%	57%
American Crystal Sugar	$2,091,499	56%	44%
National Rural Electric Cooperative Association	$2,070,022	28%	72%
Carpenters & Joiners Union	$2,032,750	78%	22%
American Federation of Teachers	$2,025,000	99%	1%
General Electric	$2,014,500	39%	61%

Congressional candidates raised billions of dollars in the 2014 midterm elections, a significant increase from the 2006 election cycle. In 2006, House candidates raised $544 million, up 18 percent from 2002, while Senate candidates raised $350 million dollars, up 15 percent from 2002. In 2014, congressional candidates and outside groups spent over $3.67 billion, shattering all records.

The Difference Between Lobbyists, PACs, Super PACs (Independent Expenditure Committees), 527 Super PACs, and Social Welfare Organizations 501(c)4 Groups

There is confusion regarding the differences between lobbyists, political action committees (PACs), Super PACs (Independent Expenditure Committees) and Social Welfare organizations also known as 501(c)4 groups:

> There are different types of Political Action Committees that have different regulations governing their operations. The one thing they all have in common is the goal of influencing the outcome of elections on the local, state, and federal levels.

- Lobbyists: As previously described, lobbyists represent special interest groups. They provide information to legislators and advocate their group's positions. Lobbyists do not contribute money to candidates or office holders. Congressional law dictates how much money a lobbyist can spend when meeting with a legislator.
- Political Action Committees (PACs): PACs can be formed by special interest groups, elected officials, and candidates running for office. PACs formed by special interest groups can raise money, contribute money to candidates, and spend money advocating their positions. PACs formed by elected officials and candidates running for office can raise money and spend money on advancing their own campaigns, or they can contribute money to other candidates. An example of this type of PAC was "Ready for Hillary," the political action committee that was formed to encourage Hillary Clinton to run for president in 2016.
- Super PACs, aka Independent Expenditure Committees: These committees are regulated by the Federal Election Commission, and they are supposed to act independently from any candidate or campaign. Independent Expenditure Committees cannot contribute directly to any campaign. They raise money for the purpose of supporting a candidate's positions on specific issues through political advertisements. The Club for Growth is an independent committee that supports candidates who pledge that they would not vote to raise taxes.
- 527 Super PACs: Also independent expenditure committees, these PACs can create independent expenditure accounts that can accept donations without limits from individuals, corporations, labor unions, and other political action committees (thanks to the decision made by the U.S. Supreme Court in the Citizens United case). 527 groups have proliferated and play a significant role in congressional and presidential elections. Examples of 527 groups are Priorities USA (supporting Democratic candidates), American Crossroads, and Americans for Prosperity (supporting Republican candidates). By law, they cannot coordinate their spending with the candidates they support.
- Social Welfare Organizations aka 501(c)4 groups: These Super PACs are recognized by the Internal Revenue Service as "Tax Exempt Social Welfare Organizations" formed for the purpose of improving the social welfare of society. There are no limits on how much money they can raise. They can spend money on political advertising that supports their goals, as long as that political activity is not the sole purpose of the group. They differ from 527 groups because they do not have to disclose publicly the names of their contributors. Crossroads GPS is an example of a 501(c)4 group. Such groups have been criticized because of the anonymity of their donors. They have also played a major role in congressional and presidential elections.

PUBLIC AWARENESS AND EFFECTIVENESS

> The success and failure of interest groups, lobbyists, and PACs to achieve their goals depends, to a large extent, on their public image and their ultimate ability to influence the outcome of public policy.

In order for an interest group to succeed, not only must a public awareness of the group's position take place but legislators must also accept the bill of sale presented to them. There is no doubt that the National Rifle Association's membership consists of a small percentage of the American public. Yet because of its image, for example, the "We are the NRA" commercials and its advocacy of the constitutional right to bear arms, the public is certainly aware of its stand, and polls indicate that many people support its position.

The National Rifle Association is a good example of how a special interest group successfully influences public policy. From 1994 to 2012, the NRA's political influence has been felt by both parties. In 1994, they successfully campaigned against Democrats who voted for the assault weapons ban, a key to the Republicans taking over Congress. After the tragic mass shooting of elementary school children and teachers at Sandy Hook Elementary school in 2012, public opinion shifted in favor of gun control legislation. Universal background checks, penalties for gun trafficking, regulation of the number of magazine clips, and a new assault weapons ban were part of the legislative agenda. The NRA opposed these measures citing Second Amendment concerns. Ultimately Congress failed to approve any new gun control measures.

**ONE OF THE AIMS OF THE NATIONAL RIFLE ASSOCIATION
IS TO SUPPORT THE RIGHT TO BEAR ARMS**

There are very few consistent winners or losers in the attempts by special interests to control the policy agenda. What is clear is that, when the system works, compromise and bipartisanship take place. What is also evident is that when the system breaks down, gridlock occurs, and special interests are called to task. Whether Madison was right in his concern about factions is debatable. They are an important part of the political process. They have major constituencies who rely on them as much as they rely on elected officials.

Section 1: Multiple-Choice Questions

1. An interest group is most likely to have influence in Congress with which of the following situations?

    (A) An issue that is narrow in scope and low in public visibility
    (B) An issue that is part of the president's legislative package
    (C) An issue that has been highly dramatized by the media
    (D) An issue that engages legislators' deeply held convictions
    (E) An issue that divides legislators along party lines

2. All of the following statements concerning interest groups are true EXCEPT

    (A) they are policy experts
    (B) they attempt to appeal to a broad spectrum of political interests
    (C) they often run their own candidates for public office
    (D) they lobby different levels of government
    (E) they have specific policy goals

3. Special interest groups do all of the following EXCEPT

    (A) testify at congressional hearings
    (B) donate money to federal judges
    (C) endorse candidates for political office
    (D) try to influence the media
    (E) work on the campaigns of candidates

4. All of the following arguments are essential to the special interest theory of politics EXCEPT

    (A) Interest groups compete with each other.
    (B) Interest groups provide linkage between people and government.
    (C) One or two interest groups may dominate the debate over legislation.
    (D) Interest groups encourage membership from diverse groups that may disagree with their goals.
    (E) Interest groups have been protected by Supreme Court decisions.

5. Which of the following represents a major reason for the proliferation of special interests and lobby groups?

    (A) The reactive nature of interest groups and lobbyists to new issues
    (B) The increase in donations received by interest groups from their membership
    (C) The trust citizens have in the legislative process
    (D) The ability of lobbyists and special interest groups to get members from their own group to run for political office
    (E) The increasing demand for campaign reform

6. Which of the following officials do lobbyists most succeed with?

   (A) Officials who have a basic philosophical affinity with the lobbyist
   (B) Officials who have a basic philosophical difference with the lobbyist
   (C) Officials who are neutral with the lobbyist's position
   (D) Officials who have strong convictions
   (E) Officials who are very conservative

7. A significant amount of PAC money most likely goes to

   (A) candidates challenging Republican seats
   (B) candidates challenging Democratic seats
   (C) candidates who are new to the political scene
   (D) candidates who have wide philosophical differences with the PAC
   (E) candidates who hold incumbent status

8. Which of the following statements represents the main function of special interest groups?

   (A) They eventually want to end up as political office holders.
   (B) They nominate candidates for political office.
   (C) They have the primary function of funding political campaigns.
   (D) They want to influence officeholders and achieve legislative goals.
   (E) They attempt to recruit an elite membership in order to become influential.

9. All of the following are techniques used by lobbyists EXCEPT

   (A) testifying at congressional hearings
   (B) providing officials with research information
   (C) appearing on the floor of Congress as staff assistants to senators and representatives
   (D) taking senators and representatives to conferences sponsored by a special interest group
   (E) giving senators and representatives feedback from their constituents

10. Which of the following statements represents a potential conflict of interest?

   (A) Lobbyists work closely with the interest groups that hired them.
   (B) Lobbyists are former government officials who have close ties with current legislators.
   (C) Lobbyists are persistent in making sure that the results they get do not change before a vote.
   (D) Lobbyists know as much and sometimes even more than legislators about pending legislation.
   (E) Lobbyists attempt to convince senators and representatives that if they support their position they will receive the support of their constituency.

Answer Explanations

1. **(A)** Type of Question: Hypothetical
Even though interest groups are involved with all the situations that are described, because of the nature of special interest groups, a narrowly scoped issue with low visibility has the greatest chance of lobbying success. For instance, the NRA may fail to stop the Congress from passing an assault weapons ban, but it could prevent other related legislation from passing.

2. **(C)** Type of Question: Negative
Even though interest groups support candidates for political office through their political action committees, it is highly unlikely that they will actually run their own candidates for elective office. One of the problems that arises is a clear conflict of interest. Another problem is that, because a special interest group usually is interested in a specific issue, running a candidate would attract only a small segment of the electorate.

3. **(B)** Type of Question: Negative
Just as in the previous question, the role of special interest groups is analyzed. It should be obvious that special interest groups cannot donate money to federal judges. Therefore, choice B is the correct answer.

4. **(D)** Type of Question: Negative
By definition, a special interest group is formed over a very specific issue. Whether it is abortion, guns, or a general category of supporting labor or business interests, these groups still recruit membership from the sphere they are trying to influence. Therefore, to say that interest groups attempt to attract a diverse membership is contradictory. Choice E may throw some students because there have been Supreme Court decisions protecting interest groups.

5. **(A)** Type of Question: Cause-and-effect relationships
For most issues brought up before Congress, you will be able to find some interest group that exists and hopes to influence the legislative process. Even though some interest groups are getting increased donations from their members, that is the exception rather than the rule. And even if there is an increased demand for campaign reform, it does not follow that more interest groups would form. Choice C is clearly not the perception of the public, and interest groups do not run their own members for political office.

6. **(A)** Type of Question: Hypothetical
The problem with this kind of question is that in some situations lobbyists may be able to accomplish their task with all the officials described in the question. But the best chance for success comes with the elected official who, going into the situation, basically agrees with the position of the special interest group or has a constituency who has strong feelings about the issue being discussed.

7. **(E)** Type of Question: Hypothetical
Although millions of dollars are pumped into the political coffers of both political parties and even candidates who are new to the political scene, most PAC money goes to incumbents. It is rare for money to be invested in candidates who most likely will vote against the position the PAC is taking.

8. **(D)** Type of Question: Generalization
By definition, a special interest group attracts membership as a result of an identification process. People who believe that every woman has the right to have an abortion will look

for pro-choice groups; gun advocates will look for a group like the NRA. Choices A and B are incorrect because these groups' major function is to endorse candidates. Choice C is wrong because funding is not their primary function. And choice E is incorrect since most likely a special interest group can attract only a narrowly based membership.

9. **(C)** Type of Question: Solution to a problem

According to political history the term lobbyist came about because special interest groups hired individuals to "hang out" in the lobby of Congress so that, when senators and representatives entered or left the floor the lobbyist could approach the representative without an appointment. There are strict rules regarding who actually can be on the floor of Congress—lobbyists are not permitted.

10. **(B)** Type of Question: Generalization

Although the other choices are all factually correct, the only answer that represents a conflict of interest is that many lobbyists are former senators, representatives, or executive staffers who may have retired, resigned, or been defeated. In some cases these individuals have abused the system and have been accused of ethical misconduct.

Section 2: Free-Response Question (6 points)

> There are distinct differences in the roles that special interest groups, lobbyists, and political action committees play as linkage groups in the political process.
> (a) Define the terms special interest group, lobbyist, and political action committee.
> (b) Give one example for each term you defined in (a) of the tactics used by each to accomplish their goals.

SAMPLE RESPONSE

(a) The classic definition of an interest group is an organization, affiliation, or committee whose prime incentive is to publicize its members' viewpoint. Lobbyists and PACs are usually formed through a common interest that unites a group as it gains strength. These types of interest groups usually try to advance their goals through political means. Lobbyists are defined as instruments used to enhance a special interest group's goals through government officials, while PACs raise money from the group's constituents through committees that become directly involved in the political process. All three groups are interconnected, yet they each have different goals and duties. These groups utilize a variety of tactics to accomplish their individual goals; because of these tactics, the public views them in negative ways.

Special Interest Groups

(b) Special interest groups have a common goal of persuading public policymakers to act according to the group's perspective. The actual carrying out of these interest groups' goals are reserved to the lobbyists and PACs. Special interest groups are formed out of a common interest that unites its members through group identification and group affiliation. They try to influence elected officials; because they only concentrate on one issue, they have a very focused constituency. For the same reason, however, special interest groups can attract a great number of people from large sections of the United States. Internal functions, such as promises of succession, benefit the social, economic, and political needs of their members and help to attract membership. Mothers Against Drunk Driving (MADD) is an example of a special interest group that has benefited socially and politically from its accomplishments, which include a federal law that created a national minimum drinking age. Special interest groups by themselves offer a base to which lobbyists and PACs can add to, creating a more powerful group that can have a great impact on public policy.

Lobbyists

Lobbyists are the next step in forming a more powerful special interest group. Lobbyists are the people, in the eyes of legislators, who actually write letters to United States congressmen and voice support for or opposition to a particular issue. Lobbyists use a variety of techniques to achieve success in obtaining their goals. Some of these techniques include knowing as much as they can about the political situation and the people involved, being truthful to the people they deal with, and understanding the goals of the group and determining who they want to see. For example, the National Rifle Association (NRA) is so powerful that it literally threatened a Florida senator's seat when the Crime Bill came up for a vote. The success of lobbyists, like PACs and special interest groups, depends upon their public image and their ability to influence public policy.

PACs

PACs are the committees that raise money and make contributions to political campaigns. Labor unions began forming PACs during the 1940s, but corporations were barred from doing so until passage of the Federal Campaign Act of 1971 (FECA). By lifting the prohibition against using corporate money to set up PACs, FECA and its 1974 and 1976 amendments legalized a new and much larger role for trade associations and corporations in politics. Thus, FECA brought about a dramatic change in the way political money is raised and fostered an enormous growth in the numbers of PACs involved in active politics. The amount of money raised over the last few elections has been exorbitant. Individual political campaigns have received over $5 million from PACs and other sources. In 2000, about 4,200 PACs distributed $284 million to congressional candidates, most of them incumbents.

SCORING GUIDELINES FOR FREE-RESPONSE QUESTION (6 POINTS)

Part (a) 3 Points

One point is earned for defining each term: "special interest group," "lobbyist," and "political action committee":

- special interest group—an organization or affiliation whose prime incentive is to publicize its members' viewpoint
- lobbyists—instruments used to enhance a special interest group's goal through government officials
- political action committees (PACs)—raise money from the group's constituents through committees and spend money on behalf of a candidate, campaign, or party committee

Part (b) 3 Points

One point is earned for giving an example of a tactic used by special interest groups, lobbyists, and political action committees to accomplish their goals.

Answers may include but are not limited to:

- special interest groups—use their special knowledge to influence elected officials, donate money to political parties, and pay for political ads
- lobbyists—one-on-one meetings with elected officials giving them important information about specific issues related to the lobbyist's cause, developing a trust with elected officials, and gaining knowledge that they can share with elected officials
- political action committees—raise money and make contributions to political campaigns and pay for political ads

PART FIVE
Public Policy Issues

The Economy, the Federal Budget, Social Welfare, and Entitlements

15

- → BALANCED BUDGET
- → BLOCK GRANT
- → CONGRESSIONAL BUDGET OFFICE (CBO)
- → CONSUMER PRICE INDEX
- → CONTINUING RESOLUTION
- → CULTURE OF POVERTY
- → DEBT CEILING
- → DEFICIT SPENDING
- → DIRECT TAX
- → DISCOUNT RATES
- → ENTITLEMENTS
- → FEDERAL RESERVE SYSTEM
- → FISCAL CLIFF
- → FISCAL POLICY
- → FLAT TAX
- → FOOD STAMP PROGRAM
- → GROSS DOMESTIC PRODUCT
- → GROSS NATIONAL PRODUCT
- → INCOME DISTRIBUTION

- → INDIRECT TAX
- → LAISSEZ-FAIRE
- → MANDATORY SPENDING
- → MEDICAID
- → MEDICARE
- → MONETARY POLICY
- → NORRIS-LA GUARDIA ACT (1932)
- → OFFICE OF MANAGEMENT AND BUDGET (OMB)
- → OPEN MARKET
- → POVERTY LINE
- → PRICE SUPPORTS
- → PROGRESSIVE TAX
- → REGRESSIVE TAX
- → REGULATORY POLICY
- → SAFETY NET
- → SEQUESTRATION
- → SOCIAL WELFARE
- → WAGNER ACT
- → WORKFARE

CONTEMPORARY CONNECTION

According to the U.S. Treasury, the national debt has more than doubled over the past decade. The chart on the following page traces the increase.

Congress needs to raise the debt limit in order for the United States to meet its obligations. In 2011, the Republican majority in the House of Representatives threatened not to raise the debt ceiling unless President Obama made cuts in spending to offset the increase. A crisis was averted in the eleventh hour when a compromise was reached and the debt ceiling was raised. This chapter explores the issues facing the U.S. economy, how the federal budget is prepared, its components, and the impact social welfare programs and entitlements have on the economy.

Date	Dollar Amount
09/30/2014	17,824,071,380,733.82
09/30/2013	16,738,183,526,697.32
09/30/2012	16,066,241,407,385.89
09/30/2011	14,790,340,328,557.15
09/30/2010	13,561,623,030,891.79
09/30/2009	11,909,829,003,511.75
09/30/2008	10,024,724,896,912.49
09/30/2007	9,007,653,372,262.48
09/30/2006	8,506,973,899,215.23
09/30/2005	7,932,709,661,723.50
09/30/2004	7,379,052,696,330.32
09/30/2003	6,783,231,062,743.62
09/30/2002	6,228,235,965,597.16
09/30/2001	5,807,463,412,200.06
09/30/2000	5,674,178,209,886.86

The final section of the review part of this book concerns the definitive measure of whether the institutions of government and the components of our political system succeed—the implementation of public policy. The following areas serve as yardsticks to gauge the successes and failures of public policy:

- the economy
- the federal budget
- social welfare and entitlements

THE ECONOMY

This section explores the government's attempt to regulate economic policy. By evaluating the monetary policies of the Federal Reserve System and the fiscal policies of the government, you will be able to see how specific public policy is developed and how it affects the major areas of American life—agricultural, business, labor, and consumer. Viewing the history of government regulation, we will conclude the chapter by looking at recent attempts at deregulation and focus on the economy's future.

Perhaps the most definitive indicator of the overall public policy direction the government is taking is the development of the federal budget. It involves key players, a prescribed process, and inherent problems. We will explain the players' roles and what happens each step of the way in the budget process. There are problems caused by the growing budget and decisions must be made by the president and congress when considering budget priorities.

We will also look at the specific type of taxes that exist, how they affect people who have different levels of income and wealth, and the types of welfare and entitlement programs—Social Security, Medicare, Medicaid, food stamps, aid to the disabled, and welfare.

ECONOMIC DIFFERENCES

Basic differences between Republicans and Democrats and ideological differences between conservatives and liberals are great when economic issues are raised. Traditionally, Republicans have been identified as the party favoring the rich and big business, whereas the Democrats have been viewed as being sympathetic to labor and the poor. Democrats have accused Republican presidents of having unsuccessful "trickle-down, supply-side" economic policies, resulting in a recessionary trend and higher unemployment. Republicans accuse Democratic presidents of following a "tax and spend, regulatory" program, causing runaway inflation. The conservative congressional coalition sides with policies aimed at dramatically reducing the deficit, whereas liberals believe government-sponsored economic stimulus programs result in a strong economy.

Government plays a dual role in being linked to the nation's economy. It measures the economic status of the nation and attempts to develop effective measures to keep the economy on the right track. The Department of Labor (Bureau of Labor Statistics), the Congressional Budget Office, and the Executive Office of the Council of Economic Advisers all report to the country vital economic statistics such as the

- unemployment rate (adjusted index of people obtaining jobs)
- Consumer Price Index (CPI)—According to the U.S. Census Bureau, "the CPI is a measure of the average change in prices over time in a fixed 'market basket' of goods and services purchased either by urban wage earners and clerical workers or by all urban consumers." It is also a primary measure of inflation when the index rises over a defined period of time.
- Gross National Product (GNP)—The Census Bureau defines GNP as "the total output of goods and services produced by labor and property located in the United States, valued at market prices."
- Gross Domestic Product (GDP)—Lately the GDP has become the key economic measure analyzing an upward or downward economic trend, on a quarterly basis, of the monetary value of all the goods and services produced within the nation. Other factors such as consumer confidence, the actual inflation rate, and the stock market give a complete picture of the economy.

The government's primary policy role, therefore, is to develop a healthy economic policy. Programs such as the New Deal's three Rs—Relief, Recovery, and Reform—set in motion policies that have succeeded in preventing the country from experiencing a depression of the magnitude of the one that occurred in the 1930s. Many of Roosevelt's programs such as Social Security (relief), the Securities and Exchange Commission (reform), and jobs program prototypes (recovery) are still part of the economic fabric of the country today.

MONETARY POLICY OF THE FEDERAL RESERVE

Monetary policy is defined as the control of the money supply and the cost of credit. Many leading economists feel that there is a direct relationship between the country's money supply and the rate of economic growth. The Federal Reserve System, or as it is called "the Fed," was established in 1913. It consists of a seven-member board of governors serving by appointment of the president for staggered 14-year terms. Its chairman, appointed by the president and confirmed by the Senate, is a powerful spokesperson of the Fed and serves for four-year renewable terms. The Federal Reserve Board is an independent agency, free of presidential or congressional control. Its chairman during the 1990s, Alan Greenspan,

> Economic policy has a direct relationship to politics, political parties, elections, and government.

> The Federal Reserve System plays a large role in regulating monetary policy. It has been applauded by its supporters as a key watchdog agency and criticized by its critics as too powerful.

was very effective and influential in setting monetary policy. There are more than 6,000 member banks that are affected by Fed policy and then influence monetary policies of other banks, ultimately having an impact on the interest rates consumers pay.

The Federal Reserve System regulates the money supply through:

- Open-market operations—buying and selling of government securities, which affects the money supply and cost of money.
- Reserve requirements—establishing the legal limitations on money reserves that banks must keep against the amount of money they have deposited in Federal Reserve Banks (which give the banks interest). These limits affect the ability of banks to loan money to consumers because actions in this area can increase the availability of money for credit.
- Discount rates—determining the rate at which banks can borrow money from the Federal Reserve System. If rates are raised, interest rates for consumers also rise. The Federal Reserve System uses this tactic to keep inflation in check. This is probably the most publicized action taken by the Fed.

A good example of how the Federal Reserve's monetary policy is used in conjunction with a president's fiscal policy was in 1981 after Ronald Reagan was inaugurated. The country's number one economic problem was double-digit inflation. The Federal Reserve forced a recession by raising the discount rate. The action had the immediate impact of reducing inflation. However, unemployment continued to be a problem. Reagan's fiscal policies (which we will discuss fully in the next section), although eventually creating a long period of prosperity, also saw the greatest increase in the deficit in the nation's history. In 1999, after President Clinton's deficit reduction economic package succeeded in reversing some of the nation's deficit and increased employment, the Fed was forced to raise discount rates as a precautionary measure. It feared that, because the economy was again improving, inflation would tend to increase. The question of having an independent agency be the sole arbiter in these very important functions upsets many economists. On the other hand, the board must be immune from political pressure and pressure from special interests who would benefit if they had the inside track or could influence the monetary policy of the Fed. Most economists give the Federal Reserve high praise for the way it monitored the economy during the 1990s. The Federal Reserve has also been a key player, lowering interest rates during the economic recession that began in 2008.

An example of other actions taken by the Federal Reserve was in 2010 and 2012—the Federal Reserve launched a controversial program to buy $600 billion in longer-term Treasury securities by mid-2011 to support a weak economic recovery that was failing to generate jobs. As the economy improved, the Fed reduced the amount of securities they bought.

FISCAL POLICY

Fiscal policy of different administrations is characterized by an active or passive government economic policy.

Fiscal policy is primarily established by an economic philosophy that determines how the economy is managed as a result of government spending and borrowing and the amount of money collected from taxes. The two contrasting philosophies related to fiscal policy are Keynesian economics, developed by English economist John Maynard Keynes, and supply-side economics, developed by Ronald Reagan's economic team. Keynes advocated an increase in national income so that consumers could spend more money either through investments or purchases of goods and services. He also felt that the best strategy to counter an economic recession was an increase in government spending. A corollary to this viewpoint would be that government would also adopt regulatory, distributive, and redistributive policies as tools to ensure consumer enterprise.

The differing philosophies to a large extent can be traced to the laissez-faire philosophy of Hoover versus the regulatory philosophy of Roosevelt. Both fiscal policies attempted to handle the country when it was facing an economic downturn or when the country was facing too much growth. The key to success is to find the best way to balance the tools available to the government. Should it raise or lower taxes? Should it increase or decrease spending levels? How much regulation is really necessary? These are the issues that have perplexed economists and presidents since the Great Depression.

REGULATION AND DEREGULATION

As much as we have seen the government involved in regulations, during the 1970s and 1980s there has also been significant government deregulation of the airline industry, trucking and railroads, and the banking industry. Though the government continued on a course of environmental regulation during the 1990s and 2000s, the government continued deregulation of the banking industry and charted the country through deregulation of the housing industry. As a result, abuses led to a housing bubble that burst in 2008 as well as a collapse of many major financial institutions, ushering in a major economic recession. In 2009 and 2010, President Obama signed legislation that reversed the trend creating regulatory reform for banks and Wall Street.

> Deregulation of the economy has been favored by both liberals and conservatives in the hope that it would encourage more competition and decrease government involvement in key areas of American life.

Banking

When the banking industry was deregulated in the 1980s, it caused one of the most far-reaching scandals in banking history. The savings and loan (S&L) problems included consumers losing money that was not protected under the Federal Savings and Loan Insurance Corporation, banks closing, and heads of S&Ls under investigation for improprieties. The federal government under President Bush was forced to bail out the industry, resulting in an increase in the already inflated federal deficit. His administration was highly criticized for allowing the banks to mismanage their affairs, and after congressional oversight hearings took place, there was no doubt that the federal government would have to again regulate that industry. That regulation took place in the form of a massive government bailout of the banking industry in 2008, after the country's worst recession since the Great Depression. The largest banks came close to collapsing as a result of their investments in what was called "sub-prime" mortgages. Both the George W. Bush and Obama administrations, working closely with the Federal Reserve, the Treasury Department, and Congress, had to pump money into the failing banks. New laws were passed tightening banking regulations and consumer rights.

In looking at the federal budget, we will also trace the history of key legislation affecting the players and the process. Then we will analyze the components of the budget, including where the government gets its income and how it is allocated. Finally, we will discuss some of the reforms that have been proposed to keep the budget in check.

QUICK CONSTITUTIONAL REVIEW: THE BASIS OF THE FEDERAL GOVERNMENT'S BUDGETARY POWER

- In Article I, Section 8, Clause 1, the Congress is given the power to "lay and collect taxes, to pay the debts, and provide for the common defense and general welfare of the United States."

- Article I also gives the House of Representatives the power to initiate the process of passing all appropriations.

- Article I establishes the power of Congress to impose excise taxes in the form of tariffs.

- However, Article I Section 9 prohibits export taxes.

- Article I directs Congress to impose taxes that are equally apportioned.

- Thus, as a result of the ratification of the Sixteenth Amendment, the income tax is the only direct tax levied.

- Any indirect taxes, such as gasoline, tobacco, and liquor, must be uniform.

- The Supreme Court's decision in *McCulloch v Maryland* (1819) established the principle that states could not tax the federal government.

- Congress is also given the power to "borrow money on the credit of the United States" in Article I.

- Congress can appropriate only money that is budgeted.

BUDGET APPROVAL

Even though Congress is given the constitutional power of the purse, the players involved in the process include

- the president,
- executive staff and agencies,
- special interest groups,
- the media, and
- the public.

The process of budget development and passage involves the key players in the political game.

The president by law must submit a budget proposal to Congress the first Monday after January 3rd. Prior to that date, each federal agency submits detailed proposals outlining the expenses for each department over the next fiscal year. This spending plan is submitted to the Office of Management and Budget, responsible for putting the budget requests together. Following a budget review and analysis, the OMB revises many of the recommendations and prepares a budget for the president to submit to Congress. By the middle of February, the Congressional Budget Office (CBO) evaluates the president's budget and submits a report to the House and Senate Budget Committees. It is interesting to note that the CBO is a staff agency of the Congress, whereas the OMB is a staff agency of the president. Therefore, the results of budgetary analysis by each group may differ.

Once the appropriations committees of each house receive the budget, they review it and submit budget resolutions to their respective chambers. These resolutions include estimates of expenditures and recommendations for revenues. By April 15th a common budget direction must be passed. This provides the basis for the actual passage of the following year's budget.

The fiscal year begins each October 1st, and both houses must pass a budget that includes 13 major appropriations bills by that date. If any of these bills are not passed, Congress must then pass emergency spending legislation, called a continuing resolution, to avoid the shutdown of any department that did not receive funding from legislation passed. Shutdowns have occurred during the Reagan, Bush, and Clinton administrations. The battle over the 1995–1996 budget was particularly significant. It caused not only the most prolonged government shutdown, but also created unique political consequences. After the Republicans assumed control of Congress in 1994, led by conservative freshmen and spurred on by what was called the "Gingrich Revolution," the GOP believed they could force President Clinton to capitulate when the Congress passed a balanced budget.

By September 30, 1995, the end of the fiscal year, it became apparent that the Republicans' balanced budget, which included major social program reductions and an overall objective of reducing the size and scope of the federal government, would be vetoed by President Clinton. After Clinton's veto, the budget battle began. Republicans refused to pass continuing resolutions—a stopgap measure to keep the government operating—unless the president agreed in principle to their budgetary demands. President Clinton, using his bully pulpit in a most effective manner, refused and in fact went on the offensive by suggesting that the Republicans were holding the American people hostage. When the media focused their attention on how the shutdown was affecting government workers, and showing dramatic pictures of signs posted outside government agencies and national parks, the Republicans were forced to pass continuing resolutions and reformulate their own budget proposal.

In addition to losing public opinion, the budget battle (the temporary funding of the government) also had a longer lasting impact on presidential politics. It reestablished President Clinton's image after the devastating midterm election defeat in Congress. The 1995 and 1996 government shutdowns created an election issue that would carry through the entire 1996 campaign. The last government shutdown took place in 2013.

During this entire process, special interest groups, heads of bureaucratic agencies, the media, and the public are also involved in trying to influence the nature of the budget. Private sector lobbyists argue for increased funding for programs such as entitlements and federal aid, whereas bureaucratic chiefs attend congressional hearings to fight for their departments. The media publicizes the process through objective news reports and editorials. The public through its contacts with legislators (letter writing and phone calls) also gives its viewpoint regarding such issues as a tax increase.

Deficit Spending

What exactly is deficit spending? Ross Perot, during the 1992 campaign, suggested that the problem was so serious that his grandchildren would potentially face the problem of a nation going broke. Very simply put, deficit spending is when expeditures exceed revenues. Beginning with the Revolutionary War, the United States has been forced to be a nation in debt. The debt usually increased after the United States had to react to either a domestic or foreign policy crisis. For instance, during the Depression the country faced one of the largest deficits in its history as a result of the implementation of Roosevelt's New Deal programs. However, the extent of the deficit became unmanageable beginning in the 1980s and reaching new heights in 2010 because of its size and the interest on the debt.

To place the figures in some perspective, during World War I we borrowed $23 billion; during the Depression, another $13 billion, and during World War II, $200 billion. By 2009 the deficit was up to over $1 trillion. The federal government is the only level of government able to borrow more money than it receives. State budgets must be balanced by law. To make matters worse, the interest on the deficit also increases the size of the debt. So, even if the government can reduce the size of

Serious problems, such as how to reduce the nation's deficit while maintaining social programs, face the key players.

the debt over a number of years, it still must repay the interest. Who does the federal government borrow money from? It borrows from

- trust funds such as Social Security,
- foreign investors,
- Federal Reserve banks,
- commercial banks,
- state and local governments,
- individuals who own savings bonds,
- money market funds in the form of treasury bonds,
- insurance companies,
- corporations, and
- other areas such as pension funds, brokers, and other groups.

Because the Constitution does not place limits on the extent or method of borrowing, Congress sets limits on the debt. However, the limit has been inching upward and until the passage of the 1993 budget had not decreased since the last time the country showed a surplus, in 1969. By 1997, the deficit was reduced by more than half of what it was when President Clinton assumed the presidency in 1992. As a result of the Balanced Budget Agreement in 1996, and an economy that showed high economic growth, the 1998 proposed budget eliminated the deficit and actually reflected a budget surplus. This surplus was projected to increase throughout the first decades of the new century. But because of a recession in early 2000, the effects of 9/11, and the impact of the war on terrorism, the surplus vanished and record deficits returned.

The deficit increased so rapidly in the 1980s due partly to a massive tax decrease proposed by Reagan and passed by Congress without a corresponding cut in expenses. In fact, the defense budget showed a dramatic increase, while the cost of entitlement programs continued to escalate. Bush made campaign promises to reduce the deficit but became frustrated with the Democratic-controlled Congress, which refused to cut social programs. George H. W. Bush was forced to renege on his "read my lips, no new taxes" pledge made during the campaign in order to get a budget passed. The consequences of this debt and runaway deficit for the country was a recession that retarded the rate of economic growth and caused an increase in unemployment and failed businesses. Add to the deficit a huge trade imbalance, and you can understand why Congress has attempted to find ways of setting budgetary limits. During the 1990s, President Clinton, working with the Republican-controlled Congress, signed a balanced budget that led to a surplus in 2000. After George W. Bush's election, there was a mild economic recession followed by the events of September 11th and the wars against Afghanistan and Iraq. These events, along with one of the largest tax cuts signed into law by George W. Bush, again led to large deficits. These deficits were made worse after President Obama took office and signed an $800 billion economic stimulus bill, which he said would help end the economic recession that began in 2008.

In 2010 the Congress and president faced mounting pressure by the American people to deal with the nation's unemployment rate, which was almost 10 percent, and the rising national debt and deficit that was over a trillion dollars. A bipartisan debt commission made a number of recommendations that would have reduced the deficit by dealing with spending and entitlement programs. The Democrats and Republicans have not agreed on a common approach to solve these issues.

Budget Reforms

Efforts to control the budget started with reforms of the actual process. Prior to 1974 Congress budgeted in a haphazard manner. The process was decentralized with subcommittees of each house reviewing every request on an agency-by-agency basis. Until the bottom line was totaled, there was never any certainty what the total budget would be.

The history of budget reform measures has resulted in congressional efforts to create an equitable tax structure and reasonable limits on expenditures.

The Congressional Budget and Impoundment Control Act of 1974 was passed to streamline the process. A secondary objective of the measure was to place controls on the president's ability to determine allocations without appropriate congressional checks. Before the law was passed, President Nixon used his authority to cut off funds for programs he felt would increase the deficit. Congress responded by passing this law, which placed an additional check on the president. It prevented the president from impounding previously passed allocations without congressional approval. The law also provided for

- a budget calendar with a series of built-in procedures,
- the creation of a budget committee in each house whose responsibility it was to recommend to the Congress a total budget by April 1st, and
- the creation of the Congressional Budget Office, which acted as a check on the OMB.

The law established a time line of procedural steps the Congress had to take in order to pass the budget. These included the passage of budget resolutions, budget reconciliation aimed at achieving savings from taxes, other revenue adjustments and authorization bills that established discretionary government programs, and finally appropriations bills that covered the budget year and gave final authorization for spending. Even though the deficit and debt continued to rise after passage of the law, its supporters pointed to the fact that Congress was able to view the entire process from start to finish and therefore was able to understand fully where revenue was coming from and where money was being allocated.

Response to Deficit Spending

In response to the increased deficit spending, Congress passed the Gramm-Rudman-Hollings Balanced Budget and Emergency Deficit Control Act of 1985. This law was named after its cosponsors Senators Phil Gramm of Texas, Warren Rudman of New Hampshire, and Ernest Hollings of South Carolina. The law set goals to meet the deficit. If these goals were not met, automatic across-the-board spending cuts must be ordered by the president. Programs such as Social Security and interest on the national debt were exempt. In 1989 cuts were made until a budget was approved by Congress. The law also gave direction that the 1993 budget would have to be balanced. Because these were goals and a balanced budget requirement would need a constitutional amendment, Congress has used this law as a guide for overall reductions.

Attempting to find a way of helping the economy and closing tax loopholes, President Reagan asked Congress to pass the most far-reaching tax reform measure since the income tax was instituted. Supported by liberal Democratic Senator Bill Bradley of New Jersey, this law called for tax code changes that would result in a restructuring of tax brackets and eliminating many tax deductions. The law, supported by both Democrats and Republicans, passed in 1986 and succeeded in these two objectives.

The result was that many Americans received a tax cut. And because many loopholes were addressed, it was hoped that additional income would offset the loss of revenue from the tax cut received by the middle class. The law reduced the number of brackets from 15 to 3, it slightly increased deductions for individuals and families, and eliminated many other deductions. Even though the law succeeded in its objectives, because the expense side of the budget was not kept in check, the deficit still increased dramatically. From 1981 to 1992 the overall deficit quadrupled. However, Clinton's deficit reduction programs eliminated the deficit during his administration. By the year 1998, the budget was balanced, along with an anticipated budget surplus. The political argument then arose as to what should be done with any surplus. Some of the suggested uses for the surplus included reducing the national debt, saving Social Security, decreasing tax rates for all Americans, and increasing spending for government programs. This surplus was short lived. As previously discussed, the country again faced deficits starting in 2001, which got worse after the economic recession of 2008. By 2015, the deficit had been reduced by almost 66% since its high in 2009.

The Fiscal Cliff and Sequestration

The fiscal cliff was a date (January 1, 2013) that if no action was taken by Congress, the nation's economy would be impacted in the following ways:

- The so-called Bush tax cuts would expire and income tax rates would be raised for every taxpayer.
- Unemployment insurance would run out for millions of people who were out of jobs.
- There would be mandated cuts in discretionary spending and defense spending defined by law (sequestration).

Congress passed legislation avoiding the fiscal cliff by raising tax rates only on those people earning more than $450,000, extending unemployment benefits, and delaying the mandated cuts.

Sequestration was the mandated cuts in discretionary and defense spending passed by Congress for the purpose of reducing spending after President Obama and the House Republicans agreed to raise the debt ceiling and extended the Bush tax cuts in 2011. These cuts took place in 2013 and negotiations began to avert the harmful impact on the military and discretionary programs that were cut.

The Federal Budget

Let's look at some characteristics of recent budgets adopted by Congress.

Money comes from

- federal income taxes—46 percent
- Social Security and payroll taxes—32 percent
- corporate taxes—10–15 percent
- excise taxes such as taxes on liquor, gasoline, and luxury items—2–4 percent
- customs and duties collected and other sources—2–4 percent

Money is expended for

- entitlements (Social Security, Medicare, Medicaid)—40–45 percent
- national defense—16–20 (mandatory) percent
- national defense discretionary—50–55 percent
- interest on the debt—7–12 percent
- non-defense discretionary spending—40–45 percent
- other mandatory spending—7 percent

By 2014 the total budget had risen to over $3 trillion.

Even though the defense budget was a distant second to entitlements in expenditures, if you add the components of budgets from other areas, the gap is much smaller. A second issue was why social programs have increased so dramatically. Part of the answer came about from the philosophy of the Democrats to maintain programs passed as part of FDR's New Deal and Johnson's Great Society. When Reagan became president, he made a concerted attempt and succeeded in reducing some of these programs. However, they are still the single largest area of the budget. Economists and political scientists felt that the process itself encouraged the increase in this area. They pointed to the incremental manner in which budgets are developed, where the previous year's budget is looked upon as a base and therefore the new budget must increase because of inflation and other factors.

The outcome of the budgetary process is often a result of wrangling between Democrats and Republicans. Democrats accuse Republicans of pushing through a budget that would result in "trickle-down economics." Republicans point to Democrats as "taxers and spenders."

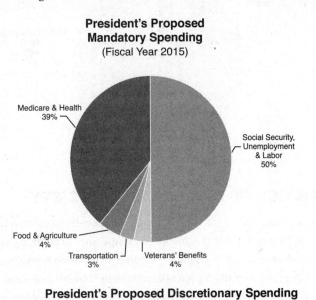

President's Proposed Mandatory Spending
(Fiscal Year 2015)

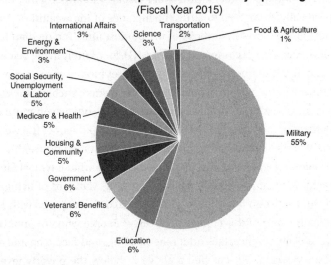

President's Proposed Discretionary Spending
(Fiscal Year 2015)

Even with attempts at what is called zero-based budgeting, where budget lines start at a ground-floor foundation so that programs can be reviewed, Congress still operated using an incremental approach. Another reason why costs have escalated is that, because entitlement programs are mandated by law, they are already built into the budget and increase as a result of the nature of the particular entitlement. For instance, the cost of Social Security has increased dramatically from $33 billion in 1970 to $265 billion in 1991. In 2010, the cost of Social Security topped $730 billion. In addition to the increase, Congress borrowed from the Social Security trust fund, and projections indicate that by the second decade of the twenty-first century the system will go broke. Congress in 1994 approved the formation of a separate Social Security Administrative agency. By 2010, both Congress and the president recognized the need for major reforms for Social Security, Medicare, and Medicaid. President Barack Obama appointed a bipartisan commission to make recommendations regarding Social Security and the federal deficit.

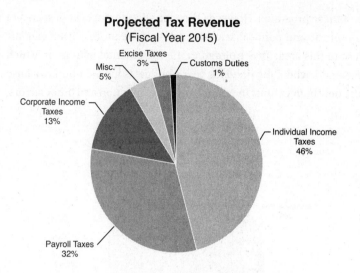

Projected Tax Revenue
(Fiscal Year 2015)

Excise Taxes 3%
Misc. 5%
Customs Duties 1%
Corporate Income Taxes 13%
Individual Income Taxes 46%
Payroll Taxes 32%

CHARACTERISTICS OF CLASS-BASED SOCIETY

> A class-based society in America is characterized by a disparity in the distribution of income and wealth. However, in the past 15 years, the percentage of Americans living below the poverty line has decreased.

First we must define some basic terms. Income distribution refers to the portion of national income that individuals and groups earn. Even though there has not been a significant comparative change in income distribution between the lowest and highest fifth of the American population from 1953 to 2012, since then there has developed over that period of time a wider disparity in levels of income for those groups. Specifically, from 1980 to 2015, the incomes of the wealthiest Americans rose at a much greater level than those of the poorest fifth. The median income in 2014 for whites was $59,754 compared with $35,416 for a family living below the poverty level.

Income is defined as the specific level of money earned over a specific period of time, whereas wealth is what is actually owned, such as stocks, bonds, property, bank accounts, and cars. Wealth, unlike levels of income, has been even more disproportionate, with the top one percent of the country's rich having about 25 percent of the wealth.

Taking into account this disparity of the distribution of income and wealth, the United States Census Bureau has adopted a poverty line. This line measures what a typical family of four would need to spend to achieve what the Bureau calls an "austere" standard of living. According to the Bureau, the poverty line for a family of four in 2007 was $20,650, compared with $23,364 in 2011.

Which groups become part of this culture of poverty? People who are poor because they cannot find work, have broken families, lack adequate housing, and face a hostile environment. The Bureau of the Census views families as being above or below the poverty level using a poverty index developed by the Social Security Administration. According to the Bureau, "the Index is based solely on money income and does not reflect the fact that many low-income persons receive noncash benefits such as food stamps, Medicaid, and public housing." People living below the poverty level include a disproportionate number of minorities living in cities when compared to the percentage of all poor people within each group.

TAXES

As stated on earlier pages, taxes are the major source of income for federal, state, and local governments. Taxes have been the brunt of comedians' jokes ("the only things certain in life are death and taxes"), but they are recognized as an essential ingredient in the ability of government to provide services to the population. The three types of personal taxes that exist are progressive taxes, regressive taxes, and proportional taxes. They each affect groups in different ways. A progressive tax such as the current federal income tax collects more money from the rich than the poor on a sliding scale. If the government takes an equal share from everybody regardless of income, it is a proportional tax. Also called a flat tax, former California Governor Jerry Brown suggested this approach during the 1992 presidential campaign. Many Republicans suggested this as an alternative to the present tax structure after the 1994 election. A regressive tax such as a sales tax has the poor paying a greater share than the rich. After the 1996 election, some Republicans even demanded the abolition of the Internal Revenue Service as well as for the implementation of a flat tax structure.

Yet, governments have few alternatives other than collection of taxes to pay for the services they provide, especially in the area of social welfare programs. The foundation for these programs stems from the grandparent of entitlement, Social Security. It mandates contributory payments in the form of payroll taxes made by the employer and employee. Part of the payments also go to a Medicare program established as part of the Great Society. Because this program is predicated on forced savings, it differs from other programs such as public assistance programs, which are based on a noncontributory approach.

Finally, if government has these programs, are they making a difference in income distribution? Studies have concluded that despite all the efforts made on the part of federal, state, and local governments the problem of income inequality still exists.

SOCIAL WELFARE PROGRAMS

The social welfare era began with New Deal relief measures under the Social Security Act. It was the most far-reaching piece of legislation ever passed. Its primary aim was to help one segment of the society—senior citizens. Previously described, the act established the principle that it was the government's responsibility to aid retirees, even if the aid came from the forced savings of the workforce.

The history of social welfare programs reflects a trend of increased government contributory and noncontributory policies.

Other aspects of the bill provided for unemployment insurance, and today the act has been expanded to include

- **Old-Age Survivors Disability Insurance (OASDI)**—covers 93 percent of the work force through FICA contributions and provides monthly payments to retired and disabled workers, spouses, and their children.
- **Social Security Disability Insurance (SSDI)**—monthly checks to disabled workers between the ages of 50 and 64.
- **Supplemental Security Income (SSI)**—gives money to the needy, aged, blind, or disabled through a formula that equalizes benefits.
- **Aid to Families with Dependent Children (AFDC)**—establishes federal grants to state governments that will provide money to low-income families with dependent children. This program is the largest welfare program. It was changed dramatically in 1996 when President Clinton signed a major welfare reform act. This law, which will be discussed at the end of the chapter, in the free-response question, gave block grants to the states. The burden of overseeing welfare was shifted from the federal government to the states.

Great Society Programs

The turning point in the federal era occurred as part of Lyndon Johnson's Great Society programs. Much legislation was passed in part as a response to the civil rights movement and also because there was a significant Democratic majority in both houses who agreed with Johnson that the government's role should be to develop programs including

- Medicare—covering hospital and medical costs of people 65 years of age and older as well as disabled individuals receiving Social Security.
- The war on poverty extending benefits to the poor.
- Food stamp program—giving food coupons to people determined to be eligible based on income and family size.
- Medicaid (a shared program between the federal and local governments)—covering hospital, doctor, prescription-drug, and nursing-home costs of low-income people.

In addition, Johnson pushed through Congress civil rights legislation that had the intent of increasing educational and job opportunities for minorities.

During the Nixon, Carter, and Ford years, the Great Society programs were sustained and, in some cases, expanded. In 1972 the Equal Opportunity Act provided for legal recourse as a result of job discrimination. In 1972 cost of living indexing was attached to Social Security and other welfare programs, and in 1973 a job training act, Comprehensive Employment Training Administration (CETA), was passed. The first hint that there were problems with Social Security also occurred in 1973 when the Board of Trustees of the Social Security System reported that the system was running a large deficit.

The "Reagan revolution" of the 1980s, with his assurance that there would always be a "safety net" for those people receiving the benefits of the many programs previously described, attempted to cut back the scope of the Great Society programs. He received the cooperation of the Democrats and cut the rate of increase to OASDI and Medicare. He also succeeded in reducing some of the need assistance programs. However, after 1984 these programs again began to increase. In addition, special interest groups such as the American Association of Retired Persons (AARP) lobbied effectively against cuts in Social Security and Medicare. During the 1995 congressional term, the Republicans passed a series of bills that would substantially cut Medicare and Medicaid in an effort to prevent their collapse and with the goal of moving toward a balanced budget. President Clinton vetoed these measures. A broader agreement was reached in 1997, however. It also became apparent that eventually there would be means testing and increased costs for senior citizens.

SEARCHING FOR SOLUTIONS

Universal healthcare became the battle cry of the Clinton administration. However, the issue had been originally placed on the public agenda by Presidents Truman and Nixon. One would expect that the United States would be a healthcare world leader. In fact other countries such as Canada and Great Britain have had universal healthcare for years. Critics of America's system pointed to the fact that the United States has a lower life expectancy and higher infant mortality rate than countries providing universal coverage. There are those who pointed out that, even without a universal system, America still spends over 15 percent of its Gross National Product on health. But because of such factors as medical malpractice suits, skyrocketing insurance, and health costs, as well as the loss of coverage for many workers who changed or lost jobs, the cry for reform was taken up. In addition, it became evident that access to health insurance was closely tied to race and income with whites, who have higher incomes on average than African-Americans, more likely to have coverage.

Even with Medicare and Medicaid, the country still lagged behind in dealing with health-related coverage. The Family Medical Leave Act of 1993 gave unpaid emergency medical leave for employees with a guarantee that their job would not be taken away in the interim. But what President Clinton hoped would be the benchmark of his administration was the adoption of a national health security plan as extensive as the original Social Security Act. Standing before Congress in 1993, Clinton held up a Health Security Card and threatened to veto any bill passed that did not include universal healthcare as its foundation. The bill itself was well over a thousand pages, and spearheading the drive was the nation's First Lady, Hillary Rodham Clinton. During the summer of 1994 both houses introduced watered-down versions of Clinton's bill. However, the legislation remained tied up as a massive lobbying effort took place. The issues of employer mandates, timing, and the extent of the coverage provided kept Congress from acting on the measure. As a result of the Republican electoral victory in the midterm elections, the issue of healthcare was placed on the back burner. However, in 1996, a health reform law guaranteeing the portability of health insurance if a worker left a job was signed into law.

In 2010, President Obama signed historic health care legislation called the Affordable Care Act of 2010. The opponents of the law called it "Obamacare," and made the claim that it was a government takeover of the health system. The law's goal was to fully insure an additional 35 million Americans, reduce the costs of health care, and reduce the federal deficit over a 10-year period. After the law was signed, those who had health insurance policies received increased benefits, such as increased coverage and protection from being dropped from a policy as a result of a preexisting condition. The law was challenged, and in 2012 the Supreme Court ruled it was constitutional. The initial rollout in 2014 had major problems. The government website crashed making it very hard to sign up. Even though President Obama promised that if you liked your current health care plan, then you can keep it, many Americans were informed that they had to change their policies to comply with the law. Even with these problems, by 2015 over 16.4 million people have gained health insurance coverage since the Affordable Care Act became law nearly five years ago. The coverage gains have delivered the largest drop in the uninsured rate in four decades, bringing that rate down to 13.2% by the end of the first quarter of 2015. The law was also challenged in 2015. The United States Supreme Court ruled in *King v Burwell* that tax credits are available to individuals purchasing health insurance on federal and state exchanges.

Welfare reform has also been high on the political agendas of state governors as well as the federal government. Workfare became an alternative to welfare, and many states have successfully instituted work programs aimed at removing welfare recipients from the rolls. President Clinton as well as the Republicans finally reached agreement on a far-reaching Welfare Reform Act.

Spotlight on Social Security

To illustrate the point, you have to go only as far as looking at the Social Security System. After its board informed the public of the program's deficit, Congress began looking at ways of saving the system. The National Commission on Social Security Reform was created in 1983 by President Reagan. Among the commission's suggestions adopted by Congress were

Social welfare programs today emphasize the need to provide solutions for homelessness, healthcare coverage, and the scourge of drug abuse.

- a six-month delay in the cost of living index adjustment in July 1983;
- a rescheduling of previously approved increases in Social Security payroll taxes, which would have the effect of kicking in scheduled increases at a slower rate;
- a gradual increase in the age when an individual could first receive Social Security benefits (as a result of an increase in life expectancy, it was felt that people could also work longer);
- having federal employees contribute to the Social Security System; and
- a portion of Social Security benefits being subject to federal taxes for those people with incomes over $20,000.

These reforms resulted in a surplus in the system. The government began borrowing from the reserve, and as a result the system is again in trouble. Projections indicate that by the second decade of the twenty-first century, the Social Security System will not be able to pay everybody who is eligible. A new bipartisan commission was appointed by President George W. Bush in 2001. Its mission was to investigate alternatives and enhancements to Social Security such as partial privatization. The report suggested that the Social Security System would need to be reformed through means testing and studied the feasibility of creating privatized Social Security accounts. Congress did not adopt these reforms. One reason that they refused to pass any legislation dealing with the recommendations was that Social Security was traditionally considered to be "the third rail" of American politics. After President George W. Bush was reelected in 2004, he made Social Security reform his number one legislative priority. He proposed the creation of Personal Retirement Accounts for anybody who was born after 1950. His critics called it privatization.

> The future of social welfare programs depends on whether they remain a public policy priority. An essential component of this debate will be the ability of government to continue to foot the bill.

The proposals were never voted on by Congress, and in 2006 a newly elected Democratic Congress refused to bring it up. In 2010, a new bipartisan debt commission came out with suggestions regarding Social Security and Medicare. The report aimed to make Social Security solvent over 75 years through a number of measures, including smaller benefits for wealthier recipients, a less generous cost-of-living adjustment for benefits, and a very slow rise in the retirement age (from 67 to 68 by 2050; rising to 69 by 2075). It also would expand over 40 years the amount of workers' income subject to the payroll tax. The report also recommends capping growth in total federal health spending—everything from Medicare to health insurance subsidies—to the rate of economic growth plus 1 percent. These recommendations were highly controversial, and they were not considered by the newly elected 2010 Congress.

Long-Term Problems Face Social Security and Medicare

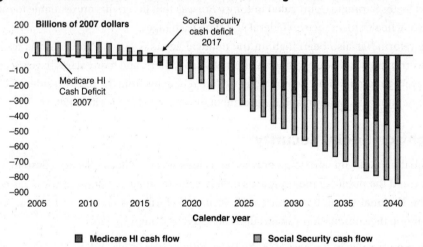

Source: GAO analysis of data from the Office of the Chief Actuary, Social Security Administration and Office of the Actuary, Centers for Medicare and Medicaid Services.
Note: Projections based on the intermediate assumptions of the 2007 Trustees' Reports. The CPI is used to adjust from current to constant dollars.

The debate regarding the nation's debt and deficit in 2012 ignored what was the major contributing factor that contributed to the deficit—the cost of Social Security and Medicare, and the viability of the two programs. Even though these entitlement programs, along with Medicaid, account for almost 40 percent of the federal budget, there has not been any serious action to curb costs such as extending the age when a senior citizen can get Social Security and Medicare, means testing the programs, or increasing the payroll tax limits for Social Security and Medicare. As the chart illustrates, until these issues are addressed it will be very difficult to sustain these programs.

Section 1: Multiple-Choice Questions

1. Traditionally, the Republican Party has been viewed as favoring which of the following groups?

   (A) Big business
   (B) The poor
   (C) The middle class
   (D) African-Americans
   (E) Hispanics

2. Traditionally, the Democratic Party has been known as

   (A) supporters of a tax-and-spend philosophy
   (B) supply-siders
   (C) believers of trickle-down economics
   (D) advocates of antiregulation of the economy
   (E) proponents of repeal of capital gains taxes

3. All of the following items are measures of the nation's economy EXCEPT

   (A) the nation's unemployment rate
   (B) the rise or fall of the Consumer Price Index
   (C) the amount of growth or decline in the Gross National Product
   (D) the amount of taxes corporations pay to the federal government
   (E) the rise or fall of the Gross Domestic Product

4. A primary way that the Federal Reserve regulates the money supply is when it

   (A) votes to increase taxes
   (B) votes to decrease taxes
   (C) adjusts the discount rate
   (D) adjusts the rate of inflation
   (E) votes to increase price supports

5. Supply-side economists urge

   (A) government stimulation of the economy
   (B) increased government spending for social programs
   (C) increased government borrowing of money
   (D) large tax cuts by the government
   (E) an increase of the management of the economy by the government

6. Which of the following presidents pursued a laissez-faire economic policy?

   (A) Theodore Roosevelt
   (B) Herbert Hoover
   (C) Franklin Roosevelt
   (D) Lyndon Johnson
   (E) Bill Clinton

7. Which of the following institutions is given specific constitutional power of the purse?

(A) Office of Management and Budget
(B) President
(C) Congress
(D) Special interest groups
(E) Executive agencies

8. If Congress does not pass a budget by the beginning of the fiscal year, then which of the following takes place?

(A) The president can impose a budget to keep the government running.
(B) The Courts can step in and create a temporary budget.
(C) The Congress must pass a continuing resolution.
(D) Government offices are automatically shut down.
(E) A contingency budget goes into effect.

9. The federal government may borrow money from all of the following EXCEPT

(A) trust funds
(B) foreign investors
(C) commercial banks
(D) money market funds
(E) the United States Treasury

10. As a result of President Nixon's practice of cutting off funds for programs he felt would increase the budget

(A) Congress passed the line item veto
(B) Congress passed the Congressional Budget and Impoundment Control Act
(C) the Supreme Court ruled the practice unconstitutional
(D) a balanced budget amendment was passed
(E) the Gramm-Rudman-Hollings Emergency Deficit Control Act was passed

11. Over the past 20 years, which of the following areas has shown the greatest increase in budgetary spending?

(A) The defense budget
(B) Federal operations
(C) Federal grants
(D) Discretionary spending
(E) Entitlements

12. Which of the following areas gives the federal government the greatest amount of income?

(A) Income taxes
(B) Social Security and payroll taxes
(C) Corporate taxes
(D) Luxury taxes
(E) Money collected from tariffs

13. Which of the following represents the main difference between a progressive income tax and a proportional income tax?

   (A) A progressive tax collects less money from the rich than the poor, whereas a proportional tax collects more from the rich.
   (B) A progressive tax collects more money from the rich than the poor, whereas a proportional tax is regressive.
   (C) A progressive tax collects more money from the rich than the poor, whereas a proportional tax collects the same.
   (D) A progressive tax collects the same amount of money from both the rich and the poor, whereas a proportional tax collects more from the rich.
   (E) A progressive tax has different brackets for different income earners, whereas a proportional tax has a greater number of brackets.

14. Which of the following is an example of a contributory entitlement program?

   (A) Supplemental Security Income
   (B) Aid to Families with Dependent Children
   (C) Social Security
   (D) Welfare
   (E) Food stamps

15. Which of the following philosophies was behind the attempt to create a safety net for individuals?

   (A) Federal government would be the exclusive agent to aid citizens.
   (B) State governments would only use block grants to help citizens.
   (C) The federal and state governments would share the costs equally.
   (D) Private businesses would provide benefits.
   (E) Even with federal government cutbacks, there would still be an assurance that people in need would receive benefits.

16. Which of the following represents legislation that guarantees unpaid emergency medical assistance for workers?

   (A) Medicare
   (B) Social Security
   (C) Family Medical Leave Act
   (D) Medicaid
   (E) Disability Insurance Act

Answer Explanations

1. **(A)** Type of Question: Cause-and-effect relationships
Choices B, C, D, and E are all groups that the Democrats like to claim as their constituency. Big business has not only been supported by the Republican Party, but it has also been a big contributor to the Republicans. This question is particularly important in the unit dealing with the economy because Republican control of the legislative agenda can mean that big business gets a tax break.

2. **(A)** Type of Question: Generalization
Choices B and C are economic issues raised by the Democrats against Republicans; choices D and E are traditional Republican causes. Choice A is an accusation made against the Democrats, but disputed by them.

3. **(D)** Type of Question: Negative
The amount of taxes corporations pay may have an impact on the nation's budget, but it is not a direct measure of how well the economy is doing. The Bureau of Labor Statistics keeps tabs on the unemployment rate and the changes in the Consumer Price Index (a measure of inflation), Gross National Product (a measure of the total growth of the country), and Gross Domestic Product (a measure of the domestic growth of the country).

4. **(C)** Type of Question: Solution to a problem
The Federal Reserve's major function is to keep tabs on the economy. One of the most effective ways the Fed tries to influence it is through the raising or lowering of the discount rate. If the economy is sluggish, the Fed will lower the interest rates. If the economy hints that inflation may set in, the Fed will raise the interest rates. The Federal Reserve Board does not have the power to increase or decrease taxes or price supports. Through the raising and lowering of the discount rate, it hopes to influence inflation. There are no guarantees that inflation will cooperate.

5. **(D)** Type of Question: Cause-and-effect relationships
The term supply-side was made popular during the Reagan administration by his director of the Office of Management and Budget, David Stockman. The term refers to an economic policy that aims to keep the economy stimulated by the private sector through tax decreases such as a capital gains tax decrease or a reduction in the personal income tax. Choices A, B, C, and E are policies supply-siders would not endorse.

6. **(B)** Type of Question: Chronological
Theodore Roosevelt was known as a "trust buster" and a president who believed in using government to further economic policy. Franklin Roosevelt developed the New Deal. Lyndon Johnson was the father of the Great Society, and Bill Clinton believed that the government should be able to stimulate the economy. Herbert Hoover was a firm believer that the private sector could extricate the country from the Depression.

7. **(C)** Type of Question: Identification and analysis
The Congress is given the specific constitutional power of appropriation, taxing, and borrowing in Article I Section 9. The president can veto proposed appropriations bills. The Office of Management and Budget prepares a preliminary budget and oversees the passed budget. Special interest groups attempt to influence spending packages, and executive agencies have defined spending limitations based on congressional approval of their budgets.

8. **(C)** Type of Question: Hypothetical

A continuing resolution prevents the federal government from shutting down if final passage of specific budget items are not approved by October 1st. Neither the president nor the Courts can intercede in this situation. Government offices remain operational when a continuing resolution is passed. A contingency budget suggests that approval is automatic and may differ from the existing budget. That is not the case when a continuing resolution is passed.

9. **(E)** Type of Question: Solution to a problem

The United States Treasury is responsible for printing currency and is the executive department responsible for dealing with many budgetary matters. It cannot print more or less money to counter economic conditions. The federal government can borrow money from trust funds such as the Social Security system, as well as foreign investors, money market funds, and commercial banks.

10. **(B)** Type of Question: Cause-and-effect relationships

The Congressional Budget and Impoundment Control Act was passed in 1974 in order to stop the president from doing away with approved programs in the name of deficit reduction. The law also streamlined the entire budgetary process. The line item veto was approved by both houses of Congress in 1995 but stalled in conference. The Supreme Court never ruled on the legality of Nixon's actions. A balanced budget amendment never passed Congress, even though a direction to balance the budget was passed by Congress in 1995. The Gramm-Rudman-Hollings Act set spending limits.

11. **(E)** Type of Question: Identification and analysis

Social Security, Medicare, Medicaid, and welfare account for more than 40 percent of the federal budget. The national defense amounts to 25 percent of the budget. Federal operations, federal grants, and discretionary spending account for the rest of the expenditures along with interest on the debt.

12. **(A)** Type of Question: Identification and analysis

Income taxes account for more than 40 percent of the income. Social Security and payroll taxes account for a little over 33 percent. Corporate taxes account for a little over 10 percent, and luxury taxes and tariffs, under 10 percent.

13. **(C)** Type of Question: Definitional

By definition a progressive tax is based on the premise that the more you earn the more you pay in taxes. A proportional tax, also known as a flat tax, is based on the premise that everybody should pay the same percentage of taxes. A regressive tax is based on the premise that everybody has to pay a tax on essential goods. An example of a regressive tax is a sales tax.

14. **(C)** Type of Question: Identification and analysis

Social Security and Medicare are examples of programs that people contribute to through payroll taxes. Supplemental Security Income, Aid to Families with Dependent Children, welfare, and food stamps are all examples of programs that are redistributive in nature based on the premise that the government uses tax money and redistributes it to other groups.

15. **(E)** Type of Question: Hypothetical

Choice A would be the philosophy of the federal era. Choice B would be the philosophy of the block grant era. Choice C has never been accepted as a practical philosophy. Choice

D has been talked about, but in practice private business does not have the resources to provide enough money to create a safety net for those in need.

16. **(C)** Type of Question: Identification and analysis

   Passed in 1992 after being vetoed by President Bush, the Family Medical Leave Act provides medical assistance and medical leave for workers without the threat of loss of job. Medicare provides healthcare benefits for senior citizens, Social Security provides money for those who contributed to the system and have reached the age set by law, and Medicaid provides for medical assistance for those who cannot afford to pay for it. Disability insurance provides for money if a person is hurt on the job and cannot return for an extended period of time.

Section 2: Data-Based Free-Response Question (5 points)

Answer the following questions based on the graph.

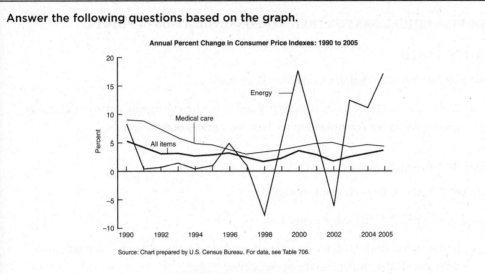

Annual Percent Change in Consumer Price Indexes: 1990 to 2005

Source: Chart prepared by U.S. Census Bureau. For data, see Table 706.

SOURCE: Bureau of the Census

The Consumer Price Index (CPI) is one of the key economic indicators released by the U.S. Bureau of the Census. The Federal Reserve evaluates the changes in the index to help them make decisions regarding the monetary policies of the Federal Reserve.

Using the information from the graph and your knowledge of U.S. government and politics:

(a) Define what is meant by the consumer price index.

(b) Identify two trends from the graph.

(c) Give two examples of actions taken by the Federal Reserve as a result of the trends in the graph.

SAMPLE RESPONSE

(a) The Consumer Price Index (CPI) is defined as the percentage increase or decrease of goods and services compared to the base year prices of those goods. Specifically, the Bureau of the Census prepares the data based on reports it receives from the Department of Labor. These reports include the market basket list of goods and services indexed to either a base year (for long-range projections) or the beginning of the calendar year (for yearly projections).

(b) The graph illustrates the following:

- In the period 1998–2004, energy-related goods and services fluctuated much more dramatically than other market-basket items.
- The rise and fall of all items calculated reflected periods of inflation, economic stability, and economic recessions.

(c) Today, the Federal Reserve Board uses a series of actions in order to try to counter inflationary and recessionary trends signaled by a rise or fall in the Consumer Price Index. If the economy seems to be heading toward higher inflation, the Federal Reserve will raise the discount and interest rates in an attempt to curb spending. If, on the other hand, the economy is sluggish and unemployment is rising along with a reduction of goods, the Fed will lower interest and discount rates to encourage spending. The Board can also borrow more money from member banks in order to stimulate the economy.

SCORING GUIDELINES FOR FREE-RESPONSE QUESTION (5 POINTS)

Part (a) 1 Point

One point is earned for defining Consumer Price Index:

- The Consumer Price Index (CPI) is defined as the percentage increase or decrease of goods and services compared to the base year prices of those goods.

Part (b) 2 Points

One point is earned for each trend identified.

Answers may include but are not limited to:

- In the period 1998–2004, energy-related goods and services fluctuated much more dramatically than other market-basket items.
- The rise and fall of all items reflected period of inflation, economic stability, and economic recessions.
- Inflation based on all items in the index was low during the period of 1990–2005.

Part (c) 2 Points

One point is earned for each example of an action taken by the Federal Reserve Board:

- The Federal Reserve raises the discount and interest rates to curb spending.
- The Federal Reserve lowers the discount and interest rates to stimulate spending.

PART SIX
Model Exams

ANSWER SHEET
Model Exam 1

1. Ⓐ Ⓑ Ⓒ Ⓓ Ⓔ
2. Ⓐ Ⓑ Ⓒ Ⓓ Ⓔ
3. Ⓐ Ⓑ Ⓒ Ⓓ Ⓔ
4. Ⓐ Ⓑ Ⓒ Ⓓ Ⓔ
5. Ⓐ Ⓑ Ⓒ Ⓓ Ⓔ
6. Ⓐ Ⓑ Ⓒ Ⓓ Ⓔ
7. Ⓐ Ⓑ Ⓒ Ⓓ Ⓔ
8. Ⓐ Ⓑ Ⓒ Ⓓ Ⓔ
9. Ⓐ Ⓑ Ⓒ Ⓓ Ⓔ
10. Ⓐ Ⓑ Ⓒ Ⓓ Ⓔ
11. Ⓐ Ⓑ Ⓒ Ⓓ Ⓔ
12. Ⓐ Ⓑ Ⓒ Ⓓ Ⓔ
13. Ⓐ Ⓑ Ⓒ Ⓓ Ⓔ
14. Ⓐ Ⓑ Ⓒ Ⓓ Ⓔ
15. Ⓐ Ⓑ Ⓒ Ⓓ Ⓔ

16. Ⓐ Ⓑ Ⓒ Ⓓ Ⓔ
17. Ⓐ Ⓑ Ⓒ Ⓓ Ⓔ
18. Ⓐ Ⓑ Ⓒ Ⓓ Ⓔ
19. Ⓐ Ⓑ Ⓒ Ⓓ Ⓔ
20. Ⓐ Ⓑ Ⓒ Ⓓ Ⓔ
21. Ⓐ Ⓑ Ⓒ Ⓓ Ⓔ
22. Ⓐ Ⓑ Ⓒ Ⓓ Ⓔ
23. Ⓐ Ⓑ Ⓒ Ⓓ Ⓔ
24. Ⓐ Ⓑ Ⓒ Ⓓ Ⓔ
25. Ⓐ Ⓑ Ⓒ Ⓓ Ⓔ
26. Ⓐ Ⓑ Ⓒ Ⓓ Ⓔ
27. Ⓐ Ⓑ Ⓒ Ⓓ Ⓔ
28. Ⓐ Ⓑ Ⓒ Ⓓ Ⓔ
29. Ⓐ Ⓑ Ⓒ Ⓓ Ⓔ
30. Ⓐ Ⓑ Ⓒ Ⓓ Ⓔ

31. Ⓐ Ⓑ Ⓒ Ⓓ Ⓔ
32. Ⓐ Ⓑ Ⓒ Ⓓ Ⓔ
33. Ⓐ Ⓑ Ⓒ Ⓓ Ⓔ
34. Ⓐ Ⓑ Ⓒ Ⓓ Ⓔ
35. Ⓐ Ⓑ Ⓒ Ⓓ Ⓔ
36. Ⓐ Ⓑ Ⓒ Ⓓ Ⓔ
37. Ⓐ Ⓑ Ⓒ Ⓓ Ⓔ
38. Ⓐ Ⓑ Ⓒ Ⓓ Ⓔ
39. Ⓐ Ⓑ Ⓒ Ⓓ Ⓔ
40. Ⓐ Ⓑ Ⓒ Ⓓ Ⓔ
41. Ⓐ Ⓑ Ⓒ Ⓓ Ⓔ
42. Ⓐ Ⓑ Ⓒ Ⓓ Ⓔ
43. Ⓐ Ⓑ Ⓒ Ⓓ Ⓔ
44. Ⓐ Ⓑ Ⓒ Ⓓ Ⓔ
45. Ⓐ Ⓑ Ⓒ Ⓓ Ⓔ

46. Ⓐ Ⓑ Ⓒ Ⓓ Ⓔ
47. Ⓐ Ⓑ Ⓒ Ⓓ Ⓔ
48. Ⓐ Ⓑ Ⓒ Ⓓ Ⓔ
49. Ⓐ Ⓑ Ⓒ Ⓓ Ⓔ
50. Ⓐ Ⓑ Ⓒ Ⓓ Ⓔ
51. Ⓐ Ⓑ Ⓒ Ⓓ Ⓔ
52. Ⓐ Ⓑ Ⓒ Ⓓ Ⓔ
53. Ⓐ Ⓑ Ⓒ Ⓓ Ⓔ
54. Ⓐ Ⓑ Ⓒ Ⓓ Ⓔ
55. Ⓐ Ⓑ Ⓒ Ⓓ Ⓔ
56. Ⓐ Ⓑ Ⓒ Ⓓ Ⓔ
57. Ⓐ Ⓑ Ⓒ Ⓓ Ⓔ
58. Ⓐ Ⓑ Ⓒ Ⓓ Ⓔ
59. Ⓐ Ⓑ Ⓒ Ⓓ Ⓔ
60. Ⓐ Ⓑ Ⓒ Ⓓ Ⓔ

Model Exam 1

SECTION 1: MULTIPLE-CHOICE QUESTIONS

TIME: 45 MINUTES

60 QUESTIONS

SECTION 1 IS WORTH 50 PERCENT OF THE TEST.

> **Directions:** Each of the following questions has five choices. Choose the best response and record your answer on the answer sheet on page 293. There will be no penalty for incorrect answers in the multiple-choice section. Answer as many multiple-choice questions in the time permitted, even if you are unsure of the correct answer, by eliminating wrong choices.

1. A provision in the Constitution that has been used to expand federal power over the states is
   (A) the police power
   (B) the reserved power clause
   (C) the due process clause of the Fourteenth Amendment
   (D) establishment of republican governments by the states
   (E) separation of powers

2. Which of the following statements best describes the consequences of elite class theory?
   (A) It encourages the formation of third political parties.
   (B) Competing special interests can unduly influence the legislative process.
   (C) A centrist philosophy would emerge resulting in gridlock.
   (D) The elite in society would play a dominant role in the political process.
   (E) The elite would clash with the middle class resulting in class warfare.

3. The exclusionary rule established by the Supreme Court supported the position that
   (A) policemen must knock before they enter a house with a search warrant
   (B) stop and frisk actions by police could be used only if there was probable cause
   (C) witnesses to a crime may testify for a trial on videotape rather than in person
   (D) evidence obtained that goes beyond the stated purpose of a search warrant may not be used in court
   (E) a suspect may withhold information from the police when a lawyer is not present during interrogation

4. Which of the following describes a consequence of the 2010 *Citizens United v FEC Supreme Court* ruling that dealt with campaign finance laws?
   (A) Corporate soft money donations to political parties is banned.
   (B) Corporate hard money donations to political candidates is banned.
   (C) Corporations do not have to disclose political donations.
   (D) Corporation funding of independent political advertisements is protected by the First Amendment.
   (E) Unions were allowed to collect dues from their members for the purpose of political action.

5. A major area that is affected by congressional oversight hearings is the

(A) structure of congressional committees
(B) ability of the president to recommend legislation to Congress
(C) reduction of the number of cases heard by the Supreme Court
(D) creation of new special interest groups
(E) review of the budgets of independent regulatory agencies

6. The primary function of a lobbyist is to

(A) find political candidates for special interest groups
(B) provide information to members of Congress that is favorable to a position taken by a special interest group
(C) poll the public to help determine a position that a special interest group should take
(D) raise money for political action committees
(E) increase the awareness of special interest groups to the electorate

7. In viewing the relationship between the president and Congress in the area of foreign policy, which action on the part of Congress attempted to reduce presidential authority?

(A) Congressional Impoundment Act
(B) War Powers Act
(C) Gulf of Tonkin Resolution
(D) Approval of the SALT agreement
(E) Approval of NAFTA

8. One way Congress can respond to a Supreme Court ruling that declares a law unconstitutional is to

(A) appoint new justices
(B) draft a referendum that the voters would approve
(C) pass new legislation that addresses the issues raised by the Court
(D) pass a law limiting the terms of the justices
(E) reargue the case in a state court

9. In attempting to gain public support for his agenda, the president uses all of the following techniques EXCEPT

(A) using the bully pulpit
(B) giving the media a photo op
(C) providing sound bites
(D) holding a press conference
(E) holding a private meeting with the joint chiefs of staff

10. A Supreme Court that creates precedent is described as one that relies on

(A) unanimous court decisions
(B) judicial federalism
(C) judicial restraint
(D) judicial activism
(E) stare decisis

Questions 11 and 12 should be answered based upon your knowledge of the Constitution and the U.S. government.

The powers not delegated to the United States by the Constitution, nor prohibited by it to the states, are reserved to the states respectively, or the people.

11. After the 1994 midterm election, which of the following laws was passed by the Republican Congress to achieve the objective of this amendment?

(A) Block grants for welfare
(B) Funded mandates
(C) Judicial authority to appoint federal judges
(D) Power to reject regulatory agency directives
(E) The go-ahead to make individual treaties with foreign countries

12. Which principle of government is derived from this amendment?

(A) Separation of powers
(B) Checks and balances
(C) Federalism
(D) Pluralism
(E) Republicanism

13. Whips have which of the following functions?

(A) They act as direct liaisons to the White House.

(B) They work closely with the minority party in the name of bipartisanship.

(C) They make appointments to the various House and Senate committees.

(D) They are responsible for keeping party members in line when a vote occurs.

(E) They preside over the House when the speaker is absent.

14. Which of the following is a major cause of the inability of Congress to pass legislation?

(A) The number of bills proposed by the president

(B) Lobbyists influencing Congress

(C) Divided party control of the Congress

(D) The increased number of southern Republicans elected to Congress

(E) The change in the party identification of voters

15. Sunshine laws were passed in order to give

(A) Congress greater flexibility in determining meeting times

(B) C-SPAN the ability to televise congressional sessions

(C) citizens the ability to get information from law enforcement agencies

(D) citizens the ability to attend meetings that previously were held in secret session

(E) the press the right to get information from citizens

16. Which of the following is a characteristic of the electoral college?

(A) It mandates presidential electors to vote for the candidate they are pledged to.

(B) It establishes a power base for third-party candidates.

(C) It has resulted in frequent occasions when a president wins the electoral vote but not the popular vote.

(D) It became part of the Constitution to give more power to the voters.

(E) It gives the House of Representatives the power to determine who will be president if no candidate gets a majority of the electoral votes.

17. Standing House committees such as the Ways and Means Committee are important because they

(A) do not engage in partisan behavior

(B) mark up bills before they go to the entire House for debate

(C) can act independently from established House rules

(D) receive conference committee reports

(E) are equally divided in membership between Democrats and Republicans

18. The Constitution provides that one-third of the Senate's membership is up for election every two years so that

(A) House members may decide whether to run for the Senate

(B) committee assignments can be alternated between Democrats and Republicans

(C) voters have less of a chance to change control of the Senate from one party to another

(D) the entire House and entire Senate are not elected in the same year

(E) congressional apportionment can alter the size of House districts

19. Which of the following groups voted most heavily Republican during the first decade of the twenty-first century?

   (A) Jews
   (B) Evangelical Christians
   (C) African-Americans
   (D) Asian-Americans
   (E) Labor union members

20. Proponents of the Second Amendment were most upset when Congress passed

   (A) the Civil Rights Act of 1990
   (B) the Family and Medical Leave Act of 1992
   (C) the Unfunded Mandates Act of 1994
   (D) the Line Item Veto Act of 1994
   (E) the Brady Bill of 1992

21. Procedural due process can best be found in

   (A) the First Amendment
   (B) the Second Amendment
   (C) the Fifth Amendment
   (D) plea bargaining agreements
   (E) the use of cameras in the courtroom

Question 22 is based on the following headline.

Green Party Candidate Ralph Nader Runs for President

Some people say we should have a third major political party in the country in addition to the Democrats and Republicans.

22. Which of the following reflects the best explanation for the headline?

   (A) The Democratic and Republican parties have outlasted their effectiveness.
   (B) The media's coverage of the parties has soured the voters.
   (C) Voters don't seem to detect major differences between the Democrats and Republicans.
   (D) Third political parties will have a better chance to elect their candidates.
   (E) Voter registration has been on the decline.

23. What is the result of a continuing resolution agreed upon by both houses of Congress?

   (A) It authorizes the president to borrow money in advance of an approved budget.
   (B) It allows a president to send troops abroad on a temporary basis.
   (C) It prevents the shutdown of any governmental operation if a new budget is not enacted.
   (D) It directs the Congress to meet until a budget is voted on.
   (E) It creates a new legislative agenda.

24. The trend of states joining in regional presidential primaries suggests that the states want to

   (A) lessen the cost of the presidential campaigns
   (B) have greater influence in the outcome of the nominating process
   (C) lessen the importance of the New Hampshire primary
   (D) decrease the electorate's influence on the outcome
   (E) diminish the coverage by the media

25. Which of the following reflects how the news media covers campaigns?

   (A) The media covers the candidates' positions in an in-depth manner.
   (B) The media is obligated to give equal coverage to all candidates running for office.
   (C) The media's main objective is to change public opinion through its coverage.
   (D) The media's coverage is characterized by candidates' sound bites and photo ops.
   (E) The media has shied away from looking at the personal lives of the candidates running for office.

26. In choosing members of the cabinet, the president usually seeks out people who

    (A) exclusively come from his own political party

    (B) are primarily from the business community

    (C) will remain loyal to the president

    (D) are current government officials

    (E) are former government officials

27. Which of the following is true about senatorial courtesy?

    (A) Senators have final say regarding presidential judicial appointments.

    (B) Senators of the state from which the candidate comes are consulted by the president prior to the candidate's appointment as a federal judge.

    (C) Senators rely on the expertise of their fellow senators before approving judicial appointments.

    (D) Senators consult with the American Bar Association before voting on judicial appointments.

    (E) Senators poll their constituents before deciding on whether to accept a presidential appointment.

28. All of the following are considered delegated constitutional jobs of the president EXCEPT

    (A) commander in chief of the armed forces

    (B) chief of state

    (C) making appointments of ambassadors

    (D) head of their political party

    (E) signing treaties with foreign countries

Question 29 is based on this graph:

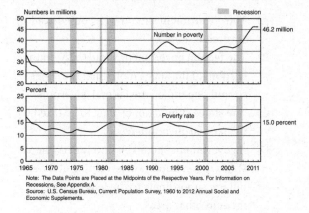

Number in Poverty and Poverty Rate: 1965–2011

Note: The Data Points are Placed at the Midpoints of the Respective Years. For Information on Recessions, See Appendix A.
Source: U.S. Census Bureau, Current Population Survey, 1960 to 2012 Annual Social and Economic Supplements.

29. The graph supports which of the following conclusions?

    (A) The poverty rate has increased from 1965 to 2011.

    (B) The number of people in poverty has increased from 1965 to 2011.

    (C) There is no correlation between the percentage of people in poverty and the poverty rate.

    (D) When the poverty rate increases, the percentage of people in poverty decreases.

    (E) The poverty rate and percentage of people in poverty increase immediately following a recession.

30. The Founding Fathers relied on which principle developed by Enlightenment thinkers?

    (A) Habeas corpus

    (B) Guarantees of life, liberty, and property

    (C) One man, one vote

    (D) The right to bear arms

    (E) A single-house legislature

31. Which of the following conclusions did Madison reach in Federalist No. 39 regarding the issue of state sovereignty in the Federal system?

(A) The government should be a confederacy of sovereign states.

(B) The federal government should rely on the wisdom of the states more than the states should depend on the federal government.

(C) The states should not be able to be taxed by the federal government.

(D) A government should be developed where states retain important governing abilities but are subordinate to the federal government in other areas.

(E) The states should have delegated powers reserved to them.

32. Which of the following is an example of the Supreme Court accepting a case based on original jurisdiction?

(A) An appeal by a state regarding the decision of a lower court to overturn the state's restrictive abortion law

(B) A habeas corpus petition from a convict who is on death row

(C) A suit on the part of a citizen who believes his First Amendment rights are being violated

(D) A dispute between environmentalists and land developers regarding the constitutionality of the Endangered Species Act

(E) A dispute between New York and New Jersey over the plans of New York to build a hotel on Ellis Island

33. A major difference between the Iowa caucus and the New Hampshire primary is

(A) greater turnout of voters in the Iowa caucus

(B) more loyal party regulars vote in New Hampshire

(C) exit polls are more accurate in caucus votes

(D) the fact that candidates must spend more money on caucus votes

(E) the fact that New Hampshire voters use a secret ballot to vote

34. Which of the following was a major reason the Supreme Court ruled that state-approved term limits for Congress were unconstitutional?

(A) State laws restricting terms varied from state to state.

(B) The age, residency, and citizenship requirements in the Constitution could be altered only by a constitutional amendment.

(C) Congress could pass their own laws changing term limits.

(D) Most people in the country voiced strong opposition to state-imposed term limit requirements.

(E) If states passed term limit laws for congressmen, it would also enable them to pass term limit laws for other elected officials.

35. Which of the following is an example of political realignment?

(A) Social conservatives voting for John McCain in 2008

(B) African-Americans voting for Barack Obama in 2008

(C) A greater percentage of Hispanics voting for Barack Obama than George W. Bush

(D) More independents voting for Barack Obama than John McCain

(E) Republican Party self-identification declining during the 2000s

36. Which of the following statements is true about the nature of modern party organizations?

(A) Local politics generates a grassroots support by party regulars.

(B) The control of the party machinery is greatest at the national level.

(C) The party's national committee has the major fundraising responsibility for local candidates.

(D) They are run by party bosses in a democratic manner.

(E) The party's chairman is selected by its congressional membership.

Base your answers to Questions 37 and 38 on the following excerpt from a Supreme Court decision:

On the other hand, the allowance of the privilege to withhold evidence that is demonstrably relevant in a criminal trial would cut deeply into the guarantee of due process of law and gravely impair the basic function of the courts. A president's acknowledged need for confidentiality in the communication of his office is general in nature. . . .

37. Which event took place as a result of this ruling?

   (A) The impeachment of Richard Nixon by the House of Representatives
   (B) The immediate resignation of Richard Nixon as president
   (C) An order requiring Nixon to turn over private documents
   (D) The release of the Watergate tapes to the Senate Watergate Committee
   (E) The erasure of 18 minutes of a critical tape by Nixon's secretary

38. The principle of executive privilege relates to which constitutional doctrine?

   (A) Division of powers
   (B) Reserved powers
   (C) Separation of powers
   (D) Judicial review
   (E) Federalism

---

39. The major impact third political parties have on presidential elections has been to

   (A) recruit leaders from the Democrats and Republicans to run for president
   (B) draw enough votes from the major parties to throw the election into the House of Representatives
   (C) generate increased party identification among the electorate
   (D) develop issues that are later adopted by the major political parties
   (E) encourage a larger voter turnout

40. A special interest group would probably have the greatest success dealing with a legislator regarding public policy issues that

   (A) were favored by the public as reflected by polls
   (B) the president also supported
   (C) were controversial in nature
   (D) the legislator needed specific information about, which the group could provide
   (E) had previously been voted on by Congress but defeated

41. Which of the following statements best describes congressional incumbency?

   (A) Incumbents are usually able to win reelection.
   (B) Incumbents have had fundraising limits imposed on them by the Federal Election Commission.
   (C) Incumbents have been able to raise less money than their opponents.
   (D) Incumbents are able to use franking privileges to their advantage.
   (E) Incumbents look to have numerous debates with their opponents.

42. Compared with marble cake federalism, Reagan's new federalism aimed to

   (A) increase the size of the federal government
   (B) reduce the number of block grants given to the states
   (C) downsize the federal government and turn more authority over to the states
   (D) increase the amount of federal taxes to reduce the deficit
   (E) reduce the size of the Defense Department and give the savings back to the states

43. Which of the following has the power to increase the size of the Supreme Court?

   (A) The voters
   (B) The president
   (C) Congress
   (D) A constitutional amendment
   (E) A vote by the Senate Judiciary Committee

44. Which statement is true about the War Powers Act?

   (A) It overturned the Gulf of Tonkin Resolution.
   (B) It gave Congress the power to appoint the head of the joint chiefs of staff.
   (C) It gave the president the authority to declare war.
   (D) It established procedures when United States troops were under the command of the UN during peacekeeping missions.
   (E) It directed the president to be accountable to the Congress if he sent troops to foreign countries.

45. The guiding principle that governs legislative apportionment is

   (A) political gerrymandering
   (B) the establishment of majority-minority districts
   (C) one man, one vote
   (D) judicial authority to create congressional districts
   (E) districts determined by the governors of each state

46. All of the following demographic criteria have had an impact on voting EXCEPT

   (A) the number of young people registered
   (B) the socioeconomic makeup of the electorate
   (C) the shift of the population to sunbelt states
   (D) the ethnic make-up of the electorate
   (E) an increase in illegal aliens

47. What conclusion can you reach from the fact that informal congressional caucus groups such as the black caucus and caucus for women's issues have been formed?

   (A) Caucus groups have had little impact on the legislative process.
   (B) Democratic caucus groups were more powerful than Republican groups.
   (C) There is an indirect relationship between these groups and special interest groups.
   (D) Caucus groups were organized to better serve voter constituents.
   (E) Republican groups were more numerous than Democratic groups.

48. Which of the following represents the attitudes of citizens with respect to the issue of separation of church and state?

   (A) A majority of the population is against a constitutional amendment authorizing silent prayer in the schools.
   (B) Liberals tend to oppose Supreme Court decisions such as *Engle v Vitale*.
   (C) Conservatives feel that more people should attend churches and synagogues on a more regular basis.
   (D) A majority of the population understands the establishment clause but feels students should be able to pray in school.
   (E) Citizens in a pluralist society reject the need to recognize the rights of minority religious groups.

49. The commerce clause of the Constitution has been viewed as a way for

   (A) Congress to exercise greater authority over state matters
   (B) the president to exercise greater authority to commit troops abroad
   (C) the states to exercise their reserved powers
   (D) the Senate to increase its authority to advise and consent the president's appointments
   (E) Congress to exercise greater authority over the Supreme Court

50. Since the 2000s the manner in which legislation passed each house of Congress suggests that

   (A) bipartisanship has been the rule of thumb
   (B) Congress has passed a greater number of bills than in previous decades
   (C) there has been an increasing tendency for the president to veto legislation
   (D) even though the House may pass its legislative agenda, it is often slowed down by the Senate
   (E) Senate-House conference committees have exercised greater influence than congressional leaders in the formulation of legislation

51. All of the following reflect devolution of federal power EXCEPT

    (A) the approval of block grants to the states

    (B) the limitations placed on the federal government to pass on unfunded mandates to the states

    (C) the Supreme Court decisions that allow death row inmates to file petitions for review in federal court

    (D) the executive orders resulting in the downsizing of the bureaucracy

    (E) the congressional legislation resulting in the elimination of regulations established by regulatory agencies

52. Since 1960, which of the following is the most significant factor in determining which candidate receives the party's nomination for president?

    (A) The economic condition facing the country

    (B) The belief that programs favored by the candidate would benefit the country

    (C) The ability of the candidate to win a majority of the delegates

    (D) The support given to the candidate by party leaders

    (E) The polls indicating that the candidate has name recognition

53. All of the following are reasons for lower voter turnout in congressional elections compared to presidential elections EXCEPT

    (A) Political advertisements use more smear tactics in presidential elections.

    (B) Voters are more aware of national issues than local issues.

    (C) There is more media coverage of presidential elections.

    (D) Voters believe that presidential elections have a greater impact on the country's future.

    (E) Candidates spend more money on presidential elections.

54. The Speaker of the House of Representatives has the primary role of

    (A) breaking tie votes in the House

    (B) presiding over the House during routine business

    (C) setting the legislative agenda for the House

    (D) settling disputes in his own party

    (E) acting as a liaison with the opposition party

55. All of the following choices are accurate statements about the nature of bureaucracies EXCEPT

    (A) There are built-in review processes for appeal of agency decisions.

    (B) There are bureaucratic agencies that oversee other agencies.

    (C) The size and scope of the federal bureaucracy increased in the 1990s.

    (D) There are political checks on agencies.

    (E) Legislative power can restrict agency appropriations.

56. Which statement is most true of the media's coverage of presidential campaigns?

    (A) Presidential endorsements by newspapers change the minds of many voters.

    (B) Sunday talk shows pay for their guests to appear.

    (C) There is an increased interest in covering the national conventions gavel to gavel by the major networks.

    (D) Networks like C-SPAN and CNN have played an increasingly important role in reporting the issues of the campaign.

    (E) The fairness doctrine has lessened the accusation that there is bias in the media toward one candidate.

57. Which of the following statements describes voting trends in recent presidential elections?

    (A) The gender gap has not been a factor.

    (B) The youth vote is declining.

    (C) The religious right is becoming less of a factor.

    (D) More people are enrolling as Independents.

    (E) White Americans vote Democratic.

58. Which of the following statements is a major reason for the increased use of public opinion polls by the media?

(A) The government assesses the validity of the polls.

(B) Candidate-sponsored polls compete for the public's attention.

(C) A smaller random sample can now be used to get accurate results.

(D) Polls are aimed exclusively at minority groups.

(E) Elected officials pay attention to poll results.

59. The Federal Reserve Board has grown in importance because it

(A) influences the trade policy of the United States

(B) has printed more money in order to reduce the deficit

(C) attempts to control inflation by raising or lowering interest rates

(D) can shut down trading on the stock market when the market drops below a certain point

(E) can create new branches of the National Bank

60. All of the following are characteristics of the media-driven presidential campaign EXCEPT

(A) 30-second political ads shown on prime-time television shows

(B) political debates that include minor party candidates

(C) the use of Twitter and Facebook by the campaigns

(D) sophisticated polling done by paid consultants

(E) candidates appearing on Sunday talk shows

STOP

If there is still time remaining, you may review your answers.

SECTION 2: FREE-RESPONSE QUESTIONS

TIME: 100 MINUTES (SUGGESTED TIME: 25 MINUTES PER QUESTION)

SECTION 2 IS WORTH 50 PERCENT OF THE TEST.

> **Directions:** Answer *all four* of the following questions in 100 minutes. Each question should take you 25 minutes, so plan your time accordingly. The questions are based on your knowledge of U.S. government and politics, and questions may contain materials from charts, graphs, and tables, which you will have to analyze and draw conclusions from. Make sure that you give specific and sufficient information and examples in your answers. Please number them clearly on your answer sheet.

1. Special interest groups are often criticized for being divisive as well as for hindering the legislative process. (5 pts.)

   (a) Define the term "special interest group."

   (b) Give one example that supports this statement and one example that refutes it.

   (c) Choose two of the following acts and explain how special interest groups helped or hindered the passage of the law.

   - The Brady Bill of 1993
   - The Equal Rights Act of 1996
   - The Americans with Disabilities Act of 1991

   (For illustrative purposes all three laws are addressed in the answer.)

2. The Constitution states that "each House shall determine the rules of its proceedings." Sometimes these rules impede the legislative process. In other cases the rules expedite the passage of laws. (6 pts.)

   (a) Define each of the following rules

   - The filibuster
   - Cloture
   - Closed rule

   (b) Describe one way two of the above rules either impedes or enhances the legislative process.

   (c) Explain how the House Rules Committee affects the legislative process.

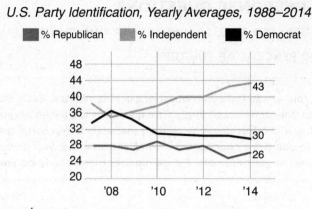

U.S. Party Identification, Yearly Averages, 1988–2014

% Republican   % Independent   % Democrat

3. From 2008–2014 party identification of the electorate could be characterized as Democratic and Republican. A segment of the population has identified themselves as Independents. There have been shifts of party allegiance among these groups, and certain factors have contributed to shifts of party loyalty. (7 pts.)

(a) Identify two trends from the data in the graph.

(b) Explain how each of the following factors has led to increased voter dissatisfaction with the major parties.

- Age
- Education
- Party identification

(c) Define "political socialization."

4. The Constitution gives the Senate the power to advise and consent for presidential appointments. (6 pts.)

(a) Describe how this constitutional process applies to the president's authority to advise and how the Senate carries out its responsibility to consent.

(b) Give two examples of a presidential appointment that met opposition in the Senate.

(c) Discuss what the consequences were to the outcome of the examples you gave in (b).

ANSWER KEY
Practice Test 1

1.	**C**	16.	**E**	31.	**D**	46	**E**
2.	**D**	17.	**B**	32.	**E**	47.	**D**
3.	**D**	18.	**D**	33.	**E**	48.	**D**
4.	**D**	19.	**B**	34.	**B**	49.	**A**
5.	**E**	20.	**E**	35.	**C**	50.	**D**
6.	**B**	21.	**C**	36.	**A**	51.	**C**
7.	**B**	22.	**C**	37.	**D**	52.	**C**
8.	**C**	23.	**C**	38.	**C**	53.	**A**
9.	**E**	24.	**B**	39.	**D**	54.	**C**
10.	**D**	25.	**D**	40.	**D**	55.	**C**
11.	**A**	26.	**C**	41.	**A**	56.	**D**
12.	**C**	27.	**B**	42.	**C**	57.	**D**
13.	**D**	28.	**D**	43.	**C**	58.	**E**
14.	**C**	29.	**E**	44.	**E**	59.	**C**
15.	**D**	30.	**B**	45.	**C**	60.	**B**

ANSWERS EXPLAINED

1. **(C)** Type of Question: Identification and analysis

   Choice A refers to a reserved power of the states. Choice B refers to the Tenth Amendment and gives states powers such as education, health, and safety. Choice C, the correct answer, established that the states could not make laws that violate the rights of individuals living in those states. It also incorporated the Bill of Rights into the states. Choice D establishes state governments. Choice E refers to checks and balances.

2. **(D)** Type of Question: Definitional

   Choice D, the correct answer, is the definition of elite class theory. Choice A is a consequence of factions. Choice B is the definition of hyperpluralism. Choice C refers to pluralism and then gives an incorrect consequence of it. Choice E may take place, but is not necessarily a consequence of the elite playing a dominant role in the political process.

3. **(D)** Type of Question: Definitional

   Choice D, the correct answer, is the definition of exclusionary rule. Choices A and B echo Supreme Court rulings. Choice C is factually correct, but has nothing to do with the exclusionary rule, and choice E is an incorrect statement as a result of the Miranda ruling.

4. **(D)** Type of Question: Identification and analysis

   Choice D correctly identifies the finding of the U.S. Supreme Court in the *Citizens United v FEC* (2010) case. Corporations prior to this decision were prohibited from using money to make independent political advertisements. Choices A and B are incorrect because corporations are allowed to give soft money to political parties and hard money through their political action committees to candidates. Choice E is incorrect because the Citizens United case did not hand down an opinion regarding unions' ability to collect dues from their members for the purpose of political action, which they are permitted to do.

5. **(E)** Type of Question: Cause-and-effect relationships

   Choice E, the correct answer, is one function of congressional oversight. Another one is to review aspects of laws passed by Congress related to specific governmental agencies or departments. Choice A is wrong because the majority party has the power to review the structure of congressional committees. Choice B is incorrect because the president can recommend legislation independently of congressional oversight. Choices C and D are incorrect statements related to the question raised.

6. **(B)** Type of Question: Definitional

   Choice B is the correct answer. Special interest groups hire lobbyists for the purpose of influencing legislation favorable to that group. For instance, the National Rifle Association (NRA) will hire lobbyists to provide information to congressmen that will encourage them to vote against gun control legislation. Choice A is incorrect because political parties, not lobbyists, find candidates to run for office. Choice C is incorrect because special interest groups hire pollsters to determine public opinion. Choice D is incorrect because special interest groups contribute money to political action committees or have those of their own. Choice E is incorrect because lobbyists work behind the scenes and do not attempt to influence the electorate at large.

7. **(B)** Type of Question: Cause-and-effect relationships

   Choice B, the correct answer, was a direct result of the president's escalation of the Vietnam War. Choice C was the action by Congress that gave President Johnson the green light to send more troops to Vietnam. Choice A refers to a budgetary action and domestic policy and does decrease presidential authority in that area. Choice D refers to Strategic Arms Limitation Talks, and choice E refers to the North American Free Trade Agreement, both treaties the Senate had to approve.

8. **(C)** Type of Question: Cause-and-effect relationships

Choice C, the correct answer, is the only manner, other than a constitutional amendment, Congress can act on a ruling by the Supreme Court that declares a law unconstitutional. Choice A is wrong because the Senate approves new justices only when there is an opening on the Court. Choice B is an incorrect statement. Choice D requires a constitutional amendment. Choice E is an incorrect statement.

9. **(E)** Type of Question: Negative

Choice E is the only incorrect choice because a meeting of the joint chiefs of staff, the heads of the military, is usually behind closed doors and would have a negligible impact on influencing public support compared to the other choices.

10. **(D)** Type of Question: Definitional

Choice D, the correct answer, requires that you understand the definition of judicial activism. The other choices are incorrect because by definition they refer to aspects of the Supreme Court that do not support what the question is asking. (Refer to glossary for definitions of each of the terms.)

11. and 12. **(A), (C)** Type of Question: Stimulus-based short quotation

In both questions you must recognize that the quote is from the Tenth Amendment to the Constitution—commonly referred to as the reserved power clause. The clause defines federalism and explains where states get their powers. Once you have determined this, you can see that in question 11, choice A would be the correct choice because block grants give funds for the states to spend without federal strings attached. In Question 12, choice C, the correct answer, relates to the principle of federalism, the division of powers between the federal government and state governments.

13. **(D)** Type of Question: Definitional

Choice D, the correct answer, is one of the jobs whips have. Choices A, B, C, and E are incorrect statements. A whip may sometimes preside over a House session, but it is not a function of the job.

14. **(C)** Type of Question: Cause-and-effect relationships

Choice C, the correct answer, is a primary reason that Congress does not pass legislation. Even though lobbyists may influence legislation (choice B) in a negative way, they are not singularly responsible for gridlock. The other choices are incorrect in relation to the question.

15. **(D)** Type of Question: Definitional

Choice D, the correct answer, is an application of the definition of sunshine laws. These laws were passed to stop the practice of legislative bodies meeting in secret executive sessions late at night. Along with the Freedom of Information Act, both laws gave citizens more rights in obtaining information from the government.

16. **(E)** Type of Question: Identification and analysis

Choice E, the correct answer, gives the circumstances when the House of Representatives is mandated by the Constitution to select a president if a majority is not reached in the electoral college. Choice A is incorrect because presidential electors are only morally obligated to vote for the candidate the elector supported. Choices B, C, and D are incorrect statements about the nature of the electoral college.

17. **(B)** Type of Question: Definitional

Choice B, the correct answer, explains a function of a standing committee in the House of Representatives. The question is made even easier because it gives an example of a standing committee. Choices A and C are easy to eliminate as incorrect answers. Choice D may be true in rare instances, but it does not describe the primary importance of standing committees. Choice E is incorrect because standing committees are divided proportionally between Democrats and Republicans based on the majority/minority split in the House.

18. **(D)** Type of Question: Cause-and-effect relationships

Choice D, the correct answer, is the most obvious reason that the entire Senate is not elected in six-year cycles. A direct result could be a dramatic upheaval of both houses under certain circumstances. Choices A, B, and C are incorrect statements based on fact or circumstance. Choice E is incorrect because apportionment does not relate to the Senate.

19. **(B)** Type of Question: Chronological

Choice B, the correct answer, is an important Republican constituency. The other choices are all traditional Democratic constituents.

20. **(E)** Type of Question: Cause-and-effect relationships

Choice E, the correct answer, is the only law that deals with the right to bear arms. The Brady Bill mandated a waiting period before an individual could purchase a gun. The NRA and other gun proponents were against the bill.

21. **(C)** Type of Question: Definitional

Choice C, the correct answer, is a constitutional example of procedural due process. The Fifth Amendment provides a road map for due process, including the right to life, liberty, and property. Plea bargaining, choice D, is incorrect because it is not a guaranteed right. The other choices do not have direct procedural guarantees even though through application or court challenge due process questions may arise.

22. **(C)** Type of Question: Stimulus-based short narrative passage

Choice C, the correct answer, reflects voter discontent with the major political parties and the reason why Ralph Nader decided to run for president in 2000. Choice A is incorrect because there is still a viable two-party system. Choice B may be true but does not directly relate to the poll results. Choice D is an inaccurate conclusion, and choice E is wrong as a result of the Motor Voter Act.

23. **(C)** Type of Question: Definitional

Choice C, the correct answer, is the basic result of what happens when a continuing resolution is adopted. Choice A represents an illegal action on the part of the president. Choices B, D, and E are factually incorrect.

24. **(B)** Type of Question: Sequencing a series of events

Choice B, the correct answer, reflects the impact of regional primaries such as Super Tuesday. A new regional primary started in 1994, when New England states joined together in what became known as Junior Tuesday, in order to have more of an impact on the process.

25. **(D)** Type of Question: Generalization

Choice D, the correct answer, requires that you understand the definitions of sound bites and photo ops. Choices A, B, and E are factually incorrect. And choice C is deceptive because, although public opinion may change through the media's coverage, that answer does not reflect the purpose of the news media's coverage of campaigns.

26. **(C)** Type of Question: Generalization

Choice C, the correct answer, has become the main criterion related to how and why cabinet appointments are made. Choice A is incorrect because of the use of the word *exclusively*. Choices B and E are incorrect because, although the statements have a degree of factual accuracy, they do not reflect the main criterion. Choice D is factually incorrect because most cabinet members come from the upper levels of the socioeconomic life.

27. **(B)** Type of Question: Definitional

Choice B, the correct answer, is the primary result of senatorial courtesy. Even though choices A, C, D, and E are factually correct, they do not relate to the concept of senatorial courtesy.

28. **(D)** Type of Question: Negative

Choice D is the incorrect answer because it is an assumed duty that is not part of the written Constitution. Choices A, B, C, and E are all constitutionally delegated powers or jobs of the president.

29. **(E)** Type of Question: Stimulus-based

Choice E is the correct answer because, in evaluating this graph, you should be able to see an increase in the poverty rate and the number of people in poverty after recessions. Choices A–D are incorrect interpretations of the graph.

30. **(B)** Type of Question: Sequencing a series of events

Choice B, the correct answer, comes directly from John Locke's writings and was changed in the Declaration of Independence to "life, liberty and the pursuit of happiness." The other choices are all part of our constitutional foundations but do not derive from the Enlightenment thinkers.

31. **(D)** Type of Question: Sequencing a series of events/generalization

Choice D, the correct answer, is a basic principle of the Federalist Papers. Choices A, B, and C reflect Anti-Federalist thinking. Choice E is factually incorrect.

32. **(E)** Type of Question: Definitional

Choice E, the correct answer, is an example of how original jurisdiction, which is defined constitutionally, works. Choices A–D are all examples of appellate jurisdiction.

33. **(E)** Type of Question: Definitional/sequencing a series of events

Choice E is the correct answer because the New Hampshire primary uses a secret ballot while the Iowa caucus is an open vote.

34. **(B)** Type of Question: Cause-and-effect relationships

Choice B, the correct answer, comes straight from the Supreme Court ruling *Thorton v Arkansas* decided in 1995. Choice A, although true, was not a primary reason for the decision. Choice C is incorrect because the decision made it clear that the only way to accomplish term limits would be through a constitutional amendment. Choice D is factually incorrect, and choice E is a legal action states can act upon.

35. **(C)** Type of Question: Hypothesis

Choice C, the correct answer, is a good example of realignment, the movement of voters from one political party to another, resulting in a major shift in succeeding elections. In this case, there was a major movement of Hispanic voters away from the Republican Party. Choices A and B are incorrect because social conservatives have voted for Republicans, and African-Americans have voted for Democrats in past presidential elections. Choice D and Choice E, though factually correct, do not define realignment.

36. **(A)** Type of Question: Generalization/definitional

Choice A, the correct answer, is a political axiom. Choices B, C, D, and E are factually incorrect. Control of party machinery is greatest at the local level. Major fundraising for local candidates is done by the local candidates and on the grassroots level. Party bosses play much less of a role in party organizations than in the days of Boss Tweed, and even those local parties dominated by a party boss are not run in a democratic manner. And the party's chair is selected by the National Committee.

37. and 38. **(D), (C)** Type of Question: Stimulus-based

The quote comes from the Supreme Court case *Nixon v United States*, also known as the Watergate tapes case. In Question 37, you first had to identify the passage as a Watergate-related quote. Then you had to sequence the event and know that the result of the ruling was that Nixon had to turn over the Watergate tapes (choice D). In Question 38 you had to know the definition of executive privilege and apply the case to the principle of separation of powers (choice C).

39. **(D)** Type of Question: Generalization

Choice D, the correct answer, is derived from the fact that throughout political history many third-party platforms are eventually incorporated into the platforms of the major parties. Examples are the populist reforms and the issue of deficit spending raised by Ross Perot in 1992. The other choices are not factually correct.

40. **(D)** Type of Question: Sequencing a series of events

Choice D, the correct answer, is true because the actions of lobbyists are measured by whether the lobbyist can convince the legislator to vote for a particular bill. Besides using other means, when a lobbyist is armed with facts and figures, legislators are more likely to respond to the position taken by the lobbyist. Choices A, B, C, and E are all possible but do not relate directly to the issue the question is raising.

41. **(A)** Type of Question: Cause-and-effect relationships

Choice A, the correct answer, reflects the importance of incumbency. During national presidential elections, most incumbents have an advantage going into the election. Choice B is factually correct. Choice D, although true, does not get to the heart of the issue of incumbency—the ability to win reelection. Choice E is a false statement.

42. **(C)** Type of Question: Definitional

Choice C, the correct answer, requires a working knowledge of the characteristics of both marble cake federalism and Reagan's new federalism. Choices A, B, and E are factually incorrect. Choice D, although factually correct, does not reflect a practice of Reagan's policies.

43. **(C)** Type of Question: Sequencing a series of events

Choice C, the correct answer, is the prescribed constitutional way the size of the Court can be changed. Historically, when Franklin Roosevelt was unhappy with the decisions made by the Court, he attempted to "pack the court" and Congress rejected the proposal. Even though a constitutional amendment could be an alternative, it is not the answer because it has never been proposed.

44. **(E)** Type of Question: Generalization

Choice E, the correct answer, is a component of the War Powers Act. Choices A, B, C, and D are factually incorrect.

45. **(C)** Type of Question: Identification and analysis

Choice C, the correct answer, derives from the Supreme Court ruling *Baker v Carr* and mandates state legislatures to take into account the make-up and size of congressional districts when redistricting based on population changes. Although political gerrymandering (choice A) or majority-minority districts may be the result, they are not the guiding principles in creating legislative apportionment. Choices D and E are factually incorrect.

46. **(E)** Type of Question: Negative

Choice E, the correct answer, though impacting on an election issue, does not affect voting because illegal aliens cannot vote. Choice D is a different issue since ethnic make-up refers to heritage.

47. **(D)** Type of Question: Cause-and-effect relationships

Choice D, the correct answer, reflects the fact that most congressional caucuses have as their purpose a constituent base. Choices A, C, and E are factually incorrect. Choice B is incorrect because there is little relationship between power and the existence of a caucus group.

48. **(D)** Type of Question: Generalization

Choice D, the correct answer, is based on numerous poll results. Choices A, B, and E are incorrect factually. Choice C is factually accurate but has nothing to do with the issue of separation of church and state.

49. **(A)** Type of Question: Identification and analysis

Choice A, the correct answer, requires you to know that the commerce clause has been used to pass legislation such as the Civil Rights Act of 1964. Even though choices B, C, and D can take place, they have nothing to do with the commerce clause. Choice E is incorrect because congressional authority relates to the size of the Court.

50. **(D)** Type of Question: Hypothetical

Choice D, the correct answer, is true especially if you consider what happened in the first year the Republicans gained control of Congress in 1994. Although the House passed almost every component of the Republican Contract with America, the Senate took much longer to pass the bills it received from the House. Choice A is incorrect because traditionally there has been bickering between the parties. Choices B, C, and E are incorrect factually.

51. **(C)** Type of Question: Negative

Choice C, the correct answer, has nothing to do with the aim of giving back power to the states. The other choices all have components that reflect the states gaining authority and the federal government giving up its control over the states.

52. **(C)** Type of Question: Solution to a problem

Choice C, the correct answer, is the practical reason why a candidate receives the nomination. Winning a majority of the delegates is crucial to receiving the party's nomination. Although choices A, B, D, and E are all factors, if the candidate does not win primaries, those issues all become irrelevant.

53. **(A)** Type of Question: Negative

Choice A, the correct answer, does not take into account that even in congressional elections candidates use smear tactics. The other choices are all valid reasons why there is lower voter turnout in off-year elections.

54. **(C)** Type of Question: Identification and analysis

Choice C, the correct answer, is a major function of the speaker. Even though the speaker has other roles described (choices A, B, D, and E), the primary role is to establish a legislative agenda. A good example of this responsibility was when Newt Gingrich pushed through the House the Republican Contract in 1994.

55. **(C)** Type of Question: Negative

Choice C, the correct answer, is not true because of President Clinton's efforts to downsize the federal government through his REGO (reinventing government) programs. The other choices are all correct.

56. **(D)** Type of Question: Generalization

Choice D, the correct answer, is a relatively new characteristic of the importance of the media in covering the political scene. Choices A, C, and E are factually inaccurate. Choice B is an exaggeration.

57. **(D)** Type of Question: Identification and analysis

Choice D correctly identifies the recent voting trend regarding party identification. Since 2008, more people are enrolling as Independents rather than Democrats or Republicans. This is called dealignment. Choice A is incorrect because in the last three presidential elections women have voted in higher numbers for the Democratic presidential candidate than men voting for either the Republican or Democratic presidential candidate. Choice B is incorrect because in the 2008 presidential election the youth vote increased for President Obama. Choice C is incorrect because the religious right vote has been a major factor in elections, especially in the 2004 election. Choice E is incorrect because white Americans tend to vote Republican in presidential elections.

58. **(E)** Type of Question: Cause-and-effect relationships

Choice E, the correct answer, is an obvious reason and may cause some confusion because it answers the question so simplistically. Choices A, B, C, and D are factually incorrect.

59. **(C)** Type of Question: Identification/definitional

Choice C, the correct answer, is a major function of the Federal Reserve Board and was used frequently in the 1990s in an attempt to head off a period of inflation. Choices A, B, D, and E are factually incorrect.

60. **(B)** Type of Question: Negative

Choice B, the correct answer, does not accurately describe the media-driven presidential campaign. Even though a political debate is a characteristic of a media-driven presidential campaign, the inclusion of minor party candidates has not occurred since the 1992 presidential debate. The other choices are all characteristics of the media-driven presidential campaign.

Section 2: Free-Response Answers

SAMPLE RESPONSE TO QUESTION 1

(More than one definition is provided.)

(a) Special interest groups are linkage institutions that, along with political parties and the media, serve as a means through which issues and the public's policy preferences get on the government's policymaking agenda. They are the policy specialists and interact with the political parties, which are recognized as the policy generalists. They provide a wealth of information that elected officials need to make accurate and important decisions.

(b) By looking at the Federalist Papers, you can see why special interest groups have been criticized. As early as 1787, James Madison warned about the "mischief of factions," his term for such groups. The U. S. Congress has periodically investigated alleged corruption and scandals in interest group activities throughout the nineteenth and twentieth centuries.

An example refuting the public's negative view of special interest groups is the fact that they have also been seen as an integral and beneficial part of the American political process, legitimized in the United States Constitution by the First Amendment, which guarantees freedom of speech and the right to "petition the Government for a redress of grievances." Lobbyists and interest groups have important and specific jobs to do. They are responsible for providing Congress with crucial information, often with assurances of financial aid in the next campaign. Although special interest groups are known to hold up legislation in Congress, they also speed up the process by saving congressmen the time needed to research particular issues. Additionally, political observers generally acknowledge that instances of outright corruption and bribery involving special groups are rare. It can also be argued that special interest groups serve a purpose by helping to develop substantive public policy issues.

(c) A good example of how special interest groups have been divisive and slowed down the legislative process is the Brady Bill. The Brady Bill was proposed shortly after James Brady was shot in 1981, during the attempted assassination of President Reagan. The bill required a waiting period before a handgun could be purchased, during which time a criminal background check of the intended buyer would be made. This waiting period would thus help to further regulate the people who could buy handguns. The National Rifle Association (NRA), one of the largest special interest groups in the country, with nearly four million members, opposed the bill. Because of the NRA's interaction with Congress, they were able to delay passage of the bill for more than ten years through a flurry of debates and arguments. It was eventually passed in a watered-down form. This is a clear example of how special interest groups can hinder the legislative process by delaying votes on a particular bill by long drawn-out congressional debates made at their request.

It can also be argued, however, that special interest groups have helped shape our nation's legislative process. Special interest groups have helped to express the views and opinions of large segments of America's population that cannot be represented by one congressional district. Good examples of this are women's rights groups, which have helped women gain treatment more equal to that of men. These groups helped to pass legislation such as the Equal Rights Act of 1966, which gave women in government jobs equal pay for the same positions held by men. Special interest groups representing handicapped Americans helped to get the Americans with Disabilities Act passed in 1991, which gives equal employment opportunities to disabled people and enables them to experience the same American dream as nondisabled Americans. Special interest groups have also been a forum for new ideas in the legislative process, helping to make our representative democracy more representative.

SCORING GUIDELINES FOR FREE-RESPONSE QUESTION 1 (5 POINTS)

Part (a) 1 Point

One point is earned for defining special interest group in one of the following ways:

- A linkage institution that serves as a mean by which issues and the public's policy preferences get on the government's policymaking agenda
- Policy specialists interacting with political parties
- Providers of information that elected officials need to make accurate decisions related to the legislative process
- Groups that donate money to political candidates, parties, and political action committees
- A specialized group that solicits members but does not nominate candidates for political office

Part (b) 2 Points

One point is earned for an example that supports the proposition that special interest groups are divisive and hinder the legislative process, and one point is earned for an example that refutes that proposition.

Any of the following can be used as examples of support of the statement:

- Madison's Federalist Paper No. 10
- Gridlock in Congress
- The number of competing special interest groups working at cross purposes

Any of the following can be used as examples refuting the statement:

- Special interest groups are an integral and beneficial part of the American political process, made legitimate by the First Amendment to the Constitution.
- Lobbyists and special interest groups provide Congress with crucial information and can speed up the legislative process after providing research to the legislators.
- Special interest groups help develop substantive public policy issues.

Part (c) 2 Points

One point each is earned for explaining how special interest groups either helped or hindered the passage of two of the following laws:

- The Brady Bill (1993)—the National Rifle Association hindered the passage of the bill
- Equal Rights Act (1966)—women's rights groups such as Emily's List helped the passage of the bill
- Americans with Disabilities Act (1991)—veteran groups such as the VFW and groups representing people with handicaps helped the passage of the bill

SAMPLE RESPONSE TO QUESTION 2

(a) The filibuster is a Senate rule that enables a Senator to initiate a debate on legislation, a presidential appointee, or any other action that requires a vote that cannot be stopped until the Senator decides to stop or until 60 senators vote to end the filibuster. Cloture is a Senate rule that is used to end a filibuster. In order for cloture to succeed, 60 senators must vote for it. A closed rule is a House rule that prevents any amendments from being considered on the floor of the House during the debate of a bill.

Please note that all the rules are answered in this response.

(b) The filibuster impedes the legislative process because a minority of Senators is able to block almost every piece of legislation by extending debate on the legislation until 60 senators vote to end the debate. Because a filibuster creates a super majority to pass legislation, if the majority party in the Senate does not have 60 senators, the minority party can prevent a piece of legislation that has majority support from ever coming up for a vote. Traditionally, a filibuster occurred when senators held the floor continuously. This has evolved to a filibuster that just had to be announced. In 2013, the Senate modified the filibuster rules to speed up the legislative process. However, after that agreement, for the first time in Senate history, a filibuster was held to block the confirmation of President Obama's nominee for defense secretary. The Senate voted to end the filibuster and the nominee was approved.

Cloture enhances the legislative process because when it is invoked and 60 senators vote to end the filibuster a vote is taken on the legislation that was being debated. Cloture votes can be taken more than once. The Senators holding the filibuster may vote for cloture if there is agreement with the sponsors of the bills regarding amendments to the legislation or other issues that caused the filibuster. Once a cloture vote is taken, often a bill that is filibustered can obtain many more than 60 votes on the bill's final passage. Without a cloture rule, the Senate would be paralyzed.

The House closed rule enhances the legislative process because it prevents numerous amendments from being voted on. If there was no rule, then hypothetically any number of amendments could be offered by the 435 members of the House. Another way this rule helps the legislative process is that sometimes if an amendment is offered and adopted, it may make the proposed legislation different from the Senate version or it may result in a presidential veto. The closed rule is adopted by the House Rules Committee.

(c) The House Rules Committee is a standing committee of the House of Representatives and acts like a steering committee for every piece of legislation that goes to the House floor for a vote. The committee makes rules on the order legislation is voted on, the length of the debate, and whether any amendments can be offered. If the committee decides there cannot be any amendments, it is called a closed rule. An open rule allows a specified number of amendments. The Rules Committee is essential for the lawmaking process because the committee establishes a defined procedure for every bill that is considered. Unlike the Senate, the House rules do not allow filibusters. The House Rules Committee is one of the key committees in the legislative process.

SCORING GUIDELINES FOR FREE-RESPONSE QUESTION 2 (5 POINTS)

Part (a) 2 Points

One point is earned for the correct definition of two of the following; filibuster, cloture, and the closed rule. Correct responses are not limited to:

- The filibuster is a Senate rule that enables a senator to initiate a debate on legislation, a presidential appointee, or any other action that requires a vote that cannot be stopped until the senator decides to stop or until 60 senators vote to end the filibuster.
- Cloture is a Senate rule that is used to end a filibuster. In order for cloture to succeed, 60 senators must vote for it.
- A closed rule is a House rule that prevents any amendments from being considered on the floor of the House during the debate of a bill.

Part (b) 2 Points

One point is earned for correctly describing how the filibuster, cloture, or the closed rule either impedes or enhances the legislative process. A second point is earned for describing how another of the three rules impedes or enhances the legislative process. Correct responses are not limited to:

Filibuster
- A filibuster impedes legislation because it creates a super majority to pass legislation. If the majority party in the Senate does not have 60 senators, the minority party can prevent a piece of legislation that has majority support from ever coming up for a vote.
- Filibusters impede legislation because they can be used to block not only legislation but also presidential appointees.
- Filibusters impede legislation because a super majority is needed for legislation to pass.

Cloture
- Cloture enhances the legislative process because when it is invoked and 60 senators vote to end the filibuster a vote is taken on the legislation that was being debated.
- Once a cloture vote is taken, often a bill that is filibustered can obtain many more than 60 votes on the bill's final passage. Without a cloture rule, the Senate would be paralyzed.

Closed rule
- The House closed rule enhances the legislative process because it prevents numerous amendments from being voted on.
- The closed rule helps the legislative process in that sometimes if an amendment is offered and adopted it may make the proposed legislation different from the Senate version or it may result in a presidential veto.

Part (c) 1 Point

One point is earned for explaining how the House Rules Committee affects legislation. A sufficient explanation of what the House Rules Committee does is necessary to receive credit. Correct responses are not limited to:

- The House Rules Committee is a standing committee of the House of Representatives and acts like a steering committee for every piece of legislation that goes to the House floor for a vote.
- The committee makes rules on the order legislation is voted on, the length of the debate, and whether any amendments can be offered.

- The Rules Committee is essential for the lawmaking process because the committee establishes a defined procedure for every bill that is considered.

SAMPLE RESPONSE TO QUESTION 3

(a) One trend shown in the graph is that because more people identified themselves as independents, that group outnumbered Republicans and Democrats in 2012 and 2014. A second trend shown is a widening decrease of self-identified Democrats from 2008 to 2014 compared with Independents.

(b) Assuming that major party dissatisfaction is on the rise, the following criteria would indicate the level:

- Age—As the age increases, the level of dissatisfaction decreases. That is the result of the fact that the so-called younger generation probably has a more liberal point of view on social issues, whereas the older people probably have a more conservative bent. Considering that there has been a Republican Party era since 1968, the age factor may have a lot to do with that trend. Young voters today may be looking for politicians and a new party that will meet their needs.
- Education—As the level of education decreases so does the voter discontent. The more educated people are, the more likely they are to be informed about the political process. Outlets such as C-SPAN and the political talk shows demonstrate the bickering between the parties and the gridlock in government. Statistically, 55–60 percent of those polled who are dissatisfied are either college graduates or have had some college education.
- Party identification—Independent voters want a third party because they are fed up with the other two. However, a significant number of members of the other parties are also calling for a third party. Party members are often splitting tickets trying to find candidates who reflect their viewpoints. Ross Perot struck a chord among the voters when he brought up the deficit as the major issue in his campaign. With the overall approval ratings of political parties being so low, the lack of party identification should be sending a message to the Democrats and Republicans. The likelihood of the emergence of a third major political party seems to be on the horizon.

(c) Political socialization is the factor that determines party identification and voting behavior such as family, religion, and educational level.

SCORING GUIDELINES FOR FREE-RESPONSE QUESTION 3 (7 POINTS)

Part (a) 2 Points

One point is earned for identifying each trend from the graph. Answers may include but are not limited to:

- Because more people identified themselves as Independents, that group outnumbered Democrats and Republicans in 2014
- A widening decrease of self-identified Democrats from 2006 to 2014 compared with Independents

Other acceptable answers:

- A decrease in self-identified Democrats after the 2010 midterm election
- An increase in self-identified Democrats after the 2008 election
- A fluctuation of self-identified Republicans from 2008 to 2014

Part (b) 3 Points

One point is earned for explaining how each factor listed led to increased voter dissatisfaction with the Democrats and Republicans:

- Age—young people tend to have less party allegiance than older voters
- Education—poorly educated people have more party dissatisfaction than highly educated people
- Party identification—strong party identification with the Democratic and Republican parties is eroding and there has been a movement toward a third party, and Independent registration has been on the increase

Part (c) 2 Points

Two points are earned for the definition of political socialization.

- Political socialization are the factors that determine party identification such as family, education, the Church, and socioeconomic status.

SAMPLE RESPONSE TO QUESTION 4

(a) Though the Senate confirmation process is as old as the Constitution itself, the controversy surrounding presidential appointments did not really reach a peak until the hearings were first televised in the late 1960s.

   The founding fathers clearly established the notion of checks and balances as a firm prerequisite before agreeing to adopt the new Constitution. Very simply, in the area of presidential appointments, the Constitution ensures that the president does not have the ability to make unchecked political appointments. The Constitution specifically gives the president the power to appoint ambassadors, cabinet-level officials, and federal judges. After a hearing is held in the appropriate Senate committee, the Senate must approve the presidential appointment by a majority vote.

(b) In the modern-day politics of the confirmation process, a president, typically, must make hundreds of lower-level appointments, mostly in the form of federal judges. Higher-level appointments include cabinet members, executive level positions, ambassadors, and Supreme Court justices. Senate confirmation of appointments in these categories generated what many political scientists have described as a perversion of the system. The controversy reached a peak during the presidency of George Bush, when Clarence Thomas was nominated as a member of the Supreme Court. The Democratic-dominated Senate Judiciary Committee heard Anita Hill testify that Thomas sexually harassed her when she worked for him. More controversy resulted with another appointment at the cabinet level when the Democrats scrutinized the personal life of John Tower, who had been nominated for the post of Secretary of Defense. The Senate committee overseeing the confirmation went as far as asking for confidential FBI files.

(c) Although, historically, most presidential appointments go unnoticed by the public and easily pass Senate scrutiny, throughout the 1980s and 1990s the Senate has used its constitutionally delegated power to approve presidential appointments as a means of airing debate regarding public policy issues. The irony is that many believe that the founding fathers never intended the confirmation process as a means of impeding a president's ability to appoint the people he thinks are best qualified. Whether it is the nomination of a Surgeon General, Defense Secretary, or Supreme Court justice, the Constitution sets up the potential for dramatic public hearings. Only when the public perceives that the Senate is abusing its power does the process hurt the democratic process.

SCORING GUIDELINES FOR FREE-RESPONSE QUESTION 4 (6 POINTS)

Part (a) 2 Points

One point is earned for describing how the Senate's power to advise and consent affects presidential power, and one point is earned for describing how the Senate carries out its power to consent:

- Presidential authority—to advise the Senate through the authority to appoint ambassadors, cabinet-level officials, and federal judges.
- Senate's power to approve—Senate approves appointments after a committee hearing moves the appointment to the Senate where the nominee needs a majority vote to be confirmed.

Part (b) 2 Points

Two points are earned for two examples of a presidential appointment that met opposition in the senate:

Answers are not limited to the following examples:

- Clarence Thomas nomination to the Supreme Court
- John Towers nomination as Secretary of Defense
- Clinton's appointment of Dr. Henry Foster for Surgeon General
- Any other nomination that a president made that had significant opposition

Part (c) 2 Points

Two points are earned for two examples of the consequences of Senate opposition of presidential appointments. Some examples are, but not limited to:

- It impedes the president's ability to make appointments as a result of the scrutiny of appointments.
- There is a perceived abuse of power by the public if the Senate denies a president's appointment.
- People become hesitant to agree to public service if they feel their privacy will be violated at the confirmation hearings.
- Politics creates delays of presidential appointments.

TEST ANALYSIS WORKSHEET

The following table provides information on how to calculate your AP exam score. First determine the number of correct multiple-choice questions from Section 1. Remember there is no penalty for incorrect answers, just positive score for those questions answered correctly. So, if you answered 45 questions correct, your multiple-choice raw score would be 45. Next, self-score the free-response answers you wrote or have your teacher score your answers based on the points allocated for each question. Then, using the free-response formula, calculate your weighted free-response raw score. Add the Section 1 multiple-choice score to the Section 2 free-response score and look at the conversion chart, which will determine your final AP score (1–5).

   Using the table below, you can determine how well you did on Model Exam 1.

Section 1: Multiple Choice

Total multiple-choice questions correct (out of 60):   _____

Raw score Section 1 multiple choice: _____

Section 2: Free-Response Questions

Question 1 =   _____   (out of 5 points)

Question 2 =   _____   (out of 5 points)

Question 3 =   _____   (out of 7 points)

Question 4 =   _____   (out of 6 points)

Raw Score:

_____ × 2.5000 = _____

Total of   Free-Response
Questions 1–4   Score

Final Score:

_____ + _____ = _____

Multiple-Choice   Free-Response   Final Score
Score   Score

**Chart to Convert Final Score to
AP U.S. Government and Politics Score**

Total Points	AP Score
91–120	5
79–90	4
62–78	3
42–61	2
0–41	1

ANSWER SHEET
Model Exam 2

1. Ⓐ Ⓑ Ⓒ Ⓓ Ⓔ   16. Ⓐ Ⓑ Ⓒ Ⓓ Ⓔ   31. Ⓐ Ⓑ Ⓒ Ⓓ Ⓔ   46. Ⓐ Ⓑ Ⓒ Ⓓ Ⓔ
2. Ⓐ Ⓑ Ⓒ Ⓓ Ⓔ   17. Ⓐ Ⓑ Ⓒ Ⓓ Ⓔ   32. Ⓐ Ⓑ Ⓒ Ⓓ Ⓔ   47. Ⓐ Ⓑ Ⓒ Ⓓ Ⓔ
3. Ⓐ Ⓑ Ⓒ Ⓓ Ⓔ   18. Ⓐ Ⓑ Ⓒ Ⓓ Ⓔ   33. Ⓐ Ⓑ Ⓒ Ⓓ Ⓔ   48. Ⓐ Ⓑ Ⓒ Ⓓ Ⓔ
4. Ⓐ Ⓑ Ⓒ Ⓓ Ⓔ   19. Ⓐ Ⓑ Ⓒ Ⓓ Ⓔ   34. Ⓐ Ⓑ Ⓒ Ⓓ Ⓔ   49. Ⓐ Ⓑ Ⓒ Ⓓ Ⓔ
5. Ⓐ Ⓑ Ⓒ Ⓓ Ⓔ   20. Ⓐ Ⓑ Ⓒ Ⓓ Ⓔ   35. Ⓐ Ⓑ Ⓒ Ⓓ Ⓔ   50. Ⓐ Ⓑ Ⓒ Ⓓ Ⓔ
6. Ⓐ Ⓑ Ⓒ Ⓓ Ⓔ   21. Ⓐ Ⓑ Ⓒ Ⓓ Ⓔ   36. Ⓐ Ⓑ Ⓒ Ⓓ Ⓔ   51. Ⓐ Ⓑ Ⓒ Ⓓ Ⓔ
7. Ⓐ Ⓑ Ⓒ Ⓓ Ⓔ   22. Ⓐ Ⓑ Ⓒ Ⓓ Ⓔ   37. Ⓐ Ⓑ Ⓒ Ⓓ Ⓔ   52. Ⓐ Ⓑ Ⓒ Ⓓ Ⓔ
8. Ⓐ Ⓑ Ⓒ Ⓓ Ⓔ   23. Ⓐ Ⓑ Ⓒ Ⓓ Ⓔ   38. Ⓐ Ⓑ Ⓒ Ⓓ Ⓔ   53. Ⓐ Ⓑ Ⓒ Ⓓ Ⓔ
9. Ⓐ Ⓑ Ⓒ Ⓓ Ⓔ   24. Ⓐ Ⓑ Ⓒ Ⓓ Ⓔ   39. Ⓐ Ⓑ Ⓒ Ⓓ Ⓔ   54. Ⓐ Ⓑ Ⓒ Ⓓ Ⓔ
10. Ⓐ Ⓑ Ⓒ Ⓓ Ⓔ   25. Ⓐ Ⓑ Ⓒ Ⓓ Ⓔ   40. Ⓐ Ⓑ Ⓒ Ⓓ Ⓔ   55. Ⓐ Ⓑ Ⓒ Ⓓ Ⓔ
11. Ⓐ Ⓑ Ⓒ Ⓓ Ⓔ   26. Ⓐ Ⓑ Ⓒ Ⓓ Ⓔ   41. Ⓐ Ⓑ Ⓒ Ⓓ Ⓔ   56. Ⓐ Ⓑ Ⓒ Ⓓ Ⓔ
12. Ⓐ Ⓑ Ⓒ Ⓓ Ⓔ   27. Ⓐ Ⓑ Ⓒ Ⓓ Ⓔ   42. Ⓐ Ⓑ Ⓒ Ⓓ Ⓔ   57. Ⓐ Ⓑ Ⓒ Ⓓ Ⓔ
13. Ⓐ Ⓑ Ⓒ Ⓓ Ⓔ   28. Ⓐ Ⓑ Ⓒ Ⓓ Ⓔ   43. Ⓐ Ⓑ Ⓒ Ⓓ Ⓔ   58. Ⓐ Ⓑ Ⓒ Ⓓ Ⓔ
14. Ⓐ Ⓑ Ⓒ Ⓓ Ⓔ   29. Ⓐ Ⓑ Ⓒ Ⓓ Ⓔ   44. Ⓐ Ⓑ Ⓒ Ⓓ Ⓔ   59. Ⓐ Ⓑ Ⓒ Ⓓ Ⓔ
15. Ⓐ Ⓑ Ⓒ Ⓓ Ⓔ   30. Ⓐ Ⓑ Ⓒ Ⓓ Ⓔ   45. Ⓐ Ⓑ Ⓒ Ⓓ Ⓔ   60. Ⓐ Ⓑ Ⓒ Ⓓ Ⓔ

Model Exam 2

SECTION 1: MULTIPLE-CHOICE QUESTIONS

TIME: 45 MINUTES

60 QUESTIONS

SECTION 1 IS WORTH 50 PERCENT OF THE TEST.

Directions: Each of the following questions has five choices. Choose the best response and record your answer on the answer sheet on page 323. There will be no penalty for incorrect answers in the multiple-choice section. Answer as many multiple-choice questions in the time permitted, even if you are unsure of the correct answer, by eliminating wrong choices.

1. Which of the following statements is true?

   (A) People have a high degree of trust in their politicians and elected officials.
   (B) Divided government has been endorsed by the electorate in numerous presidential elections.
   (C) Democrats have regained status as the majority party in the South.
   (D) Realignment has created a viable third party.
   (E) People identify themselves more as liberals than conservatives.

2. Which of the following principles of government was articulated in the Federalist Papers?

   (A) Checks and balances
   (B) A weak judicial branch
   (C) A weak executive branch
   (D) A strong House and a weak Senate
   (E) A unitary form of government

3. An example of political socialization includes which of the following statements?

   (A) Parents who vote Democratic influencing their children to vote Democratic
   (B) Children being taught about politics in school
   (C) College graduates deciding to attend law school in order to run for office
   (D) Political parties influencing voters through political ads
   (E) A newspaper running an editorial that suggests that a politician should resign

4. Executive privilege has

   (A) protected the president from standing trial while in office
   (B) protected the first lady from handing over personal materials to special prosecutors
   (C) resulted in Supreme Court decisions ordering the president to give sensitive materials to investigators
   (D) created the need for new laws defining what executive privilege means
   (E) rallied public opinion to support the president using this power

5. Which of the following reforms has been recommended to change the electoral college?

   (A) Close polls throughout the country the same time on election day.
   (B) Ban exit polling by the networks.
   (C) Eliminate the winner-take-all provision of the system.
   (D) Move up the date that electors vote.
   (E) Expand the concept of choosing electors to congressional races.

6. Supreme Court cases mainly derive from

   (A) plea bargains that fail
   (B) congressional legislation that is vetoed
   (C) state legislation that goes unchallenged
   (D) original jurisdiction cases
   (E) appellate jurisdiction cases

Question 7 is based on this table:

CONGRESSIONAL BILLS VETOED: 1961–2010

Period	President	Total vetoes	Regular vetoes	Pocket vetoes	Vetoes sustained	Bills passed over veto
1961–1963	Kennedy	21	12	9	21	0
1963–1969	Johnson	30	16	14	30	0
1969–1974	Nixon	43	26	17	36	7
1974–1977	Ford	66	48	18	54	12
1977–1981	Carter	31	13	18	29	2
1981–1989	Reagan	78	39	39	69	9
1989–1993	Bush	44	29	15	43	1
1993–2001	Clinton	37	36	1	34	2
2001–2009	Bush	10	10	—	7	3
2009–2010	Obama	1	—	1	1	—
2011–2014	Obama	1	1	—	1	—

Source: U.S. Congress, Senate Library. *Presidential Vetoes...1789–1999;* U.S. Congress. *Calendars of the U.S. House of Representatives and History of Legislation,* annual.

7. Which of the following conclusions about presidential vetoes is supported by the table?

(A) More vetoes have been overridden than sustained by Congress.

(B) Pocket vetoes are routinely rejected by Congress.

(C) President Reagan had the greatest success in having his vetoes sustained by Congress.

(D) President Ford had more vetoes overridden than any other president listed.

(E) Pocket vetoes were used by every president on the list.

8. The provisions of the Fifth Amendment have all of the following components EXCEPT

(A) prohibition of double jeopardy

(B) the right to a speedy trial

(C) the protection against self-incrimination

(D) the right of eminent domain

(E) protection of life, liberty, and property

Question 9 is based on this table:

Senate Action on Cloture Motions				
Congress	Years	Motions Filed	Votes on Cloture	Cloture Invoked
114	2015–2016	15	17	4
113	2013–2014	253	218	187
112	2011–2012	115	73	41
111	2009–2010	137	91	63
110	2007–2008	139	112	61
109	2005–2006	68	54	34
108	2003–2004	62	49	12
107	2001–2002	72	61	34
106	1999–2000	71	58	28
105	1997–1998	69	53	18
104	1995–1996	82	50	9
103	1993–1994	80	46	14
102	1991–1992	59	47	22
101	1989–1990	37	24	11

9. The table above supports which of the following trends regarding Senate actions on cloture motions?

   (A) There were more cloture motions filed in the Senate during the Bill Clinton presidency than during the George W. Bush presidency.
   (B) The Senate voted to start more filibusters between 2001 and 2014 than between 1989 and 2000.
   (C) The Senate voted to end more filibusters between 1989 and 2000 than 2001 and 2014.
   (D) George H.W. Bush had more filibusters filed in the Senate in his first year in the White House than in Barack Obama's first year as president.
   (E) Cloture votes are decreasing between 1989 and 2014.

10. Which of the following ideas advocated by Republicans during the 1994 congressional elections best describes the concept of devolution?

   (A) They encouraged a return of power to the state governments.
   (B) They promoted a strong executive branch.
   (C) They called for an evolutionary approach to checks and balances.
   (D) They advocated a better relationship between the voter and elected representatives.
   (E) They insisted on passage of a balanced budget amendment.

11. Which of the following House committees has the most influence in determining the fate of legislation?

   (A) Agricultural Committee
   (B) Rules Committee
   (C) Post Office Committee
   (D) Education Committee
   (E) Foreign Affairs Committee

12. Which of the following is considered to be the highest leadership position in the Senate?

(A) Minority Whip
(B) Majority Whip
(C) Minority Leader
(D) Majority Leader
(E) Chairman of the Senate Foreign Relations Committee

13. Elite class theory differs from pluralism in that groups from the elite believe that

(A) consensus is essential to political compromise
(B) representation of many interest groups foster good government
(C) they are best suited to run government based on their economic status
(D) sharing wealth and power are foundations of representative government
(E) gaining access to elected representatives can best be achieved through special interests

14. Libel and slander most closely come into conflict with the constitutional guarantee of

(A) due process
(B) free speech
(C) equal protection under the law
(D) a fair trial
(E) the right to an attorney

15. In the *Gibbons v Ogden* case, the Supreme Court decided for the first time that

(A) judicial review was a power of the court
(B) state contracts took precedence over federal law
(C) Congress had the exclusive right to regulate interstate commerce
(D) intrastate commerce was a legitimate federal function
(E) states could not tax the federal government

16. A constituent approach to representation reflects a

(A) congressman who consistently votes his conscience
(B) legislator who usually follows the party line
(C) lawmaker who introduces a bill that increases defense spending
(D) desire on the part of an elected official to represent the view of those who voted for him
(E) consistent approach by the representative who challenges the president's programs

17. What is a major difference between the manner in which both houses of Congress operate?

(A) The House allows unlimited debate on bills, whereas the Senate has strict time limitations.
(B) The Senate permits more amendments to bills than does the House.
(C) The rules of both houses are the same.
(D) Committee chairman terms are limited in the Senate, but not in the House.
(E) The Senate Committees always have equal numbers of Democrats and Republicans serving on them.

18. The media play what kind of role related to public policy?

(A) It raises money to support candidates running for office.
(B) It has the major function of linking the electorate to the formal institutions of government.
(C) It investigates the personal ethics of elected officials.
(D) It competes for the attention of the electorate.
(E) It influences politicians by offering them lower advertising rates.

19. What advantage did the line item veto have over a regular veto? The line item veto allowed the president to

(A) strike any provision of the 13 major appropriation bills
(B) eliminate riders attached to spending bills
(C) line out appropriation bills started in the Senate
(D) veto legislation designated as essential
(E) ignore a continuing resolution

20. Which step in the development of public policy occurs first?

(A) Enactment of the policy
(B) Formation of policy alternatives
(C) Evaluation of the policy
(D) Recognition of the problem
(E) Revision of the policy

21. Which of the following is a consequence of recent Supreme Court decisions regarding campaign finance reform?

(A) An increase in political ad spending by independent groups and corporations
(B) A ban on soft money donations
(C) A ban on hard money donations
(D) Presidential candidates accepting matching funds
(E) Public financing of congressional campaigns

22. The aim of the exclusionary rule as defined in the *Mapp v Ohio* Supreme Court case is to

(A) encourage police to knock before entering a suspected crime scene
(B) prevent law enforcement officials from stopping and frisking suspects
(C) deny the media access to places where police are conducting an investigation
(D) force police to get search warrants for evidence in plain view
(E) not allow illegally obtained evidence to be admitted into a court proceeding

23. The main criticism levied against the Articles of Confederation was that it

(A) gave too much power to the central government
(B) failed to give the national government the authority to lay and collect taxes
(C) did not allow the federal government to govern new territories
(D) created a powerful judicial branch
(E) had a term limit provision for the president

24. As a result of the Motor Voter Law, there was

(A) a decrease in registration because states challenged the law's constitutionality
(B) an increase in registration, but a decrease in turnout
(C) a decrease in registration and a decrease in turnout
(D) an increase in registration and an increase in turnout
(E) the greatest increase in registration of senior citizens

25. Which of the following statements about presidential appointments is true?

(A) All presidential appointments must be confirmed by a majority of the Senate.
(B) Presidential staff appointments must be confirmed by the Senate.
(C) Presidential appointments are reviewed by the House of Representatives before going to the Senate.
(D) Presidential appointments are first sent to a Senate committee before the full Senate votes.
(E) State judges are confirmed by the Senate.

26. The Supreme Court has the constitutional authority to check Congress by

(A) vetoing legislation signed by the president
(B) settling disputes among states
(C) applying original jurisdiction to cases brought before them on appeal
(D) declaring parts of legislation unconstitutional
(E) assigning the Chief Justice to preside over the impeachment trial of the president

27. An alternate manner in which a president can implement policy without congressional approval is by

(A) appointing a member of the opposing political party to the cabinet
(B) issuing an executive order
(C) sending controversial legislation to the electorate for a referendum
(D) making a speech in front of a group that opposes him
(E) holding a press conference

Question 28 is based on this table:

Composition of Congress by Political Party: 1997 to 2015 **(D= Democrat, R = Republican. As of the beginning of the first session of each Congress. Data reflect the immediate result of elections. Vacancies and third party candidates are noted.)**											
Congress	**Session**	**Senate**	**Dem.**	**Rep.**	**Ind.**	**Other**	**House**	**Dem.**	**Rep.**	**Ind.**	**Other**
96th	1979–1981	100	58	41	1	—	435	277	158	—	—
97th	1981–1983	100	46	53	1	—	435	242	192	1	—
98th	1983–1985	100	46	54	—	—	435	269	166	—	—
99th	1985–1987	100	47	53	—	—	435	253	182	—	—
100th	1987–1989	100	55	45	—	—	435	258	177	—	—
101st	1989–1991	100	55	45	—	—	435	260	175	—	—
102nd	1991–1993	100	56	44	—	—	435	267	167	1	—
103rd	1993–1995	100	57	43	—	—	435	258	176	1	—
104th	1995–1997	100	48	52	—	—	435	204	230	1	—
105th	1997–1999	100	45	55	—	—	435	207	226	2	—
106th	1999–2001	100	45	55	—	—	435	211	223	1	—
107th	2001–2003	100	50	50	—	—	435	212	221	2	—
108th	2003–2005	100	48	51	1	—	435	205	229	1	—
109th	2005–2007	100	44	55	1	—	435	202	231	1	1
110th	2007–2009	100	49	49	2	—	435	233	198	—	4
111th	2009–2011	100	57	41	2	2	435	256	176	—	1
112th	2011–2013	100	51	47	2	—	435	193	242	—	—
113th	2013–2015	100	54	45	1	—	435	201	234	—	—

28. The table shown above illustrates what trend regarding the relationship between the party that controlled the presidency and the party that controlled Congress?

(A) The Republicans controlled both houses of Congress in more terms than they controlled the presidency.
(B) The Democrats and Republicans alternated control of Congress in the 1980s.
(C) The party that controlled Congress usually controls the presidency.
(D) Independents are playing a greater role in the House.
(E) Divided government was a dominant feature.

29. The trend of affirmative action programs in the 2000s was to

(A) require a quota system for college admissions
(B) eliminate requirements for federally funded affirmative action programs
(C) take race as a factor only in the private sector
(D) have Congress increase the number of programs
(E) face challenges on the legality of existing laws

30. The "fighting words" doctrine outlined in Supreme Court decisions deals with

(A) freedom of the press
(B) separation of church and state
(C) freedom of speech
(D) freedom of assembly
(E) freedom to petition

31. A major characteristic of independent regulatory agencies is that they are

(A) quasi-legislative and quasi-judicial in function
(B) highly influenced by special interest groups
(C) sensitive to the needs of the electorate
(D) decreasing in size, scope, and influence
(E) minimally influential in determining public policy

32. Which of the following is characteristic of the nominating process for president in the 2008 and 2012 elections?

(A) There were more caucuses than primaries.
(B) There was a higher voter turnout in the primaries than in the general election.
(C) Women determined the outcome of the nomination for the Democratic Party.
(D) There was an incumbent running in both parties.
(E) There was an increased number of front-loaded primaries.

33. A trend toward dealignment occurred in the 2000s because

(A) voters had strong party identification
(B) the Motor Voter Law has increased registration for the Democrats and Republicans
(C) there was a general mistrust of elected officials
(D) the Republicans gained control of Congress in 1994
(E) the Freedom of Information act revealed campaign irregularities by the major parties

34. A presidential power that has been challenged by Congress since 1980 is the power to

(A) commit troops to foreign countries
(B) give the State of the Union address
(C) appoint cabinet members
(D) sign treaties
(E) receive ambassadors

35. A major difference between a freshman member and a five-term member of the House of Representatives is that the

(A) freshman was allowed to get committee chairmanship
(B) five-term representative could not run for reelection because of term limits
(C) freshman representative could not offer amendments to proposed bills
(D) five-term representative had fewer opportunities to receive PAC money
(E) freshman representative had strong convictions and was less likely to compromise

36. The concept of one man, one vote as outlined in the *Baker v Carr* Supreme Court decision applies to elections for

(A) U. S. senator
(B) president
(C) federal judges
(D) state legislatures
(E) governors

37. The original intent of the Fourteenth Amendment to the United States Constitution as interpreted by the Supreme Court was to

(A) force the states to follow the Bill of Rights
(B) provide equal protection under the law for freed slaves
(C) expand voting for women
(D) give states the right to pass laws that guaranteed separate but equal status to their citizens
(E) enable Congress to pass affirmative action legislation

38. Historically, the approval rating of the president usually

(A) remains around 50 percent during his entire term
(B) fluctuates depending on his response to national and international problems
(C) is lowest during times of war
(D) is highest toward the end of his presidency
(E) depends on the kind of media coverage he gets

39. All of the following steps are characteristic of the lawmaking process EXCEPT

(A) Revenue bills must start in the Senate.
(B) Conference committees resolve differences between bills.
(C) Filibusters in the Senate are used to stop bills from coming to a vote.
(D) Each House has standing committees that mark up legislation.
(E) A roll call vote indicates the positions taken by congressmen.

40. The use of racial quotas was made illegal in the United States as a direct result of the

(A) Supreme Court decision in *University of California v Bakke*
(B) Supreme Court decision in *Brown v Board of Education of Topeka*
(C) Proposition 209—The California Civil Rights Initiative
(D) Civil Rights Act of 1964
(E) affirmative action programs created by individual states

41. A primary election in which voters from one political party can cross over to express their choice for a candidate from another party is called

(A) a closed primary
(B) an open caucus
(C) a nonbinding primary
(D) an open primary
(E) a dual primary

42. All of the following is true about the 2010 census EXCEPT

(A) Minorities, especially Hispanics, make up a growing share of the U.S. population and are the largest ethnic group.
(B) The fastest-growing states are in the North and Rustbelt.
(C) Southern and western states gained seats in the U.S. House of Representatives, while Northeastern and Midwestern states lost seats.
(D) The fastest rates of decline tend to be in the Northeast and Midwest.
(E) Most U.S. population growth during the past century has taken place in suburbs, rather than central cities.

43. Congressional oversight committees have the main purpose of

(A) reviewing governmental operations
(B) drafting appropriation bills
(C) holding impeachment hearings
(D) establishing time limits for debates
(E) writing constitutional amendments

44. A criticism of the U.S. census is that it

(A) favors large cities over suburban areas
(B) costs the taxpayer too much money
(C) is held too frequently
(D) is biased toward the party who controls Congress
(E) does not take into account the homeless

Question 45 is based on this graph:

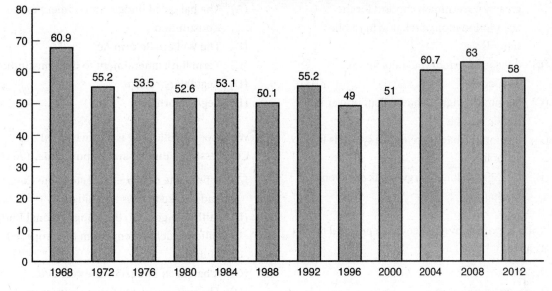

Percent of People Ages 18 and Older Who Voted in the U.S. Presidential Election, 1968 to 2012

45. According to the graph, which statement is true about voter turnout in presidential elections?

(A) Turnout is greatest when the country is at peace.

(B) Turnout is lowest in elections where there is a landslide.

(C) Turnout is determined by the number of candidates running for president.

(D) Turnout is lower after presidential scandals.

(E) Turnout is increased when a president wins a second term.

---

46. The president and Congress have all of the following powers in dealing with proposed legislation EXCEPT

(A) The president may exercise a line item veto on appropriation bills.

(B) The House and Senate may not send different versions of the same bill to the president for consideration.

(C) The president has the authority to hold on to legislation after Congress adjourns without signing it.

(D) The president may issue a veto after receiving legislation passed by both houses of Congress.

(E) Congress may override a presidential veto by a two-thirds vote of each house.

47. Campaign finance reform advocacy groups such as Common Cause favor

(A) a ban on soft money

(B) the elimination of any free television time for candidates

(C) an increase in the amount of money that labor unions can give to both parties

(D) special interest groups financing congressional campaigns

(E) greater use of personal funds by presidential candidates

48. Supreme Court decisions in the 2000s related to the separation of church and state reflect the Court's approval of

(A) greater government support for the accommodation of religion in public schools

(B) the use of school vouchers for tax deductions

(C) the limited right to have silent prayer in public schools

(D) a complete ban on religious symbols in schools

(E) the right to have clergy speak at school graduation

49. When apportionment becomes a political tool, it is called

(A) census taking

(B) gerrymandering

(C) equal representation under the law

(D) single district representation

(E) multidistrict representation

50. What kind of political action committee would most likely support Democratic candidates?

(A) Tobacco corporations

(B) Labor unions

(C) Gun advocacy groups

(D) Business corporations

(E) The Chamber of Commerce

51. All of the following powers are granted to Congress by the Constitution EXCEPT the power to

(A) collect taxes

(B) declare war

(C) appoint judges

(D) regulate interstate commerce

(E) create inferior courts

52. Which of the following provisions of the Republican Contract with America had the goal of reforming the Congress?

(A) The balanced budget amendment to the Constitution

(B) The Welfare Reform Act

(C) Term limit amendment to the Constitution

(D) Regulatory reform

(E) Legal reform

53. Which of the following is a provision of the Congressional Budget and Impoundment Act?

(A) A time line of procedural steps the Congress had to take to pass the budget

(B) Authority given to the Congressional Budget Office to delete items from the proposed budget

(C) A balanced budget by the year 2002

(D) The power given to Congress to stop mandatory spending after the budget is signed into law

(E) The ability of the president to have a line item veto

54. Which of the following events occurs first during the impeachment of a president?

(A) A media frenzy forces the House to vote to impeach the president

(B) The House Judiciary Committee votes on articles of impeachment

(C) A special prosecutor issues a report to Congress

(D) The Senate Judiciary Committee votes on articles of impeachment

(E) The Supreme Court rules on the guilt or innocence of the president

55. Southern states that created "majority-minority" congressional districts did so because they were

(A) directed to do so by the Supreme Court
(B) attempting to abide by the provisions of the Voting Rights Act of 1965
(C) hopeful that African-Americans would vote Republican
(D) confident that white candidates would be given an advantage over African-Americans
(E) responding to an executive order of the president

56. Liberal activists would probably support which of the following rulings made by the Supreme Court?

(A) An abortion case that ruled there should be a 24-hour waiting period before a woman could get an abortion
(B) A search and seizure case limiting the *Miranda* restrictions placed on the police
(C) A death penalty habeas corpus appeal to the federal courts that was turned down
(D) A free speech case where a provision of a congressional act restricting access to obscene sites on the Internet was declared unconstitutional
(E) A free press case giving school officials greater latitude in censoring school newspapers

57. A strong federal system of government has which of the following components?

(A) A central government dominated by the states
(B) Different levels of government unified by a central government
(C) Three branches of government each having separate powers
(D) A parliament with a prime minister as head of the government
(E) A loosely bound union of states

58. According to the Twenty-Fifth Amendment to the Constitution, what happens if a president is disabled when serving in office?

(A) The House and Senate must vote to allow the vice president to assume power.
(B) The first lady is given temporary power to govern.
(C) The Supreme Court decides when the vice president can take over the office.
(D) After the cabinet makes a declaration of the president's incapacity to govern, the vice president becomes president.
(E) There is a special election held to determine who will be the next president.

59. The Supreme Court has determined that racial gerrymandering is unconstitutional because it

(A) violates the reserve power clause of the Constitution
(B) deprives elected representatives of their property right
(C) ignores the one man, one vote principle of a previous Supreme Court ruling
(D) violates the equal protection clause of the Fourteenth Amendment
(E) extends affirmative action to a point that goes beyond the intent of the Voting Rights Act of 1965

60. What constitutional principle allows a president to send combat troops to a foreign country?

(A) A delegated power to declare war
(B) An enumerated power to fund the troops
(C) An implied power as Commander in Chief
(D) A delegated power as Chief of State
(E) A delegated power to sign treaties

STOP

If there is still time remaining, you may review your answers.

SECTION 2: FREE-RESPONSE QUESTIONS

TIME: 100 MINUTES (SUGGESTED TIME: 25 MINUTES PER QUESTION)

SECTION 2 IS WORTH 50 PERCENT OF THE TEST.

> **Directions:** Answer all four of the following questions in 100 minutes. Each question should take you 25 minutes, so plan your time accordingly. The questions are based on your knowledge of U.S. government and politics, and questions may contain materials from charts, graphs, and tables, which you will have to analyze and draw conclusions from. Make sure that you give specific and sufficient information and examples in your answers. Please number them clearly on your answer sheet.

1. The Supreme Court ruled in the 2010 *Citizens United* decision that corporations and other independent groups had the right to raise unlimited campaign funds that could be used in political campaigns for and against candidates. The decision had a direct impact on campaign financing and the electoral process. (6 pts.)

    (a) Identify and explain the rationale the Supreme Court used in the majority decision.

    (b) Describe two impacts the decision had on campaign financing.

    (c) Explain two ways the decision affected the electoral process.

2. The United States has a representative form of government. Yet in many states, people vote directly on legislative proposals through a process of initiative and referendum. (6 pts.)

    (a) Define initiative and referendum.

    (b) Using either Proposition 209-the California Civil Rights Initiative or Proposition 9-the California Marriage Act, explain the legislative history of the policy you selected.

    (c) Discuss one constitutional issue that the proposition or initiative you chose raised in the courts.

3. The electoral college has come under much criticism following the disputed 2000 presidential election. (7 pts.)

    (a) Identify and explain two constituational provisions regarding the electoral college.

    (b) Describe two problems with the electoral process resulting from the 2000 presidential election.

    (c) Discuss one reform that has been suggested to overhaul the electoral college.

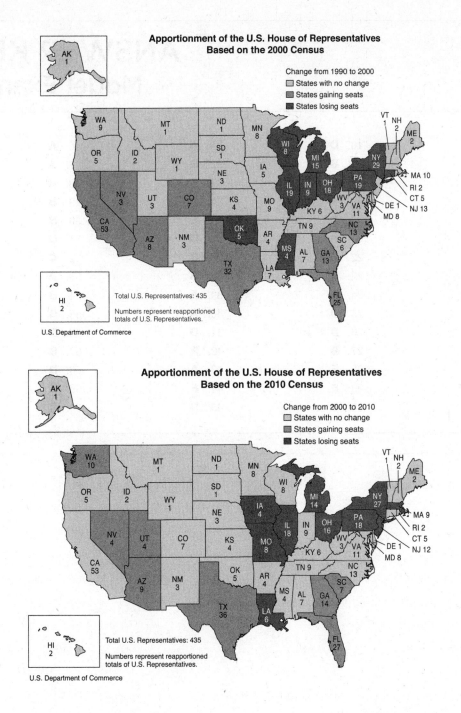

Apportionment of the U.S. House of Representatives Based on the 2000 Census

Change from 1990 to 2000
- States with no change
- States gaining seats
- States losing seats

Total U.S. Representatives: 435

Numbers represent reapportioned totals of U.S. Representatives.

U.S. Department of Commerce

Apportionment of the U.S. House of Representatives Based on the 2010 Census

Change from 2000 to 2010
- States with no change
- States gaining seats
- States losing seats

Total U.S. Representatives: 435

Numbers represent reapportioned totals of U.S. Representatives.

U.S. Department of Commerce

4. The two maps above represent apportionment of the U.S. House of Representatives based on the 2000 Census and 2010 Census. Those states that lost seats are represented by the dark-gray shade. Those states that gained seats are represented by the medium-gray shade, and those states that did not gain or lose seats are represented by the light-gray shade. (7 pts.)

(a) Define apportionment, reapportionment, and gerrymandering.

(b) Identify two trends that resulted from apportionment from 2000 to 2010.

(c) Explain how the trends identified in (b) have an impact on presidential elections.

1.	**B**	16.	**D**	31.	**A**	46.	**A**
2.	**A**	17.	**B**	32.	**E**	47.	**A**
3.	**A**	18.	**B**	33.	**C**	48.	**A**
4.	**C**	19.	**A**	34.	**A**	49.	**B**
5.	**C**	20.	**D**	35.	**E**	50.	**B**
6.	**E**	21.	**A**	36.	**D**	51.	**C**
7.	**D**	22.	**E**	37.	**B**	52.	**C**
8.	**B**	23.	**B**	38.	**B**	53.	**A**
9.	**B**	24.	**B**	39.	**A**	54.	**B**
10.	**A**	25.	**D**	40.	**A**	55.	**B**
11.	**B**	26.	**D**	41.	**D**	56.	**D**
12.	**D**	27.	**B**	42.	**B**	57.	**B**
13.	**C**	28.	**E**	43.	**A**	58.	**D**
14.	**B**	29.	**E**	44.	**E**	59.	**E**
15.	**C**	30.	**C**	45.	**D**	60.	**C**

ANSWERS EXPLAINED

1. **(B)** Type of Question: Identification and analysis

   Choice B, the correct answer, refers to the fact that since 1968 there has been a consistent pattern reflected in the election of a president from one party and the election of a majority of members of the opposite party to Congress. Choice A is the opposite of what people believe. Choices, C, D, and E are factually incorrect.

2. **(A)** Type of Question: Identification and analysis

   Choice A, the correct answer, is a central concept of the Federalist papers. The Federalists adopted Montesquieu's principle of checks and balances as the foundation of the separation of powers in the federal government. Choices B and C were weaknesses in the Articles of Confederation. Choice D was never discussed, and Choice E deals with a different form of government.

3. **(A)** Type of Question: Definitional

   Choice A is the correct answer because, by definition, political socialization is the process whereby people obtain their political values. These values, such as party identification, views on abortion, and attitudes toward affirmative action, can come from a variety of sources—primarily from parents, but also schools and churches. Choices B, C, D, and E are incorrect because they do not fit within this definition.

4. **(C)** Type of Question: Cause-and-effect

   Choice C, the correct answer, applies the definition of executive privilege to a specific situation. The Supreme Court ruled in the *United States v Nixon* and in a case where Hillary Rodham Clinton tried to use executive privilege in order to withhold Whitewater documents that in both cases the materials had to be handed over. Choices A and B are factually incorrect. Choices D and E were never part of the controversy.

5. **(C)** Type of Question: Solution to a problem

   Choice C, the correct answer, deals with the part of the electoral college system that awards a candidate the total electoral votes of a state regardless of the margin of victory. There have been suggestions to reform the system by creating a proportional allocation of electoral votes. Choices A and B are reforms suggested dealing with the coverage of national elections by the networks. Choices D and E have never been suggested.

6. **(E)** Type of Question: Identification and analysis

   Choice E, the correct answer, is the most common manner in which cases get to the Supreme Court. In order to answer the question correctly, you must know the definitions and application of original jurisdiction and appellate jurisdiction. The other choices are incorrect.

7. **(D)** Type of Question: Stimulus-based

   The table identifies the nature and number of presidential vetoes used by presidents, beginning with Kennedy and ending with Clinton. The table also defines the type of veto each president used; regular, which can be voted on by Congress, or pocket, which a president makes when Congress has completed its session or is in recess for ten days. Choice D is the correct answer because, clearly, Ford had more vetoes rejected by Congress than the other president listed. Choice A is wrong because more vetoes have been sustained than overridden. Choice B is incorrect because Congress does not vote on pocket vetoes. Choice C is incorrect because even though Reagan had the highest number of vetoes sustained, on a percentage basis, Bill Clinton was more successful. Choice E is wrong because Clinton never used a pocket veto.

8. **(B)** Type of Question: Negative

   Choice B, the correct answer, is the only answer that refers to a right not found in the Fifth Amendment. It is a Seventh Amendment right. The other choices are all part of the Fifth Amendment.

9. **(B)** Type of Question: Stimulus-based

Choice B is the correct answer because the definition of cloture is the ending of a filibuster. Therefore, there were more filibusters started by the Senate as a result of a motion filed between 2001 and 2010 than between 1989 and 2000. Choices A and D are incorrect because there were more clotures filed in George W. Bush's presidency, 2001–2008, than Bill Clinton's presidency, 1993–2000 (choice A), and there were more filibusters filed during Barack Obama's first year (2009–2010) than George H.W. Bush's first year (1989–1990). Choice E is incorrect because cloture votes increased between 1989 and 2014.

10. **(A)** Type of Question: Identification and analysis

Choice A, the correct answer, requires that you know the definition of devolution and then be able to apply it to an actual event. In this case, the Republicans wanted more power to be turned over to the states. Choice B is the opposite of devolution. Choices C and D have nothing to do with devolution, and Choice E, though having consequences for the states, does not answer the question as directly as Choice A.

11. **(B)** Type of Question: Identification and analysis

Choice B, the correct answer, is one of the most influential House committees. The other committees may be important in certain situations, but the question asked you to identify specifically a committee that can influence legislation. The Rules Committee determines which bills reach the floor.

12. **(D)** Type of Question: Identification and analysis

Choice D, the correct answer, includes those positions in the Senate that are leadership in nature even if it is a minority position (minority leader).

13. **(C)** Type of Question: Comparing and contrasting concepts

Choice C, the correct answer, is a good definition and application of the elite class theory. Choice A is a good application of pluralism. Choice B is an application of hyperpluralism. Choices D and E may have some truth in their applications, but do not answer the question.

14. **(B)** Type of Question: Sequencing a series of ideas

Choice B, the correct answer, is an application of the definition of libel and slander. If you know those definitions, then you will be able to connect them with an inherent conflict of the free speech provision of the First Amendment. Choice A may apply if a trial occurs over a libel or slander suit. Choice C is a general constitutional guarantee. Choices D and E are components needed in any trial.

15. **(C)** Type of Question: Chronological

Choice C, the correct answer, is the central result of one of the landmark cases the Marshall Court ruled on. The question is difficult because Choices A and E were results of other landmark Marshall cases—*Marbury v Madison* and *McCulloch v Maryland*. Choices B and D are false statements.

16. **(D)** Type of Question: Definitional

Choice D, the correct answer, defines the notion behind the idea of a congressman following a constituent's view when voting on legislation. In order to answer the question, you must know the definition of constituent, and you should be able to recognize the fact that there are other legitimate approaches a representative can take (Choices A, B, and E) that do not answer the question.

17. **(B)** Type of Question: Comparing and contrasting ideas

Choice B, the correct answer, is the only answer that establishes a major difference between the House and Senate. Choices A, C, and E are obviously incorrect. Choice D is tricky because the House has term limits for committee chairmen.

18. **(B)** Type of Question: Cause-and-effect relationship

Choice B, the correct answer, is a definition of the media as a linkage institution to government. Choice C may be a function of the media, but it does not apply to public policy. Choice D may be true, but it also does not have anything to do with what the question is asking.

19. **(A)** Type of Question: Identification and analysis

Choice A, the correct answer, was the only provision of the line item veto that applied to legislation before it was declared unconstitutional. The line item veto permitted the president to exercise veto power on any part of the 13 appropriation bills that fund the government and make up the discretionary spending portion of the federal budget. Choice B is wrong because it only refers to amendments attached to appropriation bills. Choice C is incorrect because it only refers to action taken in the Senate. Choice D is wrong because there are many bills that can be characterized as essential. Choice E is incorrect because the president can veto a continuing resolution.

20. **(D)** Type of Question: Sequencing a series of events

Choice D, the correct answer, is the first step in the development of public policy. There is a logic behind this procedure, because one would want to identify a problem before enacting, forming, evaluating, or revising the policy.

21. **(A)** Type of Question: Cause-and-effect

Choice A is the correct answer because a consequence of the *Citizens United* case is it allowed unlimited campaign donations to groups that were independent from any party or campaign. Choice B is incorrect because soft money donations were the type of donations allowed in the decision. Choice C is factually incorrect. Choice D is incorrect because in both the 2008 and 2012 presidential campaigns candidates stopped accepting matching funds. Choice E is incorrect because there is no public financing of congressional campaigns.

22. **(E)** Type of Question: Identification and analysis

Choice E, the correct answer, reflects the definition and application of the exclusionary rule. Choice A refers to the no-knock ruling. Choice B refers to the stop and frisk principle. Choice C can be true in certain situations but has nothing to do with the exclusionary rule. Choice D is a false statement, and in fact police do not need warrants to get evidence in plain view.

23. **(B)** Type of Question: Chronological

Choice B, the correct answer, reflects the major criticism and weakness of the Articles of Confederation. The reason why the Articles were so ineffective, besides giving too much authority to the states, was that the new central government could not pay off Revolutionary War debts by collecting taxes. The other choices are all incorrect because they do not apply to the Articles.

24. **(B)** Type of Question: Cause-and-effect

Choice B, the correct answer, requires that you understand the nature and provisions of the Motor Voter Law passed by Congress in 1993. If you knew that the law's intent was to make it easier to register, then you could eliminate Choices A and C. Choice D is partially correct, but it is wrong because there was a decrease in actual turnout. Choice E is wrong because senior citizens were already registered and did not have to take advantage of the new law.

25. **(D)** Identification and Analysis

Choice D is the correct answer because after a president makes an appointment, the Senate according to the Constitution has the power to check the appointment through its power to "consent" to that appointment. Once an appointment is announced, the appropriate Senate committee holds hearings and hears testimony from the appointee. For instance, a Supreme Court nominee appears before the Senate Judiciary Committee. Once the testimony is completed, the committee votes to send the nominee's name to the full Senate where a majority vote is needed to confirm the appointee. Choices A and B are incorrect because presidential staff appointments such as chief of staff and press secretary do not need Senate confirmation. Choice C is incorrect because the House of Representatives does not play a role in this process. Choice E is incorrect because state judges are confirmed by state legislatures or voted on by the people from that state.

26. **(D)** Type of Question: Solution to a problem

Choice D, the correct answer, is the primary manner in which the Supreme Court applies judicial review to congressional actions. Choice A is not a power of the Court. Choices B, C, and E are all powers of the Supreme Court, but they do not have anything to do with its ability to check congressional power.

27. **(B)** Type of Question: Identification and analysis

Choice B is the correct answer because an executive order defines the manner in which a president can create public policy without signing legislation. Choices A, D, and E are all legitimate tools a president can use, but they do not necessarily result in public policy. Choice C is not a power of the president.

28. **(E)** Type of Question: Stimulus-based table

Choice E, the correct answer, makes you apply the data in the table to the trend of divided government which was a dominant feature of the modern political scene. The other choices are all factually incorrect.

29. **(E)** Type of Question: Generalization

Choice E, the correct answer, comes directly from a series of court cases challenging existing affirmative action programs. Choice A is factually incorrect. Choice B would be true if it suggested a reduction of federal programs, rather than a complete elimination. Choices C and D are factually incorrect.

30. **(C)** Type of Question: Definitional

Choice C, the correct answer, is the only area in the Bill of Rights where the "fighting words" doctrine applies. It originally came from the Supreme Court case *Chaplinsky v New Hampshire*, and it was one of the few decisions that placed limitations on freedom of speech.

31. **(A)** Type of Question: Generalization

Choice A, the correct answer, is the only answer that gives a major characteristic of many bureaucratic agencies such as the Environmental Protection Agency (EPA), the Food and Drug Administration, and Federal Trade Commission (FTC). They are called quasi-legislative and quasi-judicial because they can issue regulations and then act as judges to see that the regulations are being followed.

32. **(E)** Type of Question: Sequencing a series of events

Choice E is the correct answer because both the Democratic and Republican parties had what are called front-loaded primaries, the scheduling of early presidential primaries, in 2008 and 2012. Choice A is incorrect because there are more primaries than caucuses. Choice B is incorrect because there is a higher voter turnout in the general election than in the primaries. Choice C is incorrect because women were only one voting group that helped determine the nominee. Choice D is incorrect because only in 2004 was an incumbent, George W. Bush, running.

33. **(C)** Type of Question: Definitional/cause-and-effect

Choice C, the correct answer, requires that you understand the definition of dealignment. Once you recognize that the term means a moving away from both major political parties, the question becomes relatively easy. Choice A is the opposite meaning. Choice B may be true but does not answer the question. Choices D and E may be factually correct, but they do not provide the correct answer to the question posed.

34. **(A)** Type of Question: Identification

Choice A, the correct answer, is the one area in which the Congress and the president have disagreed. After the Vietnam War, Congress became very hesitant anytime the president committed American troops to a foreign nation. Situations like Haiti and Bosnia are recent examples. The other choices all contain presidential powers that have not been challenged to any great extent by Congress.

35. **(E)** Type of Question: Comparing and contrasting ideas

Choice E, the correct answer, is a characteristic of a newly elected ideological representative. You only have to go back to the freshman class of 1994 to see how they came into Congress ready to change the rules of the game. They succeeded to a certain extent. However, they also learned that the art of compromise was essential to the implementation of public policy. The other choices are all false statements.

36. **(D)** Type of Question: Definitional

Choice D, the correct answer, is the only answer that applies the one man, one vote ruling to an election that guarantees equal representation. The original case, in fact, dealt with a state legislature in Tennessee that had major voting representation inequalities. The other choices all deal with elected offices that do not require equal representation. There are two senators in each state. Every citizen within a state has equal weight in voting for a president or governor, and people do not vote for federal judges.

37. **(B)** Type of Question: Chronological

Choice B, the correct answer, is derived from the fact that the Fourteenth Amendment was introduced and ratified after the Civil War to deal with the injustices that the freed slaves had to face. The amendment was later used to incorporate the Bill of Rights into state action (Choice A). Choice C was accomplished through another constitutional amendment. Choice D was the manner in which the Supreme Court interpreted the equal protection clause in the *Plessy v Ferguson* case. Choice E is factually correct, but not the original intent of the amendment.

38. **(B)** Type of Question: Generalization

Choice B, the correct answer, is true because public opinion is quite fickle and usually responds to very visible national and international problems. Choices A and C are factually incorrect. Choices D and E may have some elements of truth, but they do not provide a complete answer to the question asked.

39. **(A)** Type of Question: Negative

Choice A, the incorrect statement, reflects the fact that revenue bills must start in the House. The other choices all reflect important characteristics of the lawmaking process.

40. **(A)** Type of Question: Cause-and-effect

Choice A is the correct answer because the *Bakke* decision allowed states to take race into consideration when developing affirmative action programs. However, the Court also ruled that a quota system violated the equal protection clause of the Fourteenth Amendment. Choice B is wrong because the *Brown* decision only dealt with the issue of school integration and was silent about quotas. Choice C is incorrect because Proposition 209 eliminated all government-sponsored affirmative action programs in California. Choice D is incorrect because the Civil Rights Act of 1964 banned discrimination in public accommodations. Choice E is an accurate statement of fact but does not answer the question.

41. **(D)** Type of Question: Sequencing an event

Choice D, the correct answer, is the prescribed manner in which an open primary is held. You must know the definitions of the different kinds of primaries to be able to answer this question. Closed primary is limited by party affiliation. Nonbinding primary does not lock delegates to the winner. Dual primary is one in which a presidential preference and a separate slate is voted on. An open caucus does not exist.

42. **(B)** Type of Question: Negative

Choice B, the correct answer, is false because the fastest-growing states are in the West and South. Choices A, C, D, and E are all results from the 2010 census.

43. **(A)** Type of Question: Identification

Choice A, the correct answer, is the major function of congressional oversight committees. Once the oversight function is completed, appropriate legislation may be drafted to deal with the problem that was investigated. Or a criminal proceeding may result if evidence is brought out in the hearings. Two examples of oversight hearings are the campaign finance irregularities and the Whitewater hearings. The other choices, though functions of congressional committees, do not apply directly to oversight.

44. **(E)** Type of Question: Cause-and-effect

Choice E, the correct answer, is an aspect of the census that has only become a problem because the homeless do not reside in a specific residence. It is important, especially to the large urban areas, because it could easily impact on the number of representatives from a state that has a large homeless population. The other choices are factually incorrect.

45. **(D)** Type of Question: Stimulus-based graph

The graph shows the percent of eligible voters who actually voted in presidential elections from 1968 through 2012. To answer the question, you must know some presidential history. Choice D is the correct answer. Voter turnout decreased in the elections following the Watergate scandal in 1974 and President Clinton's impeachment in 1999. Choice A is incorrect because the graph indicates that turnout was greatest when the country was at war—look at the rates during the Vietnam War. Choice B is incorrect because turnout was higher in 1968 and 1980, election years where there were "landslide" victories. Choice E is wrong because turnout decreased in the years when Reagan and Clinton were reelected to second terms.

46. **(A)** Type of Question: Negative

Choices B, C, D, and E are factually correct and illustrate the powers that the president and Congress have in dealing with legislation. Choice A, the line item veto, is the correct answer because it was ruled unconstitutional by the Supreme Court and, therefore, is no longer an option available to the president or Congress.

47. **(A)** Type of Question: Identification

Choice A, the correct answer, requires that you know that advocacy groups such as Common Cause believe that soft money (the money that is unregulated and can go to political parties in large sums) should be banned. The other choices are incorrect because they are not areas that advocacy groups believe would reform campaign finances.

48. **(A)** Type of Question: Cause-and-effect

Choice A, the correct answer, is true because the Court has drawn a fine line between accommodation and practice of religion, especially in public schools. The other choices all reflect areas the Supreme Court has declared illegal.

49. **(B)** Type of Question: Hypothetical

Choice B, the correct answer, requires that you know the definition of gerrymandering (the redrawing of legislative districts after a census based on purely political factors). Though Choices C and D are characteristics of congressional districts, they do not answer the question.

50. **(B)** Type of Question: Identification

Choice B, the correct answer, is a classic supporter of the Democratic Party. In fact, labor unions are the target of both Republicans and some advocacy groups because of the manner in which the unions are able to funnel contributions to the Democratic Party. The other choices reflect PACs that traditionally support the Republican Party.

51. **(C)** Type of Question: Negative

Choice C, the correct answer, may provide some difficulty because the Senate must approve the appointment of federal judges. The other choices are specific delegated powers of Congress.

52. **(C)** Type of Question: Identification

Choice C, the correct answer, is a provision of the Contract with America that would have limited the terms of Representatives and Senators, if enacted. It was proposed as a constitutional amendment and defeated twice by the House. The other choices, though all provisions of the Contract, did not impact on the Congress itself.

53. **(A)** Type of Question: Identification

Choice A, the correct answer, is a characteristic of the act and sets in motion the manner in which the budget cycle moves in Congress. It was passed during the Nixon administration in response to Nixon's impounding funds that were budgeted. The other choices, though all aspects of budget development, are not characteristic of the Impoundment Act.

54. **(B)** Type of Question: Sequencing a series of events

Choice B is the correct answer because the Constitution requires the House of Representatives to initiate impeachment charges against the president. In order for the initiation of charges to occur, the House Judiciary Committee must first vote on articles of impeachment. If you only think back to the Clinton impeachment, you may get confused and select another choice based on the events surrounding that episode, such as the media frenzy or the use of a special prosecutor's report. Although those events were associated with the impeachment of Bill Clinton, they are not part of the formal impeachment process.

55. **(B)** Type of Question: Definitional

Choice B, the correct answer, illustrates how states had to abide by the provisions of congressional law to create equality in the voting process. In order to answer the question correctly, you have to understand the nature of majority-minority districts and the historical background. It is a difficult question because the Supreme Court declared many of these districts unconstitutional.

56. **(D)** Type of Question: Hypothetical

Choice D, the correct answer, is an application of the definition of judicial activism (those court decisions that overturn precedent or existing law). The choices are all based on actual decisions. Choices A, B, C, and D are all cases that are judicial restraint in nature.

57. **(B)** Type of Question: Identification/definitional

Choice B, the correct answer, is a major characteristic of a federal form of government. Choices A and E are more typical of a confederation. Choice C can be a part of a federal system but only if there are state governments that are part of the system. Choice D is a parliamentary form of government.

58. **(D)** Type of Question: Identification

Choice D, the correct answer, is the only choice that is a provision of the constitutional amendment that outlines what happens when a president is disabled. The other choices are all factually incorrect.

59. **(E)** Type of Question: Sequencing a series of events

Choice E, the correct answer, requires that you know the definition of racial gerrymandering and the historical reasons why it existed. Choice D would be correct if the Court ruled that these districts were constitutional. The other choices are factually incorrect.

60. **(C)** Type of Question: Identification

Choice C, the correct answer, reflects the fact that the president's stated power as Commander in Chief must be expanded into an implied power when the president sends troops into combat in a foreign country without Congress declaring war. Choices A and B are incorrect because Congress has the power to declare war and appropriate funds to support troops. Choice D is incorrect because even though the president is considered Chief of State, it is more of a ceremonial role. Choice E is incorrect because, though the president has the power to sign treaties, treaties must be approved by the Senate.

Section 2: Free-Response Answers

SAMPLE RESPONSE TO QUESTION 1

(a) In deciding the *Citizens United* case, the Supreme Court equated the use of campaign funds as free speech. Therefore, there was a violation of the First Amendment to the U.S. Constitution if corporations and independent groups were prohibited from raising and using funds for political purposes. Prior to the decision, federal law prohibited corporations, unions, and independent groups from raising unlimited money and spending their general treasury funds for speech that expressly advocates the election or defeat of a candidate. Because that law violated the First Amendment's free speech provision, the Supreme Court struck down that law.

(b) As a result of the decision, two things that happened were that corporations, unions, and independent groups were able to raise an unlimited amount of soft money, dollar amounts that are not restricted by law. Second, new independent groups were created with the specific purpose of raising funds for the purpose of running political ads during the entire campaign. Groups such as Crossroads GPS and Priorities USA raised millions of dollars. The decision was criticized by proponents of campaign finance reform and weakened the provisions of the McCain-Feingold Act dealing with soft money.

(c) Two impacts the decision had on the electoral process was that there was a record amount of money raised by the new independent groups that were formed in both the 2010 midterm election and a record amount of money spent during the 2012 presidential campaign. In the 2012 midterm election, the newly formed independent group used the money that was spent on negative political ads. Because there were many more groups formed that supported Republican candidates, the decision contributed to the electoral success of Republican candidates and their efforts to take control of the House of Representatives. In 2012, more than $1 billion was spent in the presidential campaign. Much of it came from independent expenditures. President Obama and Governor Romney had independent groups sympathetic to their campaigns. And both candidates made the decision not to accept public financing knowing that these groups could raise and spend unlimited funds.

SCORING GUIDELINES FOR FREE-RESPONSE QUESTION 1 (6 POINTS)

Part (a) 2 Points

One point is earned for identifying the rationale the Supreme Court used in the *Citizens United* majority decision and one point is earned for explaining the reason the Court decided the way they did.

- In deciding the *Citizens United* case, the Supreme Court equated the use of campaign funds as free speech. Therefore, this was a violation of the First Amendment to the U.S. Constitution.
- The reasoning behind this decision was if corporations and independent groups were prohibited from raising and using funds for political purposes, that would violate free speech. Prior to the decision, federal law prohibited corporations, unions, and independent groups from raising unlimited money and spending their general treasury funds for speech that expressly advocates the election or defeat of a candidate.

Part (b) 2 Points

Two points are earned for describing two impacts the decision had on campaign financing.
- Corporations, unions, and independent groups were able to raise an unlimited amount of soft money.
- New independent groups were formed with the specific purpose of raising funds that were used to run political ads.

Part (c) 2 Points

Two points are earned for describing two impacts the decision had on the electoral process.

- There was a record amount of money raised by new independent groups.
- There was a record amount of money spent.

SAMPLE RESPONSE TO QUESTION 2

Though the U.S. government is based on a representative model, 24 states have made the initiative and referendum process a part of their electoral system.

(a) By definition, a referendum and an initiative are used in two different contexts. A referendum occurs when the state wants voters to consider a legislative proposal that, if passed, would either amend the state's constitution or become a law. In 2004, the issue of gay marriage was a referendum that passed in 11 states. The initiative or proposition occurs when a proposal is made by the voters and is placed on the ballot. If it is passed, it becomes the law even if the state legislature has not voted on it.

The initiative differs from the referendum because it is a process that involves voters organizing themselves around a single issue, gathering signatures on a petition, and then having that issue voted on in the form of a proposition. If the proposition passes, it automatically becomes a law in that state. Sometimes these initiatives are controversial in nature. They include areas such as physician-assisted suicide, affirmative action, homosexual rights, the legalization of marijuana for medicinal purposes, and restrictions on late-term or partial-birth abortions. Other initiatives may be noncontroversial in nature, such as a simple vote to approve a bond issue.

(b) One of the most significant propositions put forward was California's Proposition 209, also called the California Civil Rights Initiative. It originated with an official in the state university system, and its goal was to eliminate all state-sponsored affirmative action programs in California. Petitions were circulated, and the required number of signatures was obtained for the proposition to appear on the ballot in 1996. Supporters of the proposition included California's Republican governor, Pete Wilson. Most Democrats opposed the ballot proposal. It became a hotly contested issue, not only in the state, but also in the presidential and Senate campaigns. Special interest groups argued that the proposition would destroy California's state university system, while other groups insisted that affirmative action programs were inherently unfair. The measure passed by over 60 percent of the vote. The governor immediately instituted new rules regarding the state's affirmative action programs.

(c) Soon after the ballot proposal was passed, opponents of Proposition 209 filed a lawsuit in federal court. They believed that Proposition 209 was unconstitutional because it violated the equal protection clause of the Fourteenth Amendment. They also felt that the proposition violated the supremacy clause of the United States Constitution, arguing that Proposition 209 conflicted with the Civil Rights Act of 1964. Opponents also pointed out that a Supreme Court case, *University of California v Bakke*, set forth rules regarding affirmative action programs that worked well in California. The proposition was implemented, and all affirmative action programs in California were eliminated.

SCORING GUIDELINES FOR FREE-RESPONSE QUESTION 2 (6 POINTS)

Part (a) 4 Points

One point is earned for defining initiative and one point is earned for describing how the initiative process works. One point is earned for defining referendum and one point is earned for describing how it works:

- An initiative involves voters organizing themselves around a single issue and getting enough signatures on a petition to get the issue voted on by the electorate. Once it passes, it becomes state law.

- A referendum is voted on after a state legislature places the measure on the ballot. If the voters approve it, then it becomes state law. There is no petition process in a referendum.

Part (b) 1 Point

One point is earned for explaining how this process works for either California's Proposition 209 or California's Proposition 9. Acceptable answers are:

- Proposition 209—petitions got enough signatures to place a measure on the ballot that would ban state-sponsored affirmative action programs. The proposition passed.
- Proposition 9—petitions got enough signatures to place a measure on the ballot that would define marriage as between a man and a woman and would outlaw gay marriage. The proposition passed.

Part (c) 1 Point

One point is earned for explaining a constitutional issue that was raised by the proposition. Acceptable answers are:

- Proposition 209—opponents raised the equal protection clause of the Fourteenth Amendment of the U.S. Constitution. Proponents argued that the proposition was legal under state law and the Tenth Amendment of the U.S. Constitution
- Proposition 208—opponents raised the equal protection clause of the Fourteenth Amendment of the U.S. Constitution. Proponents pointed to the Tenth Amendment of the U.S. Constitution and state law.

SAMPLE RESPONSE TO QUESTION 3

(More than two provisions are described for illustrative purposes.)

(a) The electoral college, as provided for in Article II of the Constitution and later changed by the Twelfth Amendment, establishes the procedure by which the president of the United States is elected. In the Federalist Papers, the founding fathers expressed their reservations about the direct election of a president by the public. Based on these reservations, the electoral college was established. As provided for by the Constitution, the number of electors that each state sends to the electoral college is based on its population. Thus, the larger a state's population, the more electors it can send to the electoral college. The actual number of electors that a state sends to the electoral college is equal to the number of representatives it has in the House of Representatives plus the number of members it has in the Senate. Therefore, the smallest number of electors a state can have is three. In 2000, California had 54 electors, representing its 52 House members and two Senators. Washington, D.C., on the other hand, had only three electors. The Constitution also provides the legislature of each state with the authority to decide the manner in which it selects its electors.

For a candidate to win the presidency, he must win a majority of the electoral votes cast. In the 2000 election, the number of electoral votes needed to win a majority was 270. If a candidate does not receive a majority of the electoral votes, the election is thrown into the House of Representatives, where each state receives one vote. The majority vote of each state's delegation to the House determines the winner of the state's vote. Thus, if the majority of a state's representatives is Democratic, its vote would probably go to the Democratic candidate. In instances where no candidate receives a majority of the electoral votes, the Senate determines the contest for vice president, with the winner determined by a simple majority vote.

Once electors are selected by the states, they pledge to cast their electoral vote for the winner of the states' popular vote. There have been rare instances, however, where electors have changed their minds and not cast their votes for the winner of the state's popular vote. These electors have been given the name "faithless" electors.

(b)   In the election of 2000, Vice President Al Gore won the popular vote by more than 500,000 votes, but on election night the winner of the electoral vote was still in doubt. The popular vote in Florida was so close that state law called for a mandatory recount. The votes in other states were also so close that absentee ballots had to be counted in order to confirm the winner. However, it was in Florida that the election of 2000 was determined.

Two problems that surfaced as a result of the 2000 election included the manner in which the ballots were counted in Florida and the big differences in the election machinery used throughout the country. After Florida began its recount, there was much criticism of the so-called butterfly ballots and the fact that many of them were not counted. Older machines could not read many of these ballots, and the issue of hanging chads resulted in a large number of disputed ballots. These votes, if counted, could have given the election to Gore. Ultimately, the United States Supreme Court stepped in and, in *Bush v Gore*, determined that the Florida recount process was flawed. The result of this decision was that George W. Bush was awarded Florida's electoral votes, giving him an electoral majority. The second problem brought to light by the 2000 election, the lack of uniform voting equipment throughout the country, was illustrated by the fact that some states had old-fashioned voting booths while others had modern optical scanners.

(c)   One reform that has been suggested to improve the electoral college is to abolish it completely and go to a direct popular vote. This could be accomplished through a constitutional amendment. Proponents of this measure point out that the electoral college is an outdated notion and that the percentage of electoral votes that a candidate receives does not actually reflect the popular vote. They also point out that the results of the 2000 election illustrate how flawed the electoral system is because a candidate can win the popular vote but lose the electoral vote. Opponents of this reform suggest that the 2000 election was an anomaly and that the system has worked well since the Twelfth Amendment was adopted.

SCORING GUIDELINES FOR FREE-RESPONSE QUESTION 3 (7 POINTS)

Part (a) 4 Points

Two points are earned for identifying and two points are earned for describing the constitutional provisions related to the electoral college. Acceptable answers include:

- The number of electors that each state sends to the electoral college is based on its population. The larger a state's population the more electors it has.
- The Legislature of each state has the authority to decide the manner in which it selects its electors.
- A candidate must win a majority of the electoral votes cast to win the election for president.
- If a candidate does not receive a majority of the electoral votes, the election is decided in the House of Representatives for president and in the Senate for vice president.
- Electors are selected by the states.

Part (b) 2 Points

Two points are earned for describing two problems resulting from the 2000 presidential election. Acceptable answers are:

- Al Gore won the popular vote but lost the electoral vote
- The manner in which the votes were counted in Florida
- The ballot layout in Florida counties
- The lack of uniform voting equipment

Part (c) 1 Point

One point is earned for describing a reform for the electoral college. Acceptable answers include:

- Abolishing the electoral college and using only the popular vote to determine the winner
- Use a proportional formula to allocate electoral votes in every state based on the percentage of votes won by the candidate
- Award electoral votes by congressional district

SAMPLE RESPONSE TO QUESTION 4

(a) The definition of apportionment is the determination of the number, size, and location of legislative and congressional districts as a result of population changes measured by the census every ten years. The definition of reapportionment is the process in which a state legislature redraws the number, size, and location of legislative and congressional districts as a result of population changes measured by the census every ten years. The definition of gerrymandering is the redrawing of legislative or congressional districts by state authorities using political considerations and redrawing the districts favoring one political party over the other, or protecting the incumbent by redrawing the district boundaries resulting in more registered party members of the incumbent in the new district.

(b) Two trends resulting from apportionment changes in 2000 and 2010 are the shifting of population from the industrial Northeast and Midwest to the sunbelt states of the South and Southwest and the movement of retired people to those areas, respectively. Specifically, states such as New York and Ohio lost more than two congressional seats, and states like Florida, Texas, and Arizona all gained more than two seats.

(c) These changes have a significant impact on presidential elections. The loss of seats in states such as New York and Ohio that result in a loss of electoral votes for those states as well as the other states shaded in dark gray. The increase of seats in states such as Florida, Texas, and Arizona that result in a gain of electoral votes for those states as well as the other states shaded in medium gray. That means that in the 2012 presidential election Barack Obama needed to win six more electoral votes because of the 2010 census. The trends also favor future Republican candidates if those candidates can win more ethnic minorities.

SCORING GUIDELINES FOR FREE-RESPONSE QUESTION 4 (7 POINTS)

Part (a) 3 Points

One point is earned for the definition of apportionment. One point is earned for the definition of reapportionment, and one point is earned for the definition of gerrymandering. Students must be able to distinguish the differences between apportionment and reapportionment and use political reasoning in the definition of gerrymandering. Acceptable answers are:

- Apportionment—the determination of the number, size, and location of legislative and congressional districts as a result of population changes measured by the census every ten years.
- Reapportionment—the process in which a state legislature redraws the number, size, and location of legislative and congressional districts as a result of population changes measured by the census every ten years.
- Gerrymandering—the redrawing of legislative or congressional districts by state authorities using political considerations and redrawing the districts favoring one political party over the other, or protecting the incumbent by redrawing the district boundaries resulting in more registered party members of the incumbent in the new district.

Part (b) 2 Points

Two points are earned for identifying two trends from the apportionment changes reflected on the 2000 and 2010 maps. Acceptable answers include trends from either or both maps or trends that are the same or different when the two maps are compared. Acceptable answers include but are not limited to:

- The shifting of the population from the industrial Northeast and Midwest to the sunbelt states of the South and Southwest in 2000 and 2010
- The movement of retired people to the sunbelt states of the South and Southwest in 2000 and 2010
- A majority of the states reflecting no change in 2000 and 2010

Part (c) 2 Points

Two points are earned for explaining how the trends identified in (b) have an impact on presidential elections. Students must be able to connect the trend with some aspect of presidential politics. Acceptable answers include:

- The loss of seats in states such as New York and Ohio that result in a loss of electoral votes for those states as well as the other states shaded in dark gray in 2000 and 2010.
- The increase of seats in states such as Florida, Texas, and Arizona that result in a gain of electoral votes for those states as well as the other states shaded in medium gray in 2000 and 2010.
- The trends also favor the Republican candidate because the states that gained electoral votes in the South and Southwest because of an increase in retirees have trended Republican in recent elections.
- Retirees tend to vote in higher numbers than other age groups and have trended voting Republican.

TEST ANALYSIS WORKSHEET

The following table provides information on how to calculate your AP exam score. First determine the number of correct multiple-choice questions from Section 1. Remember there is no penalty for incorrect answers, just positive score for those questions answered correctly. So, if you answered 45 questions correctly, your multiple-choice raw score would be 45. Next, self-score the free-response answers you wrote or have your teacher score your answers based on the points allocated for each question. Then, using the free-response formula, calculate your weighted free-response raw score. Add the Section 1 multiple-choice score to the Section 2 free-response score and look at the conversion chart, which will determine your final AP score (1–5).

Using the table below, you can determine how well you did on Model Exam 2.

Section 1: Multiple Choice
Total multiple-choice questions correct (out of 60): _____
Raw score Section 1 multiple choice: _____

Section 2: Free-Response Questions

Question 1 = _____ (out of 6 points)

Question 2 = _____ (out of 6 points)

Question 3 = _____ (out of 7 points)

Question 4 = _____ (out of 7 points)

Raw Score:

$$\underline{\hspace{3cm}} \times 2.5000 = \underline{\hspace{3cm}}$$

Total of   Free-Response
Questions 1–4   Score

Final Score:

$$\underline{\hspace{3cm}} + \underline{\hspace{3cm}} = \underline{\hspace{3cm}}$$

Multiple-Choice   Free-Response   Final Score
Score   Score

Chart to Convert Final Score to
AP U.S. Government and Politics Score

Total Points	AP Score
91–120	5
79–90	4
62–78	3
42–61	2
0–41	1

MODEL EXAM 2

Glossary

Activist court—court that makes decisions that forge new ground such as *Roe v Wade* or *Brown v Board of Education* and establish precedent that often result in some form of legislative action.

Advise and consent—power of the Senate regarding presidential appointments.

Affirmative Action—programs for minorities supported by government as a means of providing equality under the law.

Affordable Care Act 2012—In 2010, President Obama signed into law his signature initiative, the Affordable Care Act. The law was passed only by Democratic votes; the Republicans who opposed it referred to it as "Obamacare." The law provides that all Americans will have access to affordable health insurance options.

Agenda setting—policy goals typically set by political parties.

All politics is local—phrase coined by former Speaker of the House Tip O'Neill (Speaker 1977–1987) and refers to how the behavior of congressmen and women on the local level was the determining factor of the way voters perceived their representatives.

Americans with Disabilities Act (1991)—act that required employers, schools, and public buildings to reasonably accommodate the physical needs of handicapped individuals by providing such things as ramps and elevators with appropriate facilities.

Amicus curiae—"friend of the court"; briefs that may be sent to support the position of one side or the other.

Anti-Federalists—led by Thomas Jefferson, one of the first political parties urging the rejection of the Constitution. Its members were farmers and represented the interest of the common people.

Appellate jurisdiction—courts that have the right to review cases from lower courts on appeal. The highest federal court, the Supreme Court, is the final court of appeal.

Apportionment—the determination of legislative district boundaries as a result of population changes measured every 10 years by the census.

Appropriation bill—congressional legislation that has spending as a basic characteristic. There are 13 appropriation bills that make up the federal budget.

Arms control—agreements reached by countries with the aim of reducing the proliferation of military weapons such as the Antiballistic Missile Treaty (1972), the first Strategic Arms Limitation Treaty (1972), the second Strategic Arms Limitation Treaty (1979), the Intermediate-Range Nuclear Forces Treaty (1987), the first Strategic Arms Reduction Treaty (1991), and the second Strategic Arms Reduction Treaty (1993).

Arraignment—court hearing where a person accused of a crime is formally charged.

Articles of Confederation—the first adopted written constitution of the newly independent United States. Because of its weaknesses, the period of time (1781–1789) became known as the critical period.

Baker v Carr—case that established the principle of one man, one vote. This decision created guidelines for drawing up congressional districts and guaranteed a more equitable system of representation to the citizens of each state.

Balanced budget—public policy that advocates that the federal budget spend as much money as it receives. Attempt made to pass a constitutional amendment mandating this policy failed.

Battleground states—also called "swing states," refers to those states in a presidential election, such as Florida, Missouri, and Ohio, that are closely contested.

Bicameral—a two-house legislature.

Bill of attainder—the constitutional prohibition of the legislature determining a judicial outcome without a trial.

Bill of Rights—adopted in 1791 by the states two years after the ratification of the Constitution, it established the basis of civil liberties for Americans.

Bipartisan—refers to two political parties working together to reach a common policy goal.

Bipartisan Campaign Act of 2002—also known as the McCain-Feingold Act, it banned soft money donations by individuals to presidential candidates and set aggregate limits for individuals contributing to individual candidates.

Block grants—a form of fiscal federalism where federal aid is given to the states with few strings attached.

Brandeis Brief—a friend of the court opinion offered by Louis Brandeis, in the Supreme Court case *Muller v Oregon* (1908), which spoke about inherent differences between men and women in the workplace.

Bully pulpit—the ability to use the office of the presidency to promote a particular program and/or to influence Congress to accept legislative proposals.

Bureaucracies—large administrative agencies reflecting a hierarchical authority, job specialization, and rules and regulations that drive them.

Burger Court—Warren Burger was appointed by Richard Nixon in 1969 as the 15th Chief Justice of the Supreme Court. The Court he presided over was more conservative than the Warren Court, handing over more power to the states through the Court's decisions.

Bush v Gore (2000)—Supreme Court ruled that the Florida recount held after the 2000 presidential election between Republican Governor George W. Bush and Vice President Al Gore violated the equal protection clause of the Fourteenth Amendment, which resulted in Bush winning Florida's electoral votes and the presidential election.

Cabinet—part of the "unwritten Constitution," it was first established by George Washington and includes federal departments such as state, defense, etc.

Campaign finance reform—legislation aimed at placing limits on political candidates accepting money and gifts from individuals and special interest groups.

Casework—also known as constituent service, a congressman or woman provides different services such as helping an immigrant get a green card to people who reside in the district or state that elected the representative.

Categorical grants—include project and formula grants and aim at assisting the states in areas such as health, income security, and education.

Caucus—party regulars meeting in small groups asking questions, discussing qualifications regarding the candidate, and voting on whether to endorse a particular candidate. The Iowa caucus has taken on almost as much importance as the New Hampshire primary because of its timing.

Census—official count of the population of a district, state, or nation, which includes recording of statistics such as age, sex, occupation, and property ownership.

Checks and balances—a key aspect of the Constitution of the United States protecting the balance of power among the three branches of government. The concept was first promoted by James Madison in the Federalist Papers.

Chief executive—used to describe the president. Powers found in Article II of the Constitution.

***Citizens United v Federal Election Commission* (2010)**—a case in which the Supreme Court ruled that corporations and other independent groups have the right to raise unlimited campaign funds that could be used in political campaigns for and against candidates because the funds were equated as free speech.

Civil liberties—those rights of the people that are protected by the Bill of Rights.

Civil rights—the application of equal protection under the law to individuals.

Civil Rights Act of 1964—act that prohibited the use of any registration requirement that resulted in discrimination and paved the way for the involvement of the federal government to enforce the law.

Clean Air Act (1970)—law that established national standards for states, strict auto emissions guidelines, and regulations, which set air pollution standards for private industry.

Clean Water Act—passed in 1987, this law established safe drinking standards and created penalties for water polluters.

Clear and Present Danger Doctrine—established in *Schenck v United States* (1919), it gives the government the right to censor free speech if, during national emergencies such as war, it can be proven that the result of the speech will significantly hurt national security.

Closed rule—bans amendments to a bill once the bill reaches the House floor.

Cloture—the process in which it takes 60 senators to cut off a filibuster and that is aimed at protecting minority interests.

Coalition building—the alliance of special interest groups with the purpose of achieving the same goal using both direct lobbying and grassroots lobbying.

Cold War—an era of American foreign policy lasting from the end of World War II (1945) to the collapse of the Soviet Union (1991) where American policy was defined as containment of communism.

Collective security—agreement to form through treaties mutual defense arrangements, such as NATO, which guarantee that if one nation is attacked, other nations will come to its defense.

Commander-in-chief—delegated power of the president.

Commerce clause—Article I Section 8 Clause 3 of the Constitution giving Congress the authority to regulate interstate commerce and commerce with foreign countries.

Common law—based on the legal concept of stare decisis, or judicial precedent.

Competitive federalism—begun under Richard Nixon and known as the new federalism, this approach stressed the downsizing of the federal government and more reliance on revenue sharing and grants.

Concurrent power—power shared by the state and federal government, such as the power to tax.

Concurring opinion—additional opinion in a Court decision written by a member of the majority.

Confederation—approach to government that decentralizes power, giving more power to the individual states than to the central government.

Conference committee—a committee consisting of senators and representatives that meets to resolve differences in legislation.

Congressional Budget Office (CBO)—set up by the Congress, this office evaluates the cost of legislative proposals.

Congressional District—defined by the U.S. Constitution as the people in each state should choose their representatives based on its population determined by the census. The number of citizens per congressional district has risen from an average of 33,000 in 1790 to almost 709,000 as of 2012.

Congressional oversight—power used by Congress to gather information useful for the formation of legislation, review the operations and budgets of executive departments and independent regulatory agencies, conduct investigations through committee hearings, and bring to the public's attention the need for public policy.

Connecticut Compromise—offered at the Constitutional Convention at Philadelphia, it was adopted by the delegates and created a bicameral legislature, where one house is represented by population, and the other house is represented by the states.

Consent of the governed—a derivative of the doctrine of natural rights; a philosophy, later adopted by Jefferson when he drafted the Declaration of Independence, that puts the authority of the government in the people's hands.

Conservative—A person who believes in less government, lower taxes, a strong national defense, and more responsibility.

Constituent—person living in the district of an elected official.

Constituent service—a member of Congress providing services to voters such as providing help with federal agencies, federal grants, and students who want to attend the U.S. military academies, who live in the district the representative or senator serves.

Constitution—provides the basic framework of government. It is the supreme law of the land.

Consumer Price Index (CPI)—a primary measure of inflation determined by the increase in the cost of products compared to a base year.

Continuing resolution—emergency spending legislation that prevents the shutdown of any department simply because its budget has not been enacted.

Contract with America—a blueprint for legislative action and congressional reform that House Republicans led by Newt Gingrich successfully campaigned for in the 1994 midterm elections resulting in what was called "the Republican revolution."

Convention bump—an increase reflected in presidential preference polls immediately following a party's nominating convention.

Cooperative federalism—developed during the New Deal, it is characterized by the federal government's becoming more intrusive in what were traditionally state powers.

Council of Economic Advisors—White House staff agency created to give the president advice regarding economic and fiscal policy.

Creative federalism—developed during President Lyndon Johnson's administration, it was characterized by the Great Society programs, which placed a major responsibility on federally funded programs.

Critical election—an election that results in a party realignment caused by the movement of voters from one party to another. The election of 1980 was a critical election because traditional Democrats voted for Ronald Reagan. They became known as Reagan Democrats.

Cruel and unusual punishment—doctrine found in the Eighth Amendment to the Constitution that prohibits the federal government from imposing excessive penalties for crimes committed.

Culture of poverty—the establishment of an income level by government that references the point at which an individual is considered to be living in poverty.

Daily tracking poll—polls that are released every day during a campaign. They differ from other tracking polls because unlike weekly or monthly polls, they are more of an instant snapshot of how a candidate is performing.

Dark horse—candidate running for office who is not well known, considered to be the underdog in the race.

Debt ceiling—the point at which the federal government will run out of money to pay the interest to the creditors of the United States. The debts of the United States are guaranteed by the full faith and credit clause in the Constitution.

De facto segregation—segregation of schools and other public facilities through circumstance with no law supporting it.

De jure segregation—segregation by law, made illegal by *Brown v Board of Education*.

Declaration of Independence—blueprint for the American Revolution containing three parts. The first part—an introduction including ideas such as natural rights as related to life, liberty, and property, the consent of the governed, and the concept of limited government. The second part—a list of grievances against the King of England and the third part—a declaration of independence.

Declaration of Sentiments and Resolutions (1848)—Drafted at the Seneca Falls Convention and taken from *The History of Woman Suffrage*, Vol. 1, by E.C. Stanton, S. B. Anthony, and M. J. Gage, the document outlines the case for the right to vote for women, as well as other rights denied to women at that time.

Defense of Marriage Act—also known as DOMA. It was signed into law by President Clinton in 1996. The act defines marriage as "a legal union between one man and one woman as husband and wife." The law also allows states not to recognize gay marriages performed legally in other states. The law also prohibits gay couples that are legally married or are recognized as a couple as a result of a civil union from collecting any federal benefits that married couples receive.

Deficit spending—refers to a budget where expenditures exceed revenues resulting in an increase of interest on the debt.

Delegated Powers—defined in the Constitution as those powers that are listed in the Constitution as belonging to the federal government.

Delegate model of representation—also known as the representational view. Voters elect their representatives as their own delegates representing them for the primary purpose of acting exclusively as their voice in Congress.

Democratic Party—political party that evolved from the original Democratic-Republican Party. It is one of the two major political parties.

Democratic-Republicans—led by Thomas Jefferson, they were characterized as the party of the "common man." They believed in a more limited role of the central government.

Demographics—characteristics of a population, including age, sex, and race. Demographics are often used to determine changes in the make-up of a population.

Détente—a foreign policy started by Richard Nixon and supported by Ronald Reagan that resulted in an improvement of relations with the Soviet Union during the Cold War.

Devolution—political theory of returning power to the states.

Direct democracy—type of government characterized by citizens attending a town meeting and voting on issues raised, with the majority prevailing.

Direct lobbying—the attempt by lobbyists to directly influence legislation through communication with a member of a legislative body or government official who has a connection with the formulation of legislation.

Direct primary—voters, including cross-over voters from other political parties, can express a preference for candidates.

Direct tax—money paid directly to the government in the form of income taxes.

Discount rates—interest levels established by the Federal Reserve that affect the ability of the consumer to borrow money. Raising and lowering rates is used as a tool to combat inflation.

Discretionary spending—Those appropriation items in the budget that are not mandatory. In the federal budget, discretionary spending consists of measures in the 13 appropriation bills that must be passed by Congress by October 1 in such categories as transportation, agriculture, and education.

Dissenting opinion—judicial written opinion that is contrary to the ruling of the full court.

Distributive policy—results in the government giving benefits directly to people, groups, farmers, and businesses. Typical policies include subsidies, research and development funds for corporations, and direct government aid for highway construction and education.

Divided government—characterized by political gridlock as the result of different political parties having control of different branches of the government.

Division of labor—skilled workers each have a specialized function, resulting in increased productivity.

Double jeopardy—legal concept wherein once a verdict is handed down, you cannot be tried again for the same crime.

Dual federalism—the earliest type of relationship established between the federal government and the states where the federal government's powers were defined as delegated and the state government's powers were reserved.

Dual primary—where presidential candidates are selected and a separate slate of delegates is also voted on. New Hampshire uses this type of primary.

Earmarks—pet projects added to appropriation bills by congressmen, called "wasteful spending" and "pork barrel legislation" by critics.

Elastic clause—found in Article I Section 8 of the Constitution, it gives Congress the power to make "all laws necessary and proper" to carry out the other defined powers of Congress.

Electoral college—consists of presidential electors from each state. The number of electors is based on the state's population. The states with the greatest population have the most electoral votes. When the voter casts a vote for president, in reality the vote goes to one of the presidential electors designated by the candidate in that state. The number of electors for each state equals the number of senators and representatives that state has in Congress. The candidate with a majority of the electoral votes is elected to office. If no candidate receives a majority, the House of Representatives will determine the outcome of the election.

Elite and class theory—a group theory that revolves around an economic stratum of society controlling the policy agenda.

Entitlements—those benefits guaranteed by law paid to individuals by the federal government, such as Social Security.

Enumerated powers—delegated powers of Congress, including the power to collect taxes, pay debts, provide for the common defense and general welfare, regulate commerce among the states, coin money, and declare war.

Environmental Protection Agency (EPA)—regulates air and water pollution, pesticides, radiation, solid waste, and toxic substances. It is the main environmental regulatory agency.

Equal Protection Under the Law—phrase found in the Fourteenth Amendment of the Constitution that furthers the legal concept of civil rights. Originally intended to protect freed former slaves, the clause was later expanded by court interpretation to protect other minority groups.

Establishment clause—component of the First Amendment to the Constitution that defines the right of the citizens to practice their religions without governmental interference. It also places a restriction on government creating a "wall of separation" between church and state.

Ex post facto laws—laws that take effect after the act takes place. Congress is prohibited from enacting this type of legislation.

Exclusionary rule—rule that resulted from the *Mapp v Ohio* decision determining that police may obtain only that evidence that can be had through a legitimate search warrant. Other evidence found at the scene of the crime is not admissible, or is excluded, in the trial.

Executive agreement—agreement made between the president and a leader of a foreign country that does not have to be ratified by the Senate.

Executive office of the president—created by Franklin Roosevelt in 1939; it has four major policymaking bodies today—the National Security Council, the Council of Economic Advisors, the Office of Management and Budget, and the Office of National Drug Control Policy.

Executive order—order signed by the president that has the effect of law, even though it is not passed by Congress. An example of an executive order includes President Clinton's order legalizing the abortion pill, RU486.

Executive privilege—the ability of the president to protect personal material.

Exit poll—a survey of randomly selected voters that is taken outside the voting area after the voter leaves it with the purpose of finding out who the voters cast their ballots for, demographic information, and where the voter stands on different issues.

Expressed power—specific power of the president as listed in Article I of the Constitution.

Faction—term used by Madison in the Federalist #10 to describe groups that are formed that threaten minority rights.

Fairness doctrine—scrapped in 1987, it provided that the media air opposing opinions of the same issue.

Family Medical Leave Act (1993)—act that gave unpaid emergency medical leave for employees with a guarantee that their job would not be taken away in the interim.

Favorable balance of trade—refers to a country exporting more than it imports. The United States has had an unfavorable balance of trade since World War II.

Favorite son—the presidential candidate backed by the home state at the party's nominating convention.

Federal Election Campaign Acts (FECA)—in 1971 it set up restrictions on the amount of advertising used by a candidate, created disclosure of contributions over $100, and limited the amount of personal contributions a candidate could make on his or her own behalf. In 1974 it set up a Federal Election Commission and established a system of federal matching funds for presidential candidates.

Federal Election Commission—made up of three Democrats and three Republicans, in 1975 Congress created the Federal Election Commission (FEC) to administer and enforce the Federal Election Campaign Act (FECA). The duties of the FEC, which is an independent regulatory agency, are to disclose campaign finance information, to enforce the provisions of the law such as the limits and prohibitions on contributions, and to oversee the public funding of presidential elections.

Federal Reserve System—federal body that regulates the money supply by controlling open-market operations; buying and selling of government securities; and establishing reserve requirements, the legal limitations on money reserves that banks must keep against the amount of money they have deposited in Federal Reserve Banks and through discount rates, and the rate at which banks can borrow money from the Federal Reserve System.

Federalism—the overall division of power between the federal government and state governments; as defined in the Tenth Amendment of the Constitution. It specifically tells the states that they have reserved powers. Powers not delegated to the government by the Constitution are given to the respective states.

Federalist Papers—written using the pen name Publius; John Jay, Alexander Hamilton, and James Madison wrote a series of articles urging the adoption of the Constitution. They argued for a Constitution that would establish a government that could deal with "the tyranny of the majority" by creating three branches of government having distinctive and separate powers.

Federalist Party—headed by Alexander Hamilton, this party, made up of the country's upper class, supported a strong national government and set a policy agenda that would solve the nation's economic problems.

Fighting words doctrine—established in *Chaplinsky v New Hampshire* (1942), the decision incorporated into state law the concept that the government can limit free speech if it can be proved that the result of speech will cause physical violence.

Filibuster—tactic used in the Senate whereby a vote on legislation can be delayed through debate. The longest continuous filibuster was made by Strom Thurmond and lasted 24 hours.

Fiscal cliff—on January 1, 2013, if no action was taken by Congress, the so-called Bush tax cuts would expire and income tax rates would be raised for every taxpayer, unemployment insurance would run out for millions of people who were out of jobs, and there would be mandated cuts in discretionary spending and defense spending defined by law (sequestration). An agreement was reached before these actions took place.

Fiscal federalism—a concept of federalism where funding is appropriated by the federal government to the states with specific conditions attached. The legislation can be in the form of mandates.

Fiscal policy—policy that determines how the economy is managed as a result of government spending and borrowing and the amount of money collected from taxes.

***Fletcher v Peck* (1810)**—decision that established the precedent that the Supreme Court could rule a state law unconstitutional.

Focus group—technique used by pollsters to determine how a cross section of voters feels about a particular topic.

Food stamp program—federally funded program that gives food coupons to low-income people based on income and family size.

Franking—privilege enjoyed by members of Congress entitling them to free postage for any mailings made as part of their official duties.

Free Exercise Clause—phrase found in the First Amendment to the United States Constitution that guarantees an individual the right to pray and believe in the religion of his or her choice by making it illegal for Congress to pass laws that restrict this right.

Freedom of Information Act (1974)—act that incorporates sunshine laws; opened up the government's meetings of record to the public and media.

Front loading—refers to the scheduling of the early presidential primaries and its impact on the selection of the majority of presidential delegates.

Front runner—designation given to the candidate who leads in the polls.

Full faith and credit—phrase used to describe the mutual respect and legality of laws, public records, and judicial decisions made by states.

Funded mandates—those regulations passed by Congress or issued by regulatory agencies to the states with federal funds to support them.

Gender gap—a significant deviation between the way men and women vote.

General Agreement on Tariffs and Trade (GATT)—agreement wherein new trade barriers would be avoided by member nations, existing tariffs would be eliminated, and protective tariffs would be used only for emergency situations.

Gerrymandering—state legislatures, based on political affiliation, create congressional districts, many of which are oddly shaped and favor the political party in power in the state making the changes.

Gibbon v Ogden (1824)—case established the principle that Congress has sole authority over interstate commerce.

Gitlow v New York (1925)—landmark decision in that the Supreme Court incorporated the First Amendment to a state case for the first time.

Global interdependence—the degree of linkage among the community of nations.

Good neighbor policy—a foreign policy established by Franklin Roosevelt that aimed at improving relations with Latin America.

Government—those institutions that create public policy.

Government corporation—such as the Tennessee Valley Authority, created during the New Deal, having specific responsibilities that facilitate a specific operation of the government.

Grand Old Party—known as the GOP, another way of identifying the Republican Party.

Grants-in-Aid—money provided by the federal government to the states including categorical grants, aid that meets the criteria of a specific category, project grants that are competitive, formula grants that have specific rules and a formula for who is eligible, and block grants that are given for specific purposes.

Grassroots—political participation at the local level.

Great Compromise—created a bicameral legislature at the Constitutional Convention held in Philadelphia in 1787. The compromise came about after delegates could not agree on the New Jersey plan that advocated one legislative house based on equal representation and the Connecticut plan that favored one house based on population.

Gridlock—describes people's perception that Congress and the president are in a state of disagreement that results in little legislation passing.

Gross domestic product (GDP)—currently the key economic measure that analyzes an upward or downward economic trend of the monetary value of all the goods and services produced within the nation on a quarterly basis.

Gross national product (GNP)—the total of all goods and services produced in a year.

Gulf of Tonkin Resolution—passed by Congress in 1964 giving President Lyndon Johnson authority to take whatever action necessary to defend American troops fighting in Vietnam. The resolution became the trigger for our escalation in Vietnam without a formal declaration of war by Congress.

Habeas corpus—right that safeguards a person from illegal imprisonment. *Habeas corpus* is Latin for "you should have the body." It refers to the writ requiring that a person be brought before a court to determine whether he is being detained legally.

Hard money—federally regulated campaign contributions made to political candidates and political parties. Under current law, hard money contributions cannot exceed $1,000 per individual, per election cycle.

High-tech campaign—a major characteristic of the modern presidential campaign. The use of paid political ads, 30- and 60-second spots, paid infomercials incorporating charts and graphs, and sophisticated polling techniques have all been used in recent campaigns.

Horserace journalism—the claim that the media is more interested in covering a campaign like a horserace focusing more on who is ahead rather than in-depth coverage of issues.

Immigration Act of 1991—act that shifted the quota of immigrants to Europe and aimed to attract immigrants who were trained workers.

Impeachment—listing of accusations against a federal official of "high crimes and misdemeanors" for the purpose of removing that official from office for such misconduct. President Clinton was the only elected president to be impeached but not removed from office.

Imperial Congress—describes a Congress that succeeds in establishing itself as dominant in legislative and foreign policy.

Imperial presidency—term developed by historian Arthur Schlesinger Jr.; refers to presidents who dominate the political and legislative agenda.

Implied Powers—those powers in the Constitution that are not listed or delegated. An example of an implied power is the Elastic Clause, giving Congress the right to make laws that are "necessary and proper."

Incorporation of the Fourteenth Amendment—doctrine that made the Bill of Rights apply to the states as a result of Supreme Court decisions. Even though the Fourteenth Amendment was ratified in 1868, incorporation started to take place in the 1920s. It reached a peak during the Warren Court in the late 1950s and 1960s.

Incumbents—those elected officials who are running for new terms of office.

Independent executive agency—such as the General Services Administration, which handles government purchasing and has a specific responsibility that facilitates the day-to-day operation of the government.

Independent expenditures—non-federally regulated campaign contributions made by special interest groups, labor unions, and corporations to political action committees and political parties; also called soft money.

Independent regulatory agencies—agencies that are quasi-legislative and quasi-judicial in nature and operation. Examples include the Food and Drug Administration and Environmental Protection Agency.

Indictment—a formal list of charges made by a grand jury and guaranteed in the Fifth Amendment.

Indirect tax—money paid to the government as a result of purchased goods.

Inflation—economic situation characterized by steadily rising prices and falling purchasing power. It is, in part, caused by wage rates increasing faster than productivity.

Infomercials—paid political commercials usually lasting longer than the average 30- or 60-second paid political ad.

Information superhighway—a linked conglomerate of computer-generated information also known as the Internet.

Inherent power—assumed powers of the president not specifically listed in the Constitution. Inherent powers are derived from the president's role as chief executive.

Initiative—ballot proposal put forth by the public and voted on as a result of the petition process.

Interest group—a public or private organization, affiliation, or committee that has as its goal the dissemination of its membership's viewpoint.

International Monetary Fund (IMF)—a clearinghouse for member nations to discuss monetary issues and develop international plans and policies to deal with monetary issues. Regulating monetary exchange rates is its primary task.

Invisible primary—the first phase of the presidential nomination process, where candidates attempt to gain front-runner status and raise the most money.

Iowa caucus—the first-in-the-nation presidential preference vote usually held in January or early February. The results reflect the organizational ability and strength of presidential candidates. The majority of candidates who win the Iowa caucus go on to win their party's nomination.

Iowa Straw Poll—an informal vote held by the Republican Party at the Iowa State Fair that gauges the support for a candidate. It is nonbinding and reflects a small portion of the voters. It is held in

July preceding the Iowa Caucus (which takes place the following January or February) and reflects which candidate has good organizational support.

Iron triangle network—the interrelationship among bureaucracies, the government, interest groups, and the public, which also establishes a pattern of relationships among an agency in the executive branch, Congress, and one or more outside clients of that agency.

Jim Crow laws—legislation that legalized segregation even after the adoption of the Fourteenth Amendment.

Joint committee—congressional committee made up of members of both political parties from the Senate and House of Representatives.

Judicial activism—a philosophy of judicial review that results in decisions that overturn precedent.

Judicial conference—following oral arguments, Supreme Court justices convene and review the case they heard before taking a vote that determines the decision.

Judicial restraint—a court that maintains the status quo or mirrors what the other branches of government have established as current policy.

Judicial review—derived from the *Marbury v Madison* decision, it gives the Supreme Court the power to interpret the Constitution and specifically acts of Congress, the president, and the states.

Judiciary committee—key Senate committee that is responsible for recommending presidential judicial appointments to the full Senate for approval.

Keynote address—key speech at the national nominating convention that outlines the themes of the campaign.

Laissez-faire—French term literally meaning "hands off." Used to describe an economic philosophy of nongovernment intervention in economic matters such as regulation of business or establishing tariffs.

Lame duck—an officeholder who is either defeated or is retiring from the office in which he is serving, but is still in office until his successor is sworn in; perceived to have little power or influence.

Landslide—election where the winning candidate wins by more than 60 percent of the votes cast.

Layer cake federalism—federalism characterized by a national government exercising its power independently from state governments.

Legislative veto—provision granting Congress the right to veto regulations made by federal agencies; ruled unconstitutional by the Supreme Court.

Libel—written publications that intentionally print false information that defames the character of an individual.

Liberal—A person who believes in greater government intervention, higher taxes, and a smaller military.

Limited government—derived from the doctrine of natural rights, it was adopted by Jefferson and restricts the power of government especially in the area of protecting the rights of the people.

Line item veto—allows the president to veto selectively what he considers unnecessary spending items contained in legislation. It was ruled unconstitutional by the Supreme Court.

Linkage institution—the means by which individuals can express preferences regarding the development of public policy. Examples of linkage institutions include political parties, special interest groups, and the media.

Litigation—an action by one party that sues another party in the form of a lawsuit. Special interest groups use litigation for the purpose of impacting and changing policy. These lawsuits can be aimed at private individuals, corporations, or a governmental agency.

Literacy laws—declared unconstitutional by the Supreme Court, they were passed by southern states after the Civil War aimed at making reading a requirement for voting so that freed slaves could not vote.

Lobbyists—the primary instruments of fostering a special interest group's goals to the policymakers. The term comes from people who literally wait in the lobbies of legislative bodies for senators and representatives to go to and from the floor of the legislatures.

Logrolling—a tactic used in Congress that is best illustrated by one legislator saying to another, "I'll vote for your legislation, if you vote for mine."

Loose construction—a liberal interpretation of the Constitution.

Majority leader—persons selected by the political party holding a majority of the seats in the House and Senate.

Majority opinion—court ruling participated in by the majority of justices hearing a case.

Mandatory spending—those appropriation items in a budget that must be allocated. In the federal budget, the majority of spending items are mandatory and include Social Security, Medicare, Medicaid, payment on the national debt, and certain components of defense spending.

Marble cake federalism—also known as cooperative federalism, it developed during the New Deal and is characterized by the federal government's becoming more intrusive in what was traditionally states' powers.

Marshall Court—John Marshall's tenure as Chief Justice of the Supreme Court, whose leadership resulted in the landmark decisions of *Marbury v Madison, McCulloch v Maryland,* and *Gibbons v Ogden.* These cases shifted power to the judiciary and federal government.

Marshall Plan—developed by President Truman's Secretary of State, George C. Marshall, and implemented after World War II beginning in 1947, it gave massive aid to help rebuild Europe after the war.

Mass media—consisting of television, radio, newspapers, and magazines, they reach a large segment of the population. It is also considered one of the linkage institutions.

Matching funds—limited federal funds given to presidential candidates that match private donations raised during the campaign.

McCulloch v Maryland **(1819)**—case that established the principle that the federal government was supreme over the state.

McGovern-Fraser Commission—commission that brought significant representation changes to the Democratic Party. It made future conventions more democratic by including more minority representation.

Media—one of the linkage institutions, along with special interests groups and political parties, that connects citizens to a group that influences public policy. The old media represents print and broadcast journalism. The new media represents social sites like Facebook and Twitter and Internet-driven sites.

Medicaid—a shared program between the federal and local governments that covers hospital and nursing home costs of low-income people.

Medicare—program that covers hospital and medical costs of people 65 years of age and older as well as disabled individuals receiving Social Security.

Minority leader—persons selected by the political party holding a minority of the seats in the House and Senate.

Minority opinion—a dissenting opinion written by a justice representing a minority point of view in the losing side of a Supreme Court decision.

Miranda rights—those rights directing police to inform the accused upon their arrest of their constitutional right to remain silent, that anything said could be used in court, that they have the right to consult with a lawyer at anytime during the process, that a lawyer will be provided if the accused cannot afford one, that the accused understands these rights, and that the accused has the right to refuse to answer any questions at any time and request a lawyer at any point.

Monetary policy—policies developed by the Federal Reserve Board, such as raising or lowering interest rates, aimed at creating and maintaining a healthy economy.

Motor Voter Act of 1993—signed into law by President Clinton, it enables people to register to vote at motor vehicle departments.

National committee—the governing body of a political party made up of state and national party leaders.

National convention—political forum in which each major political party selects its candidate for president and vice president and finalizes its respective platform.

National nominating conventions—the governing authority of the political party. They give direction to the national party chairperson, the spokesperson of the party, and the person who heads the national committee, the governing body of the party. They are also the forums where presidential candidates are given the official nod by their parties.

National Security Council—chaired by the president, it is the lead advisory board in the area of national and international security. The other members of the council include the vice president, secretaries of state and defense, director of the Central Intelligence Agency, and chair of the joint chiefs of staff.

Nationalization of the Bill of Rights—a judicial doctrine of the Fourteenth Amendment that applied the Bill of Rights to the states in matters such as segregation.

Natural rights—part of Locke's philosophy; rights that are God given such as life, liberty, and property.

New Democrat—a term created by the Democratic Leadership Council in 1992, it denotes a less liberal, centrist Democrat.

New federalism—political theory first espoused by Richard Nixon and carried out by Ronald Reagan. New federalism advocates the downsizing of the federal government and the devolution of power to the states.

New Hampshire primary—the first-in-the-nation presidential vote differing from the Iowa caucus because it is a secret ballot where voters use ballots and where registered voters and nonaffiliated Independents can vote.

New Jersey Plan—offered at the Constitutional Convention at Philadelphia, it urged the delegates to create a legislature based on equal representation by the states.

New world order—President Bush's vision for world peace centering around the United States taking the lead to ensure that aggression be dealt with by a mutual agreement of the United Nations, NATO, and other countries acting in concert.

Nominating convention—party delegates selected from caucus and primary votes officially select their party's candidate for president and vice president based on a majority vote of the delegates attending the convention.

Nonpreferential primary—where voters choose delegates who are not bound to vote for the winning primary candidate.

Nonrenewable resources—those natural resources such as oil, which, based on consumption, are limited.

Norris-La Guardia Act (1932)—act that prohibited employers from punishing workers who joined unions and gave labor the right to form unions.

North American Free Trade Agreement (NAFTA)—agreement that called for dramatic reductions of tariffs among the United States, Canada, and Mexico.

Nuclear Nonproliferation Treaty of 1968—agreement that stopped and monitored the spread of nuclear weapons to countries who did not have the bomb.

Nuclear Regulatory Commission—created as a part of the Energy Reorganization Act of 1974, it was given jurisdiction to license and regulate commercial use of nuclear technologies and monitor waste storage and transportation of materials arising from its use.

Nuclear Test Ban Treaty of 1963—agreement that banned atmospheric testing of nuclear weapons.

Office of Management and Budget (OMB)—its director, appointed with the consent of the Senate, is responsible for the preparation of the massive federal budget, which must be submitted to the Congress in January each year. Besides formulating the budget, the OMB oversees congressional appropriations.

Oral argument—legal argument made by each attorney in proceedings before the court in an attempt to persuade the court to decide the issue in their client's favor.

Original jurisdiction—cases heard by the Supreme Court that do not come on appeal and that "affect ambassadors, other public ministers and consuls, and those in which a State shall be a party."

Pardon—power to excuse an offense without penalty or grant release from a penalty already imposed.

Partnership for peace—President Clinton announced in 1993 a policy that allowed for the gradual admission into NATO of new member nations from the former Warsaw Pact and gave the designation of associate status in NATO to Russia.

Party caucus—also known as the party conference, it is a means for each party to develop a strategy or position on a particular issue.

Party dealignment—a shift away from the major political parties to a more neutral, independent ideological view of party identification.

Party eras—a time period characterized by national dominance by one political party. There have been four major party eras in American history—the era of good feeling, the Republican era following the Civil War, the Democratic era following the election of Franklin Roosevelt, and the Republican era following the election of Richard Nixon.

Party identification—the manner in which a person acts when belonging to a political party.

Party machine—the party organization that exists on the local level and uses patronage as the means to keep the party members in line. Boss Tweed and Tammany Hall are examples.

Party organization—formal structure of a political party on the national, state, and local levels.

Party platforms—voted on by the delegates attending the National Convention, they represent the ideological point of view of a political party.

Party realignment—the movement of voters from one political party to another resulting in a major shift in the political spectrum (characterized by the start of a party era).

Party regulars—enrolled party members who are usually active in the organization of a political party and support party positions and nominated candidates.

Photo ops—photo opportunities.

Plank—any of the principles contained in a political party's platform.

***Plessy v Ferguson* (1896)**—case that ruled that states had the right to impose "separate but equal" facilities on its citizens as well as create other laws that segregated the races.

Pluralism—a group theory that involves different groups all vying for control of the policy agenda. No single group emerges, forcing the groups to compromise.

Plurality—winning number of votes received in a race containing more than two candidates but which is not more than half of the total votes cast.

Pocket veto—rejection of legislation that occurs if the president does not sign a bill within 10 days and the Congress also adjourns within the same time period.

Police power—power reserved to the states by the Tenth Amendment to the Constitution.

Policy agenda—agenda that results from the interaction of linkage institutions.

Political action committees—known as PACs, they raise money from the special interest constituents and make contributions to political campaigns on behalf of the special interest group.

Political consultant—person who specializes in running a political campaign. James Carville and Karl Rove are examples of political consultants.

Political culture—the fundamental values that people have about their government and how these values translate into voting patterns.

Political participation—the different ways an average citizen gets involved in the political process ranging from conventional means of influencing government to more radical unconventional tools that have influenced our elected officials.

Political party—a group of people joined together by common philosophies and common approaches with the aim of getting candidates elected in order to develop and implement public policy. It is characterized by an organization that is responsible to the electorate and has a role in government.

Political socialization—the factors that determine voting behavior such as family, religion, and ethnic background.

Politics—who gets what, when, how, and why.

Poll tax—made illegal by the Twenty-Fourth Amendment to the Constitution, it was a tax instituted by mainly southern states as a condition to vote and had the effect of preventing African-Americans from voting.

Popular sovereignty—political doctrine that believes that government is created by and subject to the will of the people.

Pork barrel legislation—the practice of legislators obtaining funds through legislation that favors their home districts.

Poverty line—references the point at which an individual is considered living in what has been called a "culture of poverty."

Preamble—the introduction to the Constitution, outlining the goals of the document.

Precedent—legal concept, also known as stare decisis, by which earlier court decisions serve as models in justifying decisions in subsequent cases.

President pro tempore—temporary presiding officer of the Senate.

Presidential primary—elections held in individual states to determine the preference of the voters and to allocate the number of delegates to the party's national convention.

Press secretary—key White House staff position; the press secretary meets with the White House press corps.

Price supports—the government's price guarantees for certain farm goods. The government subsidizes farmers to not grow certain crops and also buys food directly and stores it, rather than let the oversupply in the market bring the prices down.

Prior restraint—the actions of a governmental body that result in the censorship of written material. In the "Pentagon Papers" case, President Nixon asked for an injunction to halt the publication of the confidential Defense Department documents by *The New York Times*.

Privileges and immunities—the guarantees that the rights of a citizen in one state will be respected by other states. Also a clause in the Fourteenth Amendment that protects citizens from abuses by a state.

Procedural due process—a series of steps that are established by the Fifth, Sixth, and Seventh Amendments that protect the rights of the accused at every step of the investigation.

Progressive tax—a tax based upon the amount of money an individual earned, such as an income tax. Became legal as a result of the ratification of the Sixteenth Amendment to the Constitution.

Public opinion polls—scientific surveys aimed at gauging public preference of candidates and issues.

Public policy—the final action(s) taken by government in promotional, regulatory, or distributive form.

Quasi-judicial—a characteristic of independent regulatory agencies that gives them judicial power to interpret regulations they create.

Quasi-legislative—a characteristic of independent regulatory agencies that gives them legislative powers to issue regulations.

Ranking committee member—the senior member of the minority party serving on a congressional committee who works closely with the committee chair deciding on committee business.

Reagan Democrats—traditional Democratic middle-class voters turning to Ronald Reagan during the 1980s.

Reapportionment—the process in which a state legislature redraws congressional districts based on population increases or declines.

Reapportionment Act of 1929—act that provides for a permanent size of the House and for the number of seats, based on the census, each state should have.

Recess appointment—a presidential appointment made when the Congress is not in session that usually lacks enough votes in the Senate for confirmation. The position must be confirmed by the Senate by the end of the next session of Congress, or the position becomes vacant.

Recession of 2008—caused by a collapse of the housing market, the mismanagement of housing mortgages by banks, and the bankruptcy of major investment firms, it resulted in a 10 percent unemployment rate, a precipitous drop in the global markets, and an economic slowdown that lasted until the middle of 2009.

Red tape—used to describe the difficulty it takes to get answers from a bureaucratic agency.

Redistricting—process that takes place every ten years, as a result of the federal census, mandating state legislatures to redraw their congressional districts based on population gains and losses.

Referendum—practice of submitting to popular vote a measure proposed by a legislative body; also called a proposition.

Regressive tax—a tax that is imposed on individuals regardless of how much they earn, such as a sales tax.

Regulatory policy—policy that results in government control over individuals and businesses. Examples of regulatory policy include protection of the environment and consumer protection.

Rehnquist Court—first nominated by Richard Nixon in 1971, William Rehnquist was confirmed as the 16th Chief Justice of the Supreme Court after Warren Burger retired in 1986. He was known as a conservative jurist and his stewardship over the court reflected a court of judicial restraint and conservative tendencies.

Religious right—an evangelical conglomeration of ultraconservative political activists, many of whom support the Republican Party.

Renewable resources—those natural resources such as solar energy that can be used over again.

Representative democracy—form of government that relies on the consent of the people and is often called a republican government.

Republican form of government—describes the manner in which the U.S. Constitution defines our democracy, one that is characterized by representation by the people and for the people.

Republican Party—political party that evolved from the Whig Party, coming to power after Lincoln's election. It is one of the two current major political parties.

Reserved power clause—found in the Tenth Amendment, it gives states powers not delegated to the national government.

Reverse discrimination—discrimination against whites or males, usually with regard to employment or education. Those who oppose affirmative action programs often claim reverse discrimination as a result of such programs. Alan Bakke is an example.

Riders—amendments to bills, often in the form of appropriations, that sometimes have nothing to do with the intent of the bill itself and many times are considered to be pork barrel legislation.

Rule of four—judicial concept employed by the Supreme Court requiring the approval of at least four justices before a case can be heard on appeal.

Rules Committee—one of the most important committees of the House of Representatives; its function is to create specific rules for every bill to be debated by the full House.

Rust Belt—the geographic area that is characterized by industries that have been in decline in the western part of the Northeast and upper Midwest including western Pennsylvania, western New York, Ohio, Michigan, Wisconsin, and northern Illinois and Indiana. The name came from residue from industrial plants that caused outdoor machinery to rust. It is a politically important area because these states have become swing states in presidential elections.

Safe seat—an elected official who, as an incumbent, has an easy reelection as a result of his incumbency or the political makeup of the district.

Safety net—a minimum government guarantee that ensures that individuals living in poverty will receive support in the form of social welfare programs.

Sampling error—refers to a statistical error, usually within three percentage points, inherent in the polling process.

Second Treatise of Civil Government—written by John Locke, it contains the blueprint principles found in the Declaration of Independence.

Select committees—specially created congressional committees that conduct special investigations. The Watergate Committee and Iran-Contra investigators were select Senate committees.

Senate confirmation—the process outlined in Article Two of the Constitution, giving the Senate the authority to approve appointments made by the president.

Senatorial courtesy—policy that gives senators the right to be notified by the president of pending judicial nominations. Once informed, the approval of the senators from the state from which the judge comes is obtained and the appointment process moves on. This courtesy does not apply to Supreme Court justice nominations.

Seniority—a system guaranteeing that those who serve in office the longest get preferential treatment. In Congress, those representatives who serve the longest get seniority in their committee assignments.

Separate but equal—the judicial precedent established in the *Plessy v Ferguson* decision that enabled states to interpret the equal protection provision of the Fourteenth Amendment as a means of establishing segregation.

Separation of church and state—also known as the "establishment clause," it is part of the First Amendment to the Constitution prohibiting the federal government from creating a state-supported religion.

Separation of powers—originally developed by Montesquieu in *The Spirit of Natural Laws* written during the Enlightenment and used by James Madison in Federalist No. 48. This important doctrine resulted in the establishment of three separate branches of government—the legislative, executive, and judicial branches, each having distinct and unique powers.

Sequestration—sequestration was the mandated cuts in discretionary and defense spending passed by Congress after President Obama and the House Republicans agreed to raise the debt ceiling in 2011. Sequestration was put in place in 2013 after Congress and the president could not agree on an alternative.

Shared powers—those powers that are concurrent, or overlapping, between the federal and state governments. Taxation is a shared power, for instance.

Shays' Rebellion—a failed attempt by Daniel Shays, a farmer who lost his property, to revolt against the state government.

Signing statement—made by the president at the time the president signs a bill into law that enables the president to give explanatory views and interpretation of the intent of the law.

Simpson-Marzzoli Act (1987)—act that resulted in more than 2 million illegal aliens who were living in this country since 1982 being allowed to apply for legal status.

Slander—Speech that intentionally gives false information or defames the character of an individual.

Soccer mom—term coined in 1996 presidential election referring to those suburban women, some of whom are single parents, who supported President Clinton because of his articulation of their values.

Social media—social media include e-mail, personal opinion pages called "blogs," Facebook and Twitter, and other sites that promote personal interaction. Social media became a political force starting with the 2008 presidential campaign with candidates setting up Facebook pages and Twitter accounts.

Social welfare—entitlement programs such as Social Security and programs such as Aid to Dependent Children paid for by the federal government.

Soft money—unrestricted and unregulated legal campaign contributions made to political parties and intended for party development. Significant abuses of soft money contributions were discovered during the 1996 election.

Solid South—dominance by the Democratic Party in the South following the Civil War. The Republicans made strong inroads when Ronald Reagan was elected President in 1980 and after the Republicans gained control of the Congress in 1994.

Sound bites—30- or 60-second statements by politicians aired on the evening news shows or Sunday morning talk shows.

Speaker of the House—the representative from the majority party in the House of Representatives who sets the House agenda, presides over House meetings, recognizes speakers, refers bills to committees, answers procedural questions, and declares the outcome of votes.

Spin doctor—name given to political consultants who try to shape the story or actions of their clients to the media in a positive manner.

Standing committees—committees that deal with proposed bills and also act in an oversight function. They are permanent, existing from one Congress to the next, such as the House Ways and Means and Senate Appropriations.

Stare decisis—Latin for judicial precedent, this concept originated in England in the twelfth century when judges settled disputes based on custom and tradition.

State of the Union address—constitutional requirement imposed on the president to deliver an annual report regarding the current state of the nation to Congress. Traditionally, the president delivers the State of the Union address every January, in the form of a speech before a joint session of Congress.

Straw vote—nonbinding vote used to determine the views of a small cross section of voters.

Strict constructionists—individuals who believe in a conservative interpretation of the Constitution.

Stump speech—speech given by a candidate on the campaign trail containing the candidate's key talking points and given to many different audiences with the purpose of driving home the candidate's message.

Substantive due process—legal process that places limits related to the content of legislation and the extent government can use its power to enact unreasonable laws.

Suffrage—the right to vote guaranteed to African-Americans in the Fifteenth Amendment and women in the Nineteenth Amendment.

Sunshine laws—those measures that open up governmental meetings to the public and prohibit government entities from conducting business in private session.

Super PACs—independent political action committees that can endorse or criticize a political candidate by raising unlimited funds, sometimes anonymous, from corporations, unions, and individuals.

Super Tuesday—the Tuesday on which a number of primary votes take place.

Superdelegates—Democratic Party leaders and elected party officials who automatically are selected as delegates to the National Convention.

Supremacy clause—clause that states that "the Constitution, and the laws of the United States . . . shall be the supreme law of the land."

Symbolic speech—form of free speech interpreted by the Supreme Court as a guarantee under the First Amendment to the Constitution, such as wearing a black armband to protest a governmental action or burning an American flag in protest for political reasons.

Taft-Hartley Act (1947)—act that outlawed the closed union shop and certain kinds of strikes, permitted employers to sue unions for violations of contracts, allowed the use of injunctions to stop union activities, and allowed states to adopt right-to-work laws, giving employers more rights regarding the establishment of union shops. Finally, the act gave the president the right to step in and prevent a strike by an entire industry, such as the steel or auto industry, if such an action would threaten the nation's health and safety.

Talking heads—politicians who use sound bites or other means to present a superficial look at a policy position rather than an in-depth approach in explaining their views.

Third political parties—political parties that can be described as ideological, single-issue oriented, economically motivated, and personality driven. Examples include the Free Soil Party, Know-Nothings, Populist, and Bull Moose Parties. In 1996 Ross Perot created a new national third party called the Reform Party.

Thirty-second spots—paid political ads 30 seconds in duration.

Three-Fifths Compromise—offered at the Constitutional Convention at Philadelphia, it was adopted by the delegates and counted every five slaves as three people for representation and tax purposes.

Ticket splitting—process by which voters choose a candidate from one political party for one elective office and another candidate from a different party for another elective office.

Tracking poll—polls conducted by media outlets to gauge the potential outcome of a political election on a periodic basis.

Trial balloons—selective leaks aimed at testing the political waters.

Trustee model of representation—also known as the attitudinal view. Voters elect their representatives as their own trustees giving them the autonomy to act for the good of the constituents enabling the congressman or woman to act of out of conscience even if the majority of voters might disagree.

Twenty-Fifth Amendment—constitutional amendment outlining the criteria for presidential selection and presidential disability.

Two-party system—two political parties controlling representation in the government. In the United States, the Democrats and Republicans have dominated elections because of the "winner-take-all" electoral system.

Unalienable rights—rights such as life, liberty, and the pursuit of happiness, which are derived from the doctrine of natural rights.

Unanimous decision—a decision made by the Supreme Court that has no dissent. A unanimous decision by the Court is 9-0.

Unconventional political participation—the means by which people get involved in the political process when conventional means fail such as protests and civil disobedience.

Unfunded mandates—those regulations passed by Congress or issued by regulatory agencies to the states without federal funds to support them.

Unitary system of government—type of government that centralizes all the powers of government into one central authority.

Universal suffrage—right of all qualified adults to vote.

Unwritten Constitution—traditions, precedent, and practice incorporated into our form of government that add to the Constitution's elasticity and its viability. Political parties, the president's cabinet, political action committees, and the federal bureaucracy are important examples.

Veto—power of the president to prevent enactment of legislation passed by Congress. A two-thirds majority vote of each house is required to override a presidential veto.

Virginia Plan—offered at the Constitutional Convention at Philadelphia, it urged the delegates to create a legislature based on the population of each state.

Voting Rights Act of 1965—act that finally made the Fifteenth Amendment a reality. As a result of this act, any state not eliminating the poll tax and literacy requirements would be directed to do so by the federal government. It also resulted in the establishment of racially gerrymandered congressional districts in the 1980s and 1990s.

Wagner Act—also called the National Labor Relations Act of 1935, it gave workers involved in interstate commerce the right to organize labor unions and engage in collective bargaining and prevented employers from discriminating against labor leaders and taking action against union leaders.

War Powers Act—1973 act that states that a president can commit the military only after a declaration of war by the Congress, by specific authorization by Congress, if there is a national emergency, or if the use of force is in the national interest of the United States.

Warren Court—nominated by President Eisenhower in 1954, Earl Warren is best known for the court's unanimous decision in *Brown v Board of Education* (1954) soon after he took office. His court also had the reputation of often being a liberal, activist court.

Watergate—refers to the office complex in Washington, D.C., where members of the committee to reelect Richard Nixon, posing as burglars, broke into the offices of the Democratic Party's national headquarters. They were caught, and the scandal ultimately led to Nixon's resignation.

Wave election—an election where one political party wins, resulting in a change of control in the presidency and Congress, increased control of the Congress, or change of control in one or both houses of Congress. Examples of wave elections are the 2008 presidential election (change of control of the presidency and an increase of Democrats in both houses of Congress) and the 1994, 2006, and 2010 midterm elections where one party took control of one or both houses of Congress.

Whips—also known as assistant floor leaders, they check with party members and inform the majority leader of the status and feelings of the membership regarding issues that are going to be voted on. Whips are responsible for keeping party members in line and having an accurate count of who will be voting for or against a particular bill.

White House staff—managed by the White House Chief of Staff, who directly advises the president on a daily basis, it includes the more than 600 people who work at the White House, from the chef to the advance people who make travel arrangements. The key staff departments include the political offices of the Office of Communications, Legislative Affairs, Political Affairs, and Intergovernmental Affairs. It includes the support services of Scheduling, Personnel, and Secret Service and the policy offices of the National Security Affairs, Domestic Policy Affairs, and cabinet secretaries.

Workfare—an alternative to the traditional welfare, where an individual is trained to work instead of receiving welfare.

World Bank—called the International Bank for Reconstruction and Development, it provides monetary assistance to nations for the development of industries and aims to stimulate economic growth of third-world nations.

Writ of certiorari—Latin for "to be made more certain," the process in which the Supreme Court accepts written briefs on appeal based on the rule of four.

Index

How to Use the CD-ROM

The software is not installed on your computer; it runs directly from the CD-ROM. Barron's CD-ROM includes an "autorun" feature that automatically launches the application when the CD is inserted into the CD-ROM drive in your PC (it does not autorun on Mac). In the unlikely event that the auto-run feature is disabled, follow the manual launching instructions below.

Windows®

Insert the CD-ROM and the program should launch automatically. If the software does not launch automatically, follow the steps below.
1. Click on the Start button and choose "My Computer."
2. Double-click on the CD-ROM drive, which will be named **AP_US_Government.**
3. Double-click **AP_US_Government.exe** application to launch the program.

Macintosh®

1. Insert the CD-ROM.
2. Double-click the CD-ROM icon.
3. Double-click the **AP_US_Government** icon to start the program.

SYSTEM REQUIREMENTS

This CD is intended to run on systems meeting the minimum requirements below.

Windows	**Mac OS**
2.33GHz or faster x86-compatible processor, or Intel® Atom™ 1.6GHz or faster processor for netbooks. Windows Server® 2003 (32-bit) or higher. 512MB of RAM (1GB of RAM recommended for netbooks); 128MB of graphics memory CD-ROM drive 1024 x 768 color display Flash Player 10.2 or higher is recommended.	Intel Core™ Duo 1.83GHz or faster processor MAC OS X 10.6 or higher 512MB of RAM; 128MB of graphics memory CD-ROM drive 1024 x 768 color display Flash Player 10.2 or higher is recommended.